世界名校经典演讲

BORN EXTRAORDINARY

新东方图书研发中心 编著

浙江教育出版社·杭州

图书在版编目（CIP）数据

生而不凡：世界名校经典演讲：英汉对照 / 新东方图书研发中心编著. -- 杭州：浙江教育出版社，2025. 6. -- ISBN 978-7-5722-9875-2

Ⅰ. H319.4

中国国家版本馆CIP数据核字第2025QC5349号

生而不凡 世界名校经典演讲
SHENG'ERBUFAN SHIJIE MINGXIAO JINGDIAN YANJIANG
新东方图书研发中心　编著

责任编辑	赵清刚
美术编辑	韩　波
责任校对	马立改
责任印务	时小娟
产品监制	王秀荣
特约编辑	刘姜榕　刘红静
装帧设计	路丽佳
出版发行	浙江教育出版社
	地址：杭州市环城北路177号
	邮编：310005
	电话：0571-88900883
	邮箱：dywh@xdf.cn
印　　刷	炫彩（天津）印刷有限责任公司
开　　本	710mm×1000mm　1/16
成品尺寸	170mm×230mm
印　　张	28.25
字　　数	340 000
版　　次	2025年6月第1版
印　　次	2025年6月第1次印刷
标准书号	ISBN 978-7-5722-9875-2
定　　价	88.00元

版权所有，侵权必究。如有缺页、倒页、脱页等印装质量问题，请拨打服务热线：010-62605166。

目录 Contents

第一章 梦想的力量

每个成功者都是大梦想家 / 1

2 / Stay Hungry, Stay Foolish
求知若饥，虚心若愚
——乔布斯 2005 年在斯坦福大学毕业典礼上的演讲

20 / Be Honest with Yourself and the World
对自己和世界诚实
——雪莉·桑德伯格 2014 年在哈佛大学毕业典礼上的演讲

42 / Never Surrender to Complexity
永远不要向复杂低头
——比尔·盖茨 2007 年在哈佛大学毕业典礼上的演讲

66 / It's Time to Take an Adventure
是时候去冒险了
——埃隆·马斯克 2014 年在南加州大学马歇尔商学院毕业典礼上的演讲

76 / Always Have a Dream
永不放弃梦想
——贝拉克·奥巴马 2009 年在亚利桑那州立大学毕业典礼上的演讲

第二章 奋斗的力量

因为努力,才有选择 / 99

100 / Doing the Right Thing in the Digital World
在数字世界中做正确的事
——蒂姆·库克 2017 年在麻省理工学院毕业典礼上的演讲

116 / We Are Shaped by Our Own Choices
我们的选择塑造了我们
——杰夫·贝索斯 2010 年在普林斯顿大学毕业典礼上的演讲

130 / Speak Up When You Disagree with the Voice of Authority
听从内心,追随直觉
——史蒂文·斯皮尔伯格 2016 年在哈佛大学毕业典礼上的演讲

148 / Investment and Personality Growth
关于投资与人格成长
——沃伦·巴菲特 1998 年在佛罗里达大学商学院的演讲

第三章 主动的力量

成功是失败再往前走一步 / 235

236 / The Benefits of Failure and the Importance of Imagination
失败的好处和想象力的重要性
——J. K. 罗琳 2008 年在哈佛大学毕业典礼上的演讲

256 / Learn from Your Failures
在失败中成长
——奥普拉·温弗瑞 2013 年在哈佛大学毕业典礼上的演讲

282 / Don't Be Afraid. We'll Make It out of This Mess
别怕犯错，勇敢向前
——泰勒·斯威夫特 2022 年在纽约大学毕业典礼上的演讲

302 / Make Your Inexperience an Asset
让经验匮乏成为优势
——娜塔莉·波特曼 2015 年在哈佛大学毕业典礼上的演讲

第四章 勇气的力量

真正的成长是向死而生 / 327

328 / This Is Water
这就是水
——大卫·福斯特·华莱士 2005 年在凯尼恩学院毕业典礼上的演讲

354 / Thirteen Lessons on Life
十三堂人生课
——马修·麦康纳 2015 年在休斯敦大学毕业典礼上的演讲

398 / Life Is Too Short to Live Empty-Handed
生命太过短暂，不能空手走过
——朱棣文 2009 年在哈佛大学毕业典礼上的演讲

420 / Ten Suggestions for Life
人生的十个建议
——本·伯南克 2013 年在普林斯顿大学毕业典礼上的演讲

436 / The Last Lecture
最后一课
——兰迪·波许 2008 年在卡内基梅隆大学毕业典礼上的演讲

第一章

梦想的力量

每个成功者都是大梦想家

梦想 Dream

Stay Hungry, Stay Foolish
求知若饥，虚心若愚

——乔布斯 2005 年在斯坦福大学毕业典礼上的演讲

简介 Profile

史蒂夫·乔布斯
Steve Jobs

1955 年，乔布斯出生于加利福尼亚州的旧金山，养父母把他抚养长大，并倾尽积蓄送他进了大学。但遗憾的是，出于对未来的规划和繁重的经济压力，乔布斯读了六个月便退学了。

离开大学两年后，1976 年，乔布斯和史蒂夫·沃兹尼亚克、龙·韦恩共同创办了苹果公司，同年，苹果第一款个人电脑"Apple I"问世。

1985 年，经过一系列激烈的公司内部权力斗争，乔布斯被这个自己一手创办的公司给踢了出去。

离开苹果公司后，乔布斯并未一蹶不振，很快又创办了皮克斯动画工作室。

1997 年，苹果公司收购了乔布斯的创业公司 NeXT，乔布斯得以重新回归苹果，担任首席执行官（CEO）。

此后十几年间，这位充满创造力与行动力的 CEO 几次力挽狂澜，带领苹果公司走出困境，一步步走向辉煌。

直到 2011 年 8 月，乔布斯递上一纸辞呈，再次离开了苹果公司。但这次的离开是永久的，两个月后，56 岁的乔布斯因癌症离开人世。

尽管人已不在，但乔布斯创造的产品直至今天依然家喻户晓。Macintosh、iPhone、iPod……他掀起了一次次技术和时尚的浪潮，也改变了人们的思考方式和生活方式。而他留下的精神也不曾随着时间流逝而磨灭，仍然激励着无数不甘平凡、勇敢向上的人们。正如微软创始人比尔·盖茨在评价乔布斯时说的那样："很少有人对世界产生像乔布斯那样的影响，这种影响将是长期的。"

他生前面向斯坦福大学毕业生的这场演讲，全面回顾了自己的一生，讲述了生命中尤为重要的三个故事，其中蕴含的人生经验和力量将会使那些正在人生岔路口迷茫徘徊的人受益匪浅。

演讲 Speech

扫描二维码
获取本篇演讲原视频、音频

Thank you. I'm honored to be with you today for your commencement from one of the finest universities in the world. Truth be told, I never graduated from college, and this is the closest I've ever gotten to a college graduation.

Today, I want to tell you three stories from my life. That's it. No big deal. Just three stories.

The first story is about connecting the dots.

I dropped out of Reed College after the first six months, but then stayed around as a drop-in for another 18 months or so before I really quit. So why did I drop out?

It started before I was born. My biological mother was a young, unwed graduate student, and she decided to put me up for adoption. She felt very strongly that I should be adopted by college graduates, so everything was all set for me to be adopted at birth by a lawyer and his wife—except that when I popped out they decided at the last minute that they really wanted a girl.

So my parents, who were on a waiting list, got a call in the middle of the night asking, "We've got an unexpected baby boy. Do you want him?" They said, "Of course." My biological mother found out later that my mother had never graduated from college and that my father had never graduated from high school. She refused to sign the final adoption papers. She only relented a few months later when my parents promised that I would go to college. This was

谢谢大家。今天能与你们一起参加这所世界顶尖大学的毕业典礼，我感到很荣幸。说实话，我大学没有毕业，这是我离大学毕业最近的一次。

今天，我想给大家讲讲我的三个人生故事。仅此而已，没什么特别的，只是三个故事。

第一个故事讲的是点和点之间的串联。

我在里德学院读了半年就退学了，但之后我又作为旁听生待了一年半左右，才真正离开学校。那么，我为什么退学呢？

故事还要从我出生前说起。我的生母那时还是研究生，很年轻，也没结婚，她决定让别人收养我。她坚定地认为，收养我的人应该有大学学历。所以，在我出生前，一切都安排好了，我将被一位律师和他的妻子收养——只是等到我呱呱坠地了，到了最后关头，他们才发现自己真正想要收养的是女孩。

我的养父母当时在排队名单上，他们半夜三更接到电话："我们这里意外多了一个男婴，你们想要吗？"他们说："当然啦。"我的生母后来发现，我的养母大学没毕业，养父高中都没毕业，于是拒绝在最终的收养文件上签字。几个月后，养父母承

> *Much of what I stumbled into by following my curiosity and intuition turned out to be priceless later on.*
>
> 我追随着好奇心和直觉，邂逅了很多人生体验，而后的人生证明，它们都是无价之宝。

the start in my life.

And 17 years later I did go to college. But I naively chose a college that was almost as expensive as Stanford, and all of my working-class parents' savings were being spent on my college tuition. After six months, I couldn't see the value in it. I had no idea what I wanted to do with my life and no idea how college was going to help me figure it out. And here I was spending all of the money my parents had saved their entire life.

So I decided to drop out and trust that it would all work out okay. It was pretty scary at the time, but looking back it was one of the best decisions I ever made. The minute I dropped out I could stop taking the required classes that didn't interest me, and begin dropping in on the ones that looked far more interesting.

It wasn't all romantic. I didn't have a dorm room, so I slept on the floor in friends' rooms. I returned[1] coke bottles for the five-cent deposits to buy food with, and I would walk the seven miles across town every Sunday night to get one good meal a week at the Hare Krishna temple. I loved it. And much of what I stumbled into[2] by following my curiosity and intuition turned out to be priceless later on. Let me give you one example:

Reed College at that time offered perhaps the best calligraphy instruction in the country. Throughout the campus every poster, every label on every drawer, was beautifully hand calligraphed. Because I had dropped out and didn't have to take the normal classes, I decided to take a calligraphy class to learn how to do this. I learned about serif and san serif typefaces, about varying the amount of space between different letter combinations, about what makes great typography[3] great. It was beautiful, historical, artistically subtle in a way that science can't capture, and I found it fascinating.

None of this had even a hope of any practical application in my life. But ten years later, when we were designing the first Macintosh computer, it all

诺一定会让我上大学，我的生母才松了口。这便是我人生的开端。

17年后，我的确上了大学，但当年太幼稚了，选择了一所学费昂贵得比肩斯坦福大学的学校，工薪阶层的父母把毕生积蓄都用来给我付了学费。读了半年大学，我觉得不值得。我不知道自己想做什么，也不知道大学怎么帮我找到答案，可是上大学却要花掉父母一生的积蓄。

所以我决定退学，相信一切都会向好的方向发展。当时我心里直打鼓，但如今回头看，这是我生命中最明智的决定之一。从退学的那一刻起，我就不必再上自己不感兴趣的必修课了，而是开始旁听那些看起来有趣得多的课程。

那段时光于我而言并不全是美好的回忆。我没有宿舍，只能在朋友的房间里打地铺。我去捡可以换5美分的可乐瓶，仅仅为了填饱肚子。每个星期天晚上，我都要走7英里（约合11.27公里）的路，穿过小镇，去哈雷克里希纳神庙，吃每周限定一顿的好饭。我喜欢这样的生活。我追随着好奇心和直觉，邂逅了很多人生体验，而后的人生证明，它们都是无价之宝。我给大家举个例子吧：

当时，里德学院的书法课或许在全国也是数一数二的。整个校园里，每张海报和每个抽屉上的每个标签，都写着漂亮的手写体。因为我已经退学了，不用正常上课，所以我决定去上书法课，学习怎么写出一手好字。我学习了衬线字体和无衬线字体的知识，学习了如何调整不同字母组合之间的间距，学习了如何在版面设计上精益求精。这是一种科学无法捕获的美丽，蕴含着深厚的历史底蕴和精妙的艺术魅力，我对它很是着迷。

这门学问在我的实际生活中毫无施展的余地。但10年后，在设计第一台麦金

---

1. return：*v.* 把（空瓶或空罐头盒）送到回收站。——编者注（如无特别说明，本书注释均为编者注）
2. stumble into：偶然遇到。
3. typography：*n.* 印刷术；版面设计。

came back to me. And we designed it all into the Mac. It was the first computer with beautiful typography. If I had never dropped in on that single course in college, the "Mac" would have never had multiple typefaces or proportionally spaced fonts[4]. And since Windows just copied the Mac[5], it's likely that no personal computer would have them. If I had never dropped out, I would have never dropped in on that calligraphy class, and personal computers might not have the wonderful typography that they do. Of course it was impossible to connect the dots looking forward when I was in college. But it was very, very clear looking backwards 10 years later.

Again, you can't connect the dots looking forward; you can only connect them looking backwards. So you have to trust that the dots will somehow connect in your future. You have to trust in something—your gut, destiny, life, karma, whatever, because believing that the dots will connect down the road will give you the confidence to follow your heart, even when it leads you off the well-worn path, and that will make all the difference.

My second story is about love and loss.

I was lucky—I found what I loved to do early in life. Woz and I started Apple in my parents' garage when I was 20. We worked hard, and in 10 years Apple had grown from just the two of us in a garage into a two billion dollar company with over 4,000 employees. We'd just released our finest creation—the Macintosh—a year earlier, and I had just turned 30.

And then I got fired. How can you get fired from a company you started? Well, as Apple grew we hired someone who I thought was very talented to run the company with me, and for the first year or so things went well. But then our visions of the future began to diverge and eventually we had a falling out. When we did, our Board of Directors sided with him. And so at 30, I was out. And very publicly out. What had been the focus of my entire adult life was gone, and it was devastating.

塔电脑时，这些知识又回到了我的脑海中。我们把它融入了Mac电脑的设计中，打造出了第一台拥有漂亮字体版式的计算机。如果我没在大学里随兴旁听这一门课程，那么Mac电脑就不会有那么多种字体版式，也不会有合理安排的字距。加上Windows依葫芦画瓢地抄袭了Mac，所以也可以说如果我没有退学去旁听书法课，所有的个人电脑可能都不会有这么漂亮的字体版式。当然，大学时的我不可能看到这些点和点之间的串联，但10年后回头看，这种串联一目了然。

还是那句话，向前看是没法将这些点串联起来的，只有回头看才行。所以我们必须相信，这些点会在未来以某种方式串联起来。我们必须相信一些东西——直觉、命运、生活、因果等。因为相信这些点终将在前路上串联起来，会让人有信心去追随内心，即使这意味着要踏上人迹罕至的道路，但一切都将变得不同。

第二个故事讲的是爱与失去。

我很幸运，很早就找到了自己热爱的事业。20岁时，我和沃兹在我父母的车库里创办了苹果公司。经过我们10年的不懈努力，苹果公司从车库里只有两个人的公司发展成为一家拥有4000多名员工、市值20亿美元的大公司。而此前一年，我们刚刚推出了最得意的作品——麦金塔电脑，其时我刚满30岁。

然后我被炒了。怎么会有人被自己亲手创办的公司炒了呢？是这样的：随着苹果公司的发展，我们向一位我认为颇有天赋的英才抛出了橄榄枝，聘请他来和我一起管理公司。头一年一切顺利，但随后，我们对公司未来发展的看法出现了分歧，最终我们闹翻了。闹翻后，董事会站在了他那边。于是，30岁那年，我出局了，而且闹得沸沸扬扬。我成年以来整个生活的重心就这样没了，这对我来说是毁灭性的打击。

---

4. font: *n.* 字体。
5. 1980年代，Mac率先推出图形界面。乔布斯发现Windows在界面等方面与Mac极为相似，认为微软抄袭。1988年苹果起诉微软，称Windows 2.0窃取Mac 189个元素。但法官裁定部分元素在授权范围内，未认定Windows抄袭。

I really didn't know what to do for a few months. I felt that I had let the previous generation of entrepreneurs down—that I had dropped the baton as it was being passed to me. I met with David Packard and Bob Noyce and tried to apologize for screwing up so badly. I was a very public failure, and I even thought about running away from the valley. But something slowly began to dawn on me: I still loved what I did. The turn of events at Apple had not changed that one bit. I had been rejected, but I was still in love. And so I decided to start over.

I didn't see it then, but it turned out that getting fired from Apple was the best thing that could have ever happened to me. The heaviness of being successful was replaced by the lightness of being a beginner again, less sure about everything. It freed me to enter one of the most creative periods of my life.

During the next five years, I started a company named NeXT, another company named Pixar, and fell in love with an amazing woman who would become my wife. Pixar went on to create the world's first computer-animated feature film, *Toy Story*, and is now the most successful animation studio in the world. In a remarkable turn of events, Apple bought NeXT, and I returned to Apple, and the technology we developed at NeXT is at the heart of Apple's current renaissance. And Laurene and I have a wonderful family together.

I'm pretty sure none of this would have happened if I hadn't been fired from Apple. It was awful tasting medicine, but I guess the patient needed it. Sometimes life's going to hit you in the head with a brick. Don't lose faith. I'm convinced that the only thing that kept me going was that I loved what I did. You've got to find what you love.

And that is as true for your work as it is for your lovers. Your work is going to fill a large part of your life, and the only way to be truly satisfied is to do what you believe is great work. And the only way to do great work is to love

头几个月我真的不知道该做什么。我觉得自己辜负了初代创始人们的期望——接力棒传到我手中，我却掉了链子。我与大卫·帕卡德、鲍勃·诺伊斯会面，想为自己的惨败道歉。我是一个尽人皆知的失败者，我甚至想过逃离硅谷。但我逐渐明白：我仍然热爱我所做的一切。苹果公司的变故并未改变这一点。我被拒之门外，但仍然满心热爱。因此，我决定重新开始。

当时很难看清楚，但事实证明，被苹果公司解雇是我这辈子碰到的最好的事情。保持成功的重担消失了，取而代之的是重新出发的轻松感，对一切都不那么确定。我获得了自由，踏入了我人生中最具创造力的时期之一。

随后五年里，我创办了一家名为 NeXT 的公司和一家名为皮克斯的公司，爱上了一位了不起的女性，后来还和她结为夫妻。皮克斯打造了世界上首部电脑动画长片《玩具总动员》，如今已成为全球最成功的动画工作室。事情发生了戏剧性转变，苹果公司收购了 NeXT，我又回到了苹果公司，NeXT 研发的技术在苹果公司的再度崛起中发挥了核心作用。另外，我和劳伦还组建了一个美满的家庭。

我确信，倘若苹果公司没把我炒了，这一切都不会发生。良药苦口利于病。有时生活会给你当头一棒，但不要灰心丧气。我确信，对事业的爱是让我坚持下来的唯一原因。我们必须找到自己的真爱。

这一点适用于工作，也适用于爱情。工作将占据生活的很大一部分，唯有做自己认为伟大的工作，才能真正获得满足感。而成就一番伟大事业的唯一途径就是热

Sometimes life's going to hit you in the head with a brick. Don't lose faith.

有时生活会给你当头一棒，但不要灰心丧气。

what you do. If you haven't found it yet, keep looking—and don't settle. As with all matters of the heart, you'll know when you find it. And like any great relationship, it just gets better and better as the years roll on. So keep looking—don't settle.

My third story is about death.

When I was 17, I read a quote that went something like: "If you live each day as if it was your last, someday you'll most certainly be right." It made an impression on me, and since then, for the past 33 years, I've looked in the mirror every morning and asked myself: "If today were the last day of my life, would I want to do what I am about to do today?" And whenever the answer has been "No" for too many days in a row, I know I need to change something.

Remembering that I'll be dead soon is the most important tool I've ever encountered[6] to help me make the big choices in life, because almost everything—all external expectations, all pride, all fear of embarrassment or failure—these things just fall away in the face of death, leaving only what is truly important. Remembering that you are going to die is the best way I know to avoid the trap of thinking you have something to lose. You are already naked. There is no reason not to follow your heart.

About a year ago I was diagnosed[7] with cancer. I had a scan at 7:30 in the morning, and it clearly showed a tumor on my pancreas. I didn't even know what a pancreas was. The doctors told me this was almost certainly a type of cancer that is incurable, and that I should expect to live no longer than three to six months. My doctor advised me to go home and get my affairs in order, which is doctor's code for "prepare to die." It means to try and tell your kids everything you thought you'd have the next 10 years to tell them in just a few months. It means to make sure everything is buttoned up so that it will be as easy as possible for your family. It means to say your goodbyes.

I lived with that diagnosis all day. Later that evening I had a biopsy[8],

爱你所做之事，如果尚未找到，那就继续寻找，不要将就。就像心之所求的一切，遇上自会知晓；就像真挚的情谊，只会随着岁月更迭更添醇香。所以继续寻找，不要将就。

第三个故事讲的是死亡。

17岁时，我读到过一句话，大概是这么说的："若把每一天都设想为人生的最后一天来活，终有一天设想会成真。"这句话给我留下了深刻的印象，自那之后的33年里，每天早上我都会对镜自问："倘若今天是我生命中的最后一天，我会想做今天计划要做的事吗？"如果一连数日得出的答案都是"不想"，我就知道，是时候做出改变了。

提醒自己生命随时可能迎来终结，这一点帮助我做出了很多重大的人生抉择。因为几乎所有的事情，包括外界的期望、引以为傲的一切以及对尴尬或失败的恐惧，在死亡面前都会烟消云散，只有真正重要的东西会留下。时刻谨记生命随时会结束，就能消除害怕失去身外之物的恐惧。如果一无所有，那就没有理由不遵从自己的内心。

大约一年前，我确诊患上了癌症。早上 7 点半我做了扫描检查，扫描结果清楚地显示，我的胰腺上有一个肿瘤。当时我甚至不知道胰腺是什么。医生告诉我，这类癌症几乎可以断定是不治之症，我最多只能再活 3～6 个月。医生建议我回家把事情安排妥当，其实就是暗示我"安排后事"。这意味着，在短短几个月内，我就得努力把本该在接下来的 10 年里告诉孩子们的话讲完，确保把一切都安排妥当，不给家人添麻烦。这也意味着，我要和世界告别了。

诊断结果一整天都在我的脑子里挥之不去。当晚我做了活组织检查，医生用内

---

6. encounter: *v.* 偶然碰到，意外遇见。
7. diagnose: *v.* 诊断（疾病）；判断（问题的原因）。
8. biopsy: *n.* 活组织检查。

where they stuck an endoscope[9] down my throat, through my stomach into my intestines, put a needle into my pancreas and got a few cells from the tumor. I was sedated, but my wife, who was there, told me that when they viewed the cells under a microscope the doctors started crying because it turned out to be a very rare form of pancreatic cancer that is curable with surgery. I had the surgery and, thankfully, I'm fine now.

This was the closest I've been to facing death, and I hope it's the closest I get for a few more decades. Having lived through it, I can now say this to you with a bit more certainty than when death was a useful but purely intellectual concept: No one wants to die.

Even people who want to go to heaven don't want to die to get there. And yet death is the destination we all share. No one has ever escaped it. And that is as it should be, because Death is very likely the single best invention of Life. It's Life's change agent. It clears out the old to make way for the new. Right now the new is you, but someday not too long from now, you will gradually become the old and be cleared away. Sorry to be so dramatic, but it's quite true.

Your time is limited, so don't waste it living someone else's life. Don't be trapped by dogma[10]—which is living with the results of other people's thinking. Don't let the noise of others' opinions drown out your own inner voice. And most important, have the courage to follow your heart and intuition. They somehow already know what you truly want to become. Everything else is secondary.

When I was young, there was an amazing publication called *The Whole Earth Catalog*, which was one of the "bibles" of my generation. It was created by a fellow named Stewart Brand not far from here in Menlo Park, and he brought it to life with his poetic touch. This was in the late 60s, before personal computers and desktop publishing, so it was all made with typewriters, scissors, and Polaroid cameras. It was sort of like Google in paperback form,

窥镜插入我的喉咙，穿过胃进入肠道，把一根针插入胰腺，从肿瘤中取出一些细胞。我当时麻醉了，不过我的妻子在场。她后来告诉我，医生在显微镜下观察细胞的时候喜极而泣，因为他们发现，原来我患上的是一种非常罕见的胰腺癌，可以通过手术治愈。我接受了手术，谢天谢地，我现在没事了。

　　这是我离死亡最近的一次，但愿也是我未来几十年离死亡最近的一次。经历过这一切之后，死亡对我来说不再仅仅是个有用但抽象的概念，我可以更肯定地告诉你们：没有人想死。

　　即使是向往天堂的人，也不想为上天堂而死。然而，死亡是我们共同的归宿，没有人能够逃脱死亡。这也是理所应当的，因为死亡很可能是生命最伟大的发明。它是生活变革的推动者。它清除旧人，为新人让路。现在的你们是新人，但不久之后的某一天，就会逐渐变成旧人，被清除掉。不好意思，我说得很夸张，但事实就是如此。

　　你的时间有限，不要浪费在学别人的活法上。不要拘于教条主义——那是按照别人的想法来活。不要让世人的喧嚣淹没内心的声音。最重要的是，要勇于追随内心和直觉。对于究竟想要成为什么样的人，内心和直觉在某种程度上已有答案。其他一切都是次要的。

　　我年轻的时候，有一本很棒的刊物叫作《全球概览》，它是我们这一代人的"圣经"之一。斯图尔特·布兰德在离这里不远的门洛帕克创办了这份刊物，用诗意的笔触将它带到这个世界。在20世纪60年代末，个人电脑和桌面出版尚未问世，所以这份刊物是用打字机、剪刀和宝丽来相机打造的。它有点像平装本的谷歌，比谷

---

9. endoscope：*n.* 内窥镜。
10. dogma：*n.* 教条；教义；信条；教理。

35 years before Google came along. It was idealistic, overflowing with neat tools and great notions.

Stewart and his team put out several issues of *The Whole Earth Catalog*, and then when it had run its course, they put out a final issue. It was the mid-1970s, and I was your age. On the back cover of their final issue was a photograph of an early morning country road, the kind you might find yourself hitchhiking on if you were so adventurous. Beneath it were the words: "Stay Hungry, Stay Foolish." It was their farewell message as they signed off. Stay Hungry, Stay Foolish. And I've always wished that for myself.

And now, as you graduate to begin anew, I wish that for you.

Stay Hungry, Stay Foolish.

Thank you all very much.

歌早了 35 年。它洋溢着理想主义色彩，汇聚了实用的工具和卓越的理念。

　　斯图尔特及其团队相继发行了数期《全球概览》，这本刊物即将走到尽头时还发布了终刊。那是 20 世纪 70 年代中期，那时我和你们一样大。终刊的封底是一张清晨乡村小路的照片，爱冒险的人会在那种地方搭便车。这张照片下方写着："求知若饥，虚心若愚。"这是他们的停刊告别辞。求知若饥，虚心若愚。这也是我一直以来对自己的期望。

　　现在，你们即将毕业，开启新征程，我把这句话送给你们。

　　求知若饥，虚心若愚。

　　非常感谢大家。

- You have to trust in something—your gut, destiny, life, karma, whatever. Because believing that the dots will connect down the road will give you the confidence to follow your heart.
  我们必须相信一些东西——直觉、命运、生活、因果等。因为相信这些点终将在前路上串联起来，会让人有信心去追随内心。

- Much of what I stumbled into by following my curiosity and intuition turned out to be priceless later on.
  我追随着好奇心和直觉，邂逅了很多人生体验，而后的人生证明，它们都是无价之宝。

- Sometimes life's going to hit you in the head with a brick. Don't lose faith.
  有时生活会给你当头一棒，但不要灰心丧气。

- The only way to do great work is to love what you do. If you haven't found it yet, keep looking—and don't settle.
  成就一番伟大事业的唯一途径就是热爱你所做之事，如果尚未找到，那就继续寻找，不要将就。

- Remembering that I'll be dead soon is the most important tool I've ever encountered to help me make the big choices in life.
  提醒自己生命随时可能迎来终结，这一点帮助我做出了很多重大的人生抉择。

- Your time is limited, so don't waste it living someone else's life.
  你的时间有限，不要浪费在学别人的活法上。

Be Honest with Yourself and the World
对自己和世界诚实

——雪莉·桑德伯格 2014 年在哈佛大学毕业典礼上的演讲

简介 Profile

雪莉·桑德伯格
Sheryl Sandberg

1969年，雪莉·桑德伯格出生于美国华盛顿。18岁时，她被哈佛大学录取，主修经济学，师从著名经济学家劳伦斯·萨默斯，其出色的学术表现为她后续的职业生涯奠定了坚实的基础。

2001年，她加入了彼时还是初创公司的谷歌，凭借出色的能力迅速晋升为副总裁，见证了谷歌从初创企业到全球科技巨头的崛起。2008年，桑德伯格加入Facebook（2021年改名为Meta），彼时的Facebook尚处发展初期，虽已小有名气，但商业模式并不成熟。桑德伯格的到来，为Facebook带来了至关重要的商业洞察力和运营策略。她主导搭建起Facebook广告业务体系，精准定位受众、创新投放形式，吸引众多品牌入驻，助力平台全球扩张，广告营收持续增长，成就社交网络巨头地位，她也成为Facebook的核心人物。

除此之外，桑德伯格还非常关注女性在职场中的地位和权益。2010年，桑德伯格在TED发表了一场名为《为何女性领导太少》的演讲。她以自身经历为切入点，坦诚分享了女性在职场中面临的诸多隐形阻碍，比如晋升时遭遇的性别偏见、工作与家庭平衡的艰难抉择等。演讲中，她言辞恳切地呼吁社会重视这些问题，鼓励女性打破心理枷锁，勇敢争取领导职位。2013年，桑德伯格发起了一项名为"向前一步"的运动，旨在鼓励女性勇敢面对职场挑战，提高女性在职场中的地位和影响力。这一运动在全球范围内产生了广泛影响，激发了无数女性追求自己的梦想。

雪莉·桑德伯格不仅是一位杰出的商业领袖，更是一位激励人心的榜样。2014年，她来到了母校哈佛大学，跟毕业生们分享了自己的人生经历，以及她作为女性在职场中所面临的挑战和机遇。她衷心建议毕业生们一定要找到自己的人生目标，因为只有找到了真正热爱的事情，才能全力以赴地追求它。

扫描二维码
获取本篇演讲原视频、音频

Congratulations everyone, you made it.

And I don't mean to the end of college, I mean to class day, because if memory serves[1], some of your classmates had too many scorpion bowls[2] at the Kong last night and are with us today.

Given the weather, the one thing Harvard hasn't figured out how to control, some of your other classmates are someplace warm with a hot cocoa, so you have many reasons to feel proud of yourself as you sit here today.

Congratulations to your parents. You have spent a lot of money, so your child can say she went to a "small school" near Boston. And thank you to the class of 2014 for inviting me to part of your celebration. It means a great to me. And looking at the list of past speakers was a little daunting. I can't be as funny as Amy Poehler[3], but I'm gonna be funnier than Mother Teresa.

25 years ago, a man named Dave I did not know at the time but who would one day become my husband was sitting where you are sitting today. 23 years ago, I was sitting where you are sitting today. Dave and I are back this weekend with our amazing son and daughter to celebrate his reunion, and we both share the same sentiment, Harvard has a good basketball team.

Standing here in the yard[4] brings memories flooding back for me. I arrived here from Miami in the fall of 1987, with big hopes and even bigger hair. I was assigned to live in one of Harvard's historic monuments to great architecture,

祝贺大家，你们成功了。

我指的不是成功毕业，而是成功出席毕业日活动，因为没记错的话，今天在场的同学当中，有些昨晚还在香港餐厅畅饮蝎子碗鸡尾酒。

鉴于今天的天气——这事儿哈佛目前还控制不了——你们有些同学正在暖和的地方喝热可可，所以你们有足够的原因为自己今天能坐在这里而感到骄傲。

我也要祝贺家长们。你们花了很多钱，孩子们才能对别人说自己上了波士顿附近的一所"小学校"。感谢2014届毕业生邀请我参加你们的庆典，这对我来说意义非凡。我看了一遍先前的演讲者名单，觉得有些紧张。我没法儿像艾米·波勒那么风趣，但我会比特蕾莎修女幽默一点。

25年前，一个名叫戴夫的男人坐在你们今天坐的位置上，当时我还不认识他，但他后来成了我的丈夫。23年前，我就坐在你们今天坐的位置上。这个周末，我和戴夫带着可爱的儿女回到这里，参加他的校友会，我们一致认为，哈佛的篮球队真的很棒。

站在校园里，回忆便如潮水般涌上我的心头。1987年的秋天，我从迈阿密来到这里，心怀高高的期待，头顶夸张的大背头发型。我分配到的住宿地点是哈佛的历

> *Listening to criticism is never fun, but it's the only way we can improve.*
>
> 挨批评从来都不是好玩的事，但我们只能在批评中进步。

---

1. if memory serves：如果没有记错的话。
2. scorpion bowl：一种混合鸡尾酒。
3. Amy Poehler：艾米·波勒，美国喜剧演员，参演过《周六夜现场》。
4. yard：指哈佛园（Harvard Yard），包含大部分的哈佛大一新生宿舍、图书馆等建筑，每年的毕业典礼就在哈佛园中心的三百周年剧场（Tercentenary Theatre）举行。

Canaday[5]. My go-to outfit, and I'm not making this up, was a jean skirt, white leg warmers and sneakers and a Florida sweatshirt, because my parents who were here with me then as they're here with me now, told me everyone would think it was awesome that I was from Florida. At least we didn't have Instagram.

For me, Harvard was a series of firsts. My first winter coat, we didn't need those in Miami. My first 10-page paper, they didn't assign those in my high school. My first C, after which my proctor told me that she was on the admissions committee, and I got admitted to Harvard for my personality not my academic potential. The first person I ever met from boarding school. I thought that was for really troubled kids. The first person I ever met who shares a name with a whole building, or so I met when the first classmate I met was Sarah Wigglesworth, who bore no relation at all to the dorm[6], which would have been nice to know at that very intimidating moment. But then I went on to meet others, Francis Straus, James Weld, Jessica Science Center B. My first love, my first heartbreak, the first time I realized that I love to learn, and the first and very last time I saw anyone read anything in Latin.

When I sat in your seat all those years ago, I knew exactly where I was headed. I had it all planned out. I was going to the World Bank to work on global poverty. Then I would go to law school. Then I would spend my life working in a nonprofit or in the government. At Harvard's commencement tomorrow as your dean described, each school is gonna stand up and graduate together, the college, the law school, the med school and so on. At my graduation, my class cheered for the PHD students and then booed the business school. Business school seemed like such a sellout[7].18 months later, I applied to business school.

It wasn't that I was wrong about what I would do decades after graduating. I had it wrong a year and a half later. And even if I could have predicted I would

史遗迹建筑卡纳迪楼。我当时的标配穿搭是牛仔裙、白色护腿袜、运动鞋和佛罗里达运动衫,这可不是我编出来的。我的父母当时和我在一块(他们现在也和我在一块),他们告诉我,每个人都会觉得来自佛罗里达是件很酷的事。至少那时候我们还没有照片墙。

哈佛给我带来了很多新体验。我有了第一件冬装,而在迈阿密不需要穿冬装。我写出了第一篇长达10页的论文,高中的时候没布置过这么长的论文。我的成绩得到了第一个C,监考老师后来告诉我,她是招生委员会成员,哈佛录取我是看中我的个性,而不是我的学术潜力。我第一次遇到来自寄宿学校的人,此前我还以为寄宿学校是为问题儿童开设的。我第一次遇到和楼同名的人——莎拉·威格尔斯沃思,其实她和宿舍楼并无瓜葛,要是当时就知道这一点,我可能就不会觉得震撼了。后来我又认识了其他人,弗朗西斯·斯特劳斯、詹姆斯·维尔德、杰西卡·科学中心·B。我第一次坠入爱河,第一次心碎,第一次意识到自己喜欢学习,以及第一次也是最后一次见到有人看拉丁语读物。

多年前,我坐在你们现在的位子上,清楚地知道自己要去往何方。我规划好了一切。我要进世界银行,为解决全球贫困问题而奋斗,然后我会进法学院,再然后,我会为非营利组织或政府工作一辈子。就像你们的院长所说的那样,在明天的哈佛毕业典礼上,本科部、法学院、医学院等各个学院将全体起立,一起毕业。在我的毕业典礼上,我们全班为博士生欢呼喝彩,却对商学院报以嘘声,毕竟商学院看上去就像会做出叛卖行为的势利之徒。一年半后,我申请了商学院。

我对自己毕业几十年后的人生规划其实并没有出错,出错的是对一年半后的规划。即使我能预测到有朝一日我会进私企工作,也不可能预测到会进"脸书",因为

---

5. Canaday:指Canaday Hall,哈佛大一新生的宿舍楼,以沃德·M.卡纳迪(Ward M. Canaday,1885—1976)的名字命名。沃德·M.卡纳迪于1907年在哈佛取得学士学位,在二战期间开发和生产了军用车"吉普"(Jeep)。
6. dorm:指哈佛的Wigglesworth Hall。
7. sellout:*n.* 背叛。

one day work in the private sector, I never could have predicted Facebook, because there was no Internet, and Mark Zuckerberg was at elementary school, already wearing his hoody. Not locking into a path too early, give me an opportunity to go into a new and life-changing field. And for those of you who think I owe everything to good luck, after Canaday I got Quadded[8]. What's that, Barron?

There is no straight path from your seat today to where you are going. Don't try to draw that line. You will not just get it wrong. You will miss big opportunities and I mean big, like the Internet.

Careers are not ladders—those days are long gone—but jungle gyms[9]. Don't just move up and down. Don't just look up. Look backwards, sideways, around corners. Your career and your life will have starts and stops and zigs and zags. Don't stress out about the white space, the path you can't draw, because therein lies both the surprises and the opportunities.

As you open yourself up to possibility, the most important thing I can tell you today is to open yourself up to honesty, to telling the truth to each other, to being honest with yourselves, and to being honest about the world we live in.

If you watch children, you will immediately notice how honest they are. My friend Betsy was pregnant and her son for their second child, son Sam was 5, he wanted to know where the baby was in her body. So he asked: "Mommy, are the baby's arms in your arms?" And she said, "no, no, Sam, the baby's in my tummy, the whole baby." "Mom, are the baby's legs in your legs?" "No, Sam, the whole baby's in my tummy." "Then Mommy, what's growing in your butt?"

As adults, we are almost never this honest and that can be a very good thing. When I was pregnant with our first child, I asked my husband Dave if my butt was getting big. At first, he didn't answer but I pressed. So he said, "Yeah, a little."

For years my sister-in-law[10] said about him what people will now say about

那时还没有互联网，马克·扎克伯格还在上小学——已经开始穿他的套头衫了。没有过早地把自己限制在某条职业路径上，让我有机会进入一个足以改变人生轨迹的新领域。对于那些认为我的一切都归功于好运的人来说，在卡纳迪楼之后，我又被分到了方院。我说得对吧，巴伦？

从你们今天的位置到未来的目标之间，并没有一条笔直的路。不要试图把那条线画出来，你不仅会画错，还会错过很多重大机遇，比如互联网。

职业发展不再是阶梯式上升，那样的时代早已过去，如今更像是攀爬架。不要只是上下移动，也不要只是抬头向前。要回头看，观察四周，探索角落。事业和生活会有潮起潮落，也会有曲折迂回。不要为留白和绘不出的路径而焦虑，因为那里蕴藏着意外之喜和无限可能。

我今天要说的关键点是，拥抱可能性的同时，也要坦诚——坦诚待人，坦诚待己，坦诚对待我们居住的这个世界。

观察一下孩子，你们就会立即发现，他们非常坦诚。我的朋友贝琪怀孕了，她5岁的儿子山姆好奇宝宝在她身体里的什么地方。于是他问："妈妈，宝宝的胳膊在你的胳膊里吗？"她说："不是的，山姆，整个宝宝都在我肚子里。""妈妈，宝宝的腿在你的腿里吗？""不，山姆，整个宝宝都在我肚子里。""那么妈妈，你的屁股里长了什么？"

作为成年人，我们几乎从来没有这么坦诚过，这或许是件好事。我怀第一个宝宝的时候，曾经问我的丈夫戴夫我的屁股是不是变大了。起初，他没有回答，但我继续追问。于是他说："是的，变大了一点。"

"那个家伙竟然上过哈佛"是戴夫的姐妹多年来对他的评价，也是你们将来犯蠢

---

8. got Quadded：在哈佛大学的住房分配体系中，学生如果被分到拉德克利夫方院，就可以说自己"got Quadded"。拉德克利夫方院是哈佛大学本科校园的一部分，位于马萨诸塞州剑桥市，曾是拉德克利夫学院女生的宿舍区，现在是哈佛大学学生的居住区域之一。
9. jungle gym：儿童攀爬游戏架。
10. sister-in-law：指因婚姻产生的姐妹关系，如嫂子、弟媳、大姑子等。

you for the rest of your life when you do something dumb, "and that guy went to Harvard."

Hearing the truth at different times along the way would have helped me. I would not have admitted it easily when I sat where you sit. But when I graduated, I was much more worried about my love life than my career. I thought I only had a few years, very limited time, to find one of the good guys, before he was to, or before they were all taken, or I got too old. So I moved to DC. I met a good guy, and I got married at the nearly decrepit[11] age of 24. I married a wonderful man, but I had no business making that kind of commitment. I didn't know who I was or who I wanted to be. My marriage fell apart within a year, something that was really embarrassing and painful at the time, and it did not help that so many friends came up to me and said, "I never knew that, never thought that was going to work" or "I knew you weren't right for each other." No one had managed to say anything like that to me before I marched down an aisle when it would have been far more useful.

And as I lived through those painful months of separation and divorce, boy, did I wish they had? And boy, did I wish I had asked them? At the same time in my professional life, someone did speak up. My first boss out of college was Lant Pritchett[12], an economist who teaches at the Kennedy School who is here with us today. After I deferred law school for the second time, Lant sat me down and said, "I don't think you should go to law school at all. I don't think you want to go to law school. I think you think you should because you told your parents you would many years ago." He noted that he had never once heard me talk about the law with any interest.

I know how hard it can be to be honest with each other, even your closest friends, even when they're about to make serious mistakes, but I bet sitting here today, you know your closest friends' strengths, weaknesses, what cliff they might drive off, and I bet for the most part you've never told them, and

的时候会听到的话。

要是能够听到真话，对各个人生阶段的我都会很有好处。当我尚且坐在你们的位置上时，我是不会轻易承认这一点的。不过，毕业的时候，更令我忧心的是爱情，而不是事业。我觉得自己只有几年非常有限的时间来找到一个好男人把自己嫁出去，趁着他或他们没被人抢光，趁着我还没变老。所以我搬到了哥伦比亚特区。我遇到了一个好男人，赶着在24岁这个还不算老的年纪步入了婚姻。我嫁的男人还不错，但我还没有能力经营好婚姻。我不知道自己是什么样的人，也不知道自己想成为什么样的人。仅仅一年，我的婚姻就破裂了，当时我觉得难堪又痛苦。朋友们纷纷过来对我说，"我从来不觉得你们能顺利走下去"或者"我早就知道你们不合适"。这样的话其实毫无帮助，要是说在我步入婚姻殿堂之前，会有用得多，但那时没有人对我说这样的话。

我经历了几个月痛苦的分居和离婚。天哪，我真希望他们能早点给我建议，也真希望我曾向他们寻求建议。而在我的职业生涯中，我的确遇到了直言相劝的人。兰特·普里切特是我大学毕业后的第一位老板，一位经济学家，曾执教于肯尼迪学院，今天他也在场。在我第二次推迟上法学院的计划后，兰特让我坐下来，跟我说："我觉得你根本不应该进法学院，我也不认为你想去。我觉得，你之所以认为你应该读法学院，只是因为多年前你告诉父母你会去读。"他指出，我谈论法律时，从未表现出任何兴趣。

我知道彼此坦诚有多难，即使对方是最亲密的朋友，即使对方即将犯下大错，但我敢打赌，在场的各位知道密友的优缺点，知道他们会在哪里跌落悬崖，但多数情况下，你从来没有告诉过他们，他们也从来没有问过。问一问吧，问问他们的真

---

11. decrepit: *adj.* 衰老的。
12. Lant Pritchett: 兰特·普里切特，美国发展经济学家，曾在哈佛大学肯尼迪学院任教。

they've never asked. Ask them. Ask them for the truth because it will help you. And when they answer honestly, know that that's what makes them real friends.

Asking for feedback is a really important habit to get into, as you leave the structure of the school calendar and exams and grades behind. On many jobs if you want to know how you're doing, you're going to have to ask and then you're going to have to listen without getting defensive. Take it from me[13], listening to criticism is never fun, but it's the only way we can improve.

A few years ago, Mark Zuckerberg decided he wanted to learn Chinese, and in order to practice he started trying to have work meetings with some of our Facebook colleagues who are native speakers. Now you would think his very limited language skills would keep these conversations from being useful. One day he asked a woman who was there how it was going, how did she like Facebook. She answered with a long and pretty complicated sentence. So he said, "Simpler please." She spoke again. "Simpler please." This went back and forth a couple of times. So she just blurted out in frustration, "My manager is bad." That he understood.

So often the truth is sacrificed to conflict avoidance, or by the time we speak the truth, we've used so many caveats[14] and preambles that the message totally gets lost. So as you ask each other for the truth and other people, can you elicit it in simple and clear language? And when you speak your truth, can you use simple and clear language?

As hard as it is to be honest with other people. It can be even more difficult to be honest with ourselves. For years after I had children, I would say pretty often I don't feel guilty working even when no one asked. Someone might say, "Sherly, how's your day today?" And I would say, "Great. I don't feel guilty working." Or "Do I need a sweater?" "Yes, it's unpredictably freezing and I don't feel guilty working." I was kinda[15] like a parrot with issues.

Then one day on the treadmill, I was reading this article in the *Sociology*

话，因为这会让你受益匪浅。当他们说真话时，你要知道，正是这逆耳忠言让他们成为真正的朋友。

在离开学校日程、考试和分数的体系之后，寻求反馈是要养成的一个非常重要的习惯。在很多工作中，若想知道自己表现如何，必须主动去问，必须认真地听，不要觉得被冒犯。相信我，挨批评从来都不是好玩的事，但我们只能在批评中进步。

几年前，马克·扎克伯格决定学习中文，为了练习，他开始尝试在"脸书"工作会议中和以中文为母语的同事交流。你们可能会觉得，他的语言水平有限，没法实现有效沟通。有一天，他在会上问一位女士工作进展如何，问她是否喜欢"脸书"。她回答了一个很复杂的长句。于是他说："请说得简单一点。"她重新回答了一遍，可扎克伯格又说："请说得再简单一点。"来回几轮后，她沮丧地脱口而出："我的经理很差劲。"扎克伯格这下就明白了。

为了避免冲突，真相常常被掩埋，或者说，当我们说真话时，我们用了太多的事先声明和开场白把真正的信息淹没了。那么，当你们向彼此以及他人寻求真话时，你们能用简单明了的语言表达吗？自己说真话时，你们能用简单明了的语言来表达吗？

坦诚待人难，坦诚待己更难。在我有了孩子之后的几年里，即使没有人问，我也经常会说，我对工作问心无愧。可能有人问我："雪莉，你今天过得怎么样？"我会说："过得很好，我对工作问心无愧。"或者"今天要穿毛衣吗？""是的，外面冷得出奇，我对工作问心无愧。"我有点像一只有毛病的鹦鹉。

有一天，我在跑步机上读到《社会学杂志》上的一篇文章。文章指出，谎言不

---

13. take it from me：相信我说的话。
14. caveat：*n.* 警告；事先声明。
15. kinda：有点；常用于笔语中，表示非正式会话中 kind of 的发音。

Journal about how people don't start out lying to other people, they start out lying to themselves, and the things we repeat most frequently are often those lies.

So as sweat was pouring down my face, I started wondering, well, what do I repeat pretty frequently. And I realized I feel guilty working. I then did a lot of research, and I spent an entire year with my dear friend Nell Scovell[16] writing a book talking about how I was thinking and feeling, and I'm so grateful that so many women around the world connected to it. My book of course was called *Fifty Shades of Grey*[17]. I can see a lot of you connected to it as well.

We have even more work to do in being honest about the world we live in. We don't always see the hard truths, and once we see them, we don't always have the courage to speak out.

When my classmates and I were in college, we thought the fight for gender equality was one that was over. Sure, most of the leaders in every industry were men, but we thought changing that was just a matter of time. Lamont library[18] right over there, one generation before us didn't let women through its doors. But by the time we sat in your seat, everything was equal. Harvard and Radcliffe[19] was fully integrated.

We didn't need feminism because we were already equals. We were wrong. I was wrong. The world was not equal then and it is not equal now. I think nowadays, we don't just hide ourselves from the hard truths and shut our eyes to the inequities, but we suffer from the tyranny[20] of low expectations.

In the last election cycle in the United States, women won 20% of the Senate seats, and all the headlines kept screaming out: Women take over the Senate. Women take over the Senate. I felt like screaming back, wait a minute everyone. 50% of the population getting 20% of the seats. That's not a takeover. That's an embarrassment.

Just a few months ago this year, a very well-respected and well-known

是始于欺人，而是始于自欺，经常挂在嘴边的往往就是谎言。

我脸上汗如雨下。我开始回忆自己常把什么挂在嘴边，这才意识到，我工作时是感到内疚的。然后我做了很多研究，花了整整一年的时间，与我的好友尼尔·斯科维尔一同写了一本书，在书中讲述我的想法和感受。世界各地许多女性都与这本书产生了共鸣，对此我由衷欣慰。我的书当然是叫《五十度灰》啦。我看得出来，你们中很多人对这本书的内容也颇有感触。

在坦诚面对我们所居住的世界这方面，我们有更多的工作要做。我们并非总是看清残酷的真相，即使看清了，我们也未必勇于发声。

读大学时，我和同学们认为，争取性别平权的斗争早已结束。当然，各行各业的领导者多数是男性，但我们认为变化是迟早的事。就在那边的拉蒙特图书馆，直到我们的上一代，还不允许女性进入。但当年我们坐在你们的座位上时，一切都平等了。哈佛和拉德克利夫完全合并了。

我们不需要女权主义了，因为我们已经平等了。我们错了。我错了。世界过去不平等，现在也不平等。我认为，如今，我们不仅对残酷的事实避而不谈，对不平等视而不见，而且还受到低期望的桎梏。

在美国上一届选举周期中，女性赢得了20%的参议院席位，所有的头条新闻都在叫嚷：女性接管了参议院。我真想喊回去：别急着说这种话，50%的人获得20%的席位，这不是接管，是耻辱。

就在今年几个月前，一位广受敬重的知名硅谷企业高管邀请我在他的俱乐部就

---

16. Nell Scovell：尼尔·斯科维尔，美国作家、记者、制片人，毕业于哈佛大学，曾和雪莉·桑德伯格合著《向前一步：女性、工作及领导意志》(Lean In: Women, Work, and the Will to Lead)。
17. 此处所指的书是《向前一步》，而 Fifty Shades of Grey 即《五十度灰》的作者是 E. L. 詹姆斯，此处是在开玩笑。——译者注
18. Lamont library：拉蒙特图书馆，美国第一个专门给本科生提供服务的图书馆，1967年才向女性开放。
19. Radcliffe：指拉德克利夫学院（Radcliffe College），美国女子学院，1999年全面并入哈佛，海伦·凯勒毕业于该学院。
20. tyranny：n. 暴政；暴虐；苛政；专横。

business executive in Silicon Valley invited me to give a speech to his club on social media. I've been to this club a few months before when I had been invited for a friend's birthday. It was a beautiful building and I was wandering around looking at it, looking for the women's room, when a staff member informed me very firmly that the ladies' room was over there and I should be sure not to go upstairs because women are never allowed in this building. I didn't realize I was in an all-male club until that minute.

I spent the rest of the night wondering what I was doing there, wondering what everyone else was doing there, wondering if any of my friends in San Francisco would invite me to a party at a club that didn't allow Blacks or Jews or Asians or gays. Being invited to give a business speech at this club, hit me as even more egregious[21] because you couldn't claim that it was only social. Business wasn't done there.

My first thought was, "Really? Really." A year after *Lean In*, this dude thought it was a good idea to invite me to give a speech to his literal all-boys club. And he wasn't alone, there was an entire committee of well-respected businessmen who joined him in issuing this kind invitation.

To paraphrase Groucho Marx[22], and don't worry, I won't try to do the voice. "I don't want to speak in any club that won't have me as a member." So I said no, and I did it in a way I probably wouldn't have even 5 years before. I wrote a long and passionate email, arguing that they should change their policies. They thanked me for my prompt response and wrote that perhaps things will eventually change. Our expectations are too low. Eventually needs to become immediately.

We need to see the truth and speak the truth. We tolerate discrimination and we pretend that opportunity is equal. Yes, we elected an African-American president, but racism is pervasive still.

Yes, there are women who run Fortune 500 companies, 5 percent to be

社交媒体这一主题发表演讲。几个月前，我应邀去参加朋友的生日聚会，去过那家俱乐部。那是一栋漂亮的建筑，我四处转悠，寻找女士洗手间，这时，一位工作人员为我指出了女士洗手间的方向，并特别严肃地提醒我绝对不能上楼，因为这栋楼不允许女性进入。直到那一刻我才意识到，我在一个全男俱乐部里。

整个晚上我都在思索。我到那里去干什么，其他人又是为什么聚在那里，旧金山的朋友会不会邀请我参加一个不接纳黑人、犹太人、亚洲人或同性恋的俱乐部派对。我居然收到这家俱乐部的商业演讲邀请，让我觉得这极差劲，因为这并不能归结为纯粹的社交活动，而那里根本没有商务往来。

我的第一反应是："真的吗？是真的。"《向前一步》出版一年后，这家伙觉得邀请我去他的全男俱乐部演讲是个好主意。他并不是唯一一个这样做的人，不少声望卓著的商界人士和他一起发出了邀请。

借用格劳乔·马克斯的话——别担心，我不会模仿他的腔调——"我不会去任何不愿接纳我为会员的俱乐部演讲"。于是我拒绝了，并且做了5年前的我不会做的事。我写了一封言辞恳切的长邮件，希望他们改变俱乐部的规则。他们对我的迅速回复表示感谢，并回答说，也许事情最终将会迎来变化。我们的期望太低了。"最终"应当变成"立即"才行。

我们应当看到真相，说出真相。我们容忍歧视，假装机会是平等的。没错，我们选出了一位非裔美国总统，但种族主义仍然普遍存在。

没错，财富五百强公司中确实有女性领袖，确切地说，有5%，但通往女性领袖

---

21. egregious：*adj.* 极差的；极坏的。
22. Groucho Marx：格劳乔·马克斯（1890—1977），美国电影演员。

precise, but our road there is still paved with words like pushy and bossy, while our male peers are leaders and results-focused.

African-American women have to prove that they're not angry. Latinos risk being branded as fiery hotheads. A group of Asian-American women and men at Facebook wore pins one day that said "I may or may not be good at math".

Yes, Harvard has a woman president, and in two years, the United States may have a woman president. But in order to get there, Hillary Clinton is gonna have to overcome 2 very real obstacles, unknown and often ununderstood gender bias, and even worse, a degree from Yale.

You can challenge stereotypes both subtle and obvious. At Facebook, we have posters around the wall to inspire us. Done is better than perfect. Fortune favors the bold. What would you do if you weren't afraid? My new favorite: nothing at Facebook is someone else's problem. I hope you feel that way about the problems you see in the world, because they are not someone else's problem. Gender inequality harms men along with women. Racism hurts Whites along with Minorities. And the lack of equal opportunity keeps all of us from fulfilling our true potential.

So as you graduate today, I want to put some pressure on you. I want to put some pressure on you to acknowledge the hard truths, not shy away from them, and when you see them, to address them.

The first time I spoke out about what it was like to be a woman in the workforce was less than five years ago. That means that for 18 years from where you sit to where I stand, my silence implied that everything was okay. You can do better than I did. And I mean that so sincerely.

At the same time, I want to take some pressure off you. Sitting here today you don't have to know what career you want or how to get the career you might want. Leaning in does not mean your path will be straight or smooth.

的这条路上仍然充满了"强势"和"跋扈"的恶语评价，而男性则被评价为以结果为导向的领袖。

非裔美国女性必须证明自己没有生气。拉丁裔美国人可能会轻易被贴上"脾气火暴"的标签。"脸书"员工中有一群亚裔男女，他们曾戴上胸针，上面写着"我可能擅长数学，也可能不擅长"。

没错，哈佛大学有过一位女校长，两年后，美国可能会迎来一位女总统。但为了实现这一目标，希拉里·克林顿必须克服两个非常现实的障碍：第一个是未知的、往往不被理解的性别偏见；第二个更糟糕，她还需要耶鲁大学的学位。

你们可以向那些微妙又显眼的刻板印象宣战。在"脸书"，我们在墙上贴海报来激励自己："完成胜于完美""好运垂青勇者""别怕，大胆闯"。我最近最喜欢的一条是"在'脸书'没有一件事与己无关"。我希望你们对世间顽症也能抱有同样的态度，因为没有哪个问题是只属于别人的。性别不平等伤害女性，也伤害男性。种族主义伤害少数族裔，也伤害白人。机会不平等会让所有人都无法发挥出真正的潜力。

因此，在今天毕业之际，我想给你们施加一些压力，希望你们勇于直面残酷的真相，不要回避，遇到了就要积极应对。

我首次为职场女性公开发声，距今还不到5年。也就是说，从毕业到现在，我有18年都保持沉默，好似表示一切尚可接受。你们肯定能做得比我强。我这话是发自内心的。

同时，我也想减轻你们的一些压力。今天，在座的各位不必着急弄明白自己热爱的事业是什么，又该如何追求。"向前一步"并不意味着你的职业道路一帆风顺，

> *Gender inequality harms men along with women.*
> 性别不平等伤害女性，也伤害男性。

And most people who make great contribution start way later than Mark Zuckerberg. Find a jungle gym you want to play and start climbing, not only will you figure out what you want to do eventually, but once you do, you'll crush it.

Looking at you all here today, I'm filled with hope. All of you were admitted to a "small school" near Boston, either for your academic potential, your personality, or both. You've had your firsts, whether it's a winter coat, a love or a C. You've learned more about who you are and who you want to be. And most importantly, you've experienced the power of community. You know that while you are extraordinary on your own, we are all stronger and can be louder together. I know that you will never forget Harvard, and Harvard will never forget you, especially during the next fundraising drive.

Tomorrow, you all become part of a lifelong community, which offers truly great opportunity, and therefore comes with real obligation. You can make the world fairer for everyone, expect honesty from yourself and each other, demand and create truly equal opportunity, not eventually, but now. And tomorrow, by the way, you get something Mark Zuckerberg does not have, a Harvard degree. Congratulations, everyone!

大多数做出杰出贡献的人起步比马克·扎克伯格晚得多。找一个感兴趣的攀爬架玩一玩吧，你们最终会找到自己的志向所在，而且一旦找到，你们就会大放异彩。

今天看着在座的各位，我的心中充满了希望。你们都被波士顿附近的一所"小学校"录取了，要么是因为学术潜力，要么是因为个性魅力，要么两者兼而有之。你们体验了各种第一次，无论是一件冬衣、一段爱情，还是一个C等成绩。对于"我是谁"和"我想成为谁"，你们都有了更深层次的了解。最重要的是，你们体验到了集体的力量。你们知道，虽然你一个人很出色，但同心合力会爆发出更强大的力量，喊出更响亮的声音。我知道你们永远不会忘记哈佛，哈佛也永远不会忘记你们，尤其是下次筹款募捐的时候。

明天，你们都将成为社会的终身成员，会真正遇到机遇，也将切实承担义务。你们可以把世界变得更公平，坦诚待人待己，要求并创造真正平等的机会，无须等待，就是现在。对了，明天你们会得到马克·扎克伯格没有的东西——哈佛学位。祝贺大家！

语录 Quotes

- Don't stress out about the white space, the path you can't draw, because therein lies both the surprises and the opportunities.
  不要为留白和绘不出的路径而焦虑,因为那里蕴藏着意外之喜和无限可能。

- Listening to criticism is never fun, but it's the only way we can improve.
  挨批评从来都不是好玩的事,但我们只能在批评中进步。

- So often the truth is sacrificed to conflict avoidance.
  为了避免冲突,真相常常被掩埋。

- Eventually needs to become immediately.
  "最终"应当变成"立即"才行。

- We need to see the truth and speak the truth.
  我们应当看到真相,说出真相。

- Gender inequality harms men along with women.
  性别不平等伤害女性,也伤害男性。

- The lack of equal opportunity keeps all of us from fulfilling our true potential.
  机会不平等会让所有人都无法发挥出真正的潜力。

Never Surrender to Complexity
永远不要向复杂低头

——比尔·盖茨 2007 年在哈佛大学毕业典礼上的演讲

> 简介 Profile

比尔·盖茨
Bill Gates

比尔·盖茨是一位充满传奇色彩的人物。作为微软公司的创始人以及全球最富有的人之一，他的智慧与远见引领了科技产业的发展，改变了人类生活的面貌。

1955年，盖茨出生于美国华盛顿州的西雅图市。他从小就对计算机有着极大的兴趣，当大多数人对这一新兴事物还感到陌生时，他已经看到了其中潜藏的巨大商机。于是1975年，盖茨与好友保罗·艾伦一同创办了微软公司，从此开启了他的科技帝国之路。微软成功推出了Windows操作系统，这一产品成为计算机产业的标准之一，也为微软赢得了巨大的市场份额。除了Windows操作系统，盖茨还带领微软涉足了多个领域，如办公软件、浏览器、游戏机等。这些产品不仅为微软带来了丰厚的利润，也改变了人们的工作、娱乐方式。

盖茨的成功也并非一帆风顺。他也曾面临过竞争对手的挑战、市场的变化以及企业内部的问题，但盖茨总是能够以坚定的信念和出色的领导力带领微软克服困难，继续前进。

2008年，盖茨正式辞去了微软的CEO职务，但他依然关注着科技产业的发展和微软的创新方向。他的影响力不仅仅局限于微软公司，更延伸到了整个科技产业和全球公益领域。

2007年，比尔·盖茨在面向哈佛大学毕业生发表的演讲中，提到了使他获得如此成就的最重要的思维模式，那就是永远不向任何复杂性事物低头。人性趋向简单，逃避复杂，但真正有大发展的人是敢于面对复杂问题的人。尤其是处于当下这个复杂的世界，我们无须急于求成，任何微小但持续的努力都可能带来自身和社会的发展。

演讲 Speech

扫描二维码
获取本篇演讲原视频、音频

President Bok, former President Rudenstine, incoming President Faust, members of the Harvard Corporation and the Board of Overseers, members of the faculty, parents, and especially, the graduates:

I've been waiting more than 30 years to say this: "Dad, I always told you I'd come back and get my degree."

I want to thank Harvard for this honor. I'll be changing my job[1] next year ... and it will be nice to finally have a college degree on my resume.

I applaud the graduates for taking a much more direct route to your degrees. For my part, I'm just happy that the *Crimson*[2] has called me "Harvard's most successful dropout." I guess that makes me valedictorian[3] of my own special class ... I did the best of everyone who failed.

But I also want to be recognized as the guy who got Steve Ballmer[4] to drop out of business school. I'm a bad influence. That's why I was invited to speak at your graduation. If I had spoken at your orientation, fewer of you might be here today.

Harvard was a phenomenal experience for me. Academic life was fascinating. I used to sit in on lots of classes I hadn't even signed up for. And dorm life was terrific. I lived up at Radcliffe, in Currier House[5].

There were always a lot of people in my dorm room late at night discussing things, because everyone knew that I didn't worry about getting up in the

博克校长、鲁登斯坦前校长、即将上任的福斯特校长、哈佛集团的各位成员、监管委员会的各位理事、各位老师、各位家长，尤其是各位毕业生：

等了 30 多年，我终于能够说出这句话了："爸爸，我说过我会回来拿到学位的。"

感谢哈佛授予我这一荣誉。我明年要换工作……终于能在简历上写上学士学位，这真是太好了。

我为各位毕业生感到高兴，你们拿到学位可比我简单多了。对我来说，我很高兴《哈佛深红报》称我为"哈佛最成功的辍学学生"。我想，正是这一点让我成为这个特殊班级的毕业生代表……在所有失败者当中，我做到了最好。

但我也希望大家认识到，我就是那个令史蒂夫·鲍尔默从商学院辍学的人。我是个坏榜样。这就是我受邀发表毕业典礼演讲的原因。倘若我到入学典礼上去发言，今天在场的人可能会更少。

哈佛对我来说是一段难忘的经历。学术生活令人着迷，我曾经旁听过很多未曾报名的课程。宿舍生活也极为美好，我住在拉德克利夫的柯里尔楼。

总是有很多人聚在我的宿舍里聊到深夜，因为大家都知道我不用担心早上起不

---

1. changing my job：指比尔·盖茨在 2008 年宣布退休，淡出微软的日常管理，并把 580 亿美元的个人财产捐给慈善基金会。
2. Crimson：指《哈佛深红报》(*The Harvard Crimson*)，哈佛大学学生日报，创办于 1873 年。
3. valedictorian：*n.*（毕业典礼上）致告别词的最优生。
4. Steve Ballmer：史蒂夫·鲍尔默（1956—），1980 年从斯坦福大学辍学，加入微软，2000—2014 年担任微软总裁。
5. Currier House：柯里尔楼，位于拉德克利夫四合院，哈佛大学的 12 个本科生宿舍之一，以 1967 年在飞机失事中遇难的学生奥黛丽·布鲁斯·柯里尔（Audrey Bruce Currier）命名。

morning. That's how I came to be the leader of the anti-social group. We clunged each other as a way of validating our rejection of all those social people.

Radcliffe was a great place to live. There were more women up there, and most of the guys were math-science types. The combination offered me the best odds, if you know what I mean. That is where I learned the sad lesson that improving your odds doesn't guarantee success.

One of my biggest memories of Harvard came in January 1975, when I made a call From Currier House to a company in Albuquerque, New Mexico, that had begun making the world's first personal computer. I offered to sell them software.

I worried they would realize I was just a student in a dorm and hang up on me. Instead they said: "We're not quite ready, come see us in a month," which was a good thing, because we hadn't written the software yet. From that moment, I worked day and night on the extra credit project that marked the end of my college education and the beginning of a remarkable journey with Microsoft.

What I remember above all about Harvard was being in the midst of so much energy and intelligence. It could be exhilarating, intimidating, sometimes even discouraging, but always challenging. It was an amazing privilege…and though I left early, I was transformed by my years at Harvard, the friendships I made, and the ideas I worked on.

But taking a serious look back … I do have one big regret. I left Harvard with no real awareness of the awful inequities in the world—the appalling disparities of health, and wealth, and opportunity that condemn[6] millions of people to lives of despair.

I learned a lot here at Harvard about new ideas in economics and politics. I got great exposure to the advances being made in the sciences. But humanity's

来。我也因此成为不合群学生的头头儿。我们抱团取暖，以示对一般社交人群的拒绝态度。

拉德克利夫是个住宿的好地方。那里女生很多，而且大多数男生都是理工科那种类型。你们懂我的意思吧，这种组合带来了最大的胜算。在那里我学到了一个惨痛的教训，那就是提高胜算并不能确保成功。

我对哈佛最深刻的记忆之一发生在 1975 年 1 月，当时我在柯里尔楼，给新墨西哥州阿尔伯克基的一家公司打电话。那家公司已经开始制造全球首台个人电脑，我要向他们出售软件。

那时我还担心，万一对方发现我只是一个住在宿舍里的学生，搞不好会直接挂断电话。谁知道对方说："我们还没准备好，一个月后再来找我们吧。"这是件好事，因为我们还没开始编写软件。从那一刻起，我夜以继日地在这个额外学分项目上埋头苦干，这给我的大学时光画上了句号，也标志着我与微软这段奇妙旅程的开端。

关于哈佛，我印象最深刻的是我身边的那些朝气蓬勃的聪明人。这既令人亢奋，又给人压力，有时还会让人沮丧，但在哈佛的生活总是充满挑战。能有这样的经历真的很幸运……虽然我早早地离开了，但哈佛的岁月、我结交的朋友和我折腾过的项目都对我影响很深。

但认真回想起来，我确实有一个很大的遗憾。离开哈佛时，我并没有真正意识到世界上存在着可怕的不平等——健康、财富和机会的巨大差距，使数百万人陷入绝望的生活。

我在哈佛学到了很多经济和政治方面的新思想。我非常了解科学领域的进步。

---

6. condemn：v. (情况) 迫使 (某人) 忍受 (或做) 令人不快之事。

greatest advances are not in its discoveries—but in how those discoveries are applied to reduce inequity. Whether through democracy, strong public education, quality health care, or broad economic opportunity—reducing inequity is the highest human achievement.

I left campus knowing little about the millions of young people cheated out of educational opportunities here in this country. And I knew nothing about the millions of people living in unspeakable poverty and disease in developing countries. It took me decades to find out.

You graduates came to Harvard at a different time. You know more about the world's inequities than the classes that came before. In your years here, I hope you've had a chance to think about how—in this age of accelerating technology—we can finally take on[7] these inequities, and we can solve them.

Imagine, just for the sake of discussion, that you had a few hours a week and a few dollars a month to donate to a cause—and you wanted to spend that time and money—where it would have the greatest impact in saving and improving lives. Where would you spend it?

For Melinda[8] and for I, the challenge is the same: how can we do the most good for the greatest number with the resources we have.

During our discussions on this question, Melinda and I read an article about the millions of children who were dying every year in poor countries from diseases that we had long ago made harmless in this country. Measles, malaria, pneumonia, hepatitis B, yellow fever. One disease that I had never heard of, rotavirus, was killing half a million children each year—none of them in the United States.

We were shocked. We had assumed that if millions of children were dying and they could be saved, the world would make it a priority to discover and deliver the medicines to save them. But it did not. For under a dollar, there were interventions that could save lives that just weren't being delivered.

但人类最伟大的进步并不在于发现，而是在于如何应用发现来减少不平等。无论是民主、强大的公共教育、优质的医疗保健还是广泛的经济机会，减少不平等都是人类的最高成就。

离开校园时，我并不知道这个国家有数百万年轻人被剥夺了受教育的机会。我也不知道发展中国家有数百万人生活在难以言说的贫困和疾病中。我花了几十年时间才了解到这些情况。

各位毕业生，你们进哈佛的时候，情况已经和以前不一样了。对于世界的种种不公，你们比以前的学生了解得更多。在求学生涯中，我希望你们抽出时间思考一下：在科技加速发展的时代，我们究竟该如何应对和消灭不平等。

我们来聊一聊这个问题，试想一下，假如你每周有几个小时，每月有几美元，可以捐献给某项事业，希望能在拯救生命和改善生活方面产生最大的作用，你们会用在哪里？

对于梅琳达和我来说，我们面临的挑战是一样的：如何用现有的资源帮到最多的人。

我跟梅琳达聊这个话题时，读到了一篇文章，说贫穷国家每年有数百万儿童死于美国早就能轻松治愈的疾病：麻疹、疟疾、肺炎、乙肝、黄热病。还有一种我从未听过的轮状病毒，这种疾病每年会夺走 50 万儿童的生命，但是在美国一例死亡病例也没有。

我们大为震惊。曾经我们以为，如果数百万儿童危在旦夕，但其实是有救的，那么，全世界将优先为他们研发和提供药物。但事实并非如此，有些救命的办法成本不到一美元，但就是没有送到他们手中。

---

7. take on：承担，接受（尤指艰巨工作或重大责任）。
8. Melinda：指梅琳达·法兰奇·盖茨（Melinda French Gates），美国慈善家，前微软多媒体产品开发人员和经理，入选 BBC 2021 年度百大女性；1994 年 1 月与比尔·盖茨结婚，2021 年 5 月宣布和比尔·盖茨离婚。

If you believe that every life has equal value, it's revolting to learn that some lives are seen as worth saving and others are not. We said to ourselves: "This can't be true. But if it is true, it deserves to be the priority of our giving."

So we began our work in the same way anyone here would begin it. We asked: "How could the world let these children die?" The answer is simple, and harsh. The market did not reward saving the lives of these children, and governments did not subsidize it. So the children died because their mothers and fathers had no power in the market and no voice in the system.

But you and I have both. We can make market forces work better for the poor—if we can stretch the reach of market forces so that more people can make a profit, or at least earn a living, serving people who are suffering from the great inequities. We can also press governments around the world to spend taxpayer money in ways that better reflect the values of the people who pay the taxes.

If we can find approaches that meet the needs of the poor in ways that generate profits for business and votes for politicians, we will have found a sustainable way to reduce inequity in the world. Now this task is open-ended. It can never be finished. But a conscious effort to answer this challenge can change the world.

I am optimistic that we can do this, but I talk to skeptics who claim there is no hope. They say: "Inequity has been with us since the beginning, and will be with us until the end——because people just don't care." I completely disagree.

I believe we have more caring than we know what to do with. All of us here in this Yard, at one time or another, have seen human tragedies that broke our heart, and yet we did nothing—not because we didn't care, but because we didn't know what to do. If we had known how to help, we would have acted.

The barrier to change is not too little caring; it is too much complexity. To

相信人人生而平等，却发现性命是否值得被救各有标价估量，这让人难以接受。我们对自己说："这不可能。但如果这是真的，那它就应成为我们给予帮助时优先考虑的事情。"

于是我们开始行动了，换成在座的各位，想必也是一样的。我们问："世界怎么能眼睁睁看着这些孩子死去？"答案很简单，也很残酷。拯救这些孩子的生命不会得到市场的回报，也不会得到政府的补贴。所以，这些孩子死去了，因为他们的父母在市场中没有实力，在体制中没有话语权。

但你我都具备这两点条件。倘若我们能够让市场的手伸得更远些，让救助贫苦者能够赚到钱，或者至少维持生计，那么，市场力量就能更好地服务于贫困人口。我们还可以向世界各国政府施压，让他们把纳税人的钱花在更契合纳税人价值观的地方。

减少全球不平等问题的方法应当既能解决贫困人口问题，又能为企业创造利润，为政客赢得选票，这样的可持续方法正是我们需要探索的。这项任务没有确定的结论，也永远不会有终点。然而，只要有意识地接受这一挑战，就能改变世界。

我乐观地认为我们可以做到这一点，不过我也和认为毫无希望的怀疑派聊过。他们说："不平等问题从人类诞生之初就存在，也将一直存在，因为人们根本不在乎。"我完全不同意这种观点。

我相信，我们在乎的事情太多了，只是不知道如何将爱心转化为行动。在座的各位或多或少都目睹过令人痛心的人类悲剧，但什么也没做——不是因为不在乎，而是因为不知道该做什么。如果知道如何提供帮助，我们都会行动起来。

阻碍改变的，不是关心不够，而是复杂过头。要想把关心变成行动，我们需要

> *Improving your odds doesn't guarantee success.*
>
> *提高胜算并不能确保成功。*

turn caring into action, we need to see a problem, see a solution, and see the impact. But complexity blocks all three steps.

Even with the advent of the Internet and 24-hour news, it is still a complex enterprise to get people to truly see the problems. When an airplane crashes, officials immediately call a press conference. They promise to investigate, determine the cause, and prevent similar crashes in the future.

But if the officials were brutally honest, they would say: "Of all the people in the world who died today from preventable causes, one half of one percent were on this plane. We're determined to do everything possible to solve the problem that took the lives of the one half of one percent."

The problem is not just the plane crash, but the millions of preventable deaths.

We don't read much about these deaths. The media covers what's new and millions of people dying is nothing new. So it stays in the background where it's easy to ignore.

But even when we do see it or read about it, it's difficult to keep our eyes on the problem. It's difficult to look at suffering if the situation is so complex that we don't know how to help and so we look away.

If we can really see a problem, which is the first step, we come to the second step: cutting through the complexity to find a solution.

Finding solutions is essential if we want to make the most of our caring. If we have clear and proven answers anytime an organization or individual asks "How can I help?" then we can get action—and we can make sure that none of the caring in the world is wasted. The complexity makes it hard to mark a path of action for everyone who cares—and makes it hard for their caring to matter.

Cutting through complexity to find solutions runs through four predictable stages: determine a goal, find the highest-impact approach, deliver the technology ideal for that approach, and in the meantime, use the best application of

看见问题、找到解决方案，并预测其影响。但复杂性阻碍了这三个步骤。

即使有了互联网和 24 小时新闻，想让人们真正认识到问题所在也仍然很难。倘若飞机坠毁，官员们会立即召开新闻发布会。他们承诺会进行调查、查明原因，并采取措施，防止未来发生类似的坠机事故。

但官员们要是实话实说，就会这么说："今天，全球所有可以避免的死亡之中，只有 0.5% 的人死于这架飞机的失事。我们决心尽一切可能，调查这 0.5% 的死亡原因。"

问题不仅在于这次飞机失事，还在于数以百万计的本可避免的死亡。

我们鲜少读到这些死亡的相关报道。媒体报道的是新闻，数百万人的死亡并不是什么新鲜事，所以它始终隐于背景之中，难以察觉。

但即使我们看到了，读到了，也很难对问题保持关注。情况太复杂了，我们不知道能做些什么，这就让人难以注视惨剧的发生，于是我们移开目光。

如果我们真的发现了问题所在，这是只是第一步，接着就可以进入第二步：突破复杂性，找到解决方案。

要想让爱心发挥最大限度的作用，就必须找到解决方案。每当有组织或个体问："我能帮上什么忙？"若是都能得到明确可靠的答案，那么行动便得以促成，爱心也必定不会浪费。复杂性使得有心人难以获得明确的行动路线，也使得爱心难以发挥作用。

突破复杂性，寻找解决方案，需要四个可预测的阶段：确定目标，找到最具影响力的方法，提供最适合该方法的技术，同时，最有效地利用现有的技术——可以

> *The barrier to change is not too little caring; it is too much complexity.*
>
> 阻碍改变的，不是关心不够，而是复杂过头。

永远不要向复杂低头

technology you already have—whether it's something sophisticated, like a new drug, or something simple, like a bednet[9].

The AIDS epidemic offers an example. The broad goal, of course, is to end the disease. The highest-leverage approach is prevention. The ideal technology would be a vaccine that gives life-long immunity with a single dose. So governments, drug companies, and foundations are funding vaccine research. But their work is likely to take more than a decade, so in the meantime, we have to work with what we have in hand—and the best prevention approach we have now is getting people to avoid risky behavior.

Pursuing that goal starts the four-step cycle again. This is the pattern. The crucial thing is to never stop thinking and working—and never do what we did with malaria and tuberculosis in the 20th century—which is to surrender to complexity and quit.

The final step—after seeing the problem and finding an approach—is to measure the impact of the work and to share that success or failure so that others can learn from the efforts.

You have to have the statistics, of course. You have to be able to show, for example, that a program is vaccinating millions more children. You have to be able to show, for example, a decline in the number of children dying from the diseases. This is essential not just to improve the program, but also to help draw more investment from business and government.

But if you want to inspire people to participate, you have to show more than numbers; you have to convey the human impact of the work—so people can feel what saving a life means to the families affected.

I remember going to the World Economic Forum some years back and sitting on a global health panel that was discussing ways to save millions of lives. Millions! Think of the thrill if you could save just one person's life—then multiply that by millions … Yet this was the most boring panel I've ever

复杂如新药，也可以简单如蚊帐。

艾滋病便是典型案例。当然，总体目标是消灭疾病本身。最具影响力的方法是预防。最理想的技术是一次注射终身免疫的疫苗。因此，政府、制药公司和基金会都在资助疫苗研究。但这项工作可能需要十多年的时间，所以与此同时，必须利用现有资源开展工作——现有的最佳预防方法是让大众规避危险行为。

这一目标的追求又是新一轮的四步走。这就是一种模式。关键是永远不要停止思考和工作——永远不要像20世纪对付疟疾和肺结核那样，屈服于复杂性然后放弃。

在发现问题并找到解决方法之后，最后一步是评估工作的效果，并分享成功或失败经验，以便他人学习。

当然，统计数据必不可少。例如，一个项目为数百万儿童接种了疫苗，则必须能够证明死于该疾病的儿童数量有所下降。这不仅是改进项目的关键，也有助于吸引更多企业和政府的投资。

但要想激励人们参与，仅仅摆出数字是不够的，还必须展现这项工作对个体的影响。如此一来，人们才能真切地体会到挽救一条生命对患者家庭的意义。

记得几年前，我参加了世界经济论坛的全球健康小组讨论，话题是如何拯救数百万人的生命。数百万！想想看，如果能救下一个人，那该有多激动人心——而这可是乘以数百万……然而，我从没参加过这么无聊的小组讨论，无聊到连我都受

> *Finding solutions is essential if we want to make the most of our caring.*
>
> 要想让爱心发挥最大限度的作用，就必须找到解决方案。

---

9. bednet: *n.* 蚊帐。

been on—ever. So boring that even I couldn't stand it.

What made that experience especially striking was that I had just come from an event where we were introducing version 13 of some piece of software, and we had people jumping and shouting with excitement. I love getting people excited about software—but why can't we generate even more excitement for saving lives?

You can't get people excited unless you can help them see and feel the impact. The way to do that—is a complex question. Still, I'm optimistic. Yes, inequity has been with us forever, but the new tools we have to cut through complexity have not been with us forever. They are new—they can help us make the most of our caring—and that's why the future can be different from the past.

The defining and ongoing innovations of this age—biotechnology, the personal computer, and the Internet—give us a chance we've never had before to end extreme poverty and end death from preventable disease.

60 years ago, George Marshall[10] came to this commencement and he announced a plan to assist the nations of post-war Europe. He said, I quote, "I think one difficulty is that the problem is one of such enormous complexity that the very massive facts presented to the public by press and radio make it exceedingly difficult for the man in the street to reach a clear appraisement of the situation. It is virtually impossible, at this distance, to grasp at all the real significance of the situation."

30 years after Marshall made his address, which was 30 years ago, as my class graduated without me, technology was emerging that would make the world smaller, more open, more visible, less distant. The emergence of low-cost personal computers gave rise to a powerful network that has transformed opportunities for learning and communicating.

The magical thing about this network is not just that it collapses distance

不了。

令我特别难忘的是，在参加那个无聊的小组讨论之前，我刚刚结束了某软件第 13 版的发布会，那时现场一片欢呼雀跃。我热衷于激发人们对软件的激情，可拯救生命为何无法令人迸发出这样的激情呢？

除非能让人们看到并感受到影响力，否则你无法唤起人们的激情。而做到这一点的方法是一道复杂的难题。不过，我还是很乐观。是的，不平等古已有之，但我们现在有了新工具，能帮我们搞定复杂的问题，这可是前所未有的。这些新工具能让我们把同情心发挥到极致——所以，我们真的有可能迎来一个截然不同的未来。

生物技术、个人电脑和互联网等划时代的、一直在进步的新技术带来了一个前所未有的机遇，让我们能够为极端贫困和可预防疾病造成的死亡画上句号。

60 年前，乔治·马歇尔来到这里的毕业典礼，宣布了一项帮助战后欧洲国家的计划。我引用一下他的话："我认为的一个困难是，这个问题非常复杂，媒体和广播向公众传播了海量的信息，普通人很难对形势做出清晰的评估。经过层层传播，想要完全把握局势的实际意义，几乎是不可能的事。"

30 年前，也就是马歇尔演讲的 30 年后，我的同班同学们毕业的时候（其中没有我），科技蓬勃发展，将世界变得更小、更开放、更透明，缩短了人与人之间的距离。低成本个人电脑的出现催生出强大的网络世界，变革了学习与交流的方式。

网络很神奇，它消弭了距离，令人人比邻，还大规模地汇聚人类智慧，让人们

---

10. George Marshall：乔治·马歇尔，美国第 50 任国务卿。1947 年 6 月在哈佛大学发表演讲，宣布"马歇尔计划"（又称"欧洲复兴计划"）问世。

and makes everyone your neighbor. It also dramatically increases the number of brilliant minds we can bring in to work together on the same problem—and it scales up the rate of potential innovation to a staggering degree.

At the same time, for every person who has access to this technology, five people don't. That means many creative minds are left out of this discussion—smart people with practical intelligence and relevant experience who don't have the technology to hone their talents or contribute their ideas to the world.

We need as many people as possible to gain access to this technology, because these advances are triggering a revolution in what human beings can do for one another. They are making it possible not just for national governments, but for universities, corporations, small organizations, and even individuals to see problems, see approaches, and measure the impact of their efforts to address the hunger, poverty, and desperation George Marshall spoke of 60 years ago.

Members of the Harvard Family: Here in the Yard is one of the great collections of intellectual talent in the world. For what purpose?

There is no question that the faculty, the alumni, the students, and the benefactors of Harvard have used their power to improve the lives of people here and around the world. But can we do more? Can Harvard dedicate its intellect to improving the lives of people who will never even hear its name?

Let me make a request of the deans and professors—the intellectual leaders here at Harvard. As you hire new faculty, award tenure, review curriculum, and determine degree requirements, please ask yourself: Should our best minds be more dedicated to solving our biggest problems? Should Harvard encourage its faculty to take on the world's worst inequities? Should Harvard students know about the depth of global poverty, the prevalence of world hunger, the scarcity of clean water, the girls kept out of school, the children who die from diseases we can cure?

能够共同解决问题，更是将潜在创新的速度提升到了惊人的程度。

而与此同时，世界上有条件上网的人，只占全部人口的1/6。也就是说，许多富有创造力的人被排除在网络讨论之外。很多聪明人拥有实践智慧和相关经验，但接触不到技术，无法磨炼才能，也无法为世界贡献想法。

我们要尽可能让更多的人接触到这项技术，因为科技发展正在引发一场变革，突破人类互助的桎梏。从国家政府到大学、企业、小组织乃至个人，在应对乔治·马歇尔60年前所说的饥饿、贫困和绝望问题时，都能够借助技术辅助来发现问题，找到解决方法，评估效果。

哈佛大家庭的成员们，这个校园中汇聚了世界一流人才。大家是为了什么而聚集于此呢？

毫无疑问，哈佛的教职员工、校友、学生和捐助者都以自己的力量改善了这里和世界各地人们的生活。但我们是否可以做得更多？哈佛能否将其智慧用于那些从未听过哈佛名字的人群，帮助他们改善生活？

各位院长和教授，你们是哈佛的知识领袖，我想向你们提出一个请求。在聘用新教职员工、授予终身教职、审查课程和确定学位要求时，请问问自己这些问题：顶尖人才是否更应致力于解决人类最大的难题？哈佛是否应该鼓励教职员工积极应对全球最严重的不平等现象？哈佛的学生是否应该了解全球贫困的严重性、全球饥荒的普遍性、洁净水的稀缺、失学的女孩、死于本可以被治愈的疾病的儿童？

> *From those to whom much is given, much is expected.*
>
> *所获越丰，越被寄予厚望。*

Should the world's most privileged learn about the lives of the world's least privileged? These are not rhetorical questions—you will answer with your policies.

My mother who was filled with pride the day I was admitted here, never stopped pressing me to do more for others. A few days before I was married she hosted a bridal event at which she read aloud a letter about marriage that she had written to Melinda.

My mother was very ill with cancer at the time but she saw one more opportunity to deliver her message and at the close of the letter she said, "From those to whom much is given, much is expected."

When you consider what those of us here in this Yard have been given—in talent, privilege, and opportunity—there is almost no limit to what the world has a right to expect from us.

In line with the promise of this age, I want to exhort each of the graduates here to take on an issue—a complex problem, a deep inequity, and become a specialist on it. If you make it the focus of your career, that would be phenomenal. But you don't have to do that to make an impact. For a few hours every week, you can use the growing power of the Internet to get informed, find others with the same interests, see the barriers, and find ways to cut through them.

Don't let complexity stop you. Be activists. Take on big inequities. I feel sure it will be one of the great experiences of your lives.

You graduates are coming of age at an amazing time. As you leave Harvard, you have technology that members of my class never had. You have awareness of global inequity, which we did not have. And with that awareness, you likely also have an informed conscience that will torment you if you abandon these people whose lives you could change with modest effort. You have more than we had; you must start sooner, and carry on longer.

世界上最有优势的人群是否应该了解世界上最为困顿者的生活？这些问题不能停留在讨论层面，你们要用自己制定的规则来回答。

得知我被哈佛录取的那天，我母亲感到无比自豪，她总是敦促我要多为他人做些什么。在我结婚前几天，她主持了一场婚前庆祝活动，并在活动上大声朗读了她写给梅琳达的一封关于婚姻的信。

当时，我母亲身患癌症，病得很重。尽管如此，她还是抓住机会表达了她的观点。在信的结尾，她说道："所获越丰，越被寄予厚望。"

既然哈佛学子被赋予了天分、优待和机遇，世界就有权对我们抱有无限的期待。

我想要顺应时代的期许，敦促在座的各位毕业生去关注一个课题——一道错综复杂的难题，一种根深蒂固的不公，然后成为应对它的专家。若是把它当作职业生涯的核心，那将会获得非凡的成就。不过，即使不这样做，也能影响世界。每周花几个小时，就能利用日益强大的网络资源来获取信息，找到志同道合的伙伴，识别出障碍所在，并找出解决之道。

别让复杂性成为你们的障碍，要当个行动家，去对抗那些艰巨的不平等问题。我相信，这将成为你们人生中最宝贵的经历之一。

你们这些毕业生正在一个令人惊叹的时代中走向成熟。离开哈佛之际，你们拥有我们那一届所不具备的技术手段。你们对世界的不公平有着清晰的认识，这是我们以前不具备的。你们的举手之劳能够改写很多人的命运。有了这份认知，若是选择漠视，你们将会受到良心的折磨。你们的起点高于我们当初，得尽早开始，并且

> *Don't let complexity stop you. Be activists.*
>
> 别让复杂性成为你们的障碍，要当个行动家。

And I hope you will come back here to Harvard 30 years from now and reflect on what you have done with your talent and your energy. I hope you will judge yourselves not on your professional accomplishments alone, but also on how well you have addressed the world's deepest inequities, on how well you treated people a world away who have nothing in common with you but their humanity.

Good luck.

持之以恒。

我希望你们30年后能重返哈佛，回顾一下自己的才华和精力都施展在了哪里。待到自我评判时，希望你们不仅要着眼于专业成就，还要看自己在解决全球深层次不平等问题方面做得如何，以及自己如何对待那些跟你们同为人类，但与你们毫无关系还远在千里之外的人们。

祝你们好运。

语录 Quotes

- Improving your odds doesn't guarantee success.
  提高胜算并不能确保成功。

- But humanity's greatest advances are not in its discoveries—but in how those discoveries are applied to reduce inequity.
  但人类最伟大的进步并不在于发现，而是在于如何应用发现来减少不平等。

- The barrier to change is not too little caring; it is too much complexity.
  阻碍改变的，不是关心不够，而是复杂过头。

- Finding solutions is essential if we want to make the most of our caring.
  要想让爱心发挥最大限度的作用，就必须找到解决方案。

- You can't get people excited unless you can help them see and feel the impact.
  除非能让人们看到并感受到影响力，否则你无法唤起人们的激情。

- From those to whom much is given, much is expected.
  所获越丰，越被寄予厚望。

- Don't let complexity stop you. Be activists.
  别让复杂性成为你们的障碍，要当个行动家。

It's Time to Take an Adventure
是时候去冒险了

——埃隆·马斯克 2014 年在南加州大学马歇尔商学院毕业典礼上的演讲

> 简介 Profile

埃隆·里夫·马斯克
Elon Reeve Musk

以"硅谷钢铁侠"闻名于世的马斯克在全球范围内拥有无可比拟的名气和财富。他的人生也极富传奇色彩。

1971年，埃隆·马斯克出生于南非的行政首都比勒陀利亚。他从小就对计算机和各种科学技术有着极大的兴趣，父母离婚后，马斯克跟随父亲生活，在这期间，他成功设计出一款太空游戏软件，卖出了500美元。高中毕业后，马斯克离开家，独自一人踏上求学之路。他先通过亲属关系获得了加拿大护照，然后于1990年被加拿大的女王大学录取，两年后转学到美国宾夕法尼亚大学学习经济学和物理学。1995年，马斯克被斯坦福大学的材料科学和应用物理专业录取，准备读博，但他读了两天就辍学了，转而决定投身互联网的浪潮。

1995年，他和弟弟共同创办了提供在线城市导航的软件公司Zip2。1999年，Zip2以3.07亿美元的价格被收购。2002年，马斯克创办了美国太空探索技术公司SpaceX，同年获得美国国籍。2004年，马斯克投资了电动汽车公司特斯拉，4年后出任该公司的CEO。2022年，马斯克以440亿美元的价格收购了推特；2023年，他把推特的公司名称从"Twitter"改为"X"。此外，马斯克还是脑机接口公司Neuralink的创始人、人工智能公司OpenAI的联合创始人。他在航空航天、汽车、能源等多个领域成就非凡，因此多次入选《时代周刊》全球最具影响力人物，多次位居世界首富之位。

2014年，埃隆·马斯克在南加州大学马歇尔商学院的本科毕业典礼上，向毕业生们提出了中肯、实在的建议，其中最重要的就是学会用"第一性原理"去思考，而这也正是他大学所学的物理学带给他的最重要的思维模式。他尤其希望年轻的毕业生们趁年华正盛、束缚尚少，抓紧时间找到心之所向，大胆去冒险、去开拓。

演讲 Speech

Alright, thank you. So, I've got about ... apparently I've got about five to six minutes to say the most useful things I can think of. I'm gonna do my best. It was suggested that I distill things down to 3 items. I think I'll go with four. And I'll try. I think ... I think these are pretty important ones. Some of it may kinda sound like, well, you've heard them before. But, you know, worth reemphasizing.

I think the first is, you need to work. If you, depending on how well you want to do, particularly if you want to start a company, you need to work super hard.

So what does super hard mean?

Well, when my brother[1] and I were starting our first company, instead of getting an apartment, we just rented a small office and we slept on the couch and we showered at the YMCA[2]. And we're so hard up[3] that we had just one computer. So the website was up during the day, and I was coding at night. Seven days a week, all the time. And I, sort of briefly, had a girlfriend in that period and in order to be with me, she had to sleep in the office. So, work hard, like, every waking hour.

That's the thing I would say, particularly if you're starting a company. And I mean, if you do the simple math—you say like somebody else is working 50 hours and you're working 100—you'll get twice as done, as much done, in the

好的，谢谢。看样子我大概有五六分钟的时间，得说点我能想到的最有用的东西。我会尽力的。有人建议我把内容提炼成三点来讲，我觉得还是说四点吧。我会尽量挑些重要的来说，大家可能会觉得其中一些是陈词滥调，但确实是值得反复强调的。

第一点，你们需要工作。如果想做出点成绩，特别是想要创业，就需要拼命工作。

那么，拼命工作意味着什么呢？

我们兄弟俩创办第一家公司的时候，没有租公寓，而是租了一间小办公室，我们在沙发上睡觉，到基督教青年会去洗澡。我们手头拮据，只有一台电脑，所以网站在白天运行，我在夜里编码。一周七天，天天如此。那时我短暂地交过一个女朋友，为了陪我，她也只能在办公室过夜。也就是说，清醒着的每时每刻都要用来拼命工作。

这就是我想说的第一点，特别是针对创业者来说。你可以简单算算，如果别人工作 50 个小时，而你们工作 100 个小时，那么你们公司一年能完成的工作量将是其

> *If you want to start a company, you need to work super hard.*
>
> 想要创业，就需要拼命工作。

---

1. my brother：指金巴尔·詹姆斯·马斯克（Kimbal James Musk, 1972— ），埃隆·马斯克的弟弟，现在是特斯拉和 SpaceX 的董事会成员。
2. YMCA：指基督教青年会（Young Men's Christian Association）。
3. hard up：手头拮据。

course of a year as the other company.

The other thing I'd say is that if you're creating a company, or if you're joining a company, the most important thing is to attract great people.

So either be with, join a group that's amazing, that you really respect. Or, if you're building a company, you've got to gather great people. I mean, all the company is a group of people that have gathered together to create a product or service.

So depending upon how talented and hard-working that group is, and to the degree in which they are focused cohesively in a good direction, that will determine the success of the company. So do everything you can to gather great people, if you're creating a company.

Then, I'd say focus on signal over noise.

A lot of companies get confused. They spend money on things that don't actually make the product better. So, for example, at Tesla, we've never spent any money on advertising. We've put all the money into R and D[4] and manufacturing and design to try to make the car as good as possible.

And, I think that's the way to go. For any given company, just keep thinking about, "Are these efforts that people are expending, are they resulting in a better product or service?" And if they're not, stop those efforts.

And then the final thing is, don't just follow the trend.

So, you may have heard me say that it's good to think in terms of the physics approach of first principles[5]. Which is, rather than reasoning by analogy, you boil things down to the most fundamental truths you can imagine, and you reason up from there.

And this is a good way to figure out if something really makes sense, or if it is just what everybody else is doing. It's hard to think that way. You can't think that way about everything. It takes a lot of effort. But if you're trying to do something new, it's the best way to think.

他公司的两倍。

第二点，不管是创办一家公司，还是加入一家公司，吸纳优秀人才都是最重要的。

所以，要么加入自己敬佩的优秀团队，要么为自己的初创公司招募英才。所谓公司，就是一群人聚集在一起，共同创造产品或提供服务。

因此，一个团队能不能成事，就看团队成员有多牛、有多拼，还有能不能齐心协力向好的方向迈进。所以，要创业，就要尽己所能地招揽英才。

第三点，要关注本质的信号，屏蔽表面的喧嚣。

很多公司都不明白，他们把钱花在了实际上无法改进产品的地方。举个例子，特斯拉从未在广告上花过一分钱。我们把所有资金都投入研发、制造和设计上，力求打造出最好的汽车。

我认为这是正确的道路。对任何一家公司而言，由始至终只需要考虑一点：大家付出的努力真的能让产品或服务变得更好吗？如果答案是否定的，就该叫停那些无用功。

最后一点，不要盲目跟风。

大家或许听说过我的观点，物理学的第一性原理是个思考问题的好方法。这种方法不是通过类比推理，而是尽可能把事情简化为最极致的本质，再基于此出发向上推理。

这是一种很好的方法，可以用来判断做某件事是真的有意义，还是仅仅在跟风。用这种方式思考挺费劲的，没法儿事事都这么琢磨，太耗精力了。但要是准备尝试新事物，这就是最佳的思考方式。

---

4. R and D: "research and development" 的缩写，意为"研究和开发"。
5. first principles: 第一性原理。

And that framework was developed by physicists to figure out counter intuitive things, like quantum mechanics. So it's really a powerful, powerful method.

And anyways, so that's, and then the final thing I would encourage you to do is now is the time to take risk.

You don't have kids, your obligations, well! Some of you... Hahaha, you probably don't have kids.

But as you get older, your obligations increase. So, and, once you have a family, you start taking risks not just for yourself, but for your family as well. It gets much harder to do things that might not work out. So now is the time to do that, before you have those obligations. So I would encourage you to take risks now, do something bold.

You won't regret it!

Thank you.

这套框架是物理学家们开发出来的，用于理解像量子力学这样的反直觉概念，确实是一个非常强大的方法。

我还有最后一件事要鼓励大家去做，那就是趁年轻，多去冒险。

你们还没有孩子，没什么责任要担！你们中的一些人……哈哈哈，大家应该还没有孩子吧。

但随着年龄增大，责任也越重。一旦有了家庭，要承担风险的就不仅仅是自己了，还有家人。到时候就难以去做那些未必会成功的事情了。所以，现在，趁尚且无须承担家庭义务，去冒险吧。我鼓励你们现在就去冒险，大胆做事。

你们不会后悔的！

谢谢大家。

语录 Quotes

- If you want to start a company, you need to work super hard.
  想要创业，就需要拼命工作。

- All the company is a group of people that have gathered together to create a product or service.
  所谓公司，就是一群人聚集在一起，共同创造产品或提供服务。

- Do everything you can to gather great people, if you're creating a company.
  要创业，就要尽己所能地招揽英才。

- Focus on signal over noise.
  要关注本质的信号，屏蔽表面的喧嚣。

- It's good to think in terms of the physics approach of first principles.
  物理学的第一性原理是个思考问题的好方法。

- Once you have a family, you start taking risks not just for yourself, but for your family as well.
  一旦有了家庭，要承担风险的就不仅仅是自己了，还有家人。

Always Have a Dream
永不放弃梦想

——贝拉克·奥巴马 2009 年在亚利桑那州立大学毕业典礼上的演讲

简介 Profile

贝拉克·侯赛因·奥巴马
Barack Hussein Obama

奥巴马不仅是一位杰出的政治家，更是美国历史上第一位非裔总统。

1961年，奥巴马出生于美国夏威夷州，他在印度尼西亚度过了4年的童年时光，见证了当地社会的变迁与多元文化的融合。或许是受童年时期多文化熏陶的影响，奥巴马在学业生涯中非常擅于从不同角度对国际关系进行分析与研究。在哈佛大学法学院深造期间，他以优等生身份毕业，获得了法学博士学位。这一荣誉为他日后在政坛上崭露头角奠定了坚实的基础。

完成学业后，奥巴马没有选择安逸的生活，而是投身于社区工作。他在芝加哥的街头巷尾为弱势群体争取权益，为他们发声。这段经历不仅让奥巴马积累了丰富的社会经验，也锻炼了他的组织协调能力和领导才能。

2008年，奥巴马成功当选为美国第44任总统。上任后，他推行了一系列改革措施，包括医疗改革和教育改革。在外交政策上，奥巴马展现出了卓越的智慧和手腕。他成功推动美国与古巴关系正常化，与伊朗达成核协议，并与近200个国家一道签署了应对气候变化的《巴黎协定》。这些成果都彰显了他卓越的外交才华。

2009年，奥巴马来到了亚利桑那州立大学，向毕业生们传达了勇气、责任与梦想的重要性。他希望毕业生们不要做精致的利己主义者，不要被社会上那些陈腐的名利观所侵蚀，也希望他们无论过去是大众眼里的成功者还是失败者，都不要被绊住，而是找到自己真正热爱的崇高理想，并为之不懈奋斗。

演讲 Speech

扫描二维码
获取本篇演讲原视频、音频

Now, before I begin, I'd just like to **clear the air**[1] about that little **controversy**[2] everybody was talking about a few weeks back. I have to tell you, I really thought this was much **ado**[3] about nothing, but I do think we all learned an important lesson.

I learned never again to pick another team over the Sun Devils in my **NCAA**[4] bracket. It won't happen again. President Crow and the Board of Regents will soon learn all about being audited by the **IRS**[5].

Now, in all seriousness, I come here not to dispute the suggestion that I haven't yet achieved enough in my life. First of all, Michelle concurs with that assessment. She has a long list of things that I have not yet done waiting for me when I get home. But more than that, I come to embrace the notion that I haven't done enough in my life; I heartily concur; I come to affirm that one's title, even a title like President of the United States, says very little about how well one's life has been led—that no matter how much you've done, or how successful you've been, there's always more to do, always more to learn, and always more to achieve.

And I want to say to you today, graduates, Class of 2009, that despite having achieved a remarkable milestone in your life, despite the fact that you and your families are so rightfully proud, you too cannot rest on your laurels. Not even some of those remarkable young people who were introduced

在正式开始之前，我想要先澄清一下几周前人人都在讨论的小争议。不得不说，我真的认为就这种事情而争论实在是小题大做，但我确实认为我们都从中学到了重要的一课。

我得到的教训是，在以后的全国大学体育协会的比赛中，再也不要支持其他队而不支持贵校的太阳魔鬼队。我再也不会这样了。而克罗校长和董事会得到的教训是，他们很快就会明白，国税局是怎样来查他们的账目的。

现在，我要郑重其事地说，我今天来到这里，不是来反驳那种认为我这一生还没有取得足够成就的观点的。首先，我太太米歇尔就是这样认为的。我每次回到家里，她都会拿着一张长长的单子等着我，上面写着我还没有做好的事情。但更重要的是，对于我所取得的成就还远远不够的看法，我由衷地认同。我来到这里，就是想告诉大家，一个人的头衔，即使这个头衔是美国总统，并不能说明一个人的一生如何了不起。不管你取得了多少成绩，不管你多么成功，总会有更多的事情等待你去做，有更多的东西等待你去学，有更多的成就等待你去取得。

今天，我想告诉你们，2009届的毕业生们，虽然你们达成了生命中一个重要的里程碑，虽然你们和你们的家人都理所应当为此感到自豪，但你们不能依赖过去的荣誉。即使是先前提到过的那些特别优秀的青年，甚至是今天那位获得了4个学位

---

1. clear the air：澄清事实，消除分歧。
2. controversy：争议，争论。
3. ado：纷扰；麻烦；忙乱。
4. NCAA："National Collegiate Athletic Association"的缩写，指美国全国大学体育协会，是美国负责管理大学体育运动的组织。
5. IRS："Internal Revenue Service"的缩写，指的是美国国内收入署，也被称为美国国税局。

earlier—not even that young lady who's got four degrees yet today. You can't rest. Your own body of work is also yet to come.⁶

Now, some graduating classes have marched into this stadium in easy times—times of peace and stability when we call on our graduates simply to keep things going, and don't screw it up. Other classes have received their diplomas in times of trial and upheaval, when the very foundations of our lives, the old order has been shaken, the old ideas and institutions have crumbled, and a new generation is called upon to remake the world. It should be clear to you by now the category into which all of you fall. For we gather here tonight in times of extraordinary difficulty, for the nation and for the world. The economy remains in the midst of a historic recession, the worst we've seen since the Great Depression; the result, in part, of greed and irresponsibility that rippled⁷ out from Wall Street and Washington, as we spent beyond our means and failed to make hard choices.

We're engaged in two wars and a struggle against terrorism. The threats of climate change, nuclear proliferation, and pandemic⁸ defy national boundaries and easy solutions.

For many of you, these challenges are also felt in more personal terms. Perhaps you're still looking for a job—or struggling to figure out what career path makes sense in this disrupted economy. Maybe you've got student loans—no, you definitely have student loans—or credit card debts, and you're wondering how you'll ever pay them off. Maybe you've got a family to raise, and you're wondering how you'll ensure that your children have the same opportunities you've had to get an education and pursue their dreams.

Now, in the face of these challenges, it may be tempting to fall back on the formulas for success that have been pedaled⁹ so frequently in recent years. It goes something like this: You're taught to chase after all the usual brass rings¹⁰; you try to be on this "who's who" list or that top 100 list; you chase after

的年轻女士，也不能停滞不前。你们自身的生命之作也同样尚未完成。

有些毕业班走进这座体育馆，是在轻松无忧的年代，在和平稳定的时期，那时候我们只要求毕业生们保持下去，别把好日子过得一团糟。还有的班级是在动荡不安的艰难时世中拿到文凭的，生活的基础和传统的秩序遭受重创，传统的观念和体制也分崩离析，新的一代不得不临危受命，接受拯救世界的重任。你们属于哪种范畴，现在应该是一清二楚了。因为今晚我们聚集在这里，面对的是一个困难重重的时期，不管是对美国还是对整个世界来说，都是如此。我们的经济仍然处于一个历史性的危机之中，这次危机是 1929 年经济大萧条以来最为严重的一次；究其原因，部分是因为华尔街和华盛顿的贪婪与不负责任产生的涟漪效应，也是因为我们自不量力、过度消费，没有做出理性的选择。

面对恐怖主义，我们同时卷入了两场战争和一场斗争。气候变暖、核扩散与全球流行病的威胁没有国界，也没有一蹴而就的解决方案。

对于你们许多人来说，这些挑战也和你们个人的切身利益有关。也许你还在找工作，也许你还在苦苦思考在这个经济衰败的时期从事什么职业才比较有意义。也许你办了学生贷款——不，你肯定办理了学生贷款——而且信用卡也债台高筑，你正苦恼不知怎样才能还清债务。也许你需要养家糊口，你正在苦恼怎样才能保证自己的子女拥有和你同样的机会来接受教育，并追求他们的梦想。

现在，面对这些挑战，我们很容易落入最近几年很是流行的成功秘诀的俗套。这个套路大概是这样的：你受的教育告诉你要追逐一切功名利禄；你想方设法要进入"名人录"或者"100 强"；你一门心思要赚大钱，想象着自己的高级办公室该有

---

6. 亚利桑那州立大学发言人沙伦·基勒在解释为什么不授予奥巴马荣誉学位时说，该校颁发荣誉学位是为了褒奖取得终身成就的个人，而奥巴马总统的"生命之作还没有完成"，因此现在就授予他荣誉学位并不合适。奥巴马在此引用这句话来勉励毕业生。
7. ripple：*v.* 使泛起涟漪；扩散，传播。
8. pandemic：*n.* 全球流行病，大流行病。
9. pedale：*v.* 踩踏板，这里面引申为"兜售、宣扬"的意思，在这里用了一种比喻的手法，就像不断地踩动踏板去推动或推广某些东西一样。
10. brass ring：原意是"黄铜戒指"，在这里引申为"荣誉、诱人的目标、成功的标志"等意思。

the big money and you figure out how big your corner office is; you worry about whether you have a fancy enough title or a fancy enough car. That's the message that's sent each and every day, or has been in our culture for far too long—that through material possessions, through a ruthless competition pursued only on your own behalf—that's how you will measure success.

Now, you can take that road—and it may work for some. But at this critical juncture in our nation's history, at this difficult time, let me suggest that such an approach won't get you where you want to go; it displays a poverty of ambition—that in fact, the elevation of appearance over substance, of celebrity over character, of short-term gain over lasting achievement is precisely what your generation needs to help end.

Now, ASU, I want to highlight—I want to highlight two main problems with that old, tired, me-first approach tonight. First of all, it distracts you from what's truly important, and may lead you to compromise your values and your principles and your commitments. Think about it. It's in chasing titles and status—in worrying about the next election rather than the national interest and the interests of those who you're supposed to represent—that politicians so often lose their ways in Washington. They spend time thinking about polls, but not about principle. It was in pursuit of gaudy[11] short-term profits, and the bonuses that came with them, that so many folks lost their way on Wall Street, engaging in extraordinary risks with other people's money.

In contrast, the leaders we revere, the businesses and institutions that last—they are not generally the result of a narrow pursuit of popularity or personal advancement, but of devotion to some bigger purpose—the preservation of the Union or the determination to lift a country out of a depression; the creation of a quality product, a commitment to your customers, your workers, your shareholders and your community. A commitment to make sure that an institution like ASU is inclusive[12] and diverse and giving opportunity to

多大；你担心自己没有一个足够响亮的头衔，没有一辆足够炫目的轿车。这就是我们日复一日收到的信息，也是在我们的文化中早已根深蒂固的信息——通过物质财富的占有，通过仅仅为了一己之私而进行的无情竞争——这些是你们衡量成功与否的标准。

当然，你可以走这条路——而且对有些人来说也确实可以走通。但是，在国家历史上这个关键时刻，在这个困难时期，我要说，这条路无法带你走到目的地；它只能表明你缺乏进取之心。事实上，重表面而轻实质，重名气而轻品质，重短期利益而轻长远成就，这正是你们这一代人需要去破除的风气。

各位同学，今晚，我想就这种过时的、陈腐的、以自我为中心的人生观再强调两点。首先，它会让你偏离真正重要的东西，而且可能让你妥协自己的价值观、做人原则和责任心。好好想一想。正是由于追逐名利地位——不是忧虑国家的利益，不是忧虑他们所应代表的人民的利益，而是忧虑自己下次的大选——那些政客们才在华盛顿迷失了方向。他们整天考虑的是选票问题，而不是原则问题。正是由于只追求华而不实的短期利益，以及由此带来的额外回报，很多人才在华尔街迷失了方向，才会拿别人的钱进行风险极大的投资。

相反，那些我们所尊敬的领袖人物，那些屹立不倒的企业和机构，他们并不只追求狭隘的个人名声或者个人发展，而是献身于某个更为远大的目标：要么保卫联邦的存在，或者决心使国家摆脱萧条；要么创造高质量的产品，信守对顾客、员工、股东和社会的承诺；要么致力于促使像贵校这样的机构对各种学生一视同仁、兼收

---

11. gaudy：*adj.* 华而不实的；浮夸的；俗艳的。
12. inclusive：*adj.* 包容的、兼收并蓄的。

all. That's a hallmark of real success. That other stuff—that other stuff, the trappings[13] of success may be a byproduct of this larger mission, but it can't be the central thing. Just ask Bernie Madoff[14]. That's the first problem with the old attitude.

But the second problem with the old approach to success is that a relentless focus on the outward markers of success can lead to complacency. It can make you lazy. We too often let the external, the material things, serve as indicators that we're doing well, even though something inside us tells us that we're not doing our best; that we're avoiding that which is hard, but also necessary; that we're shrinking from, rather than rising to, the challenges of the age. And the thing is, in this new, hypercompetitive age, none of us—none of us—can afford to be complacent.

That's true in whatever profession you choose. Professors might earn the distinction of tenure[15], but that doesn't guarantee that they'll keep putting in the long hours and late nights—and have the passion and the drive—to be great educators. The same principle is true in your personal life. Being a parent is not just a matter of paying the bills, doing the bare minimum—it's not just bringing a child into the world that matters, but the acts of love and sacrifice it takes to raise and educate that child and give them opportunity. It can happen to Presidents, as well. If you think about it, Abraham Lincoln and Millard Fillmore had the very same title, they were both Presidents of the United States, but their tenure in office and their legacy could not be more different.

And this not just true for individuals—it's also true for this nation. In recent years, in many ways, we've become enamored[16] with our own past success—lulled[17] into complacency by the glitter of our own achievements.

We've become accustomed to the title of "military superpower," forgetting the qualities that got us there—not just the power of our weapons, but the discipline and valor[18] and the code of conduct of our men and women in

并蓄，人人都能得到平等的机会。这才是真正成功的标志。至于其他的东西——那些成功的外在标记，可以是这一更大目标的副产品，但绝不是最重要的东西。不信你可以问问伯尼·麦道夫。这是这一陈腐人生观的第一个问题。

关于成功的陈腐人生观的第二个问题就是，过多地看重成功的外在标志会使人骄傲自满。它会使你变得懒惰。我们过多地把那些外在的、物质的东西看成自己取得成绩的标志，虽然我们内心明白自己并没有尽力；我们绕开了那些虽然困难但是必须去做的工作；面对时代的挑战，我们没有奋起迎接，而是选择了退缩。问题是，在这个高度竞争的新时代，我们当中没有任何人——没有任何人——能够付得起自满的代价。

不管你选择什么职业都是如此。教授可以获得终身教职的殊荣，但这并不能保证他们会一如既往地投入大量的时间和精力——或者拥有激情和动力——来成为伟大的教育家。同样，在你们个人生活中也是如此。做父母并不仅仅是支付账单，或者做些最起码的事情；重要的并不仅仅是把孩子带到这个世界上来，而是要用爱和无私的奉献来抚养和教育孩子，并给他们机会。对总统而言也是如此。想想看，亚伯拉罕·林肯和米勒德·菲尔莫尔都有着同样的头衔，都是美国总统，但他们的任期和成就却不可同日而语。

这一点，不仅对个人如此，对整个国家来说也是一样。最近几年，在许多方面，我们都沉醉于过去的成功之中。在成就的光芒下，我们放松了警惕，变得沾沾自喜起来。

我们都已习惯了"军事超级大国"的头衔，却忘记了使我们拥有这一头衔的品

---

13. trappings：*n.* 外部标志；装饰。
14. Bernie Madoff：伯尼·麦道夫（1938—2021），曾是华尔街的风云人物，后通过操纵巨大的"庞氏骗局"成为美国最大金融诈骗案的主犯，被判处150年监禁。奥巴马此处引用麦道夫意在强调只追求成功的外在标志是危险的，而应追求更有意义的人生目标和使命。
15. tenure：*n.* 终身教职。
16. enamored：*adj.* 迷恋的，倾心的。
17. lull：*v.* 使放松警惕，使麻痹。
18. valor：*n.* 勇气；英勇。

uniform. The Marshall Plan, and the Peace Corps, and all those initiatives that show our commitment to working with other nations to pursue the ideals of opportunity and equality and freedom have made us who we are. That's what made us a super power.

We've become accustomed to our economic dominance in the world, forgetting that it wasn't reckless deals and get-rich-quick schemes that got us where we are, but hard work and smart ideas—quality products and wise investments. We started taking shortcuts. We started living on credit, instead of building up savings. We saw businesses focus more on rebranding[19] and repackaging than innovating and developing new ideas that improve our lives.

All the while, the rest of the world has grown hungrier, more restless—in constant motion to build and to discover—not content with where they are right now, determined to strive for more. They're coming. So graduates, it's now abundantly clear that we need to start doing things a little bit different. In your own lives, you'll need to continuously adapt to a continuously changing economy. You'll end up having more than one job and more than one career over the course of your life; you'll have to keep gaining new skills—possibly even new degrees; and you'll have to keep on taking risks as new opportunities arise.

And as a nation, we'll need a fundamental change of perspective and attitude. It's clear that we need to build a new foundation—a stronger foundation—for our economy and our prosperity, rethinking how we grow our economy, how we use energy, how we educate our children, how we care for our sick, how we treat our environment. Many of our current challenges are unprecedented. There are no standard remedies, no go-to[20] fixes this time around. And Class of 2009, that's why we're going to need your help. We need young people like you to step up. We need your daring. We need your enthusiasm. We need your energy, we need your imagination. And let me

质——不仅是因为我们的武器多么强大，还因为我们的戎装战士所表现出的纪律、勇气和行为准则。"马歇尔计划"、和平队，以及我们致力于与其他国家一起追求机会、平等、自由的理想而采取的种种措施，成就了今天的我们。正是这些使我们成为一个超级大国。

我们已经习惯了美国经济在世界上的主导地位，却忘记了我们之所以取得这些成就，并不是因为那些不择手段的交易和一夜暴富的筹划，而是因为辛勤的付出和精妙的构想——那些优质产品和明智的投资。我们开始走捷径。我们开始依靠信贷生活，而不是积攒储蓄。我们看到，企业只把注意力放在产品的改头换面和包装上，而不是致力于革新产品、扩展思路来提高我们的生活水平。

与此同时，世界其他国家变得更加饥渴、更加迫切——他们不停地建造，不停地发现——不满足于他们的现状，决心要努力奋斗以获取更多。他们追上来了。因此，毕业生们，显而易见，我们需要稍微改变一下做事方式了。就个人的生活而言，你们需要不断地适应一个随时都在变化的经济环境。你们一生中可能会从事不止一种工作或者事业；你们必须不停地获得新的技能，甚至新的学位；随着新的机遇的出现，你们还必须不停地冒险。

作为一个国家，我们需要从根本上改变视角与态度。显而易见，为了经济和繁荣，我们需要打下新的根基——一个更加坚实的根基，重新思考该怎样促进经济增长，怎样使用能源，怎样教育子女，怎样照顾病人，怎样对待环境。我们目前面临的许多挑战都是前所未有的。这一次，我们没有现成的解决方案，也没有可依赖的灵丹妙药。

2009届的同学们，这就是为什么我们需要你们的帮助。我们需要你们这样的年轻人行动起来。我们需要你们的勇气、你们的热情、你们的活力以及你们的想象力。请允许我澄清一下。我所说的"年轻"，并不是指你们出生证明上的日期。我所谈的

---

19. rebrand：*v.* 重塑品牌。
20. go-to：*adj.*（因可靠或常用而）首选的，必用的。

be clear, when I say "young," I'm not just referring to the date of your birth certificate. I'm talking about an approach to life—a quality of mind and a quality of heart; a willingness to follow your passions, regardless of whether they lead to fortune and fame; a willingness to question conventional wisdom and rethink old dogmas; a lack of regard for all the traditional markers of status and prestige—and a commitment instead to doing what's meaningful to you, what helps others, what makes a difference in this world.

That's the spirit that led a band of patriots not much older than most of you to take on an empire, to start this experiment in democracy we call America. It's what drove young pioneers west, to Arizona and beyond; it's what drove young women to reach for the ballot; what inspired a 30 year-old escaped slave to run an underground railroad to freedom; what inspired a young man named Cesar[21] to go out and help farm workers; what inspired a 26 year-old preacher[22] to lead a bus boycott[23] for justice. It's what led firefighters and police officers in the prime of their lives up the stairs of those burning towers[24]; and young people across this country to drop what they were doing and come to the aid of a flooded New Orleans. It's what led two guys in a garage—named Hewlett and Packard—to form a company[25] that would change the way we live and work; what led scientists in laboratories, and novelists in coffee shops to labor in obscurity until they finally succeeded in changing the way we see the world.

That's the great American story: young people just like you, following their passions, determined to meet the times on their own terms. They weren't doing it for the money. Their titles weren't fancy—ex-slave, minister, student, citizen. A whole bunch of them didn't get honorary degrees. But they changed the course of history—and so can you, ASU. So can you, Class of 2009. So can you.

With a degree from this outstanding institution, you have everything you need to get started. You've got no excuses. You have no excuses not to change

是一种生活态度——一种精神品质和心灵品质；愿意追随自己的激情，不管它是否能带来名和利；愿意质疑传统的价值观，重新思考陈旧的教条；蔑视所有代表名声、地位的传统标志，取而代之的是投身于对自己有意义的事情，能帮助他人的事情，能改变这个世界的事情。

正是这种精神，使一群爱国者向一个帝国叫板，开始了我们称之为"美国"的民主试验，这些爱国者那时的年龄并不比你们中的绝大多数人大多少。正是这种精神，使年轻的先驱者走向西部，走向亚利桑那和更远的地方。正是这种精神，促使年轻的妇女们争取选举权，促使一名30岁的黑奴通过"地下铁路"组织逃向自由，促使一位名叫塞萨尔的年轻人全力帮助农场工人，促使一位26岁的牧师为了正义发起了一场抵制乘坐公交车的运动。正是这种精神，使得正值盛年的消防队员和警察们冲向熊熊燃烧的双子塔的楼梯，也使得全国的年轻人扔下手中的工作前来支援遭受洪灾的新奥尔良人。它使得两个年轻人——休利特与帕卡德——在车库里组建了一个公司，改变了我们生活和工作的方式；使得实验室里的科学家们、咖啡厅里的小说家们默默无闻地工作，直到最终成功地改变了我们看待这个世界的方式。

这就是美国的伟大故事：这些像你们一样的年轻人，决意追随自己的激情，用自己的方式迎接时代的挑战。他们这样做不是为了金钱。他们没有响亮的头衔——他们是曾经的奴隶、牧师、学生、市民。他们都没有得到过荣誉学位。但他们改变了历史的进程——你们也可以！亚利桑那州立大学的同学们，你们也可以！2009届的毕业生们，你们也可以！

有了这所优秀大学的学位，你们就有了开始一番事业的所有资本。你们没有借口和理由不去改变这个世界。你是学商务的吗？去开家公司吧，或者也可以去帮助

---

21. Cesar：指塞萨尔·查维斯（Cesar Chavez），墨西哥裔美国劳工运动者，联合农场工人联盟的领袖。
22. a 26 year-old preacher：指马丁·路德·金，他曾于1955年领导蒙哥马利公交车抵制运动，时年26岁。
23. boycott：*n.* 抵制。
24. 此处指2001年的9·11事件。
25. a company：指惠普公司。前文的"Hewlett and Packard"即惠普公司的两位创始人威廉·休利特（William Hewlett）和戴维·帕卡德（David Packard）。

the world. Did you study business? Go start a company. Or why not help our struggling non-profits find better, more effective ways to serve folks in need. Did you study nursing? Understaffed clinics and hospitals across this country are desperate for your help. Did you study education? Teach in a high-need school where the kids really need you; give a chance to kids who can't—who can't get everything they need maybe in their neighborhood, maybe not even in their home, but we can't afford to give up on them—prepare them to compete for any job anywhere in the world. Did you study engineering? Help us lead a green revolution—developing new sources of clean energy that will power our economy and preserve our planet.

But you can also make your mark[26] in smaller, more individual ways. That's what so many of you have already done during your time here at ASU—tutoring children; registering voters; doing your own small part to fight hunger and homelessness, AIDS, and cancer. One student said it best when she spoke about her senior engineering project building medical devices for people with disabilities in a village in Africa. Her professor showed a video of the folks they'd been helping, and she said, "When we saw the people on the videos, we began to feel a connection to them. It made us want to be successful for them." Think about that: "It made us want to be successful for them." That's a great motto for all of us—find somebody to be successful for. Raise their hopes. Rise to their needs. As you think about your life after graduation, as you look into the mirror tonight after the partying is done—that shouldn't get such a big cheer—you may look in the mirror tonight and you may see somebody who's not really sure what to do with their lives. That's what you may see, but a troubled child might look at you and see a mentor. A homebound senior citizen might see a lifeline. The folks at your local homeless shelter might see a friend. None of them care how much money is in your bank account, or whether you're important at work, or whether you're famous around town—they just know that

那些勉强支撑的非营利机构找到更好的、更有效的方法来为那些需要他们的人服务。你是学护理的吗？全美国医护人员不足的诊所和医院急需你的帮助。你是学教育的吗？去一所师资不足、孩子们真正需要你的学校教书吧。给孩子们一个机会，给那些或许在社区中，甚至在家庭中无法得到帮助的孩子们一个机会，我们不能放弃他们。去帮助他们，让他们有能力去竞争世界上任何地方的任何工作。你是学工程的吗？帮助我们发动一场绿色革命吧——开发新的清洁能源，为我们的经济提供动力，保护我们的地球。

  但是你也可以以自己的方式从更小的方面取得成就。这也是你们中很多人在亚利桑那州立大学学习期间就已经做过的事情——给孩子们做家教，登记选民，为消除饥饿和无家可归现象、对抗艾滋病和癌症尽一份微薄之力。一名学生在谈及她为非洲某村庄的残疾人打造医疗设备的高级工程项目时，说过一段很精彩的话。她的教授播放了一段录像，展示了他们正在帮助的那些人。她说："看到录像里的这些人，我们开始感到与他们之间有了一种联系。它使我们想为了他们而成功。"想想这句话："它使我们想为了他们而成功。"这应该成为我们所有人的座右铭：找到某个你想为他而成功的人。唤起他们的希望，满足他们的需求。当你考虑毕业后的生活，当你在今天的晚会结束后照镜子时——这似乎不值得你们这样欢呼吧——你在今晚照镜子时，看到的也许是一个不知毕业后该做什么的人。这也许只是你自己所看到的。但当一个迷茫的孩子看着你，他看到的也许是一个良师益友；一个困居家中的老人看到的也许是生命的希望；你们当地收容所里那些无家可归的人看到的也许是一个朋友。他们不会去考虑你银行账户里有多少钱，你在工作上是否担任重要职务，或者你在当地是否很有名气——他们只知道你是一个关心他们的人，是一个改变他们

---

26. make one's mark：产生影响；取得成就；留下印记。

you're somebody who cares, somebody who makes a difference in their lives.

So Class of 2009, that's what building a body of work is all about—it's about the daily labor, the many individual acts, the choices large and small that add up over time, over a lifetime, to a lasting legacy. That's what you want on your tombstone. It's about not being satisfied with the latest achievement, the latest gold star—because the one thing I know about a body of work is that it's never finished. It's cumulative; it deepens and expands with each day that you give your best, each day that you give back and contribute to the life of your community and your nation. You may have setbacks, and you may have failures, but you're not done—you're not even getting started, not by a long shot[27].

And if you ever forget that, just look to history. Thomas Paine was a failed corset[28] maker, a failed teacher, and a failed tax collector before he made his mark on history with a little book called *Common Sense* that helped ignite a revolution. Julia Child didn't publish her first cookbook until she was almost fifty. Colonel Sanders didn't open up his first Kentucky Fried Chicken until he was in his 60s. Winston Churchill was dismissed as little more than a has-been, who enjoyed Scotch a little bit too much, before he took over as Prime Minister and saw Great Britain through its finest hour. No one thought a former football player stocking shelves at the local supermarket would return to the game he loved, become a Super Bowl MVP, and then come here to Arizona and lead your Cardinals to their first Super Bowl. Your body of work is never done.

Each of them, at one point in their life, didn't have any title or much status to speak of. But they had passion, a commitment to following that passion wherever it would lead, and to working hard every step along the way. And that's not just how you'll ensure that your own life is well-lived. It's how you'll make a difference in the life of our nation. I talked earlier about the selfishness and irresponsibility on Wall Street and Washington that rippled out

生活的人。

　　所以，2009届的毕业生们，这才是打造生命之作的真实含义——它就是我们日常的工作，是众多个人的行为，是我们长期积累下来的大大小小的选择，是我们一生的积累，是我们留下的永久的遗产。那是你想要铭刻在你墓碑上的东西。它不是满足于目前的成就，哪怕是最新、最炫目的成就——因为，据我所知，生命之作是永远不会结束的。它是日积月累的。每天，当你竭尽全力，当你回报社会和国家，为社会和国家做贡献，你的生命之作就会变得更加深厚、更加丰富。你也许会遇到挫折，你也许会遇到失败，但你不会倒下——因为你甚至还没有开始，你离成功还很远。

　　如果你忘记这一点，就请回头看看历史。托马斯·潘恩曾经是一个失败的紧身衣裁缝，一个失败的老师，一个失败的税务员，但他最后却名垂青史，他的那本名叫《常识》的小书引发了一场革命。朱丽娅·查尔德直到将近50岁时才出版了她的第一部烹饪书。桑德斯上校直到60多岁才开办了第一家肯德基餐厅。温斯顿·丘吉尔曾被斥为一个太爱喝威士忌的过时的人物，但后来却又成为英国首相，带领英国走过了一段最为辉煌的时期。一个在当地超市摆货架的前橄榄球运动员，谁能想到他又会重返他热爱的球场，成为超级碗比赛的"最有价值球员"，然后又来到亚利桑那，率领你们的红雀队打了第一场超级碗比赛。人的生命之作永远不会结束。

　　上述人物中的每一位，在生命中的某一时刻，都没有响亮的头衔和显赫的地位值得炫耀。但他们有激情，他们追随着这种激情，不管这激情把他们带到哪里，而且他们每一步都不辞辛苦，扎实工作。这种激情，并不仅仅是让你去考虑怎样才能把自己的生活过好，它让你考虑怎样才能使我们国家的生活得到改变。刚才我谈到了华尔街与华盛顿的自私和不负责任以及由此而产生的涟漪效应，它导致我们今天

---

27. not by a long shot：固定短语，表示"根本不，根本没有"。
28. corset：*n.* 紧身衣。

and led to so many of the problems that we face today. I talked about the focus on outward markers of success that can help lead us astray.

But here's the thing, Class of 2009: It works the other way around too. Acts of sacrifice and decency without regard to what's in it for you—that also creates ripple effects, ones that lift up families and communities; that spread opportunity and boost our economy; that reach folks in the forgotten corners of the world who, in committed young people like you, see the true face of America: our strength, our goodness, our diversity, our enduring power, our ideals.

I know starting your careers in troubled times is a challenge. But it is also a privilege, because it's moments like these that force us to try harder and dig deeper, and to discover gifts we never knew we had—to find the greatness that lies within each of us. So don't ever shy away from that endeavor. Don't stop adding to your body of work. I can promise that you will be the better for[29] that continued effort, as will this nation that we all love.

Congratulations, Class of 2009, on your graduation. God bless you, and God bless the United States of America.

所面临的许多问题,我也谈到了只关注成功的外在表现会使我们误入歧途。

  但是,关键是在这里,2009届的毕业生们:我们倒过来看这些问题也同样有效。正直无私的奉献,从不考虑自己能从中得到什么,这种行为也会产生涟漪效应。这种效应能提升家庭和社会生活;能创造机遇,繁荣经济;能影响到那些在世界上被人遗忘的角落里生活的人们,让他们从你们这些具有奉献精神的青年的脸上,看到美国真正的面貌——我们的力量,我们的美德,我们的多样性,我们的耐力以及我们的理想。

  我深知,在困难时期开创一番事业是一种挑战,但它同时也是一种特殊的机遇。因为这种困难迫使我们加倍努力,深挖自身的潜力,发现我们未知的才华——找到我们每个人身上潜在的能力。所以,永远不要回避这种努力。永远不要停止书写自己的生命之作。我相信,如果你持续努力,你一定会成为优胜者,我们深爱的国家也一定会更加美好。

  祝贺你们,2009届的毕业生们,祝贺你们顺利毕业!上帝保佑你们!上帝保佑美利坚合众国!

---

29. be the better for:因……而更好。

语录 Quotes

- That no matter how much you've done, or how successful you've been, there's always more to do, always more to learn, and always more to achieve.

  不管你取得了多少成绩，不管你多么成功，总会有更多的事情等待你去做，有更多的东西等待你去学，有更多的成就等待你去取得。

- The elevation of appearance over substance, of celebrity over character, of short-term gain over lasting achievement is precisely what your generation needs to help end.

  重表面而轻实质，重名气而轻品质，重短期利益而轻长远成就，这正是你们这一代人需要去结束的风气。

- In this new, hypercompetitive age, none of us—none of us—can afford to be complacent.

  在这个高度竞争的新时代，我们当中没有任何人——没有任何人——能够付得起自满的代价。

- It wasn't reckless deals and getrich-quick schemes that got us where we are, but hard work and smart ideas—quality products and wise investments.

  我们之所以取得这些成就，并不是因为那些不择手段的交易、一夜暴富的筹划，而是因为辛勤的付出和精妙的构想——那些优质产品和明智的投资。

- Find somebody to be successful for. Raise their hopes. Rise to their needs.

  找到某个你想为他而成功的人。唤起他们的希望，满足他们的需求。

第二章

奋斗的力量
因为努力，才有选择

奋斗 Struggle

Doing the Right Thing in the Digital World
在数字世界中做正确的事

——蒂姆·库克 2017 年在麻省理工学院毕业典礼上的演讲

简介 Profile

蒂姆·库克
Tim Cook

蒂姆·库克，这个名字与苹果公司紧密相连，他的一举一动都牵动着全球科技市场的神经。这位低调而务实的领导者将苹果公司带向了新的高度。

1960年，库克出生于美国亚拉巴马州的一个农村家庭。从小就极为勤勉的他成绩非常出色，而且早早就对科技有着浓厚的兴趣。大学毕业后，库克加入了国际商业机器公司（IBM），由于能力出众，很快便脱颖而出，被列入高潜人才计划，负责领导IBM个人电脑产品在北美和拉丁美洲市场的生产和配送业务。1998年，受乔布斯邀请，库克进入苹果公司担任苹果全球运营高级副总裁。后来，库克凭借出色的业绩逐渐崭露头角。2005年，库克被任命为苹果公司的首席运营官，负责全球销售和运营。2011年，史蒂夫·乔布斯因病辞世，库克接任了苹果公司CEO。尽管面临巨大的压力和挑战，但库克依然坚定地引领着苹果公司前进，并且以实际行动践行着乔布斯留给苹果的精神遗产——专注。他深知创新的重要性，推动了一系列新产品和服务的推出，如iPhone X、Apple Watch、Apple Music等。这些产品不仅赢得了消费者的喜爱，也为苹果带来了丰厚的收入。

库克不仅是一位杰出的企业家，更是一位关注社会议题的公益倡导者。他积极地参与公益事业，关注气候变化、隐私保护和教育等议题，并倡导企业社会责任。

2017年，库克出席了麻省理工学院的毕业典礼，向即将步入社会的毕业生们分享了自己对科技、价值观和未来的看法。他鼓励毕业生们要坚守自己的价值观，勇敢面对未来的挑战，利用科技的力量为社会进步做出贡献。

演讲 Speech

Hello, MIT!

Thank you. Congratulations, Class of 2017. I especially want to thank Chairman Millard, President Reif, distinguished faculty, trustees, and members of the Class of 1967. It is a privilege to be with you today, with your families and your friends on such an amazing and important day.

MIT and Apple share so much. We both love hard problems. We love the search for new ideas, and we especially love finding those ideas, the really big ones, the ones that can change the world. I know MIT has a proud tradition of pranks[1] or as you would call them, hacks. And you have pulled off[2] some pretty great ones over the years.

I'll never figure out how MIT students sent that Mars rover to the Kresge Oval[3], or put a propeller beanie on the Great Dome, or how you've obviously taken over the president's Twitter account. I can tell college students are behind because most of the Tweets happen at 3 a.m.

I'm really happy to be here. Today is about celebration. And you have so much to be proud of. As you leave here to start the next leg of your journey in life, there will be days where you will ask yourself, "Where is all this going?" "What is the purpose?" "What is my purpose?" I will be honest. I asked myself that same question and it took me nearly 15 years to answer it. Maybe by talking about my journey today, I can save you some time.

麻省理工学院的各位，你们好！

谢谢。祝贺 2017 届毕业生。我想特别感谢米勒德主席、赖夫校长、杰出的教职工们、董事们和 1967 届的校友们。能在这个意义非凡的重要日子里和你们以及你们的家人和朋友共同庆祝，我感到十分荣幸。

麻省理工学院和苹果公司有很多共同之处。我们都喜欢攻克难题，寻找新思路，尤其喜欢寻找那些真正宏大的、可以改变世界的思路。我知道麻省理工学院有个引以为豪的恶搞传统，就是你们称之为"骇客"的传统。这些年来，你们已经完成了不少大事。

我永远想不明白麻省理工学院的学生是如何把火星漫游车送到克雷斯格椭圆形草坪上的，也想不明白你们是如何给礼堂大圆顶戴上"螺旋桨帽子"的。显然，你们还接管了总统的推特账号。就凭这个账号大部分的推文都是凌晨 3 点发的，我就可以断定这事儿的幕后主使肯定是大学生。

今天能来到这里，我真的很高兴。今天是值得庆祝的日子，你们有太多值得骄傲的地方了。当你们离开这里，即将开始人生的下一段旅程时，你将会问自己："人生去向何方？""目标是什么？""我的目标是什么？"实话说，我曾问过自己同样的问题，并且花了将近 15 年的时间才得到答案。今天说说我的人生旅程，或许会为你们节省些时间。

---

1. prank：*n.* 恶作剧；玩笑。
2. pull off：(成功地或艰苦地) 完成，做成。
3. 此处指麻省理工学院校园内的一片大型草坪区域，其中 "Kresge" 是捐赠者的名字，而 "Oval" 在英文中指椭圆形的场地或草坪。

在数字世界中做正确的事　103

The struggle for me started early on. In high school, I thought I discovered my life's purpose when I could answer that age-old question, "What do you want to be when you grow up?" Nope. In college I thought I would discover it when I could answer, "What's your major?" Not quite. I thought that maybe I'd discovered it when I found a good job. Then I thought I just needed to get a few promotions. That didn't work either.

I kept convincing myself that it was just over the horizon, around the next corner. Nothing worked, and it was really tearing me apart. Part of me kept pushing ahead to the next achievement, and the other part kept asking, "Is this all there is?"

I went to grad school at Duke looking for the answer. I tried meditation. I sought guidance in religion. I read great philosophers and authors. And in a moment of youthful indiscretion[4], I might even have experimented with a Windows PC and obviously that didn't work.

After countless twists and turns, at last, 20 years ago, my search brought me to Apple. At the time, the company was struggling to survive. Steve Jobs had just returned to Apple, and had launched the "Think Different" campaign. He wanted to empower the crazy ones—the misfits, the rebels, the troublemakers, the round pegs, and the square holes[5]—to do their best work. If we could just do that, Steve knew we could really change the world.

Before that moment, I had never met a leader with such passion or encountered a company with such a clear and compelling purpose: to serve humanity. It was just that simple. Serve humanity.

And it was in that moment, after 15 years of searching, something clicked. I finally felt aligned: aligned with a company that brought together challenging, cutting-edge[6] work with a higher purpose, aligned with a leader who believed that technology which didn't exist yet could reinvent tomorrow's world, aligned with myself and my own deep need to serve something greater.

我的困惑很早就开始了。高中时，我以为当我能够回答"你长大想做什么"这个老掉牙的问题时，我就找到了人生目标。但不是这样的。大学时，我以为能够回答"你学什么专业"时，就是找到了人生目标。也不完全如此。我想，当我找到一份好工作时，我可能就找到人生目标了，之后我又认为，只需要几次升职就能找到人生目标了，但都不对。

我不断告诉自己，答案就要浮出水面，就在前方不远处，但是无一奏效。这真的让我痛苦不堪。我一边为下一个成就努力奋进，一边不停地问自己："就是这样了吗？"

我去杜克大学读研，寻找答案。我尝试过冥想。我到宗教中寻找指点。我阅读伟大的哲学家和作家的作品。年轻的我一时头脑发热，甚至尝试过用安装了 Windows 系统的电脑寻找答案，显然这并不奏效。

经过无数次的痛苦辗转，20 年前，我的寻觅最终把我引向苹果公司。那时苹果公司正艰难求生：史蒂夫·乔布斯刚刚回到苹果，发起了"非同凡'想'"运动。他想要让那些疯狂的人——不合群的、叛逆的、爱惹麻烦的、在错误的位置上未尽其才的人——最大程度地发挥自己的才能。史蒂夫明白，如果能做到这一点，我们就可以真正地改变世界。

在此之前，我从未遇到过如此充满激情的老板，也从没见过这样的公司——它有着明确的、催人奋进的目标：服务人类。就是这么简单，服务人类。

就在那一刻，在历经了 15 年的追寻和求索后，我终于醍醐灌顶。我终于有了归属感，那就是加入一个把具有挑战性的尖端工作和高远目标结合在一起的公司，同一位相信未知技术可以深刻改变未来世界的领导者并肩作战，找到了自我和内心深处服务更远大理想的渴望。

---

4. indiscretion：*n.* 不慎重，草率。
5. square hole：在英语中，有"square pegs in a round hole"这一谚语，字面意思是"嵌入圆孔里的方桩"，引申义指那些不适宜从事某一工作或担任某一职位的人。
6. cutting-edge：*adj.* 尖端（的），前沿（的）。

在数字世界中做正确的事　105

Of course, at that moment I didn't know all of that. I was just grateful to have that psychological burden lifted. But with the help of hindsight, my breakthrough makes a lot more sense. I was never going to find my purpose working someplace without a clear sense of purpose of its own. Steve and Apple freed me to throw my whole self into my work, to embrace their mission and make it my own. How can I serve humanity? This is life's biggest and most important question. When you work towards something greater than yourself, you find meaning; you find purpose. So the question I hope you will carry forward from here is: How will you serve humanity?

The good news is since you are here today you are already on a great track. At MIT, you have learned how much power science and technology have to change the world for the better. Thanks to the discoveries made right here, billions of people are leading healthier and more productive, more fulfilling lives. And if we are ever going to solve some of the hardest problems still facing the world today, everything from cancer to climate change to educational inequality, then technology will help us do it. But technology alone isn't the solution, and sometimes it's even part of the problem.

Last year I had the chance to meet with Pope Francis. It was the most incredible meeting of my life. This is a man who has spent more time comforting the inflicted in slums than he has with heads of state.

This may surprise you, but he knew an unbelievable amount about technology. It was obvious to me that he had thought deeply about it—its opportunities, its risks, its morality. What he said to me at that meeting, what he preached, really, was on a topic that we care a lot about at Apple. But he expressed a shared concern in a powerful new way. Never has humanity had such power over itself, yet nothing ensures that it will be used wisely, he has said.

Technology today is integral to almost all aspects of our lives and most of

当然，我那时并没有意识到那么多，只是很高兴自己卸下了心理负担。但是事后想来，我的突破意义非凡。在没有明确目标的地方工作，我永远也不会找到自己的目标。史蒂夫和苹果解救了我，让我全身心地投入工作，去接受他们的使命并以之为己任。我该如何服务人类？这是人生中最重大的问题。当你向着比自身更宏大的东西奋斗时，你就发现了意义，发现了目标。所以，我希望你们带着这个问题从这里出发：你们该如何服务人类？

可喜的是，你们今天坐在这里就意味着已经踏上了一条光明之路。在麻省理工学院，你们已经了解到科技拥有多么巨大的改善世界的力量。得益于这里做出的发现，让数十亿人得以过上更健康、更高效、更美满的生活。如果我们要解决当今世界仍面临的一些最棘手的问题，不论是癌症、气候变化还是教育不公，技术都将会助我们一臂之力。但只有技术并不能解决问题，它有时甚至也是问题的一部分。

去年，我有幸见到了教皇方济各。这是我人生中最不可思议的一次会面。相比会见国家领导人，教皇更多的时间是在贫民窟里抚慰不幸的人。

你们也许会感到惊讶，但他对技术的了解到了令人难以置信的程度。在我看来，他显然对技术有过深入的思考——技术带来的机遇、风险，还关乎它的道德性。见面时他跟我说的话——事实上是对我的告诫——的的确确都和我们在苹果公司关心的问题息息相关。但他以一种崭新的方式有力地表达了我们共同关切的问题。他说，人类从未对自己有过如此大的支配力量，但是没什么能够保证这种力量得到正确地使用。

技术如今几乎融入了我们生活的方方面面。大部分时候都是积极的影响。但是，

> *If science is a search in the darkness, then the humanities are a candle that shows us where we've been and the danger that lies ahead.*
>
> 如果说科学是在黑暗中探索，那么人性就是蜡烛，照亮我们的所在，指明前方的危险。

the time it's a force for good. And yet the potential adverse consequences are spreading faster and cutting deeper than ever before—threats to our security, threats to our privacy, fake news, and social media that becomes antisocial. Sometimes the very technology that is meant to connect us divides us.

Technology is capable of doing great things. But it doesn't want to do great things. It doesn't want anything. That part takes all of us. It takes our values and our commitment to our families and our neighbors and our communities, our love of beauty and belief that all of our faiths are interconnected, our decency, our kindness.

I'm not worried about artificial intelligence giving computers the ability to think like humans. I'm more concerned about people thinking like computers without values or compassion, without concern for consequences. That is what we need you to help us guard against, because if science is a search in the darkness, then the humanities are a candle that shows us where we've been and the danger that lies ahead.

As Steve once said, technology alone is not enough. It is technology married with the liberal arts, married with the humanities, that make our hearts sing. When you keep people at the center of what you do, it can have an enormous impact. It means an iPhone that allows a blind person to run a marathon. It means an Apple Watch that catches a heart condition before it becomes a heart attack. It means an iPad that helps a child with autism[7] connect with his or her world. In short, it means technology infused with your values, making progress possible for everyone.

Whatever you do in your life, and whatever we do at Apple, we must infuse it with the humanity that each of us is born with. That responsibility is immense, but so is the opportunity. I'm optimistic because I believe in your generation, your passion, your journey to serve humanity. We are all counting on you.

潜在的负面作用也正在以前所未有的速度扩散，并造成前所未有的伤害，比如对我们安全和隐私的威胁、虚假的新闻、变得反社交的社交媒体。有时，旨在把我们联结起来的科技反而分裂了我们。

科技可以做好事，但是它并不想做好事。它无欲无求。科技的这一特性会吞噬我们所有人，会夺走我们的价值观，夺走我们对家庭、邻里、社区的承诺，夺走我们对美的热爱、我们的信念、我们的体面和善良。

我不担心人工智能赋予电脑像人类一样的思考能力。我更担心人类像电脑一样思考，价值观缺失，毫无同情心，不计后果。这就是我们需要你们帮助防范的地方。如果说科学是在黑暗中探索，那么人性就是蜡烛，照亮我们的所在，指明前方的危险。

正如史蒂夫说过的，单靠技术是不够的。技术与人文科学和人性结合才能让我们的心灵放声歌唱。如果你做的事以人为本，那么它将会产生巨大的影响。这意味着 iPhone 可以让盲人跑马拉松，Apple Watch 可以在心脏病发作前诊断出心脏疾病，iPad 可以让患有自闭症的孩子和他们的世界连接起来。简单来说，这意味着将技术注入你的价值观，让每个人都有进步的可能。

不管你这一生要做什么，也不论我们在苹果做什么，我们都必须将之与每个人与生俱来的人性融合在一起。这样的责任巨大，但是机遇也同样巨大。我很乐观，因为我相信你们这一代，相信你们的激情以及你们致力于服务人类的旅程。我们全都指望你们了。

> *When you keep people at the center of what you do, it can have an enormous impact.*
>
> 如果你做的事以人为本，那么它将会产生巨大的影响。

---

7. autism：*n.* 自闭症。

There is so much out there conspiring to make you cynical. The Internet has enabled so much and empowered so many, but it can also be a place where basic rules of decency are suspended and pettiness and negativity thrive. Don't let that noise knock you off course. Don't get caught up in the trivial aspects of life. Don't listen to trolls[8] and for God's sake don't become one. Measure your impact on humanity not in likes, but in the lives you touch; not in popularity, but in the people you serve. I found that my life got bigger when I stopped caring what other people thought about me. You will find yours will too. Stay focused on what really matters.

There will be times when your resolve to serve humanity will be tested. Be prepared. People will try to convince you that you should keep your empathy out of your career. Don't accept this false premise.

At a shareholders' meeting a few years back, someone questioned Apple's investment and focus on the environment. He asked me to pledge that Apple would only invest in green initiatives that could be justified with a return on investment. I tried to be diplomatic. I pointed out that Apple does many things, like accessibility features for those with disabilities that don't rely on an ROI[9]. We do these things because they are the right thing to do, and protecting the environment is a critical example. He wouldn't let it go and I got my blood up. So I told him, "If you can't accept our position, you shouldn't own Apple stock."

When you are convinced that your causes are right, have the courage to take a stand. If you see a problem or an injustice, recognize that no one will fix it but you. As you go forward today, use your minds and hands and your hearts to build something bigger than yourselves. Always remember there is no idea bigger than this.

As Dr. Martin Luther King said, "All life is interrelated. We are all bound together into a single garment of destiny." If you keep that idea at the forefront

这个世界有太多的东西让你们变得愤世嫉俗。网络赋予了我们太多的能力，让太多的人获得了力量，但它也是道德沦丧、负能量爆棚的地方。不要让（网上的）那些喧嚣诱你偏离轨道，不要陷入生活的琐碎中去，不要听信网络喷子，更不要变成网络喷子。你对人类的影响力不取决于你获得的点赞数，而是取决于你触及的生命；不取决于你受欢迎的程度，而是取决于你服务的人们。我发现当我不再在意别人的眼光时，我的生命变得更加有意义。终有一天，你们也会发现自己的生命变得更有意义。请持续专注于真正重要的东西。

你们服务人类的决心有时会受到考验，要做好准备。有人会试图说服你把同理心排除在事业之外，请不要接受这个谎言。

几年前，在一次股东大会上，有人质疑苹果的投资，尤其聚焦在我们投资的环保事业上。他要我保证苹果只会给有利润回报的绿色环保项目投资。我试着婉转地向他解释，指出苹果做了很多不看投资回报率的事，例如给残障人士提供辅助功能。我们做这些事是因为这是正确的事情，保护环境就是其中一个重要的例子。但他还是咬紧不放，我热血上头，跟他说："你如果接受不了我们的立场，就不该拥有苹果的股份。"

当你坚信你的事业是正确的，就要勇敢地坚守你的立场。当你碰到问题或不公的现象时，请你意识到自己就是那个解决问题、维持正义的人。今天，你们就要前行，用思想、双手和心灵去缔造比你自己更宏大的事业。要始终记得，没什么比这一思想更宏大。

正如马丁·路德·金博士所说："所有生命都是有内在联系的，我们休戚与共。"

---

8. troll：*n.* 原意指斯堪的纳维亚传说中的怪物，现常用作网络用语，指那些具有挑衅、攻击性意味的网络帖子，或恶意散发挑衅性帖子的人，也可指这一类行为。
9. ROI："Return On Investment"的缩写，意为"投资回报率"。

of all that you do, if you choose to live your lives at that intersection between technology and the people it serves, if you strive to create the best, give the best, do the best for everyone, not just for some, then today all of humanity has good cause for hope.

Thank you very much and congratulations, Class of 2017!

如果你们以此作为每件事的指导思想，如果你们选择活在技术和受益于技术的人们的相交之处，如果你努力为所有人竭尽所能，而不仅仅是为某些人，那么今天，整个人类都有理由抱有希望。

非常感谢各位，祝贺 2017 届毕业生！

语录 Quotes

- If science is a search in the darkness, then the humanities are a candle that shows us where we've been and the danger that lies ahead.
  如果说科学是在黑暗中探索,那么人性就是蜡烛,照亮我们的所在,指明前方的危险。

- When you keep people at the center of what you do, it can have an enormous impact.
  如果你做的事以人为本,那么它将会产生巨大的影响。

- Measure your impact on humanity not in likes, but in the lives you touch; not in popularity, but in the people you serve.
  你对人类的影响力不取决于你获得的点赞数,而取决于你触及的生命;不取决于你受欢迎的程度,而取决于你服务的人们。

- I found that my life got bigger when I stopped caring what other people thought about me.
  我发现当我不再在意别人的眼光时,我的生命变得更加有意义。

- People will try to convince you that you should keep your empathy out of your career. Don't accept this false premise.
  有人会试图说服你把同理心排除在事业之外,请不要接受这个谎言。

- When you are convinced that your causes are right, have the courage to take a stand. If you see a problem or an injustice, recognize that no one will fix it but you.
  当你坚信你的事业是正确的,就要勇敢坚守你的立场。当你碰到问题或不公现象的时候,请你意识到自己就是那个解决问题、维持正义的人。

We Are Shaped by Our Own Choices
我们的选择塑造了我们

——杰夫·贝索斯 2010 年在普林斯顿大学毕业典礼上的演讲

> 简介 Profile

杰夫·贝索斯
Jeff Bezos

杰夫·贝索斯出生于 1964 年，成长于美国新墨西哥州的一个普通家庭。1986 年，他获得普林斯顿大学的电气工程与计算机科学学士学位。毕业后的最初几年里，贝索斯先后在华尔街的几家公司工作过，但他内心深处始终渴望着创业。

1994 年，贝索斯看到了互联网的巨大潜力，认为创业的时机已然来临，于是决定辞职创办亚马逊公司。他将自己家的车库作为第一个办公室，招募了几名员工，开始在互联网上销售图书。随着业务的不断壮大，亚马逊迅速拓展到其他商品领域，成为全球最大的在线零售商。

除了商业领域的成功，贝索斯还积极投身于太空探索和慈善事业。他创立了蓝色起源公司，致力于降低太空旅行的成本。同时，他还捐出了自己的部分财产，用来支持教育和环保等公益事业。贝索斯的慈善事业不仅关注当下，更着眼于未来，为人类社会的可持续发展做出了贡献。

贝索斯的人生充满了传奇色彩。他的成功不仅来自对科技的敏锐洞察力和商业模式的创新，更来自他的冒险精神和不断追求卓越的决心。他曾说过一句名言："如果你想要成功，就必须愿意去冒险。"这句话也是他一生的真实写照。贝索斯的影响力不仅局限于亚马逊公司，更延伸到了整个科技和商业领域。他的无畏探索和创新精神将继续激励更多的人去追求自己的梦想和目标。

在 2010 年普林斯顿大学的毕业演讲上，杰夫·贝索斯向毕业生们分享了他的人生经验和见解，鼓励毕业生们要努力追求自己的梦想，成为一个善良和为他人着想的人，以此来创造一个更加美好的未来。

演讲 Speech

扫描二维码
获取本篇演讲原视频、音频

As a kid, I spent my summers with my grandparents on their ranch in Texas. I helped fix windmills, vaccinate cattle, and do other chores. We also watched soap operas every afternoon, especially "*Days of Our Lives*."

My grandparents belonged to a Caravan Club, a group of Airstream[1] trailer owners who travel together around the U.S. and Canada. And every few summers, we'd join the caravan. We'd hitch up the Airstream to my grandfather's car, and off we'd go, in a line with 300 other Airstream adventurers. I loved and worshipped my grandparents and I really looked forward to these trips.

On one particular trip, I was about 10 years old. I was rolling around in the big bench seat in the back of the car. My grandfather was driving. And my grandmother had the passenger seat. She smoked throughout these trips, and I hated the smell.

At that age, I'd take any excuse to make estimates and do minor arithmetic. I'd calculate our gas mileage—figure out useless statistics on things like grocery spending. I'd been hearing an ad campaign about smoking. I can't remember the details, but basically the ad said, every puff of a cigarette takes some number of minutes off of your life: I think it might have been two minutes per puff. At any rate[2], I decided to do the math for my grandmother. I estimated the number of cigarettes per day, estimated the number of puffs per cigarette

在我还是一个孩子的时候，总是跟我的祖父母在得克萨斯州的牧场过夏天。我帮着修理风车，给牛接种疫苗，做其他家务。每天下午我们还会一起看肥皂剧，尤其是《我们的日子》。

我的祖父母加入了一个车队旅行俱乐部，这是一个由清风房车车主组成的团体，他们会一起环游美国和加拿大。每隔几个夏天，我们就会随队出游。我们会把房车挂到我祖父的小汽车后面，然后和另外 300 位清风房车探险家一起出发。我很爱祖父母，很崇拜他们，也非常期待旅行。

我大约 10 岁那年的旅行很特别。那时，我在车后座的大长椅上打滚，祖父在开车。祖母坐在副驾驶座上，一路上都在抽烟。我讨厌那股烟味。

那个年纪的我热衷于找各种机会做估算和简单的算数。我计算油耗和食品杂货支出之类没什么用的统计数据。我听过一个关于吸烟的广告，细节我不记得了，只记得大致是说，每吸一口烟都会折寿几分钟，好像是每口烟折寿两分钟。总之，我决定为祖母算一下这笔账。我估算了每天抽烟的次数、每支烟吸多少口等。

> *It's harder to be kind than clever.*
>
> 善良比聪明更难。

---

1. Airstream：清风房车，美国的一个房车品牌，旗下房车以铝制车身为特色。
2. at any rate：无论如何。

and so on.

When I was satisfied that I'd come up with a reasonable number, I poked my head into the front of the car, tapped my grandmother on the shoulder, and proudly proclaimed, "At two minutes per puff, you've taken nine years off your life!"

I have a vivid memory of what happened, and it was not what I expected. I expected to be applauded for my cleverness and arithmetic skills. "Jeff, you're so smart. You had to have made some tricky estimates, figure out the number of minutes in a year and do some division."

That's not what happened. Instead, my grandmother burst into tears. I sat in the backseat and did not know what to do. While my grandmother sat crying, my grandfather, who had been driving in silence, pulled over onto the shoulder[3] of the highway. He got out of the car and came around and opened my door and waited for me to follow.

Was I in trouble? My grandfather was a highly intelligent, quiet man. He had never said a harsh word to me, and maybe this was to be the first time? Or maybe he would ask that I get back in the car and apologize to my grandmother. I had no experience in this realm[4] with my grandparents and no way to gauge[5] what the consequences might be.

We stopped beside the trailer. My grandfather looked at me, and after a bit of silence, he gently and calmly said, "Jeff, one day you'll understand that it's harder to be kind than clever."

What I want to talk to you about today is the difference between gifts and choices. Cleverness is a gift. Kindness is a choice. Gifts are easy—they're given after all. Choices can be hard. You can seduce yourself with your gifts if you're not careful, and if you do, it'll probably be to the detriment of your choices.

This is a group with many gifts. I'm sure one of your gifts is the gift of a

我满意地得出了一个合理的数字，把头探进车的前排，拍了拍祖母的肩膀，得意扬扬地宣布："每口烟折寿 2 分钟，你已经折寿 9 年了！"

接下来的事儿跟我想的完全不一样，我记得可清楚了。我以为祖母会夸我聪明，夸我算术好，以为她会说："杰夫，你真聪明。你肯定是做了一番精细的估算，算出一年里有多少分钟，然后又做了除法。"

结果完全不是那么回事儿。祖母突然大哭起来，坐在后座上的我手足无措。祖母哭泣的时候，一直默默开车的祖父把车停在了公路的路肩上。他下了车，绕过来，打开车门，等我下车跟他走。

我惹麻烦了吗？祖父是一个非常聪明而又沉默寡言的人，从来没有对我说过一句难听的话，也许这会是第一次？或许他会要求我回到车上向祖母道歉。我和祖父母之间没经历过这种情况，也无法判断后果是什么。

我们在拖车旁边停了下来。祖父看着我，沉默了一会儿，温和而平静地说："杰夫，总有一天你会明白，善良比聪明更难。"

今天我想和你们谈谈天赋和选择之间的区别。聪明是一种天赋，善良是一种选择。天赋来得轻松——毕竟是与生俱来的。选择则可能很艰难。一不留神，人就可能会被天赋所迷惑，从而做出不利于选择的事情。

在座的各位都有不少天赋。我敢肯定，你们的天赋之一就是聪明发达的大脑。

Cleverness is a gift, kindness is a choice. Gifts are easy. Choices can be hard.

聪明是一种天赋，善良是一种选择。天赋来得轻松。选择则可能很艰难。

---

3. shoulder：*n.* 路肩，公路旁的紧急停车道。
4. realm：*n.* 领域。
5. gauge：*v.* 判定，判断（尤指人的感情或态度）。

smart and capable brain. I'm confident that's the case because admission is competitive and if there weren't some signs that you're clever, the Dean of Admissions wouldn't have let you in.

Your smarts will come in handy because you will travel in a land of marvels. We humans—plodding as we are—will astonish ourselves. We'll invent ways to generate clean energy and a lot of it. Atom by atom, we'll assemble small machines that can enter cell walls and make repairs. This month comes the extraordinary but inevitable news that we've synthesized life. In the coming years, we'll not only synthesize it, but engineer it to specifications. I believe you'll even see us understand the human brain. Jules Verne, Mark Twain, Galileo, Newton—all the curious from the ages would have wanted to be alive, most of all, right now.

As a civilization, we will have so many gifts. Just as you, as individuals, have so many individual gifts as you sit before me. How will you use these gifts? And will you take pride in your gifts or pride in your choices?

I got the idea to start Amazon 16 years ago. I came across the fact that Web usage was growing at 2,300 percent per year. I'd never seen or heard of anything that grew that fast.

The idea of building an online bookstore with millions of titles—something that simply couldn't exist in the physical world—was very exciting to me. I had just turned 30 years old, and I'd been married for a year. I told my wife MacKenzie that I wanted to quit my job and go do this crazy thing that probably wouldn't work since most startups don't, and I wasn't sure what would happen after that. MacKenzie (also a Princeton grad and sitting here in the second row) told me I should go for it. As a young boy, I'd been a garage inventor. I'd invented an automatic gate closer out of cement-filled tires, a solar cooker that didn't work very well out of an umbrella and aluminum foil, baking-pan alarms to entrap my siblings. I'd always wanted to be an inventor,

我相信情况就是这样，因为入学竞争激烈，你们要是显露不出聪明的迹象，招生委员会就不会让你们入学。

你们的智慧将会派上用场，因为你们将行走在一片充满奇迹的土地之上。我们人类，尽管步履蹒跚，却会令自己惊叹不已。我们想方设法生产大量清洁能源。我们将原子逐一组装成小型机器，让它进入细胞壁并实施修复工作。本月发生了一件不同寻常却注定发生的事，那就是人类已经合成了生命。在未来几年里，我们不仅会合成生命，还会对生命进行规范化设计。我相信，各位甚至会见证人类揭开人类大脑之谜的那一刻。儒勒·凡尔纳、马克·吐温、伽利略、牛顿——古往今来所有满怀好奇心的人都会希望自己活在当下这个时代。

人类文明将拥有这么多技术，就像在座各位拥有这么多天赋一样。你们将如何使用这些天赋？你们会为天赋感到自豪，还是为选择感到自豪？

16年前，我萌生了创办亚马逊的想法。我发现网络使用量每年增长2300%。增长如此之快的事物，我实在是闻所未闻，见所未见。

创办一个拥有百万图书的在线书店——这个在现实世界中无法实现的想法令我心潮澎湃。那时我刚到而立之年，已结婚一年。我告诉妻子麦肯齐，我想辞掉工作去追梦，而这个创业计划未必能成功，毕竟大多数初创企业都以失败告终，我也无法预知未来。麦肯齐（她也毕业于普林斯顿大学，现在坐在第二排）鼓励我大胆尝试。小时候的我是车库发明家。我用装满水泥的轮胎发明过一个自动闭门器，用雨伞和铝箔做过一个不太好用的太阳能炉子，还做过用来捉弄兄弟姐妹的烤盘警报器。

> *We humans—plodding as we are—will astonish ourselves.*
>
> 我们人类，尽管步履蹒跚，却会令自己惊叹不已。

and she wanted me to follow my passion.

I was working at a financial firm in New York City with a bunch of very smart people, and I had a brilliant boss I much admired. I went to my boss and told him I was going to start a company selling books on the Internet. He took me on a long walk in Central Park, listened carefully to me, and finally said, "That sounds like a really good idea, but it would be an even better idea for someone who didn't already have a good job."

That logic made some sense to me, and he convinced me to think about it for 48 hours before making a final decision. Seen in that light, it really was a difficult choice, but ultimately, I decided I had to give it a shot. I didn't think I'd regret trying and failing. And I suspected I would always be haunted by a decision to not try at all. After much consideration, I took the less safe path to follow my passion, and I'm proud of that choice.

Tomorrow, in a very real sense, your life—the life you author from scratch on your own—begins.

How will you use your gifts? What choices will you make?

Will inertia be your guide, or will you follow your passions?

Will you follow dogma, or will you be original?

Will you choose a life of ease, or a life of service and adventure?

Will you wilt under criticism, or will you follow your convictions?

Will you bluff it out[6] when you're wrong, or will you apologize?

Will you guard your heart against rejection, or will you act when you fall in love?

Will you play it safe, or will you be a little bit swashbuckling[7]?

When it's tough, will you give up, or will you be relentless?

Will you be a cynic, or will you be a builder?

Will you be clever at the expense of others, or will you be kind?

I will hazard a prediction. When you are 80 years old, and in a quiet

我一直想成为一名发明家，她支持我追随内心的热爱。

　　我当时在纽约市的一家金融公司工作，和一群非常聪明的人当同事，我的老板也很厉害，我非常钦佩他。我去找老板，告诉他我要创办一家在网上卖书的公司。他领着我在中央公园走了很长一段路，认真听我说完，最后说："听起来确实是个好主意，不过要是你没眼下这份好工作，这主意就更好了。"

　　这个逻辑对我来说挺有道理的，他劝我考虑48个小时再做最终决定。从这个角度来看，这真是一个艰难的选择，但最终，我还是决定要试一试。如果尝试了，即使失败，我也不会后悔；而如果试都不试，我可能会惦记一辈子。经过深思熟虑，我选择了追随热爱，踏上一条不太稳妥的道路，我为这个选择感到自豪。

　　明天，非常现实地说，你们从零开始塑造自己人生的时代就要开启了。

　　你们将如何使用自己的天赋？又会做出怎样的选择？

　　是听从惯性的指引，还是追随热爱？

　　是循规蹈矩，还是选择创新？

　　是选择安逸，还是奉献和冒险？

　　被批评了，是退缩不前，还是坚守信念？

　　犯错了，是硬撑着不承认，还是道歉？

　　在坠入爱河时，是因为害怕拒绝而封闭心灵，还是勇往直前？

　　是求稳，还是冒险？

　　遇到困难，是选择放弃，还是不屈不挠？

　　是要当愤世嫉俗者，还是建设者？

　　是损人利己，还是厚道良善？

　　我冒昧地做个预测。等到你们80岁的时候，哪天闲下来回想往事，也许会为自

---

6. bluff it out：以虚张声势的方式渡过难关。
7. swashbuckling：*adj.* 惊心动魄的。

moment of reflection, narrating for only yourself the most personal version of your life story, the telling that will be most compact and meaningful will be the series of choices you have made. In the end, we are our choices. Build yourself a great story.

Thank you and good luck!

己讲述那些只属于自己的故事。那个最充实、最有意义的故事，会是你们做过的一系列选择。归根结底，我们是自己选择的总和。为自己编写一个精彩的故事吧！

谢谢大家，祝你们好运！

语录 Quotes

- It's harder to be kind than clever.
  善良比聪明更难。

- Cleverness is a gift, kindness is a choice. Gifts are easy. Choices can be hard.
  聪明是一种天赋,善良是一种选择。天赋来得轻松。选择则可能很艰难。

- You can seduce yourself with your gifts if you're not careful, and if you do, it'll probably be to the detriment of your choices.
  一不留神,人就可能会被天赋所迷惑,从而做出不利于选择的事情。

- We humans—plodding as we are—will astonish ourselves.
  我们人类,尽管步履蹒跚,却会令自己惊叹不已。

- I didn't think I'd regret trying and failing. And I suspected I would always be haunted by a decision to not try at all.
  如果尝试了,即使失败,我也不会后悔;而如果试都不试,我可能会惦记一辈子。

- In the end, we are our choices.
  归根结底,我们是自己选择的总和。

Speak Up When You Disagree with the Voice of Authority
听从内心，追随直觉

——史蒂文·斯皮尔伯格 2016 年在哈佛大学毕业典礼上的演讲

> 简介 Profile

史蒂文·艾伦·斯皮尔伯格
Steven Allan Spielberg

　　1946 年，斯皮尔伯格出生于美国俄亥俄州，他从小就对电影有着浓厚的兴趣。12 岁时，他以火车失事为主题，拍摄了人生中的第一部家庭电影。1963 年，在父亲的资助下，17 岁的斯皮尔伯格用 500 美元的预算，自编自导了他的第一部独立电影《火光》。斯皮尔伯格申请了南加利福尼亚大学的电影学院，但是因为成绩一般而被拒绝。之后，他申请了加州州立大学长滩分校，随后入学就读。

　　1968 年，斯皮尔伯格自编自导的爱情短片《安培林》给时任环球影业副总裁的西德尼·辛伯格留下了深刻的印象，他因此和环球影业签下了一份为期 7 年的导演合同。一年后，他从大学辍学，开始为环球影业拍电影。在和好莱坞主要电影公司签订长期合约的导演中，他是最年轻的一个。

　　在随后的导演生涯里，斯皮尔伯格拍出了一部部家喻户晓的好莱坞大片。1975 年，29 岁的斯皮尔伯格执导了惊悚片《大白鲨》，其全球票房超 4.7 亿美元，成为当时全球票房最高的电影，斯皮尔伯格也因此声名大噪。在之后的 40 多年里，他执导了《夺宝奇兵》《E.T. 外星人》《侏罗纪公园》《辛德勒的名单》《拯救大兵瑞恩》《头号玩家》等不同题材的电影。

　　这些优秀的作品也奠定了史蒂文·斯皮尔伯格在影视领域不可动摇的地位，他曾 3 次获得奥斯卡金像奖，4 次获得美国导演工会奖。1995 年获美国电影学会终身成就奖，2015 年获总统自由勋章，2023 年获柏林电影节终身成就金熊奖。

　　2016 年，斯皮尔伯格在哈佛大学的毕业典礼上，以自己执导过的电影为线索，寄予毕业生们肺腑之言：听从内心，追随直觉，别辜负梦想。

演讲 Speech

Thank you, thank you, President Faust, and Paul Choi, thank you so much. It's an honor and a thrill to address this group of distinguished alumni and supportive friends and kvelling[1] parents. We've all gathered to share in the joy of this day, so please join me in congratulating Harvard's Class of 2016.

I can remember my own college graduation, which is easy, since it was only 14 years ago. How many of you took 37 years to graduate? Because, like most of you, I began college in my teens, but sophomore year, I was offered my dream job at Universal Studios, so I dropped out. I told my parents if my movie career didn't go well, I'd re-enroll. It went all right.

But eventually, I returned for one big reason. Most people go to college for an education, and some go for their parents, but I went for my kids. I'm the father of seven, and I kept insisting on the importance of going to college, but I hadn't walked the walk[2]. So, in my fifties, I re-enrolled at Cal State, Long Beach, and I earned my degree.

I just have to add: It helped that they gave me course credit in paleontology[3] for the work I did on *Jurassic Park*[4]. That's three units for *Jurassic Park*, thank you.

Well, I left college because I knew exactly what I wanted to do, and some of you know, too—but some of you don't. Or maybe you thought you knew but are now questioning that choice. Maybe you're sitting there trying to figure out

感谢福斯特校长和保罗·崔校长，非常感谢你们。能够在杰出的毕业生、热心的朋友和自豪的家长面前发表演讲，我感到既荣幸又激动。我们齐聚一堂，分享今日之喜，就请和我一起祝贺哈佛大学2016届的毕业生吧。

我还记得自己的大学毕业典礼，这不难记，毕竟才过去14年。你们中有多少人像我一样花了37年才毕业？和你们大多数人一样，我十几岁就上了大学，但在大二那年，环球影城给了我一份我梦寐以求的工作，所以我退学了。我告诉父母，如果电影事业不顺利，我会重新回到学校。后来一切都挺顺利的。

不过，出于一个很重要的原因，我终究还是回来了。大多数人上大学是为了接受教育，有些人是为了父母，而我是为了孩子。我是7个孩子的父亲，我一直向孩子们强调上大学的重要性，但我自己并没有好好上大学。所以，50多岁的时候，我重新进入加州州立大学长滩分校，并获得了学位。

我必须补充一点：因为在电影《侏罗纪公园》中的工作，学校给了我古生物学的学分。《侏罗纪公园》给我带来了3个学分呢，我太感谢了。

我退学，是因为确切地知道自己想做什么。就这一点而言，你们当中有些同学心中也有数，但有些同学还很迷茫。有些同学或许原本以为自己知道，但现在正在质疑当初的选择。也许有同学正坐在这里，绞尽脑汁地琢磨着如何向父母坦白，说

> *Life is one strong, long string of character-defining moments.*
>
> 生活是一长串影响深远的关键时刻。

---

1. kvelling：*adj.* 扬扬得意的。
2. walk the walk：说到做到。
3. paleontology：*n.* 古生物学。
4. *Jurassic Park*：《侏罗纪公园》，史蒂文·斯皮尔伯格执导的经典科幻电影，1993年上映。电影讲述人类培育的恐龙逃出了公园，给人类生活带来混乱的故事，该片全球票房超10亿美元。

how to tell your parents that you want to be a doctor and not a comedy writer.

Well, what you choose to do next is what we call in the movies the character-defining moment. Now, these are moments you're very familiar with, like in the last *Star Wars: The Force Awakens*, when Rey realizes the force is with her, or Indiana Jones choosing mission over fear by jumping into a pile of snakes.

Now in a two-hour movie, you get a handful of character-defining moments, but in real life, you face them every day. Life is one strong, long string of character-defining moments. And I was lucky that at 18 I knew what I exactly wanted to do. But I didn't know who I was. How could I? And how could any of us? Because for the first 25 years of our lives, we are trained to listen to voices that are not our own. Parents and professors fill our heads with wisdom and information, and then employers and mentors take their place and explain how this world really works.

And usually these voices of authority make sense, but sometimes, doubt starts to creep into our heads and into our hearts. And even when we think, "that's not quite how I see the world," it's kind of easier to just nod in agreement and go along. And for a while, I let that going along define my character, because I was repressing my own point of view, because like in that Nilsson[5] song, "Everybody was talkin' at[6] me, so I couldn't hear the echoes of my mind."

And at first, the internal voice I needed to listen to was hardly audible, and it was hardly noticeable—kind of like me in high school. But then I started paying more attention, and my intuition kicked in.

And I want to be clear that your intuition is different from your conscience. They work in tandem[7], but here's the distinction: Your conscience shouts, "here's what you should do," while your intuition whispers, "here's what you could do." Listen to that voice that tells you what you could do. Nothing will define your character more than that, because once I turned to my intuition,

自己其实想当个医生，而不是喜剧作家。

接下来的选择，电影里管这叫塑造角色的关键时刻。我来举几个你们非常熟悉的例子，比如，在最近的电影《星球大战：原力觉醒》中，蕾伊发现原力与她同在的时刻，或者印第安纳·琼斯跳进蛇堆，选择了抛开恐惧、执行任务的时刻。

如今在一部两个小时的电影中，你们会看到若干个塑造角色的关键时刻，而在现实生活中，你们每天都要面对这样的时刻。生活是一长串影响深远的关键时刻。我很幸运，18 岁就想明白了自己到底想做什么。但我那时不知道自己是谁。我怎么可能知道呢？我们又怎么可能知道呢？毕竟在生命最初的 25 年里，我们被训练的是去倾听他人的声音。父母和教授向我们灌输智慧和信息，然后雇主和职场导师接替他们，向我们解释世界的运作模式。

这些权威的声音通常是有道理的，可有时候，疑惑却悄然潜入我们的脑海和内心。即使我们心想"这不是我看待世界的方式"，也还是会觉得，点头赞同和随波逐流会更轻松。我就曾一度任由随波逐流来定义自己，因为我在压抑自己的观点，因为就像尼尔森的歌里唱的那样，"每个人都在对我说话，所以我听不到自己心灵的回声"。

起初，我需要听的内心声音几不可闻，也难以察觉——高中时的我大概就是这样。但后来我开始留心倾听，直觉便开始发挥作用。

我想明确一点，直觉和意识不同。二者相互协作，但区别在于，意识大喊道，"这是你应该做的"，而直觉低语道，"这是你可以做的"。倾听直觉的声音吧，没有什么比这更能定义个性了。一旦我转而依靠直觉，并与之同频共振，我就会受到某

---

5. Nilsson: 哈里·尼尔森（Harry Nilsson, 1941—1994），美国歌手，代表作有 Everybody's Talkin' 等。
6. talk at:（不理会对方反应）对某人大发议论。
7. in tandem: 协力。

and I tuned into it, certain projects began to pull me into them, and others, I turned away from.

And up until the 1980s, my movies were mostly—I guess what you could call escapist. And I don't dismiss any of these movies—not even *1941*[8]. Not even that one. And many of these early films reflected the values that I cared deeply about, and I still do. But I was in a celluloid[9] bubble, because I'd cut my education short, my worldview was limited to what I could dream up in my head, not what the world could teach me.

But then I directed *The Color Purple*[10]. And this one film opened my eyes to experiences that I never could have imagined, and yet were all too real. This story was filled with deep pain and deeper truths, like when Shug Avery[11] says, "Everything wants to be loved." My gut, which was my intuition, told me that more people needed to meet these characters and experience these truths. And while making that film, I realized that a movie could also be a mission. I hope all of you find that sense of mission. Don't turn away from what's painful. Examine it. Challenge it.

My job is to create a world that lasts two hours. Your job is to create a world that lasts forever. You are the future innovators, motivators, leaders and caretakers. And the way you create a better future is by studying the past. *Jurassic Park* writer Michael Crichton, who graduated from both this college and this medical school, liked to quote a favorite professor of his who said that if you didn't know history, you didn't know anything. You were a leaf that didn't know it was part of a tree. So history majors[12]: Good choice, you're in great shape—NOT in the job market, but culturally.

The rest of us have to make a little effort. Social media that we're inundated and swarmed with is about the here and now. But I've been fighting and fighting inside my own family to get all my kids to look behind them, to look at what already has happened, because to understand who they are is to

些项目的吸引，并且参与其中，同时避开另外一些项目。

直到 20 世纪 80 年代，我想我的电影大体上是你们可能称之为逃避现实的电影。我不会贬低这些电影——即使是《1941》也不会。我早期的许多电影反映了我看重的价值观，当初看重，现在也仍然看重。但我那时候就像是被困在电影胶片的泡泡里，因为我没能完成学业，我的世界观局限于我能够在脑海中构想出来的东西，而不是世界能教给我的东西。

但后来我执导了电影《紫色》。这部电影让我大开眼界，带我见识了我从未想象过却又极度真实的故事。这个故事充满了深重的痛苦和深刻的真理，比如当莎格·艾弗里所说，"一切事物都渴望被爱"。直觉告诉我，要让更多人认识这些角色，体悟这些真理。在这部电影的制作过程中，我意识到，电影也可以肩负使命。我希望你们所有人都能找到那份使命感。不要逃避痛苦，而要审视痛苦、挑战痛苦。

我的工作是创造一个时长两个小时的世界，你们的任务是创造一个永续的世界。你们是未来的创新者、激励者、引领者和守护者。而要想创造更美好的未来，就要以史为鉴。《侏罗纪公园》的原著作者迈克尔·克莱顿毕业于哈佛大学和哈佛医学院，他喜欢引用自己最喜欢的一位教授的话：如果不懂历史，那你就是一无所知；你是一片叶子，却不知道自己是树的一部分。所以，学历史的同学们，你们的专业选得很好——在就业市场上不一定，但在文化上很有优势。

我们其余人得努努力了。社交媒体上的信息铺天盖地、蜂拥而至，但都是关于此时此刻的。在我自己家里，我一直努力让孩子们回顾过去，看看已然发生的事情。因为了解先人是什么样的人，就是在了解我们是什么样的人；了解祖父母是什么样

---

8. *1941*：《1941》，史蒂文·斯皮尔伯格执导的喜剧电影，1979 年上映。该片讲述了 1941 年 12 月日本偷袭美国珍珠港后，洛杉矶被恐慌包围的故事。观众对此片的评价褒贬不一。
9. celluloid：*n.* 电影（总称）。
10. *The Color Purple*：《紫色》，史蒂文·斯皮尔伯格执导的电影，1985 年上映。该片反映了 20 世纪初期非裔美国女性面临的贫穷、家暴、种族歧视、性别歧视等问题。
11. Shug Avery：莎格·艾弗里，《紫色》中的角色。
12. major：*n.* 主修学生。

understand who we were, and who their grandparents were, and then, what this country was like when they emigrated here. We are a nation of immigrants—at least for now.

So to me, this means we all have to tell our own stories. We have so many stories to tell. Talk to your parents and your grandparents, if you can, and ask them about their stories. And I promise you, like I have promised my kids, you will not be bored. And that's why I so often make movies based on real-life events. I look to history not to be didactic[13], because that's just a bonus, but I look because the past is filled with the greatest stories that have ever been told. Heroes and villains are not literary constructs, but they're at the heart of all history.

And again, this is why it's so important to listen to your internal whisper. It's the same one that compelled Abraham Lincoln and Oskar Schindler to make the correct moral choices. In your defining moments, do not let your morals be swayed by convenience or expediency[14]. Sticking to your character requires a lot of courage. And to be courageous, you're going to need a lot of support.

And if you're lucky, you have parents like mine. I consider my mom my lucky charm. And when I was 12 years old, my father handed me a movie camera, the tool that allowed me to make sense of this world. And I am so grateful to him for that. And I am grateful that he's here at Harvard, sitting right down there.

My dad is 99 years old, which means he's only one year younger than Widener Library[15]. But unlike Widener, he's had zero cosmetic work. And dad, there's a lady behind you, also 99, and I'll introduce you after this is over, okay?

But look, if your family's not always available, there's backup. Near the end of *It's a Wonderful Life*[16]—you remember that movie, *It's a Wonderful*

的人，就了解了当初他们移民到这里时，这个国家是什么样子的。我们是一个移民国家——至少目前如此。

所以对我来说，这意味着必须讲述自身的故事。我们有很多故事可以讲。如果可以的话，和父母、祖父母谈谈，听听他们的故事。我向你们保证，就像我向自家孩子保证的那样，你们不会觉得无聊的。这就是为什么我经常把真实事件改编成电影。我研究历史，并不是想教育谁——虽然那也算是个额外收获吧——而是因为过去充满了有史以来最伟大的故事。英雄与反派并非虚构的文学形象，而是历史的核心部分。

重申一遍，这就是为何倾听内心的低语如此重要。这种声音曾驱使亚伯拉罕·林肯和奥斯卡·辛德勒做出正确的道德抉择。在人生的关键时刻，不要让道德受制于便利或权宜。坚守个性需要极大的勇气，而要有勇气，就需要来自四面八方的支持。

要是运气够好，你们会拥有像我父母那样的家长。我把我的母亲看作我的幸运护符。我12岁的时候，我父亲递给我一台摄影机，而这个工具成了我解读世界的方式。为此我非常感激他。他现在人在哈佛，就坐在那里，对此我也很感激。

我的父亲如今99岁了，只比怀德纳图书馆小一岁，不过他可没像怀德纳那样修修补补过。爸爸，你身后有一位女士，也是99岁，等演讲结束了，我就介绍你们认识，好吗？

不过你们看，如果家人并不总在身边，还有朋友。还记得电影《生活多美好》

---

13. didactic：*adj.* 说教的。
14. expediency：*n.* 权宜之计。
15. Widener Library：哈佛大学怀德纳图书馆，藏书约350万册，1915年开放使用。
16. *It's a Wonderful Life*：《生活多美好》，弗兰克·卡普罗执导的电影，1946年上映。电影讲述主人公乔治为了帮助身边的人而放弃个人梦想的故事。当乔治想在平安夜结束自己的生命时，他的守护天使克拉伦斯告诉他，他为别人做出的贡献是多么重要。

Life? Clarence the Angel inscribes a book with this: "No man is a failure who has friends." And I hope you hang on to the friendships you've made here at Harvard. And among your friends, I hope you find someone you want to share your life with.

I imagine some of you in this yard may be a tad[17] cynical, but I want to be unapologetically sentimental. I spoke about the importance of intuition and how there's no greater voice to follow. That is, until you meet the love of your life. And this is what happened when I met and married Kate[18], and that became the greatest character-defining moment of my life.

Love, support, courage, intuition. All of these things are in your hero's quiver[19], but still, a hero needs one more thing: A hero needs a villain to vanquish. And you're all in luck. This world is full of monsters. And there's racism, homophobia, ethnic hatred, class hatred. There's political hatred, and there's religious hatred.

As a kid, I was bullied for being Jewish. This was upsetting, but compared to what my parents and grandparents had faced, it felt tame, because we truly believed that anti-Semitism was fading. And we were wrong. Over the last two years, nearly 20,000 Jews have left Europe to find higher ground. And earlier this year, I was at the Israeli embassy when President Obama stated the sad truth. He said: "We must confront the reality that around the world, anti-Semitism is on the rise. We cannot deny it."

My own desire to confront that reality compelled me to start, in 1994, the Shoah[20] Foundation. And since then, we've spoken to over 53,000 Holocaust survivors and witnesses in 63 countries and taken all their video testimonies. And we're now gathering testimonies from genocides in Rwanda, Cambodia, Armenia and Nanking, because we must never forget that the inconceivable doesn't just happen—it happens frequently. Atrocities are happening right now. And so we wonder not just, "when will this hatred end?" but, "how did it begin?"

吗？在影片接近尾声时，天使克拉伦斯在一本书上写道："有朋友的人都不会是失败者。"我希望你们能珍惜在哈佛结下的友谊，希望你们能够在朋友中找到想共度一生的人。

我想，在座的有些人可能会对此嗤之以鼻，但我并不打算掩盖自己对感情的重视。我已经说了直觉的重要性，以及没有比直觉更重要的东西值得追逐。不过，当你遇到生命中的真爱时，那可是另外一回事了。遇到凯特，和她结婚，我体会到了这一点，而这是我一生中最重要的角色塑造时刻。

爱、支持、勇气、直觉，所有这些都将成为英雄箭袋中的箭矢。不过，英雄还需要一样东西：反派。你们都很幸运。这个世界到处都是怪物：种族主义、恐同、种族仇恨、阶级仇恨、政治仇恨、宗教仇恨。

我小时候因为犹太血统而受人欺凌。这很让人难受，但与我的父母和祖父母所经历的相比，就算不上什么了，因为我们深信反犹主义正在退潮。然而，我们错了。在过去两年中，近两万名犹太人离开了欧洲，去寻求一方更加安全的土地。今年早些时候，我在以色列大使馆听奥巴马总统说出了一个可悲的事实。他说："我们必须面对一个现实，那就是，世界各地的反犹主义正在上升。我们不能否认这一点。"

出于直面现实的渴望，我于1994年成立了大屠杀基金会。自那以后，我们采访了来自63个国家的超过53 000名大屠杀的幸存者和目击者，并记录了视频证词。如今我们正在收集发生在卢旺达、柬埔寨、亚美尼亚和南京的种族灭绝证据。因为这些匪夷所思的事件并不仅仅是发生了，而是反复上演，这一点我们必须牢牢记住。暴行正在上演。因此，我们不仅要知道仇恨何时终结，还要知道仇恨是如何产生的。

---

17. a tad：少量。
18. Kate：凯特·卡普肖（Kate Capshaw，1953— ），美国女演员、画家，斯皮尔伯格的妻子。
19. quiver：*n.* 箭囊。
20. Shoah：*n.*（希伯来语）大屠杀。

Now, I don't have to tell a crowd of Red Sox fans that we are wired[21] for tribalism. But beyond rooting for the home team, tribalism has a much darker side. Instinctively and maybe even genetically, we divide the world into "us" and "them." So the burning[22] question must be: How do all of us together find the "we"? How do we do that? There's still so much work to be done, and sometimes I feel the work hasn't even begun. And it's not just anti-Semitism that's surging—Islamophobia's on the rise, too. Because there's no difference between anyone who is discriminated against, whether it's the Muslims, or the Jews, or minorities on the border states, or the LGBT community—it is all big one hate.

And to me, and, I think, to all of you, the only answer to more hate is more humanity. We got to repair—we have to replace fear with curiosity. "Us" and "them"—we'll find the "we" by connecting with each other, and by believing that we're members of the same tribe, and by feeling empathy for every soul—even Yalies[23].

My son graduated from Yale, thank you.

But make sure this empathy isn't just something that you feel. Make it something you act upon. That means vote. Peaceably protest. Speak up for those who can't and speak up for those who may be shouting but aren't being heard. Let your conscience shout as loud as it wants if you're using it in the service of others.

And as an example of action in service of others, you need to look no further than this Hollywood-worthy backdrop of Memorial Church. Its south wall bears the names of Harvard alumni—like President Faust has already mentioned—students and faculty members, who gave their lives in World War II. All told, 697 souls, who once tread the ground where we stand now, were lost. And at a service in this church in late 1945, Harvard President James Conant—which President Faust also mentioned—honored the brave and called

人类天生就喜欢搞小团体，这一点咱们这些红袜队的球迷都知道。但除了为自家球队加油，小团体心理还有更为阴暗的一面。我们几乎是本能地，甚至可能是与生俱来地，将世界分为了"我们"和"他们"。因此，当务之急必然在于：所有人如何共同找到作为"我们"的认同感？我们该怎么做呢？要做的工作还有很多，有时我甚至觉得工作尚未展开。不仅是反犹太主义在涌动，仇视穆斯林的情绪也在上升。任何被歧视的人都没有区别，无论是穆斯林、犹太人、边境州的少数民族，还是性少数群体，所有这些人都承受着深重的恶意。

对我来说，我想对你们也一样，面对日益增长的恶意，只能用更多的人性来应对。我们必须修复这个世界，必须以好奇取代恐惧。"我们"和"他们"会找到同属"我们"的认同感，通过相互建立联系，通过相信我们属于同一个共同体，通过对每一个人都抱有同理心——即使是耶鲁大学的学生。

我儿子就毕业于耶鲁大学，谢谢大家。

不过，感同身受不能只是心里想想而已，还要转化为实际行动。也就是说，要积极参与投票、和平抗议，为无法发声者发声，为发声却无人理会者发声。去帮助他人时，就让良知尽情高呼吧。

要想找到帮助他人的行动楷模，无须舍近求远，只需看看这个堪比好莱坞布景的纪念教堂。它的南墙上刻着哈佛校友的名字——就像福斯特校长已经提到的那样，他们是在第二次世界大战中献出生命的学生和教职员工。总共有 697 个曾踏过你我脚下这块土地的灵魂逝去。1945 年末，在这座教堂的一次仪式上——这件事福斯特校长也提到过——哈佛校长詹姆斯·柯南特向这些勇者致敬，并号召全体师生"将

---

21. wired：*adj.* 兴奋的。
22. burning：*adj.* 十分重要的。
23. Yalie：*n.* 耶鲁大学学生。

upon the community to "reflect the radiance of their deeds."

Seventy years later, this message still holds true, because their sacrifice is not a debt that can be repaid in a single generation. It must be repaid with every generation. Just as we must never forget the atrocities[24], we must never forget those who fought for freedom. So as you leave this college and head out into the world, continue please to "reflect the radiance of their deeds," or as Captain Miller in *Saving Private Ryan*[25] would say, "Earn this."

And please stay connected. Please never lose eye contact. This may not be a lesson you want to hear from a person who creates media, but we are spending more time looking down at our devices than we are looking in each other's eyes. So, forgive me, but let's start right now. Everyone here, please find someone's eyes to look into. Students, and alumni, and you too, President Faust, all of you, turn to someone you don't know or don't know very well. They may be standing behind you, or a couple of rows ahead. Just let your eyes meet. That's it. That emotion you're feeling is our shared humanity mixed in with a little social discomfort.

But, if you remember nothing else from today, I hope you remember this moment of human connection. And I hope you all had a lot of that over the past four years, because today you start down the path of becoming the generation on which the next generation stands. And I've imagined many possible futures in my films, but you will determine the actual future. And I hope that it's filled with justice and peace.

And finally, I wish you all a true, Hollywood-style happy ending. I hope you outrun the T. rex[26], catch the criminal, and for your parents' sake, maybe every now and then, just like E.T.[27]: Go home.

Thank you.

他们的功勋发扬光大"。

  70 年后，这番话仍然适用，因为他们的牺牲不是一代人就能偿还的债务，必须由世世代代来偿还。我们决不能忘记暴行，也决不能忘记为自由而战的人们。因此，当你们离开大学，走向世界时，请继续"将他们的功勋发扬光大"，或者像电影《拯救大兵瑞恩》中的米勒上尉所说的那样，"好好活着，别辜负了大家"。

  请大家保持连接，不要放弃面对面的眼神交流。你们可能没料到会从一个媒体人这里听到这样的告诫，但是我们确实把更多的时间花在了盯着手机屏幕上，而不是看着彼此的眼睛。所以，容我冒昧提议，不如现在就开始吧。在场的各位，请和身边某个人对视。学生们、毕业生们、福斯特校长、你们所有人，去找一个不认识或者不熟的人对视。可以是身后的人，也可以是站在自己前面几排的人，让目光交汇，就是这样。你们感受到的这种情绪，是我们作为人类所共有的情感体验，还掺杂了社交上的一丝尴尬。

  如果今天的演讲你们什么都没记住，请至少记得这一刻人与人之间的连接。我希望你们在过去的四年里都有过很多这样的体验，因为从今天开始，你们将成为下一代所依赖的一代。我在电影里设想过很多种未来，但真正的未来由你们来决定。我希望，那会是个充满正义与和平的未来。

  最后，祝大家都能拥有真正的好莱坞式大团圆结局。我希望你们能从霸王龙爪下逃脱，将罪犯绳之以法，并且偶尔可以像 E.T. 一样，回家看看。

  谢谢大家。

---

24. atrocity：n.（尤指战争中的）残暴行为。
25. *Saving Private Ryan*：《拯救大兵瑞恩》，史蒂文·斯皮尔伯格执导的战争片，1998 年上映。该片讲述了在二战中，瑞恩一家有四个儿子上了前线，三个牺牲，米勒上尉带队拯救这家仅存的儿子瑞恩的故事。该片被称为电影史上最伟大的电影之一。
26. T. rex：Tyrannosaurus rex 的缩写，意为"霸王龙"。
27. E.T.：《E.T. 外星人》，史蒂文·斯皮尔伯格执导的科幻电影，1982 年上映。该片讲述了一个叫 E.T. 的小外星人不小心留在地球，并在人类小朋友的帮助下重返外星的故事。

语录 Quotes

- Life is one strong, long string of character-defining moments.
  生活是一长串影响深远的关键时刻。

- Listen to that voice that tells you what you could do. Nothing will define your character more than that.
  倾听直觉的声音吧，没有什么比这更能定义个性了。

- Don't turn away from what's painful. Examine it. Challenge it.
  不要逃避痛苦，而要审视痛苦、挑战痛苦。

- If you didn't know history, you didn't know anything.
  如果不懂历史，那你就是一无所知。

- Talk to your parents and your grandparents, if you can, and ask them about their stories.
  如果可以的话，和父母、祖父母谈谈，听听他们的故事。

- In your defining moments, do not let your morals be swayed by convenience or expediency.
  在人生的关键时刻，不要让道德受制于便利或权宜。

- We wonder not just, "when will this hatred end?" but, "how did it begin?"
  我们不仅要知道仇恨何时终结，还要知道仇恨是如何产生的。

Investment and Personality Growth
关于投资与人格成长

——沃伦·巴菲特 1998 年在佛罗里达大学商学院的演讲

> 简介 Profile

沃伦·巴菲特
Warren Buffett

1930 年，沃伦·巴菲特出生于美国内布拉斯加州的奥马哈市。巴菲特家族在奥马哈经营杂货铺，以销售食品和日用品为主，秉持薄利多销的理念。受家庭环境影响，巴菲特自幼对商业产生兴趣，展现了敏锐的市场洞察力和商业头脑，为日后的投资生涯奠定了基础。

巴菲特小时候就将大部分时间都用来思考和读书，之后又到知名的宾夕法尼亚大学沃顿商学院、哥伦比亚商学院深造，在理论和实践方面都有着很深的造诣。1957 年，27 岁的巴菲特成立了非约束性的巴菲特投资俱乐部，收购及投资了一大批颇具前景的企业，其中包括《波士顿环球报》《华盛顿邮报》以及可口可乐等世界知名企业。2008 年，巴菲特位列《福布斯》年度全球富豪榜第一，成为全球首富。

巴菲特现任伯克希尔·哈撒韦公司董事长和首席执行官。作为价值投资、长期投资的代表人物，他被人们称为"股神"，也被尊为"奥马哈的先知""奥马哈的圣贤"，多年来备受人们的尊崇，很多人甚至以能和他吃一顿饭为荣。因此，他自 2000 年便发起了"巴菲特午餐"拍卖，所得款项均捐给了慈善机构。不仅如此，巴菲特还承诺他去世后 99% 以上财富也都将捐给慈善机构。

1998 年，沃伦·巴菲特来到了佛罗里达大学的商学院，以问答的方式向即将毕业的学生们讲述了自己对人生的看法，以及对"得失""对错""有为与无为"的理解。巴菲特不仅传授了关于商业及投资的诸多真知灼见，更揭示了个人成功背后最重要的思维和认知。这次讲座也因此被很多人誉为巴菲特最经典的演讲，没有之一。

演讲 Speech

扫描二维码
获取本篇演讲原视频、音频

Buffett: I would like to just say a few words primarily and then the highlight for me will be getting your questions in a few minutes. I want to talk about what is on your mind.

I urge you to throw hard balls. It's more fun for me if you put a little speed on the pitches as they come in. You can ask about anything except last week's Texas A&M Game. That's off limits.

I would like to talk for just one minute to the students about your future when you leave here, because you are gonna learn a tremendous amount about investments and you will learn enough to do well. You've all got the IQ to do well. You've all got the initiative and energy to do well, or you wouldn't be here. And most of you will succeed in meeting your aspirations. But in determining whether you succeed there is more to it than intellect and energy. I would like to talk just a second about that.

In fact, there was a fellow, Pete Kiewit in Omaha[1], who used to say that he looked for three things in hiring people: integrity, intelligence and energy. And he said if the person did not have the first two, the latter two would kill him, because if they don't have integrity, you want them dumb and lazy. You don't want them smart and energetic. I'd really like to talk about the first one, because we know you've got the second two.

Play along with me in a little game for just a second in terms of thinking

巴菲特：我先简单说几句，然后把大部分时间留给问答环节，聊聊大家关心的话题。

大家问的问题一定要够有挑战性。问题越难，我越觉得有意思。大家什么都可以问，唯独不能问上个星期得克萨斯农工大学的比赛，那个不在讨论范围之内。

我只会用一分钟的时间和同学们谈谈毕业后的未来，因为你们将会学到海量投资知识，会学得很好，也会做得很好。对于做好投资来说，你们有足够高的智商，有足够的拼劲和精力，否则你们就不会在这里。你们中的大多数人会实现自己的抱负。但是，决定成败的不仅仅是智力和精力。我想稍微谈一下这个问题。

奥马哈有个人叫皮特·基威特，他过去常说，他招人就看重三点：品行、头脑和精力。他说，如果一个人头脑聪明、勤奋努力，但品行不好，也会害了自己。因为对于品行不端的人，大家宁愿他们又笨又懒，不会希望他们聪明又有活力。我很想谈谈第一个特质，因为后两个你们都已经有了。

针对这个问题，我们花一点时间来玩个小游戏。在场的各位，我想你们几乎都

The chains of habit are too light to be felt until they are too heavy to be broken.

习惯的枷锁先是轻得难以察觉，后来便重得难以打破。

---

1. Omaha：奥马哈市，位于美国内布拉斯加州东部，是该州最大的城市，也是巴菲特的故乡和伯克希尔·哈撒韦公司总部的所在地。

about that question. You've all been here. I guess almost all of you are second-year MBA students and you've gotten to know your classmates. Think for a moment that I granted you the right to buy 10% of one of your classmates' earnings for the rest of his or her lifetime. You can't pick one with a rich father. That doesn't count. I mean you've got to pick somebody who is going to do it on their own merit. And I'll give you an hour to think about it. Which one are you gonna pick among all your classmates as the one you want to own 10% for the rest of his or her lifetime.

Are you gonna give them an IQ test and pick the one with the highest IQ? I doubt it. Are you gonna pick the one with the best grades? I doubt it. You are not gonna pick the most energetic one necessarily. You are the one who displays the most initiative. You will start looking for qualitative factors in addition to (quantitative factors) because everybody's got enough brains and energy.

And I would say that if you thought about it for an hour and decided who you are gonna place that bet on, you'd probably pick the one who you responded the best to, the one who is going to have the leadership qualities, the one who is going to be able to get other people to carry out their interests, and that would be the person who is generous, honest, and who gave credit to other people even for their own ideas. All kinds of qualities like that. And you could write down those qualities that you admire, whomever you admire the most in the class.

And then, I would throw in a hooker. I would say as part of owning 10% of this person, you had to agree to go short 10% of somebody else in this class. That is more fun, isn't it? And you think, "Who do I want to go short of?" And again you wouldn't pick the person with the lowest IQ. You would start thinking about the person, really, who turned you off for one reason or another. They have various qualities quite apart from their academic achievement.

是 MBA 二年级的学生，同学之间相互都认识。想象一下，假如能够买下一位同学的今后终生收入的 10%，你们会选谁？不能选富二代，这不算数。我的意思是，你得选一个靠自己白手起家的。你们有一个小时的时间思考这个问题。你们会买下哪一位同学 10% 的个人终生收入呢？

你们会选择让他们做一次智商测试，从中挑一个智商最高的吗？未必吧。会选成绩最好的那个吗？未必吧。你们也未必会选择最勤奋的那个。大家都很有进取心。你们会抛开定量因素，着眼于定性因素，因为你们很有头脑，精力旺盛。

我想说的是，如果有一个小时来考虑要把宝押在谁身上，大家选中的可能是和自己最合拍的人，是看起来能带团队的人，是能让他人去实现自身利益的人。这个人呢，肯定是那种大方又真诚的人，哪怕是自己的点子也会分享给别人。你们会考虑到各种诸如此类的品质，可以把自己欣赏的品质写下来，也写下自己最欣赏的同学。

接下来，我会再加一个变数。我会说，作为拥有这个人 10% 收入的代价，你必须同意做空另一位同班同学今后 10% 的终生收入。事情变得更好玩了，不是吗？你们想要做空谁？同样，你们不会选择智商最低的人，而是会选择自己出于种种原因

> *You already own 100% and you are stuck with it. So you might as well be that person, that somebody else.*
>
> *每个人都拥有自己 100% 的股份，而且无法卖出。所以，不如亲自成为那个理想的投资人选。*

关于投资与人格成长　153

But they have various qualities, in the end, you really don't want to be around with them, and other people don't want to be around with them. What were the qualities that lead to that? That would be a whole bunch of things. You know it's the person who is egotistical, or the person who is greedy, the person who is slightly dishonest and cuts corners. All of these qualities. You can write those down on the right-hand side of the page.

As you look at those qualities on the left and right-hand side, there is one interesting thing about them. It's not the ability to throw a football 60 yards. It's not the ability to run the 100-yard dash in 9.3 seconds. It is not being the best-looking person in the class. They are all qualities that if you really want to have the ones on the left-hand side, you can have them.

I mean they are qualities of behavior, temperament, character that are achievable. They are not forbidden to anybody in this group. And if you look at the qualities on the right-hand side, the ones that you find turn you off in other people, there is not a quality there that you have to have. If you have you can get rid of it. You can get rid of it a lot easier at your age than you can at my age, because most behaviors are habitual. And they say the chains of habit are too light to be felt until they are too heavy to be broken. There is no question about it. I see people with these self-destructive behavior patterns at my age or even ten or twenty years younger. They really are entrapped by them. They go around and do things that turn off other people right and left. They don't need to be that way but by a certain point they get so they can hardly change it. But at your age you can have any habits, any patterns of behavior that you wish. It is simply a question of which you decide. I mean, if you're like …

Ben Graham[2] did this … Ben Franklin did this before him. But Ben Graham did this in his low teens and he looked around at the people he admired and he said, "You know, I want to be admired, so why don't I just behave like them?" And he found that there was nothing impossible about behaving like

非常讨厌的人。他们学业优异,但身上有很多特质招人烦,不仅你们烦他们,大家都烦他们。什么特质会造成这种结果?那可太多了,比如自私、贪婪、为人滑头虚伪、做事偷工减料等。你们可以把所有这些特质写在纸的右边。

对比一下左右两种特质,就可以发现一件有趣的事情。不像是把橄榄球扔出 60 码(约合 54.86 米)远的能力,也不是在 9.3 秒内跑完 100 码(约合 91.44 米)冲刺的能力,更不是成为班里最漂亮的人。这些特质在于,如果你真的想要拥有左边的那些特质,你就能拥有。

我是说,这些是行为、气质和性格方面可达成的特质,且在这个群体中对任何人都是开放的。来看看右边的那些讨人厌的特质,它们也并不会强加到任何人身上,如果身上有,那也是可以摆脱的。你们还年轻,戒除恶习比我这个年纪的人容易得多,因为大多数行为都是习惯成自然。人们常说,习惯的枷锁先是轻得难以察觉,后来便重得难以打破。这一点毋庸置疑。我见过不少有这些自毁行为模式的人,他们有的和我同龄,有的甚至比我小十几二十岁。他们真的被困住了,成天到处做些讨人厌的事情。他们本来可以不必变成这样,但积重难返。不过,在你们这个年纪,想培养出什么习惯和行为模式都行,这完全取决于你们自身。我是说,比如……

本杰明·格雷厄姆就做到了。在他之前的本杰明·富兰克林也做到了。但本杰明·格雷厄姆在十几岁的时候就做到了,他观察身边令他钦佩的人,说道:"我也想受人钦佩,何不效仿他们呢?"他发现,效仿他们的为人处世之道是可以做到的。同样地,他观察身边讨人厌的人,摆脱相似的缺点。所以我建议,可以把各种好的品

---

2. Ben Graham:本杰明·格雷厄姆(1894—1976),英国证券分析师,被誉为"华尔街教父""现代证券分析之父"。

them. Similarly he did the same thing on the reverse side in terms of getting rid of those qualities. So I would suggest that if you write those qualities down and think about them a little while and make them habitual, you will be the one you want to buy 10% of when you get all of them. The beauty of it is that you already own 100% and you are stuck with it. So you might as well be that person, that somebody else. Well, that is a short little sermon.

So let's get on to what you are interested in and like I said you can go all over the lot. I don't know exactly how we're going to handle this. But let's start with the hand in some place or other. Where do we go with the first one? You, right here!

Question 1: What about Japan? Your thoughts about Japan?

Buffett: My thoughts about Japan? I am not a macro guy. Now I say to myself Berkshire Hathaway[3] can borrow money for 10 years at one percent in Japan now. One percent! I say to myself, gee, I took Graham's class 45 years ago and I have been working hard at this all my life. Maybe I can earn more than 1% annually, it doesn't seem impossible. I wouldn't want to get involved in currency risk, so it would have to be Yen-denominated. I would have to be in Japanese Real Estate or Japanese business or something of sort and all I have to do is beat one percent. That is all the money that is going to cost me and I can get it for 10 years. So far I haven't found anything. It is kind of interesting. The Japanese companies earn very low returns on equity. They have a bunch of businesses that will have 4% to 6% on equity, and it is very hard to earn a lot as an investor when the business you are in doesn't earn very much money.

Now some people do it. In fact, I've got a friend, Walter Schloss, who worked with Graham at the same time I did. And it was the first way I went at stocks to buy stock selling way below working capital, very cheap, quantitative approach to stocks. I call it the cigar butt approach to investing. You walk down the street and you look around for a cigar butt someplace. Finally you see one

质都写下来，好好思考一下，把它们养成习惯，待集齐所有这些品质，你们就会成为自己想买下那 10% 的人选。妙处在于，每个人都拥有自己 100% 的股份，而且无法卖出。所以，不如亲自成为那个理想的投资人选。这是我的一点小小说教。

接下来聊聊你们感兴趣的话题。就像我先前说的那样，大家可以随便问。我也不清楚咱们具体该怎么做。那就先随便挑一位举手的同学。第一个挑谁呢？就是你了！

问题 1：您对日本股市怎么看？考虑过投资日本股市吗？

巴菲特：对日本股市的看法？我不是专注于宏观经济分析的投资者。现在我告诉自己，伯克希尔·哈撒韦公司现在能以 1% 的利率在日本借到 10 年期的资金。百分之一！我告诉自己，天哪，我 45 年前就学了格雷厄姆的课，而且一辈子都在投资领域打滚，年回报率超过 1% 应该不成问题。我不愿意承担汇率风险，所以投资必须以日元计价。我得投资日本房地产或日本企业之类的东西，只要收益率能超过 1% 就行。1% 是我 10 年的资金借贷成本。到目前为止，我还没有找到合适的投资机会。这挺有意思的。日本公司的股本回报率非常低。很多业务的股本回报率只有 4% 到 6%。如果投资的业务本身利润不高，投资者也很难赚到高额回报。

现在有些人确实这么做。我的朋友沃尔特·施洛斯和我在格雷厄姆共事过，他就是现成的例子。我最初也是这样买股票的，买入价格远低于营运资本的非常便宜的股票。这是一种量化的股票投资方法，我称之为"烟蒂投资法"。就像走在街上四

---

3. Berkshire Hathaway：伯克希尔·哈撒韦公司，是美国的一家以保险业务为主的多元化投资集团，由沃伦·巴菲特于 1956 年建立。

and it's soggy and kind of repulsive, but there's one puff left in it. So you pick it up and the puff is free. I mean, it's a cigar butt stock. You get one free puff out, then you throw it away and you walk on the street, try another one. I mean it's not elegant but it works. If you are looking for a free puff, it works. Those are low return businesses.

But time is the friend of the wonderful business; it is the enemy of the lousy business. If you are in a lousy business for a long time, you are gonna get a lousy result even if you buy it cheap. If you are in a wonderful business for a long time, even if you pay a little too much going in, you are going to get a wonderful result if you stay in a long time. I find very few wonderful businesses in Japan at present. They may change the culture in some way so that managements get more shareholder responsible over there and returns are higher. But at the present time you will find a very lot of low return businesses and that was true even when the Japanese economy was booming. I mean it is amazing; they had an incredible market without incredible companies. They were incredible in terms of doing a lot of business, but they were not incredible in terms of the return on equity that they achieved and that's finally caught up with them. So we have so far done nothing there. But as long as money is 1% there, I will keep looking.

Question 2: You were rumored to be one of the rescue buyers of Long-Term Capital[4]. What was the play there? What did you see?

Buffett: Well, there's a story and the current *Fortune Magazine*[5], one has Rupert Murdoch's picture on the cover that tells the whole story of our involvement, it is kind of an interesting story. Because it's a long story so I won't go into all the background of it. But I got the really serious call about Long-Term Capital. About four weeks ago, I got it in mid-afternoon. My granddaughter was having her birthday party that evening and I was flying that night to Seattle to go on a 12-day trip with Gates to Alaska on our private

处寻找烟蒂，最后找到了一个，虽然湿答答的，有点恶心，但还能抽一口。这就是烟蒂股，可以捡起来免费抽上一口，抽完一扔，继续在街上游荡，寻找下一个。我是说，这种方法并不高雅，但它有效。如果你想要一口免费烟，这么干确实行得通。这些都是低回报的生意。

时间是优秀生意的益友，却是糟糕生意的敌手。长期投资一门糟糕的生意，即使低价买入，最终结果也会不如意。而要是出色的生意，即使初始投入略高，长期持有也能获得丰厚的回报。目前我在日本没发现什么特别出色的生意。日本公司可能需要在文化上做一些改变，让管理层对股东更负责，提高回报率。但目前仍有许多低回报企业，即使在日本经济繁荣时期也是如此。我觉得这真的很神奇。他们拥有惊人的市场，却没有出色的公司。他们把生意做得很大，但资本回报率却表现平平，这最终也拖累了他们。因此，到目前为止，我们还没有投资日本股市。但只要利率保持在1%，我就会继续观察日本市场。

问题二：有传言说您是长期资本管理公司的救助性买家之一，到底发生了什么？能给我们讲讲吗？

巴菲特：这里头有个故事。最新的那期《财富》杂志，就是封面上有鲁伯特·默多克照片的那期，讲述了我们的完整经历，这是一个相当有趣的故事。这件事说来话长，我就不细说前情了。我接到了一通关于长期资本管理公司的电话，是一通非常严肃的电话。大约4周前，我在下午3点左右接到了这通电话。那天晚上，我的孙女要办生日会，而且我当晚要飞往西雅图，和盖茨一起坐私人飞机去阿拉斯加，

---

4. Long-Term Capital：美国长期资本管理公司，一家于1994年创立的著名的对冲基金公司。该公司创立后的头些年盈利可观，年均40%以上。但在1998年，这家基金在4个月里损失了46亿美元，震惊世界。
5. Fortune Magazine：《财富》杂志，主要刊登经济问题的研究文章，由亨利·鲁斯创办于1930年，其推出的企业排行名单是公司用来判断自身实力、规模和国际竞争力的重要指标。

plane and I was really out of communication. But I got this call on a Friday afternoon saying that things were really getting serious there. I had some other calls before the article gets published a few weeks earlier. I know those people, most of them, pretty well—a lot of them at Salomon[6] when I was there. And the place was imploding and the FED[7] was sending people up that weekend. Between that Friday and the following Wednesday when the New York Fed, in effect, orchestrated a rescue effort but without any Federal money involved. I was quite active but I was having a terrible time because we were sailing up through these canyons which held no interest for me whatsoever in Alaska. And the captain would say, you know, if we just steered over here we might see some bears and whales. And I said, "Steer where you got a good satellite connection."

We put in a bid on Wednesday morning. By then I was in Bozeman, Montana. I talked to Bill McDonough, the head of the New York Fed. But they were having a meeting with bankers at 10 o'clock that morning in New York. We actually delivered a message to him. He called me out there in Wyoming a little bit before 10:00 New York time. We made a bid, because it was being done at a long distance and it was really an outline of the bid, but in the end, the bid was for 250 million essentially for the net assets but we would have put in 3 and 3/4 billion on top of that. And it would have been $3 billion from Berkshire Hathaway, $700 million from AIG[8] and $300 million from Goldman Sachs[9]. And we submitted that, but we put a very short time fuse on it because when you are bidding on 100 billion dollars worth of securities that are moving around, you don't want to leave a fixed price bid out there very long. Plus we were worried about getting shopped. In the end the bankers made the deal, but it was an interesting period.

The whole Long-Term Capital Management, I hope most of you are familiar with it but the whole story is really fascinating because if you take

开启一场为期 12 天的旅行，到时候我会和外界断联。然而在周五下午，我接到了这通电话，说那里的情况真的很严重。在那篇文章发表的几周前，我还接到了其他一些人的电话。大多数是熟人打来的——不少是我在所罗门兄弟公司时的同事。长期资本管理公司要崩盘了，美联储在那个周末也派人过去了。从那个周五到下一周的周三，美联储纽约分行切实地展开了一场纾困行动，但没有动用联邦资金。我当时很积极地想参与，但我在船上，信号不好。我没心思欣赏周围阿拉斯加的峡谷，当时过得很不开心。船长提议说，开偏一点没准儿能看到熊和鲸鱼，我回答："哪里信号好就往哪里开吧。"

周三上午，我们给出了一个报价。那时我已经在蒙大拿州的博兹曼了。我和美联储纽约分行的行长比尔·麦克多诺谈了谈，但他们那天上午 10 点钟要在纽约和银行家们开会。我们把意向传达过去。他在纽约时间快 10 点的时候给在怀俄明州的我打了电话。我们出了个价，因为我人不在现场，实际上只是出了个大概的价格，最终出价是针对 2.5 亿美元的净资产，但我们还会在此基础上再注资 37.5 亿美元。其中伯克希尔·哈撒韦公司出资 30 亿美元，美国国际集团出资 7 亿美元，高盛集团出资 3 亿美元。我们提交了报价，但只给对方很短的时间考虑，因为要竞标的是价值 1000 亿美元的证券，而证券是不断流动的，所以固定报价有效期不能太久。而且我们还担心被别人买走了。最终，银行家们把这笔交易谈成了，不过那段时间还挺有意思的。

相信在座的大多数人都听说过长期资本管理公司的故事，那真的是个很耐人寻

---

6. Salomon：指所罗门兄弟公司（Salomon Brothers Inc.），华尔街著名的投资银行，1910 年由所罗门兄弟三人与人合伙组建，20 世纪 90 年代末被旅行者集团（现属花旗集团）并购。
7. FED：美国联邦储备局，是美国的中央银行体系，根据《联邦储备法》于 1913 年 12 月 23 日成立。
8. AIG：美国国际集团（American International Group），创立于 1919 年，是一家以美国为基地的国际性跨国保险及金融服务机构集团，总部设于纽约市的美国国际大厦。
9. Goldman Sachs：高盛集团，一家全球金融机构，创立于 1869 年，总部在美国纽约，是跨国银行控股公司集团。主要业务是为包括公司、金融机构、政府和个人在内的庞大而多元化的客户群提供广泛的金融服务。

John Meriwether, Eric Rosenfeld, Larry Hillenbrand, Greg Hawkins, Victor Haghani and the two Nobel prize winners, Merton and Scholes. If you take the 16 of them, they probably have as high an average IQ as any 16 people working together in one business in the country, including Microsoft or wherever you want a name. An incredible amount of intellect in that room. Now you combine that with the fact that those 16 had had extensive experience in the field they were operating in. These were not a bunch of guys who had made their money selling men's clothing and then all of a sudden went into the securities business. They had in aggregate[10], the 16, probably had 350 or 400 years of experience doing exactly what they were doing and then you throw in the third factor that most of them had virtually all of their very substantial networks in the business. So they had their own money up. Hundreds and hundreds of millions of dollars of their own money up, super high intellect and working in a field that they knew. Essentially they went broke.

That to me is absolutely fascinating. If I ever write a book it is going to be called, *Why Smart People Do Dumb Things*. My partner says it should be autobiographical[11]. But this might be an interesting illustration. These are perfectly decent guys, you know. I respect them and they helped me out when I had problems at Salomon, so they are not bad people at all. But to make money they didn't have and didn't need, they risked what they did have and did need. That is just plain foolish; it doesn't matter what your IQ is.

If you risk something that is important to you for something that is unimportant to you, it just doesn't make any sense. I don't care whether the odds are 100∶1 that you succeed or 1000∶1 that you succeed. If you hand me a gun with a million chambers in it. There's a bullet in one chamber and you said, "Put it up to your temple, how much do you want to be paid to pull it once?" I'm not going to pull it, you know. You can name any sum you want, but it doesn't do anything for me on the upside and I think the downside is fairly

味的故事。这家公司群英荟萃，约翰·梅里韦瑟、埃里克·罗森菲尔德、拉里·希伦布朗德、格雷格·霍金斯、维克多·哈格尼以及两位诺贝尔奖得主默顿和斯科尔斯等。你们从美国随便哪家公司挑 16 个人出来，包括微软在内，平均智商都不会比这 16 个人高。他们不仅有高智商，还有丰富的行业经验，可不是靠卖男装发家，再半路出家搞证券的。总的来说，这 16 个人的从业经验加起来搞不好有三四百年了。还有第三个因素——他们中大部分人拥有庞大的行业人脉网络。他们还把自己的钱往里投了。他们拥有数亿美元的自有资金，拥有超高的智商，行业经验丰富，却破产了。

这在我看来极其耐人寻味。如果我要写一本书的话，书名一定是《聪明人为何做蠢事》。我的搭档说我的自传就可以叫这个名字。但是，我们能从长期资本的例子中得到很多启发。他们都是很正派的人。我尊重他们。当年我在所罗门遇到问题，是他们帮助了我，所以说他们根本不是坏人。但为了赚不是自己的且自己不需要的钱，他们拿自己有的和要用的钱来冒险，这简直太蠢了，智商再高也不能掩盖其中的愚蠢。

为了得到不重要的东西，拿重要的东西去冒险，是毫无意义的。对我来说，成功的概率是 100∶1 还是 1000∶1 都无关紧要。假设我得到一把枪，里面有一百万个弹仓，但只有一个弹仓里有子弹，人家说："朝太阳穴来一枪，你要多少钱？"给多少钱我都不干。赌赢了对我没有好处，赌输了的结果显而易见。我对那种游戏不感

---

10. in aggregate：整体上。
11. autobiographical：*adj.* 自传的。

clear. I am not interested in that kind of game. Yet people do it financially without thinking about it very much. There was a lousy book with a great title written by Walter Gutman. The title was *You Only Have to Get Rich Once*. Now that seems pretty fundamental, doesn't it? If you've got $100 million at the start of the year and you're gonna make 10% if you are unleveraged and 20% if you are leveraged[12] 99 times out of 100, what difference does it make at the end of the year, whether you got $110 million or $120 million? It makes no difference at all. If you die at the end of the year, the guy who writes up the story may make a typo; he may say 110 even though you had 120. You have gained nothing at all. It makes absolutely no difference. It makes no difference to your family and makes no difference to anything.

And yet the downside, particularly managing other people's money, is not only losing all your money, but it is disgrace, humiliation and facing friends whose money you have lost. I just can't imagine an equation that makes sense for. Yet 16 guys with very high IQs who are very decent people entered into that game. I think it is madness. It is produced by an over-reliance to some extent on things. Those guys would tell me back when I was in Salomon that a Six Sigma[13] event wouldn't touch us, or a Seven Sigma event. But they were wrong. History does not tell you the probabilities of future financial things happening. They had a great reliance on mathematics. They felt that the Beta of the stock told you something about the risk of the stock. It doesn't tell you a damn thing about the risk of the stock in my view. Sigmas do not tell you about the risk of going broke in my view and maybe now in their view too.

But I don't like to even use them as an example because the same thing in a different way could happen to any of us probably, where we really have a blind spot about something that is crucial, because we know a whole lot about something else. It is like Henry Kauffman said the other day, "The people who are going broke in this situation are just of two types, the ones who know

兴趣。然而，在金融领域，大家想都不想就去干了。沃尔特·古特曼有一本书，内容很烂，名字却很棒，叫作《一生只需富一次》。这个道理算不得高深，不是吗？假设你们年初拥有 1 亿美元，不上杠杆，一年能赚 10%，上杠杆的成功率是 99%，能赚 20%，可是到年底获得 1.1 亿美元还是 1.2 亿美元有区别吗？半点区别也没有。如果你在年底去世了，说不定写讣告的人会打错字，明明身家 1.2 亿美元，他却写成 1.1 亿美元。上杠杆什么回报也没有，不会带来任何好的变化，对家人、对任何事情都一样。

要是亏损了，尤其如果管理的是别人的钱，后果不仅仅是损失钱，还有你的尊严、颜面以及面对被你赔掉钱的朋友们时的难堪。我真是想不明白这到底有什么意义，这 16 个高智商的正派人怎么会做出这样的事，真是疯了。某种程度上，促成这种结果的是对外物的过度依赖。当我还在所罗门兄弟公司的时候，那些人告诉我，六西格玛或者七西格玛事件影响不到我们。可他们错了。光研究过去的情况，没法知道未来金融事件发生的概率。他们太过依赖数学了，以为知道了股票的贝塔系数等于了解了股票的风险。在我看来，贝塔系数根本不能反映股票的风险，西格玛（标准偏差值）也不会指出破产的风险，也许现在他们也认同我这种观点了。

不过，我真不愿意拿他们举例子，毕竟同样的事情换个花样就可能会落在我们每个人头上，事实上我们都会因为了解过多细节，反而对某个关键点视而不见。正如亨利·考夫曼前几天所说："如今破产的人只有两种，一种是一无所知的人，一种

---

12. leverage：*v.* 加杠杆，指通过本金撬动更多可用资金来投资获利；通过抵押、贷款、借款等各种方式获取更多资金来从事某事业以期获得更多利润。
13. Six Sigma：六西格玛是一项以数据为依据，追求几乎完美的质量管理办法。它最初于 1986 年由摩托罗拉创立，后来被其他企业广泛应用。六西格玛采用量化的方法来分析业务流程中影响质量的因素，并找出最关键的因素进行改进，以达到更高的客户满意度，其目标是将不合格率降低到百万分之 3.4 以下，从而显著提高企业的财务绩效和竞争力。

nothing and the ones who know everything." It is sad in a way. I urge you. We never basically borrow money. I mean that we get float through our insurance business. But I never borrowed money when I had $10,000 basically. What difference did it make? I was having fun as I went along and it didn't matter whether I had $10,000 or $1,000,000 or $10,000,000 except if I had a medical emergency or something that come along like that.

I was going to do the same things when I had a lot of money as when I had very little money. If you think about the difference between me and you in terms of how we live, we wear the same clothes basically, we all have a chance to drink the juice with the gods here. We all go to McDonald's or better yet, Dairy Queen, and we live in a house that is warm in winter and cool in summer. We watch the Nebraska Texas A&M's game on a big screen. You see it the same way I see it. We do everything the same—our lives are not that different. You will get decent medical care if something happens to you, and I'll get the same medical care. The only thing we do is we travel differently. I ride around this little plane—I love it. And that takes money. But if you leave that aside—we travel differently—but other than travel, think about it, what can I do that you can't do? Now I get to work in a job that I love, but I have always worked in a job that I loved. I loved it just as much when it was a big deal if I made $1,000. I urge you to work in jobs that you love. I think you are out of your mind if you keep taking jobs that you don't like because you think it will look good on your resume.

I was with a fellow at Harvard the other day who was taking me over to talk. He was 28 and he was telling me all that he had done in life, which was terrific. And then I said, "What are you gonna do next?" "Well," he said, "Maybe after I get my MBA I will go to work for a management consulting firm because it will look good on my resume." I said, "Wait a second, you are 28 and you have been doing all these things. You got a resume that's 10 times

是无所不知的人。"这在某种程度上挺悲哀的。大家要引以为戒。我们基本上从不借钱，我的意思是我们通过保险业务获得资金周转。但手头只有 1 万美元的时候，我基本上也从不借钱。借钱有什么用？不管我手头有 1 万美元、100 万美元还是 1000 万美元都无关紧要，花起来都是一样开心。生了急病或有什么急事需要用钱则另当别论。

对我来说，不管钱多钱少，过起日子来都是一样。我和你们在生活方式上也没什么不同，衣服基本上都差不多，我们都有机会与众人在这里共饮果汁。我们都去麦当劳，或者奢侈一点，去吃 DQ 冰淇淋，我们都住在冬暖夏凉的房子里，都在大屏幕上看内布拉斯加大学和得克萨斯农工大学的比赛。你们怎么看比赛我就怎么看。我们做的事都一样——大家的活法并没有那么不同。如果出了意外，大家会得到很好的治疗，我也一样。唯一不同的是旅行方式，我有架私人小飞机可以开着到处飞，我很喜欢它。这是要花钱的。但抛开旅行方式不同这一点不谈，想想看，哪有什么是我能做而你们不能做的？我做着自己热爱的工作，但由始至终都是这样。早在我还觉得赚到 1000 美元是件大喜事的时候，我就已经很喜欢这份工作了。我强烈建议大家从事自己喜欢的工作。如果为了简历好看而一直干不喜欢的工作，那真是太糊涂了。

有一次，我去演讲，来接我的是一位哈佛的同学。这位同学 28 岁，跟我聊了聊他的工作经历。我觉得他真的很厉害了，问他说："接下来你打算做什么？"他说："等拿到 MBA 学位，我也许会进一家管理咨询公司，因为这会让我的简历好看一

> *But time is the friend of the wonderful business; it is the enemy of the lousy business.*
>
> 时间是优秀生意的益友，却是糟糕生意的敌手。

as good as anybody I have ever seen. I said if you take another job you don't like, isn't that a little like saving up sex for your old age? You know what I mean. There comes a time when you ought to just start doing what you want." I think I got the point across to him. When you get out of here, take a job you love. Don't take a job you think it's going to look good on you resume. Take a job you love. You may change later on, but you will jump out of bed in the morning. When I got out of Columbia Business School, the first thing was that I tried to go to work for Graham immediately. I offered to go to work for him for nothing. He said I was overpriced. But I kept pestering him. I went on and on. I sold securities for three years and I kept writing him and giving him ideas and finally I went to work for him for a couple of years. It was a great experience. But I always worked in a job that I loved doing. You should really take a job that if you were independently wealthy you would take. That's the job to take, because that's the one that you're going to have great fun. You will learn something, you will be excited about it, and you can't miss. You may go to do something else later on, but you will get way more out of it and I don't care what the starting salary is. I don't know how I got off on that, but there I am. So I do think that if you think you are going to be a lot happier getting 2X instead of 1X, you are probably making a mistake. You ought to find something you like then works with that. You will get in trouble if you think making 10X or 20X is the answer to everything in life, because then you will do things like borrowing money when you shouldn't or maybe cutting corners on things that your boy wants you to cut corners on. It just doesn't make any sense and you won't like it when you look back on it.

Question 3: Talk about the company you like—I don't mean the name of the company. What makes a company something that you like?

Buffett: I like businesses I can understand. Let's start with that. That narrows it down about 90%. There are all kinds of things I don't understand,

些。"我说："等等，你才28岁，就已经做了这么多事情，你的简历比我之前见过的任何人的简历都要好上10倍。要我说，要是你又找一份不喜欢的工作，不觉得有点像把性生活省下来，等老了再享受吗？你明白我是什么意思。你总有一天会去做自己想做的事。"我想他应该明白了我的意思。大家毕业的时候，要找一份喜欢的工作，而不是会给简历增色的工作。找一份你喜欢的工作。虽然喜好也会变化，但如果做喜欢的工作，早上会高兴地从床上跳起来去上班。我一从哥伦比亚商学院毕业，就想去为格雷厄姆工作。他说我要的薪水太高，我都主动说不要工资。我一直缠着他。我卖了三年证券，其间一直给他写信，把我的一些想法告诉他，最后我真的为他工作了几年。这是一段很棒的工作经历。不过我一直以来做的都是自己喜欢的工作。财务自由之后会选什么工作，就应该直接去做什么工作，因为你们会从中获得极大的乐趣，会学到东西，会满怀激情，这种体验不能错过。将来会转行也没关系，能够从中得到远超其他工作的收获，这才是最重要的，我不在乎初始薪资是多少。不知道怎么扯到这儿了，聊聊也好。总之，我真心实意地认为，如果你觉得收入翻倍会让人更快乐，那么你可能错了。你们应该找到自己热爱的事物，并为之奋斗。如果认为赚10倍或20倍的钱就能解决生活中的所有问题，那麻烦可就大了，因为你们就会因此去做一些不该做的事情，比如不该借钱的时候借钱，不该敷衍孩子的时候敷衍。这样做没有任何意义。回顾人生的时候，你们是不会喜欢这种事的。

问题三：能聊一聊您喜欢的公司吗？我不是希望您说出具体的公司名字，而是想知道有什么特质的公司能博得您的青睐。

巴菲特：我喜欢自己能懂的生意。咱们先从能不能懂说起。我用这一条标准过滤掉了90%的公司。我不懂的生意非常多，所幸也有足够多我能懂的。世界非常

but fortunately, there is enough I do understand. You have this big wide world out there and almost every company is publicly owned. So you got all American business practically available to you. Now to start with, it doesn't make sense to go with things you think you can't understand. But you can understand something. I can understand this, anybody can understand this (Buffett holds up a bottle of CocaCola). This is a product that basically hasn't been changed, since 1886 or whatever it was. It is a simple business, but it is not an easy business.

I don't want a business that's easy for competitors. I want a business with a moat[14] around it. I want a very valuable castle in the middle and then I want the Duke who is in charge of that castle to be honest, hard working and able. Then I want a moat around that castle. The moat can be various things: The moat in a business like our auto insurance business, GEICO[15], is low cost.

People have to buy auto insurance, so everybody is going to have one auto insurance policy per car or per driver basically. I can't sell them 20, but they have to buy one. What are they going to buy it on? They are going to buy based on service and cost. Most people will assume the service is fairly identical among companies, or close enough. So they will do it on cost. So I got to be the low cost producer—that is my moat. To the extent that my costs get further lower than the other guy, I have thrown a couple of sharks into the moat. But all the time if you've got this wonderful castle, there are people out there going to attack it and try to take it away from you. I want a castle that I can understand, but I want a castle with a moat around it.

30 years ago, Eastman Kodak[16]'s moat was just as wide as Coca-Cola's moat. I mean if you were going to take a picture of your six-month-old baby and you are gonna want to look at that picture 20 years from now or 50 years from now, and you are never going to get a chance—you are not a professional photographer—so you can evaluate what is going to look good 20 or 50 years

广阔，几乎所有公司都是上市公司。所以，实际上美国所有的商业领域你都能涉及。首先，明知道自己不懂，还下手，这完全没有道理。总有一门生意，你们能看懂。我能看懂这个，谁都能看懂这个。（巴菲特举起一罐可口可乐）可口可乐这个产品自1886年起基本没发生过变化。这门生意很好理解，但是并不容易做好。

我不喜欢对竞争对手来说很容易的生意。我喜欢有护城河的生意。理想的目标该是一座价值连城的城堡，守护城堡的公爵德才兼备、实干有为，城堡周围有一条护城河。护城河可以是各种各样的。像我们的汽车保险公司GEICO这样的企业，低成本就是护城河。

车险是必需品，每个有车的人基本上都需要一份车险。同一个人不可能买20份车险，但每个人都必须买一份。人们买车险的时候会看什么呢？会看服务和价格。大多数人会认为各公司之间的服务相当一致，或者相差无几，因此会选择比价。所以我必须成为低成本的生产商——这就是我的护城河。在某种程度上，我的成本越低，护城河里的鲨鱼就越多。可是，只要拥有一座美丽的城堡，总会有人进攻，企图夺其为己所有。我理想中的城堡得是我能参透的，但同时它得有护城河。

30年前，伊士曼柯达的护城河和可口可乐的一样宽。我的意思是，那时候如果想给家里6个月大的宝宝拍张照片，希望20年甚至50年后还能拿出来看，但自己又没有机会——自己又不是专业摄影师——所以没法判断什么样的照片能长期保存，那说明人们对那家影像产品公司的印象才是最重要的。因为他们向你承诺，你今天

---

14. moat：*n*. 护城河。
15. GEICO：美国政府雇员保险公司（Government Employees Insurance Company），美国第四大汽车保险公司，是沃伦·巴菲特的伯克希尔·哈撒韦公司的合伙机构。
16. Eastman Kodak：伊士曼柯达公司，简称柯达公司，是世界上最大的影像产品及相关服务的生产和供应商，总部位于美国纽约州罗切斯特市，是一家在纽约证券交易所挂牌的上市公司。

ago, what is in your mind about that photography company is what counts. Because they are promising you that the picture you take today is going to be terrific to look at 20 or 30 or 50 years from now about something that is very important to you, maybe your own child or whatever it may be. Well, Kodak had that in spades[17] 30 years ago, they owned that. They had what I call share of mind. Forget about share of market, share of mind. They had something in everybody's mind around the country, around the world—with a little yellow box—that said Kodak is the best. That is priceless. They have lost some of that. They haven't lost it all.

It is not due to George Fisher. George is doing a great job, but they let that moat narrow. They let Fuji[18] come and start narrowing the moat in various ways. They let them get into the Olympics and take away that special aspect that only Kodak was fit to photograph the Olympics. So Fuji gets there and immediately in people's minds, Fuji becomes more on a parity with Kodak.

You haven't seen that with Coke; Coke's moat is wider now than it was 30 years ago. You can't see the moat day by day but every time the infrastructure gets built in some countries that isn't yet profitable for Coke but will be 20 years from now. The moat is widening a little bit. Things are, all the time, changing that moat in one direction or another. Ten years from now, you can see the difference. Our managers of the businesses we run, I'v got one message to them, which is widening the moat. We want to throw crocodiles, sharks and everything else, gators, I guess, into the moat to keep away competitors. That comes about through service, quality of product, cost, sometimes through patents, and real estate location. So that is the business I am looking for.

Now what kind of businesses am I going to find like that? Well, I am going to find them in simple products because I am not going to be able to figure out what the moat is going to look like for Oracle, Lotus or Microsoft, ten years from now. Gates is the best businessman I have ever run into and they have got

拍摄的照片，在 20 年、30 年或 50 年后，当你回看对你来说非常重要的事物时——也许是你的孩子，或者其他任何东西——依然会很棒。30 年前柯达在这方面很出色，拥有优势。他们拥有我所说的心理份额，在心理份额面前，市场份额根本不算什么。全美国乃至全球每个人的脑海里都有一个柯达的黄色小盒子，上面写着柯达是最好的。这种信赖是无价之宝。柯达的护城河后来削弱了，但并没有完全消失。

这不能归咎于乔治·费舍尔，乔治做得很好，但还是让柯达的护城河变窄了。柯达坐视富士进攻，蚕食自己的护城河，坐视富士进军奥运会。过去在人们心目中，只有柯达才有资格拍奥运会，结果上阵的是富士。这样一来，在人们的脑海中，富士立马就与柯达平起平坐了。

可口可乐就还没碰上这种事。如今，可口可乐的护城河比 30 年前还要宽。你无法日复一日地察觉到这条护城河的变化。每次可口可乐在某个国家开新工厂，即使新工厂现在不赢利，20 年后也会赢利。护城河正一点点变宽。世事时刻皆在对护城河施加影响，事态不是向好发展便是向坏发展。10 年后，差异便显露无遗。我常对管着自家生意的高管们说，要拓宽护城河，要往护城河里扔鳄鱼、鲨鱼，把竞争对手挡在外头。想要做到这一点，要靠服务、产品质量、成本，偶尔还有专利或门店地段。我理想中的生意就是这样的。

现在来说说，该去哪里找这样的生意。我会从简单的产品里寻找，因为像甲骨文、莲花、微软这些公司，我没法预测它们的护城河十年之后会变成什么样子。盖

---

17. in spades：肯定地。
18. Fuji：富士胶片公司，又称富士胶片株式会社，创建于 1934 年，总部位于日本东京，为综合性影像、信息、文件处理类产品及服务的制造和供应商之一。

a hell of a position, but I really don't know what the business is going to look like ten years from now. I certainly don't know what his competitors businesses are gonna look like ten years from now. I'll name one I don't own. I know what the chewing gum businesses will look like ten years from now. The Internet is not going to change how we chew gum and nothing much else is going to change how we chew gum. There will be lots of new products. Is Spearmint or Juicy Fruit[19] going to evaporate? It isn't going to happen. You give me a billion dollars and tell me to go into the chewing gum business and try to make a real dent in Wrigley's. I can't do it. That is the way I think about business. I say to myself, give me a billion dollars and how much can I hurt the guy? Give me 10 billion dollars and how much can I hurt Coca-Cola around the world? I can't do it. Those are good businesses. Now give me some money and tell me to hurt somebody in some other fields, and I can figure out how to do it.

So I want a simple business, easy to understand, great economics now, honest and able management, and then I can see about in a general way where they will be ten years from now. If I can't see where they will be ten years from now, I don't want to buy it. Basically, I don't want to buy any stock where if they close the New York Stock Exchange tomorrow for five years, I won't be happy owning it. I buy a farm and I don't get a quote on it for five years and I am happy if the farm does OK. I buy an apartment house and don't get a quote on it for five years. I am happy if the apartment house produces the returns that I expect. But people buy a stock and they look at the price next morning and they decide whether they are doing well or not doing well. It is crazy. They are buying a piece of the business. That is what Graham—the most fundamental part of what he taught me. You are not buying a stock, you are buying a part ownership in the business. You will do well if the business does well, if you didn't pay a totally silly price.

That is what it is all about. You ought to buy businesses you understand.

茨是我平生所见最厉害的商人，微软也在行业内遥遥领先，但我真不知道这个行业十年后会是什么样子的，微软的竞争对手十年后又会有什么样的发展。我再来说一个我没做过的生意。我知道口香糖生意十年后会怎样。不管是互联网还是别的什么，都不会改变我们嚼口香糖的习惯。肯定会有更多新产品问世，但白箭和黄箭会消失吗？不会。给我十亿美元，让我去做口香糖生意，去挫挫箭牌的锐气，我可没这个本事。这就是我看待生意的方式。我会自问，如果给我十亿美元，我能重创这家公司吗？给我一百亿美元，让我在全球范围内和可口可乐竞争，我能重创可口可乐吗？我做不到。这样的生意就是好生意。要是说出资让我去别的行业挑战某个公司，我会想出办法的。

所以说，我想要的生意得是简单的，商业逻辑容易搞懂，当前经济效益良好，管理层德才兼备，这样的生意，我大致能预见其未来十年的发展情况。有的生意，我看不出来十年后会怎样，我就不会买。假设从明天起纽约股票交易所关门五年，某只股票如果在这种情况下我不愿意持有，那就不该买。我买一家农场，五年都不去看市场价，只要农场经营得不错，我就高兴。我买一套公寓，五年都不去看市场价，只要它能给我带来预期的回报，我就高兴。但很多人头天买完股票，第二天一早就盯着股价，看涨跌来判断买得对不对。这可太离谱了。买股票就是买公司，这是格雷厄姆教给我的最基本的道理。买的不是股票，而是企业的部分所有权。只要生意做得好，买入价格又不会高得离谱，这笔投资就算好投资。

投资就这么简单。要买能搞懂的公司，就像买农场，肯定会买自己能弄明白的。

---

19. Spearmint or Juicy Fruit：白箭和黄箭，都是美国的口香糖品牌，同属于美国箭牌糖果公司，在世界上有着广泛的销售市场。

Just like if you are buying farms, you ought to buy farms you understand. It is not complicated.

Incidentally, in calling this Graham-Buffett, this is just pure Graham. I was very fortunate because I picked up his book[20] when I was nineteen. I got interested in stocks when I was about 6 or 7. I bought my first stock when I was eleven. But I was playing around with all this stuff—I had charts and volume and I was making all kinds of technical calculations and everything. Then I picked up a little book that said you are not buying some little ticker symbol that bounces around every day, you are buying a part of the business. As soon as I started thinking about it that way, everything else followed. It is very simple.

So we buy businesses we think we can understand. There is no one here who can't understand the Coke-Cola company. I would say there's no one here that can understand some new Internet companies. I said at the annual meeting this year that if I were teaching a class at business school, on the final exam I would pass out the information on an Internet company and ask each student to value it. Anybody that gave me an answer, I'd flunk. I don't know how to do that. But people do it everyday; it is more exciting.

If you look at it like you are going to the races or something, that is a different thing. But if you are investing, investing is putting out money to be sure of getting more back later at an appropriate rate. And to do that you have to understand what you are doing. You have to understand the business. You can understand some businesses but not all businesses.

Question 4: You covered half of it which is trying to understand the business and buying the business. You also alluded to getting a return on the amount of capital invested in the business as an investor. And that comes back to what you pay for the business. What do you think is a fair price to pay for the business?

这并不复杂。

顺便说一下，别管这叫作格雷厄姆-巴菲特理念，这纯粹是格雷厄姆提出来的。我特别幸运。19 岁的时候，我有幸读到了他的书。我六七岁的时候就对股票感兴趣了，11 岁的时候第一次买股票。但我一直都在摆弄走势图，看成交量，做各种技术分析计算，等等。后来，我读到了他的书，书上说，买股票买的不是每日波动的代码，而是公司。我转变为以这种方式思考后，一切都豁然开朗。投资本身就是这么简单。

所以说，我们要买能自己能搞懂的公司。在座的各位没有看不懂可口可乐公司的。但是提到某些新兴的互联网公司呢？我敢说，在座的各位没一个能搞懂。今年在伯克希尔的年会上，我说要是我在商学院教书，我会出这样的期末试题：给出一家互联网公司的信息，让学生给该公司估值。谁要是真给出了估值，就要挂科了。我不知道怎么给互联网公司估值，但大家天天都在做这件事，大家觉得买互联网公司更刺激吧。

如果把买股票当成看赛马，那另当别论，但是如果当作投资，投资是投入资金，确定将来能以适当的收益率得到回报。要做到这一点，就得清楚地知道自己在做什么。必须懂自己要买的生意，有的生意是能搞懂的，但不是所有生意都能搞懂。

问题四：对于如何投资，您目前只说了一半，即只买自己能看懂的生意。您提到，作为投资者，要从投资中获得回报，而这就涉及买入价的问题。您认为什么样的价格才算是公允价格呢？

---

20. his book：指《聪明的投资者》，美国经济学家和投资思想家本杰明·格雷厄姆创作的投资学著作，于 1949 年出版，是一本投资实务领域的世界级和世纪级的经典著作。

Buffett: It is a tough thing to decide but I don't want to buy into any business I am not terribly sure of. So if I am terribly sure of it, it probably won't offer incredible returns. Why should something that is essentially a cinch to do well offer you 40% a year? We don't have huge returns in mind, but we do have in mind never losing anything.

We bought See's Candies[21] in 1972, See's Candies was then selling 16 million pounds of candy at a $1.95 a pound and it was making 2 bits a pound or $4 million pre-tax. We paid $25 million for it. It took no capital to speak of. When we looked at that business—basically, my partner, Charlie, and I really decide whether there was a little untapped pricing power there. In other words, $1.95 box of candy could just easily sell for $2 to $2.25. If it could sell for $2.25 or another $0.30 per pound, that was $4.8 on 16 million pounds, which on a $25 million purchase price was fine.

We never hired a consultant in our lives; our idea of consulting was to go out and buy a box of candy and eat it. What we did know was that they had share of mind in California. There was something special. Every person in California has something in their mind about See's Candies and overwhelmingly it was favorable. They had taken a box on Valentine's Day and given it to some girls and she kissed him. If she slapped him, we would have no business. As long as she kisses him, that is what we want in their minds. See's Candies means getting kissed. If we can get that in the minds of people, we can raise prices.

I bought it in 1972, and every year I raised the price on Dec. 26th, the day after Christmas, because we sell a lot at Christmas. In fact, we will make $60 million this year. We sell 30 million pounds and make $2 a pound. Same business, same formulas, same everything—60 million bucks still doesn't take any capital. And we make more money 10 years from now. But of that $60 million, we make about $55 million in the three weeks before Christmas. And

巴菲特：这很难说，不过我不想买入任何自己尚抱有疑虑的股票。但确定性高的股票可能不会带来惊人回报。很容易就能做好的事情怎么可能会带来40%的年回报率呢？我们不追求巨额回报，而是谨记绝不亏损。

我们在1972年收购了喜诗糖果，当时喜诗糖果以每磅1.95美元的价格卖出了1600万磅（约合7257.48吨）糖果，每磅赚0.25美元，税前赚400万美元。我们的收购价是2500万美元。喜诗不需要再投入任何资金了。评估喜诗的时候，我和搭档查理真正要判断的是，喜诗是否有提价的潜力。换句话说，一盒1.95美元的糖果能否以2美元到2.25美元的价格轻松卖出。如果到每磅2.25美元，或者涨价0.3美元，那么1600万磅就能多赚480美元。如果能做到的话，2500万美元的收购价是划算的。

我们这辈子从没聘请过顾问，我们找答案的方法是去买一盒来吃吃看。我们已经知道的是，喜诗在加州拥有心理份额。在加州，喜诗是特别的，每个人心里都有喜诗的一席之地，大家对喜诗印象都很好。情人节买喜诗送给女孩，会得到女孩的吻。要是得到的是巴掌，我们就没生意可做了。只要送喜诗能够得到吻，就能营造我们想要的品牌印象。喜诗糖果等于被亲吻。如果能够加深这一点在人们心中的印象，我们就能提价。

我在1972年收购喜诗，每年圣诞节后一天，也就是12月26日，我们就会涨价，因为圣诞节卖得特别好。事实上，喜诗今年能够赚6000万美元。我们卖出3000万磅（约合13 607.77吨），每磅赚2美元。同样的生意，同样的配方，什么都没变——赚6000万美元，依旧一分钱也不用投入。10年后我们会赚到更多钱。不过在这6000万美元中，有大约5500万美元是在圣诞节前三周赚的。我们公司的

---

21. See's Candies：喜诗糖果，1921年创立于旧金山，是美国西部历史最悠久最著名的糖果和巧克力食品公司。

our company song is:"What a friend we have in Jesus." It is a good business.

Think about it a little. Most people do not buy boxed chocolate to consume themselves, they buy them as gifts—somebody's birthday or more likely it is a holiday. Valentine's Day is the single biggest day of the year. Christmas is the biggest season by far. Women buy for Christmas and they plan ahead and buy over a two-or-three week period. Men buy on Valentine's Day. They are driving home; we run ads on the Radio. Guilt, guilt, guilt—guys are veering off the freeway right and left. They won't dare go home without a box of candy when we get through with them on our radio ads. So that Valentine's Day is the biggest day. Can you imagine going home on Valentine's Day—our See's Candy is now $11 a pound thanks to my brilliance. And let's say there is candy available at $6 a pound. But you really want to walk in on Valentine's Day and hand—I mean you've got all these favorable images of See's Candies over the years—and you walk in and say, "Honey, this year I took the low bid." And then hand her a box of candy. It just isn't going to work.

So in a sense, there is untapped pricing power—it is not price dependent, basically.

Think of Disney. Disney is selling, we'll say, Home Videos for $16.95 or $18.95 or whatever. All over the world—people, and we will say particularly about mothers in this case, have something in their mind about Disney. Every person in this room, when you say Disney, has something in their mind about it. If I say Universal Pictures, you don't have anything in your mind. If I say 20th Century Fox, you don't have anything special in your mind. But if I say Disney, you've got something in your mind. That is true around the world.

Now picture yourself with a couple of young kids, whom you want to put away for a couple of hours every day and get some peace of mind. You know if you get them one video, they will watch it twenty times. So you go to the video store or wherever you buy the video. Are you going to sit there and premier 10

歌是："耶稣是我们的好朋友。"这是一门好买卖。

想想看。大多数人买盒装巧克力不是为了自己吃，而是当作生日礼物，或者更有可能的是当作节日礼物。情人节是一年中单日销量最高的一天，圣诞节至今仍是最火热的销售季。女士会为圣诞节买好喜诗糖果，她们会提前规划，在两到三周的时间里采购。而男士会在情人节买。男士们开车回家的时候，电台就播着我们的广告。广告激起他们一波又一波的愧疚，让他们纷纷从高速上拐下来。在我们的电台广告攻势下，他们不敢空着手回家，必须带上一盒糖果。所以，情人节是单日销量最高的一天。想象一下情人节人们回到家，会有怎样的情景——我聪明地将喜诗糖果提到了每磅 11 美元，而假设有一种糖果的价格是每磅 6 美元。男同学们想象一下，你们的妻子这些年来对喜诗糖果的印象很好，但你们在情人节回到家，把糖果盒递给妻子，说："亲爱的，今年我买了便宜货。"这可不行。

所以从某种意义上说，喜诗有提价的潜力——基本上来说，它并不依赖于价格因素。

想想迪士尼。迪士尼电影的家庭录像带是 16.95 美元或 18.95 美元。全世界的人，尤其是做妈妈的，对迪士尼都有印象。提到迪士尼，在座的各位都能想到些什么。提到环球影业，大家的脑子里没有东西。提到 20 世纪福克斯电影公司，大家的脑子里不会有什么特别的东西跳出来。但如果我说迪士尼，大家的脑子里就会有东西浮现出来。世界各地的人们都是如此。

想象一下，你们在带几个小孩子，希望他们每天有几个小时能安静地待在一边，让自己清静一点。大家都知道，给他们放一部电影，他们会看上 20 遍。所以你们会

> *If you risk something that is important to you for something that is unimportant to you, it just doesn't make any sense.*
>
> *为了得到不重要的东西，拿重要的东西去冒险，是毫无意义的。*

different videos and watch them each for an hour and a half to decide which one your kid should watch? No. Let's say there is one there for $16.95 and the Disney there for $17.95—you know if you take the Disney video, you are going to be OK. So you buy it. You don't have to make a quality decision on something that you don't want to spend the time to do. So you can get a little bit more money if you are Disney and you will sell a lot more videos. It makes it a wonderful business. It makes it very tough for the other guy.

How would you try to create a brand—DreamWorks is trying, but how would you try to create a brand. It competes with Disney around the world to replace the concept that people have in their minds about Disney with something that says, Universal Pictures? So the mother is going to walk in and pick out a Universal Pictures video in preference to a Disney. It is not going to happen. Coca-Cola is associated with people being happy around the world. Everyplace—Disneyland, the World Cup, the Olympics—where people are happy. Happiness and Coke go together. Now you give me—I don't care how much money—and tell me that I am going to do that with RC Cola around the world and have five billion people have a favorable image in their mind about RC Cola. You can't get it done. You can fool around. You can do anything you want to do. You can have price discounts on weekends. But you are not going to touch it. That is what you want to have in a business. That is the moat. You want that moat to widen.

And if you are See's Candies, you want to do everything in the world to make sure that the experience basically of giving that gift leads to a favorable react, That means what's in the box; it means the person that sells it to you, because all our business is done, when we're terribly busy. I mean, people come in and those weeks before Christmas or Valentine's Day, there are long lines, so 5 o'clock in the afternoon some woman is selling the last person the last box of candy. And that person has been waiting in line for maybe 20 or

去音像店之类的地方买录像带。你们会在店里坐下，挑10部不同的电影，每部都看一个半小时，然后再决定买哪个给孩子看吗？不会的。假设一个是16.95美元，而迪士尼的是17.95美元，你们会想，买迪士尼的准没错，于是就买下了迪士尼的录像带。有的东西大家不会愿意花太多时间来精挑细选。所以，迪士尼卖得贵一点也能卖出更多的录像带。所以，迪士尼是一家非常棒的公司，竞争对手很难与之比肩。

如何打造品牌——梦工厂正在尝试，但如何打造品牌，才能在全球范围内与迪士尼分庭抗礼，夺走迪士尼的心理份额，而代之以别的，比如说环球影业？如何打造品牌，才能让妈妈们走进店里选择环球影业的录像带，而不是迪士尼的？这是不可能做到的。可口可乐是全世界的快乐水。迪士尼乐园、世界杯、奥运会，只要是洋溢着欢乐的地方，就有可口可乐。想要全球推广皇冠可乐，让50亿人心中建立起皇冠可乐的品牌印象，就算不计成本地砸钱也做不到。不管怎么折腾，不管你做什么，玩什么周末促销的花招，都徒劳无功。这就是投资者希望企业拥有的护城河，护城河越宽越好。

如果你们来打理喜诗糖果，就会想方设法地确保收到礼物的人会感到高兴。也就是说，要重视盒中糖果的品质，重视售货员的服务态度。因为我们所有的生意都是在非常忙碌的时候完成的。我的意思是，在圣诞节或情人节前的那几周里，顾客

> *The people who are going broke in this situation are just of two types, the ones who know nothing and the ones who know everything.*
>
> *如今破产的人只有两种，一种是一无所知的人，一种是无所不知的人。*

30 customers and if the sales person smiles at that last customer, our moat is widened. And if she snarls at them, our moat is narrowed. We can't see it. It's going on everyday but that's the key to it. I mean, it's the total part of the product delivery. It is having everything associated with See's Candies and something pleasant. And that's what business is all about.

Question 5: Have you ever bought a company where the numbers told you not to? How much is quantitative and how much is qualitative?

Buffett: The best buys have been when the numbers almost tell you not to, because then you feel so strongly about the product and not just the fact you are getting a used cigar butt cheap. It is compelling. I owned a windmill company at one time. Windmills are cigar butts, believe me. I bought it very cheap. I bought it at a third of working capital. And we made money out of it, but there is no repetitive money to be earned. There is a one-time profit in something like that. And it is just not the thing to be doing. I went through that phase. I bought streetcar companies and all kinds of things. In terms of the qualitative, I probably understand the qualitative the moment I get the phone call. Almost every business we have bought has taken five or ten minutes in terms of analysis.

We bought two businesses this year. General Re is a $18 billion deal. I have never been to their home office. I hope it is there. There could be just a few guys there saying "what number should we send Buffett this month?" I could see them coming in once a month and saying "we just tell them we've got $20 billion in the bank this month instead of $18 billion." But I have never been there.

Before I bought Executive Jet, which is fractional ownership of jets[22], before I bought it, I had never been there. I bought my family a quarter interest in the program three years earlier. And I had seen the service and it seems to develop well. And I got the numbers.

会来到店里大排长龙。假设最后一位顾客前面排了 20 或 30 个人，下午 5 点终于排到他了，如果我们的售货员能够面带微笑地将最后一盒糖果交到顾客手上，那护城河就会拓宽。如果售货员不耐烦地叫嚷，护城河就会缩窄。这种事难以察觉，但每天都在发生，而这就是关键所在。我的意思是，这就是产品交付的全部，我们要确保人们想到喜诗糖果就会觉得愉快。这就是生意的本质。

问题五：您是否曾经在数据表明不该收购一家公司的情况下仍收购了它？其中，定量和定性分析分别占多少？

巴菲特：最好的投资时机往往是数据几乎表明不该收购的时候。因为这说明自己非常看好产品，而不仅仅是因为能低价买到"烟蒂"股。这很有吸引力。我曾经买过一家风车公司。相信我，风车是"烟蒂"股。我买得很便宜。我用营运资金的三分之一买下了它。我们从这笔买卖中赚了钱，但只能赚一次。这种投资只有一次性收益。这不是我们该做的事，我经历过那个阶段。我买了电车公司之类各种各样的公司。就定性分析而言，我可能和对方在电话里聊几句就差不多完成了。几乎买入每一家企业，我们都只花 5 到 10 分钟的时间来分析。

今年我们收购了两家公司。我们收购通用再保险公司花了 180 亿美元。我从没去过他们的总部，但愿它确实在它该在的地方，搞不好只有几个人在那里商量"这个月要给巴菲特编点什么数据"，然后每个月来一次，心里想着"就告诉巴菲特他们，这个月银行里有 200 亿美元，而不是 180 亿美元"。我真的压根没有去过他们总部。

公务机航空公司是一家提供飞机分时所有权服务的公司。在我买下公务机航空公司之前，我也从来没去过他们公司。三年前，我给家人买了这家公司一个项目中四分之一的股权。我体验过他们的服务，感觉他们发展得不错。我也拿到了财务数据。

---

22. ownership of jets：译为"飞机的所有权"。在当时，拥有私人飞机是美国较为流行的趋势，然而这种花销不是一般人能承受得起的。所以可以选择买一部分飞机的拥有权，这样能拥有一段自己的飞行计划和路线。

But if you don't know enough to know about the business instantly, you won't know enough in a month or two months. You have to have sort of the background of understanding and knowing what you understand or don't understand. That is the key. It is defining what I call, your circle of competence.

Everybody has got a different circle of competence. The important thing is not how big the circle is, the important thing is staying inside the circle. And if that circle has only got 30 companies in it out of 1000s on the big board, as long as you know which 30 they are, you will be OK. And you should know those businesses well enough so that you don't need to do lots of work. Now I did a lot of work in the earlier years just in getting familiar with businesses and the way I would do that is I would go out and use what Phil Fisher[23] called the "Scuttlebutt[24] Approach." I would go out and talk to customers, suppliers, and maybe ex-employees in some cases—everybody. Every time I see somebody in an industry. Let's say, if I was interested in the coal industry, I would go around and see every coal company. I would ask every CEO, "If you only buy stock in one coal company that was not your own, which one would it be and why?" You piece those things together, and you learn a lot about the business after a while.

It's funny when you get very similar answers as long as you ask about competitors. If you got a silver bullet and you could put it through the head of one competitor, which competitor and why? You will find out who the best guy is in the industry in that case or the one that's coming up. So there are a lot of things you can learn about a business. I have done that in the past on the business I felt I could understand so I don't have to do much of that anymore. The nice thing about investing is that you don't have to learn anything new. You can do it if you want to, but if you learn about Wrigley's chewing gum forty years ago, you still understand Wrigley's chewing gum. There are not a

如果当前的知识储备不足以让你们一下子就弄懂某一门生意，那么再多花一两个月时间也没用。投资必须拥有一定的背景知识，要能弄明白自己理解什么，不理解什么。这是关键。这就是我说的能力圈。

每个人的能力圈都不一样。能力圈有多大并不重要，重要的是要待在圈子里。如果在大证券交易所数千家公司中，只有30家公司在能力圈里，只要搞清楚是哪30家，就没问题了。要对能力圈内的生意有足够的了解，事到临头就不用做很多工作了。早年为了了解各行各业，我做了很多工作。我会走出去，靠菲利普·费雪所说的"打听法"来了解各种公司。我会走出去，和那些公司的客户、供应商甚至是前员工聊天。每次我都是找业内人士打听，比如说，要是对煤炭行业感兴趣，我就会去走访各大煤炭公司。我会向每一位CEO提问："如果你要买竞争对手的股票，你会买哪一家？为什么？"把得到的信息拼凑在一起，一段时间后，就会很了解这个行业。

有意思的是，同行业内大部分公司认定的劲敌相差无几。如果你有一颗银弹，可以用它打穿一个竞争对手的脑袋，你会选谁？为什么？通过这种问题，就能找出这个行业里的佼佼者，或者即将冉冉升起的新星。各行各业都有很多学问可供钻研。我已经对自己能力圈内的公司做过这些功课了，所以现在可以省下这种功夫。搞投资的好处在于知识很难过时。愿意学新东西当然好，但只要了解40年前的箭牌口香糖，那就能看懂如今的箭牌口香糖。这些东西不会因为时间而发生多少改变。做过

---

23. Phil Fisher：菲利普·费雪（1907—2004），1907年生于旧金山，现代投资理论的开路先锋之一，成长股投资策略之父，教父级的投资大师，华尔街极受尊重和推崇的投资家之一。
24. scuttlebutt：*n.* 谣言；文中意指四处调研获取信息。

lot of great insights as you go along. So you do get a database in your head.

I had a guy, Frank Rooney, who ran Melville for many years; his father-in-law died and had owned H. H. Brown, a shoe company. And he put it up with Goldman Sachs. But he was playing golf with a friend of mine here in Florida and he mentioned it to this friend. The guy said you should call Warren. He called me at the end of the golf match and in five minutes I basically had a deal.

But I knew Frank, and I knew the kind of business. I sort of knew the basic economics of the shoe business, so I could buy it. Quantitatively, I got to decide what the price is. But, you know, that is either yes or no. I don't fool around a lot with negotiations. So if they name a price that makes sense to me, I buy it. If they don't, I was happy the day before, so I will be happy the day after without owning it.

Question 6: The Asian Crisis and how it affects a company like Coke that recently announced their earnings would be lower in the fourth quarter.

Buffett: Actually Coke just announced the third quarter earnings but few weeks ago. They tipped people off that they were going to be lower in the fourth quarter. Well, basically I love it, but because the market for Coca-Cola products will grow far faster over the next twenty years internationally than it will in the United States. It will grow in the U.S. on a per capita basis[25], but general faster elsewhere. The fact is that it will be a tough period for who knows—three months or three years—but it won't be tough for twenty years. People are still going to work productively around the world and they are going to find this is a bargain product in terms of the portion of their working day that they have to give up in order to have one of these, or better yet, five of them a day like I do. This is a product in 1936 when I first bought 6 of those for a quarter and sold them for a nickel each. It was in a 6.5 oz bottle and you paid

积累，脑子里就会有一个数据库。

我认识一个叫弗兰克·鲁尼的人，执掌梅尔维尔公司多年；他的岳父去世了，留下了一家名为 H. H. 布朗的鞋业公司。他请高盛帮忙把这家鞋业公司卖出去。我在佛罗里达有一位朋友，有一回和他一起打高尔夫球，听他提起这件事，便建议他打电话给我。弗兰克·鲁尼打完球就给我打来了电话，不到 5 分钟我们就谈成了这笔交易。

不过我早就知道弗兰克这个人，也了解这门生意。我大致了解鞋业的基本商业逻辑，所以我能做出买下它的决定。就定量来说，我必须决定多少钱合适，而且要么接受，要么不接受，我不爱讨价还价。所以如果他们给出的价格合理，我就买，否则就算了。既然前一天没这笔买卖的时候我很开心，那就算得不到，我也一样会很开心。

问题六：可口可乐近期的公告称第四季度的盈利将会下滑。您对亚洲金融危机怎么看，它对可口可乐这样的公司会有什么影响？

巴菲特：实际上，可口可乐公司刚刚公布了第三季度的收益，但几周前，他们预告说第四季度的收益会更低。基本上来说，我喜欢这种诚实的态度。可口可乐产品的国际市场增长速度将远远超过美国市场。按人均来看，它在美国的销量会增长，但在其他地方通常会增长得更快。接下来将会是一个艰难的时期，谁知道会持续多久，3 个月或 3 年，都有可能，但不至于是 20 年。世界各地的人们仍然会努力工作，他们会发现喝可乐很划算，只要从工资中拿出一点点，就能喝上一瓶，甚至像我这样一天喝 5 瓶。1936 年，我第一次买可乐，买了 6 瓶，只花了 25 美分，然后以 5 美分一瓶的价格卖出。可乐瓶是 6.5 盎司（约合 192.2 毫升）的，要付 2 美分

---

25. capita basis：人均基础量。

a two-cent-deposit on the bottle. That was a 6.5 oz bottle for a nickel at that time; it is now a 12 oz can. If you buy it on weekends or if you buy it in bigger quantities, so much money doesn't go to packaging—you essentially can buy the 12 oz for not much more than 20 cents. So you are paying not much more than twice the per oz price of 1936. This is a product that has gotten cheaper and cheaper, relative to people's earning power over the years, and which people love.

And in 200 countries, you have the per capita use going up every year for a product that is over 100 years old that dominates the market. That is unbelievable. One thing that people don't understand is one thing that makes this product worths 10s and 10s of billions of dollars is one simple fact about all colas, but we will call it Coca-Cola for the moment. It happens to be a name that I like. Cola has no taste memory. You can drink one of these at 9 o'clock, 11 o'clock, 3 o'clock and 5 o'clock. The one at 5 o'clock will taste just as good to you as the one you drank early in the morning. You can't do that with Cream Soda, Root Beer[26], Orange, Grape, you name it. All of those things accumulate on you. Most foods and beverages accumulate on you and you get sick of them after a while. And if you eat See's Candies—we get these people who go to work for See's Candies and we told them they can have all the candy they want. The first day they go crazy, but after a week they are eating the same amount as if they were buying it, because chocolate accumulates on you, everything accumulates on you.

There is no taste memory to Cola and that means you get people around the world who will be heavy users—who will drink five a day, Diet Coke[27] maybe, you know, 7 or 8 a day or something of this sort. They will never do that with other products. So you get this incredible per capita consumption. The average person in this part of the world or maybe a little north from here drinks about 64 oz. of liquid a day. You can have all 64 oz of that be Coke and you will not

的押金。在当时，一瓶6.5盎司的可乐只需要5美分；现在可乐瓶是12盎司（约合354.84毫升）的。遇上周末促销或者买量贩装会更便宜，就不用在包装上花太多钱了，基本上花不到20美分就能买到12盎司。现在每盎司可乐的价格只不过是1936年价格的两倍多一点。人们的收入越来越高，相较之下，可乐变得越来越便宜，自然讨人喜欢。

可乐在其超过100年的历史中始终主宰市场，200个国家的人均饮用量逐年上升，真是令人难以置信。所有口味的可乐——我们暂且统称为可口可乐，这个名字我很喜欢——都有一个共性，这一点少有人注意到，但就是它让这个产品价值数十亿美元。可乐没有味觉记忆。就算9点、11点、3点和5点各喝一瓶，都不会腻。奶油苏打水、根汁汽水、橙汁、葡萄汁，只要想到的，全都不行。大多数食物和饮料都是这样，多了就腻味了。喜诗糖果也是这样。我们会跟喜诗糖果的新员工说，公司里的糖果想吃多少就吃多少。他们第一天会疯狂地往嘴里塞，但一周后就不怎么吃了，像是要花钱买似的，因为巧克力之类的东西都会吃腻。

因为可乐没有味觉记忆，这意味着，世界各地的重度可乐迷会一天喝五瓶。换成健怡可口可乐，说不定要一天喝七八瓶。但没有人会一天喝这么多别的饮料。这样的人均消费量真是不可思议。在我们这一带或者稍微往北一点的地方，平均每人

---

26. Root Beer：根汁汽水，产生于19世纪，是含二氧化碳和糖的无酒精饮料，盛行于北美。最初是用檫木（产于北美东部的一种樟科植物）的根制成。
27. Diet Coke：健怡可口可乐，可口可乐公司总部1995年研发的全新产品，现已成为全球第三大饮料品牌，与普通可乐之间最大的区别在于健怡可口可乐是"低卡路里"的，但口味几乎相同。

get fed up with Coke if you like it to start with in the least. But if you did that with almost anything else; if you eat just one product all day, you will get a little sick of it after a while. It is a huge factor. So today over 1 billion 8 oz servings of Coca-Cola products will be sold in the world and that will grow year by year. It will grow in every country virtually, and it will grow on a per capita basis. And twenty years from now it will grow a lot faster internationally than in the U.S., so I really like that market better, because there is more growth there over time. But it will hurt them. It is hurting them in the short term right now, but that doesn't mean anything.

Coca-Cola went public in 1919, stock sold for $40 per share. It went back before that there was a Chandler family and they bought the whole business for $2,000 back in the late 1880s. So now he goes public in 1919, $40 per share. One year later it is selling for $19, going down 50% in one year. Now you might think it is some kind of disaster and you might think that sugar prices increased and the bottlers were rebellious[28] and a whole bunch of things. You could always find a few reasons why that wasn't the ideal moment to buy it. Years later you would have seen the Great Depression, WW II and sugar rationing and thermonuclear weapons and the whole thing—there is always a reason.

But in the end if you've bought one share for $40 and reinvested the dividends, it would be worth about $5 million now ($40 compounding at 14.63% for 86 years!). That factor overrides anything else so much. If you are right about the business you will make a lot of money. The timing part of it is a very tricky thing so I don't worry about any given event if I got a wonderful business, whether what it does the next year or something of the sort. Price controls have been in this country at various times and that has fouled up[29] even the best of businesses. I wouldn't be able to raise the prices on Dec. on See's Candies if we had price controls that we've had in this country. But that

每天摄入 64 盎司（约合 1.89 升）的液体。这 64 盎司可以都是可乐。如果你一开始就喜欢可乐，那喝再多也不会腻。但换成任何一种别的东西，吃上一整天，就会有点恶心了。这一点非常关键。如今，全球每天售出超过 10 亿份 8 盎司（约合 236.56 毫升）的可口可乐，且这个数字还将逐年增长。几乎各个国家的销量都在增长，人均饮用量也会增长。20 年后，它在国际市场上的增长速度将远远超过美国，所以我更偏爱将来增长潜力更大的国际市场。不过当前，可口可乐在国际市场面临着暂时性的挑战，但这算不了什么。

可口可乐于 1919 年上市。当时每股售价 40 美元。在此之前，19 世纪 80 年代末，钱德勒家族以 2000 美元收购了可口可乐。1919 年公司上市，每股售价 40 美元。上市一年后，售价为 19 美元，一年内下跌了 50%。现在来看，你们可能会觉得简直是灾难，担心糖价上涨，或者装瓶商在造反，多的是值得担心的事情。你总能找到理由说服自己，那不是买可口可乐股票的好时机。若干年后又会碰上大萧条、第二次世界大战、糖定量配给以及热核武器危机等——总有不买的理由。

但如果当年以 40 美元的价格买了一股，并将股息再投资，到了现在就差不多值 500 万美元了（40 美元以 14.63% 的复合年利率增长 86 年！）。买入比什么都重要。只要确实是门好生意，买入就会赚很多钱。择时难度太高了，所以如果看中了一门好生意，我就不会去担心发生任何事，不管它明年会怎么样，或其他诸如此类的事情。美国在不同时期都实行过价格管制，再厉害的企业也扛不住。如果当时美国有价格管制的话，我就没法儿在 12 月给喜诗糖果涨价了。但退一步说，喜诗糖果也不会因为价格管制而变成一门糟糕的生意，因为价格管制长久不了。我们在 20 世纪

---

28. rebellious：*adj.* 反叛的，叛逆的。
29. foul up：搞砸，弄糟。

doesn't make it a lousy business if that happens to happen, because you are not going to have price controls forever. We had them in the early 70s.

The wonderful business—you can figure out what will happen, you can't figure out when it will happen. You don't want to focus too much on when but you want to focus on what. If you are right about what, you don't have to worry about when very much.

Question 7: What about your business mistakes?

Buffett: How much time do you have? The interesting thing about mistakes is that in investments, at least for me and for my partner, Charlie Munger[30], the biggest mistakes have not been mistakes of commission, but of omission. They are where we knew enough about the business to do something and for one reason or another, we sat there sucking out thumbs instead of doing something. And so we have passed up things where we could have made billions and billions of dollars from things we understood, forget about things we don't understand.

The fact I could have made billions out of Microsoft doesn't mean anything because I never understand Microsoft. But if I can make billions out of healthcare stocks, then I should make it. And I didn't, when the Clinton health care program was proposed and they all went in the tank. We should have made a ton of money out of that because I could understand it and didn't make it.

I should have made a ton of money out of Fannie Mae[31] back in the mid-1980s. I understood it but I didn't do it. Those are billion dollar mistakes or multi-billion dollar mistakes that generally accepted accounting principles don't pick up.

The mistakes you see. I made a mistake of buying a US Air Preferred some years ago. I had a lot of money around. I make mistakes when I get cash. Charlie tells me to go to a bar instead: "Don't hang around the office." But I

70年代早期就经历过了。

对于一门好生意，我们能看出将来发展如何，但猜不出要多少时间来实现。不必过多地关注时间，而是要关注自己认定的那些特质。只要是真正的好生意，总会带来回报，是早是晚无所谓。

问题七：请问您在生意上出现过哪些失误呢？

巴菲特：你有多长时间（来听我的失误）？至少对于我和我的合伙人查理·芒格来说，投资中最大的错误不是做错事，而是没做该做的事。明明对生意有足够的了解，本该采取行动，却出于这样或那样的原因，只是坐在原地无所作为，什么都没做，这就犯错了。要是不了解的生意倒也罢了，可明明懂，明明可以赚几十亿、几百亿的，却让机会溜走了。

我本可以从微软赚到几十亿美元，但这没什么好说的，因为我从来也看不懂微软的生意。但若我本能从医疗股中赚到几十亿美元，我却没有去做，这才是错误。那时克林顿提出医保计划，医药股价格大跳水，我们本该入手，大赚一笔，因为我能看懂医药的门道，但我却没有买。

20世纪80年代中期，我本该从房利美大赚一笔，我能看懂房利美的生意，但是我没买。这些错误价值十亿或数十亿美元，而按公认的会计原则做的报表是体现不出这些损失的。

来说说大家能看得到的错误。几年前，我犯了一个错误，买了美国航空的优先股。当时我手头有很多闲钱，闲钱一多我就容易犯错。查理让我去酒吧，说："别在办公室里转悠。"但我还是待在了办公室里，口袋里有钱，就做了蠢事。这种事

---

30. Charlie Munger：查理·芒格（1924—2023），出生于美国奥马哈，美国投资家，沃伦·巴菲特的黄金搭档，生前系伯克希尔·哈撒韦公司副主席。

31. Fannie Mae：房利美，美国一家房屋抵押企业，成立于1938年，总部位于美国华盛顿，主要从事房屋贷款业务。

hang around the office and I got money in my pocket. I do something dumb. It happens every time.

So I bought this thing. Nobody made me buy it. I now have an 800 number I call every time I think about buying a stock in an airline and they talk me down. I say, "I am Warren and I am an air-aholic." Then the guy says, "Keep talking. Don't hang up yet. Don't do anything rash." Finally I get over it.

But I bought it. And it looked like we would lose all our money in that. And we came very close to losing all our money and you can say we deserved to lose all our money.

We bought it because it was an attractive security. But it was not in an attractive business. I did the same thing in Salomon. I bought an attractive security in a business that I wouldn't have bought the equity in. So you could say that is one form of mistake. Buying something because you like the terms, when you don't like the business that well. I have done that in the past and will probably do that again. The bigger mistakes are the ones of omission. Back when I had $10,000 I put $2,000 of it into a Sinclair Service Station which I lost, so my opportunity cost us about $6 billion right now—fairly big mistake. It makes me feel good when Berkshire goes down, because the cost of my Sinclair Station goes down too. My 20% opportunity cost.

I will say this—you talk about learning from mistakes—I really believe it is better to learn from other people's mistakes as much as possible. But we don't spend any time looking back at Berkshire. I have got a partner, Charlie Munger; we have been pals for forty years—never had an argument. We disagree on things a lot but we don't have arguments about it. We never look back. We just figure there is so much to look forward to. There is no sense thinking about what we might have done. It just doesn't make any difference.

You can only live life forward. You can learn something perhaps from the mistakes, but the big thing to do is to stick with the businesses you understand.

常有。

所以我做了这笔交易，没人逼我。我现在有一个 800 开头的热线电话，每当我想买航空股，我都会打这个电话，他们会说服我放弃。我说："我是沃伦，我又想买航空股了。"电话那头的人会说："继续说，先别挂电话，别冲动行事。"最后这股劲儿就会过去。

但是我确实买了美国航空，险些把钱赔光，真的差点就赔光了，可以说是活该。

我们买入美国航空，是因为美国航空是很有吸引力的证券，但航空不是一个有吸引力的行业。所罗门公司对我来说也是一样的。我觉得证券便宜，但对它的股权不感兴趣。明明不看好这门生意，只是觉得证券的条款不错就买入，这算得上是一种错误。我过去犯过这样的错，将来可能还会继续犯这种错。更严重的错误是疏忽。我当年只有 1 万美元，把其中 2000 美元投入了辛克莱尔加油站，结果亏了，这笔投资的机会成本现在都有 60 亿美元了，这个错误可太严重了。每次伯克希尔股价下跌，我都感觉心里好受了一些，毕竟这样一来，我购买加油站的成本就下降了。这可是 20% 的机会成本啊。

我想说大家都说要从错误中学习——但我真的认为大家还是尽可能地从别人的错误中学习比较好。但在伯克希尔，大家都觉得，过去的事情就让它过去吧。我有一个合伙人叫查理·芒格，我们俩做了 40 年好朋友，从来没有吵过架。虽然我们经常意见相左，但不会吵架。我们从不回头看，前方有那么多值得期待的东西在等着我们呢，没必要对过去耿耿于怀。纠结过去的事情也改变不了什么。

我们只能向前看。也许从错误中可以学到些什么，但关键还是要坚持只买能弄懂的生意。所以，如果你们也犯了这么一个普遍的错误，跳出了自己的能力圈，比

So if there is a generic mistake of getting outside of your circle of competence, like buying something that somebody tips you on or something of the sort, in an area you know nothing about, you should learn something from that which is to stay with what you can figure out yourself. You really want your decision making to be by looking in the mirror and saying to yourself, "I am buying 100 shares of General Motors at $55 because ..." It is your responsibility if you are buying it. There gotta be a reason and if you can't state the reason, you shouldn't buy it. If it is because someone told you about it at a cocktail party, not good enough. It can't be because of the volume or the chart looks good on it or anything like. It gotta be a reason you'd buy the business. That's something we stick to pretty carefully. That is one of the things Ben Graham taught me.

Question 8: What about the current tenuous economic situation and interest rates? Where are we going?

Buffett: I don't think about the macro stuff. What you really want to do in investments is figure out what is important and knowable. If it is unimportant and unknowable, you forget about it. What you talk about is important but, in my view, it is not knowable. Understanding Coca-Cola is knowable or Wrigley or Eastman Kodak. You can understand those businesses that are knowable. Whether it turns out to be important depends on where your valuation leads you and the firm's price and all of that. But we have never either bought a business or not bought a business because of any Macro feeling of any kind. We don't read things about predictions, about interest rates or business or anything like that, because it doesn't make any difference. Let's say in 1972 when we bought See's Candies, I think maybe Nixon put on the price controls a little bit later. Let's say we'd seen that, but so what! We would have missed a chance to buy something for $25 million that is earning $60 million pre-tax now. We don't want to pass up the chance to do something intelligent because of some predictions about something we are not good at anyway. So we don't

如，买了别人推荐的股票之类的，涉足了自己一无所知的领域，那就该反省反省，以后坚持只买自己能弄懂的股票。做出投资决策的时候，真应该对着镜子里的自己说："我要以 55 美元的价格买入 100 股通用汽车，因为……"投资要对自己负责，决定要买入什么，一定是有理由的，如果说不出理由，那就不应该买。在鸡尾酒会上听人推荐了某只股票，这种理由不够好。成交量或者走势图不错之类的理由也不行。理由必须是看好公司。我们严格遵从这个规则。这是本·格雷厄姆教给我的东西之一。

问题八：能否谈谈您对当前脆弱的经济形势和利率问题的看法？您认为我们将走向何方？

巴菲特：我不考虑宏观问题。投资中真正要做的是弄清楚什么是重点，什么是可知的。既不重要也不可知的事情忘记就好。这位同学问的问题是很重要，但在我看来，它是不可知的。可口可乐、箭牌、伊士曼柯达这些知名企业，只要弄懂了，就属于可知的范畴，而是否重要，取决于估值和公司的价格等因素。但我们从来不根据对宏观形势的看法来决定是否收购一家企业。我们不关注什么利率或商业发展之类的预测，因为看了也没用。1972 年我们收购喜诗糖果，不久尼克松就实施了价格管制，假设我们预先知道会发生这种事，那又怎样？我们反而会错过一门好生意，毕竟当年的收购价只有 2500 万美元，而现在税前收益是 6000 万美元。我们根本不擅长做这种预测，也不想因此而错失绝佳的投资机会。所以对于宏观因素，我们不看，不听，也不分析。投资咨询机构通常会让经济学家出来说点宏观走势，然

> *I urge you to work in jobs that you love. I think you are out of your mind if you keep taking jobs that you don't like because you think it will look good on your resume.*
>
> *我强烈建议大家从事自己喜欢的工作。如果为了简历好看而一直干不喜欢的工作，那真是太糊涂了。*

read or listen to or do anything in relation to macro factors at all, zero. The typical investment counseling organization goes out and they bring out their economist and they trot him out and he gives you this big macro picture. And then they start working from there on down. In our view that is nonsense. If Alan Greenspan[32] was on one side of me and Robert Rubin[33] on the other side and they were both whispering in my ear exactly what they were going to do the next twelve months, it wouldn't make any difference to me and what I would pay for Executive Jet or General Re insurance or anything else I do.

Question 9: What is the benefit of being an out-of-towner as opposed to being on Wall Street?

Buffett: I worked on Wall Street for a couple of years and I have got my best friends actually on both coasts. I like seeing them. I get ideas when I go there. But the best way to think about investments is to be in a room with no one else and just think. And if that doesn't work, nothing else is going to work.

The disadvantage of being in any type of market environment—Wall Street would be the extreme—is that you get over-stimulated. You think you have to do something every day. The Chandler family paid $2,000 for this company (Coke). You don't have to do much else if you pick one of those. And the trick then is not to do anything else. Even not to sell it in 1919, which the family did later on it. So what you are looking for is some way to get one good idea a year. And then ride it to its full potential and that is very hard to do in an environment where people are shouting prices back and forth every five minutes and shoving reports under your nose and all that. Wall Street makes its money on activity. You make your money on inactivity.

If everyone in this room trades their portfolio around every day with every other person, you are all going to end up broke. And the intermediary will end up with all the money. On the other hand, if you all own stock in a group of average businesses and just sit here for the next 50 years, you will end up with

后自上而下地分析一通。在我们看来，这都是无稽之谈。即使艾伦·格林斯潘和罗伯特·鲁宾一左一右地在我耳边嘀咕自己未来 12 个月要做什么，也不会动摇我的心神，不会影响我买公务机航空公司或者通用再保险公司之类的行动。

问题九：相较于在华尔街工作，身处华尔街之外有什么好处？

巴菲特：我在华尔街工作过几年，在东海岸和西海岸也都有好友，很喜欢去拜访他们。当我身处华尔街之外，我常会得到灵感。不过，考虑投资的话，最好还是自己一个人待在屋子里，除了思考什么都不做。如果这都没用，那就什么办法也没有了。

在各类市场环境中，人都容易受到过度刺激，华尔街尤其如此，那里会让人觉得每天都得做点什么才行。钱德勒家族花了 2000 美元买下了可口可乐，选中了这样的公司，别的事就都不用做了。诀窍就是之后什么也别做，甚至 1919 年也别卖，钱德勒家族后来就是在那一年把它卖掉了。所以，要做的事情是每年找到一家好公司，然后静待其潜力爆发。在华尔街，人们每五分钟就来回报价，把报告塞到我们面前。在这样的环境中，持有不动是很难做到的。华尔街靠折腾赚钱，你们则要靠不折腾赚钱。

如果在座的各位每人每天都拿自己的投资组合相互交易，你们最终都会破产，钱全被券商赚走了。而如果你们各自都持有一组普通企业的股票，在接下来 50 年里，大家最终都会得到一大笔钱，破产的将会是券商。券商就像医生，病人换药的

---

32. Alan Greenspan：艾伦·格林斯潘（1926— ），美国第十三任联邦储备委员会主席（1987—2006年任职），被称为全球的"经济沙皇""美元总统"。
33. Robert Rubin：罗伯特·鲁宾（1938— ），生于美国纽约市，美国银行家，在克林顿时期担任第 70 任美国财政部部长。

a fair amount of money and your broker will be broke. He is like a doctor who gets paid on how often he gets you to change pills. If he gives you one pill that cures you the rest of your life, he would get one sale, one transaction and that is it. But if he can convince you that changing pills every day is the way to great health, it will be great for him and the prescriptionists. And you will be out of a lot of money. You won't be any healthier and you will be a lot worse off financially.

You want to stay away from any environment that stimulates activity. And Wall Street would have the effective of doing that.

When I went back to Omaha about once every six months, I would go back with a whole list of things I wanted to check out one way or another, companies I wanted to see and I would get my money's worth out of those trips, but then I would go back to Omaha and think about it.

Question 10: How to evaluate Berkshire or Microsoft that does not pay dividends?

Buffett: It won't pay any dividends either. That is a promise I can keep. All you get with Berkshire, you stick it in your safe deposit box and then every year you take it out and fondle it, and then you put it back. There is enormous psychic[34] reward in that. Don't underestimate it.

The real question is whether we can keep retaining dollar bills and turning them into more than a dollar at a decent rate. That is what we try to do. And Charlie Munger and I have all our money in it to do that. That is all we will get paid for doing. We won't take any options or we won't take any salaries or anything. But that is what we are trying to do. It gets harder all the time. The more money we manage, the harder it is to do that. We would do way better percentage wise with Berkshire if it was 1/100 the present size. It is run for its owners, but it isn't run to give them dividends because so far every dollar that we've earned and could have paid out, we have turned into more than a

次数越多，券商赚到的钱越多。要是一颗药就根治了，那就只能赚一次钱，再没有后续了。而如果能让病人相信每天把各种药片换着吃是健康之道，那对医生和卖药的来说都是好事。病人花了大价钱，却不会变得更健康，只会让经济状况变得更糟糕。

要远离任何会刺激自己去瞎折腾的环境。华尔街就是这类环境的典型代表。

回奥马哈后，我每半年都会回华尔街一趟。我每次都会带上一整张清单，上面写着我要确认的事情以及要去调研的公司等，不让路费白花。但我会等回奥马哈再考虑一下自己做出的决定。

问题十：伯克希尔和微软都不派息，您怎么看待这种做法？

巴菲特：我保证，伯克希尔以后也不会派息。伯克希尔的股票只要放在保险箱里，每年掏出来摸一摸，再放回去，就可以了。这么干能带来极大的精神回报，可别低估了这种享受。

真正的问题是我们能否以合理的速度用留在伯克希尔的钱赚到更多钱。这就是我们要做的事。我和查理·芒格的全部身家都投进去了。这就是我们所能得到的报酬。我们不需要期权、薪水之类的东西，只是一心想实现这种增长。如今这项任务越来越难了。管理的资金越多，就越难做到这一点。如果伯克希尔的规模是现在的百分之一，投资回报率会高得多。伯克希尔是为所有股东运营的，但不是为了给股东派息运营的。到目前为止，我们赚到的每一美元，本来是可以分给股东，但我们

---

34. psychic：*adj.* 精神的，灵魂的，心灵的。

dollar. It is worth more than a dollar to keep it. Therefore, it would be silly to pay it out, even if everyone was tax free that owned it. It would have been a mistake to pay dividends at Berkshire, because so far the dollar bills retained have turned into more than a dollar. But there is no guarantee that happens in the future. At some point the game runs out on that. But it is the goal I mean, that is what the business is about. Nothing else about the business do we judge ourselves by. We don't judge it by the size of its home office building or anything, like the number of people working there. We have got 12 people working at headquarters and 45,000 employees at Berkshire, 12 people at headquarters and 3,500 sq ft. and we won't change it.

So we will judge ourselves by the performance of the company and that is the only way we will get paid. But believe me, it is a lot harder than it used to be.

Question 11: What tells you when an investment has reached its full potential?

Buffett: Well, ideally you buy in businesses where you feel that will never happen in terms of … I mean, I don't buy Coke with the idea that it will be out of gas in 10 years or 15 years. There could be something that happens but I think the chances are almost nil. So what we really want to do is buy businesses that we would be happy to own forever. It is the same way I feel about people who buy Berkshire. I want people who buy Berkshire to plan to hold it forever. They may not for one reason or another but I want them at the time they buy it to think they are buying a business they are going to own forever. And I don't say that is the only way to buy things. It is just the group I want to have join me because I don't want to have a changing group all the time. I measure Berkshire by how little activity there is in it.

If I had a church and I was the preacher and half the congregation[35] left every Sunday. I wouldn't say, "It is marvelous to have all this liquidity among my members. This terrific turnover …" I would rather go to church where all the seats are filled every Sunday by the same people.

没有，而是把它变成了更多钱。把收益留下来再投资更划算。所以说，即使股东们不用收股息，不用交税，派息也不是明智的做法。对伯克希尔来说，派息是错误的做法，因为到目前为止，留下来的每一美元都变成了不止一美元。我们没法保证将来也能做到这一点。说不准什么时候，这种游戏就玩不下去了。但这就是我们的目标，这就是商业的意义之所在。我们不会用别的标准来自我评判，不会在意总部大楼的规模、员工人数之类的东西。伯克希尔有 4.5 万名员工，但总部只有 12 个人，3500 平方英尺（约合 325.16 平方米），这一点不会改变。

资金增长是我们自我评价的唯一标准，也是我们获得回报的唯一途径。但说真的，现在比以前难多了。

问题十一：一项投资如果耗尽了潜力，会出现什么征兆？

巴菲特：理想情况下，应该买潜力永续的企业。我的意思是，我买可口可乐的时候，并不觉得它会在 10 年或 15 年后耗尽潜力。可能会发生一些意外事件，但我认为可能性几乎为零。所以，我们真正要买的，是自己愿意永远持有的企业。我希望伯克希尔的投资者也这样想，希望他们计划永远持有。虽然买下后出于这样或那样的原因可能会改变想法，但我希望他们在买入时认为伯克希尔是可以永远持有的企业。当然，股票有很多种买法，只是我更希望加入伯克希尔的是这样的投资者，因为我不希望团队总是变来变去的。我认为伯克希尔在这方面的变动越小越好。

如果我是教堂的牧师，教堂会众每个星期天都要换掉一半，我不会觉得"会众流动性这么高真是太好了"。我宁愿每个星期天坐满教堂座位的都是同一帮人。

---

35. congregation：*n.*（教堂里的）会众。

Well, that is the way we look at the businesses we buy. We want to buy something that we're really happy to own virtually forever. And we can't find a lot of those. And back when I started, I had way more ideas than money so I was just constantly having to sell what I thought was the least attractive stock in order to buy something I just discovered that looked even cheaper. But that is not our problem really now. So we hope we are buying businesses that we are just as happy with five years from now as now. And if we ever found some huge acquisition, then we would have to sell something, maybe, to make that acquisition but that would be a very pleasant problem to have.

We never buy something with a price target in mind. We never buy something at 30, saying if it goes to 40 we'll sell it or 50 or 60 or 100. We just don't do it that way. When we buy a private business like See's Candies for $25 million, we don't say it ourselves if we ever get an offer of $50 million for this business we will sell it. That is just not the way to look at a business.

The way to look at a business—is this going to keep producing more and more money over time? And if the answer to that is yes, you don't need to ask any more questions.

Questions 12: How did you decide to invest in Salomon?

Buffett: Salomon like I said, I went into that because it was a 9% security in September 1987 and the Dow[36] was up 35% that year. We sold a lot of stuff. And I had a lot of money around and it looked to me like we were never getting a chance to do anything, so I took an attractive security form in a business I would never buy the common stock of. I went in because of that and I think that's generally a mistake. It worked out OK finally on that. But it is not what I should have been doing. I either should have waited in which case I could have bought more Coca-Cola a year later or thereabouts I should have even bought Coke at the prices that was selling at then even though it was selling at a pretty good price at the time. So that was a mistake.

对我们来说，投资也是一样的。我们想买的是想到能永远持有就非常高兴的公司。这样的公司很难找。我投资刚起步的时候，想买的公司很多，但钱不多，所以为了买下更便宜的股票，必须不断地卖掉手头相对不那么看好的股票。可是今非昔比了，所以我们希望买入的公司再过 5 年也要像现在这样让我们满意。要是碰上大型收购项目，我们就不得不卖点什么来筹钱，但这是好事。

我们买入公司的时候从来不会考虑目标卖出价格，不会说 30 美元买入，等到 40 美元、50 美元、60 美元或者 100 美元就卖出。这不是我们的做事风格。当年我们以 2500 万美元收购喜诗糖果这家私企，并没有想过如果有人出价 5000 万美元就卖掉。这就不是看待一家公司该有的思路。

看待一家企业的方式是这样的：随着时间推移，它能否持续创造越来越多的收益？如果答案是肯定的，那就不用再考虑别的问题了。

问题十二：您是根据什么决定要投资所罗门兄弟公司的？

巴菲特：我买入所罗门是因为在 1987 年 9 月，它的收益率为 9%，那一年道琼斯指数上涨了 35%，我们卖出了很多股票。当时我手头资金充裕，又觉得好像永远也遇不上把钱投出去的好机会。虽然我不会买所罗门的普通股，但所罗门的另一种证券形式颇有吸引力，因此我做了这笔错误的投资。这笔投资的最终结果不算糟，但我本来不应该去做。要么我就该等等，这样一年后就可以买入更大份额的可口可乐，要么我就该立即买入可口可乐，尽管当时它的价格相当高。所以说，这是一个错误。

---

36. Dow：道琼斯指数，指的是道琼斯股票价格平均指数，它是以在纽约证券交易所挂牌上市的一部分有代表性的公司股票作为编制对象，由四种股价平均指数构成的一种算术平均股价指数。

On Long-Term Capital that is—we have learned other businesses that are associated with securities over the years—one of them is arbitrage[37]. I've done arbitrage for 45 years and Graham did it for probably 30 years before that. That is a business unfortunately I have to be near a phone for. I have to really run out of them or the office myself, because it requires being more sort of market-attuned and I don't want to do that anymore. So unless a really big arbitrage situation came along that I understood, I won't be doing much of that. But I've probably been in 300 arbitrage situations at least in my life, maybe more. It was a good business, a perfectly good business.

Long-Term Capital has a bunch of positions. They got tons of positions, but the top ten are probably 90% of the money that is at risk, and I know something about those ten positions. I don't know everything about them by a long shot, but I know enough that I would feel OK at a big discount going in and we would have the staying power to hold it out. We might lose money on something like that, but the odds are with us. That is a game that I understand. There are a few other positions we have that are not that big because they can't get that big. But they could involve yield curve relationships or on-the-run/off-the-run governments or things like that. That are just things you learn over time if you're around securities markets. They are not the base of our business. Probably on average, they have accounted for 0.5%-0.75% of our return a year. They are good little pluses that you get for actually having just been around a long time and learning a little bit about it.

First arbitrage ... not the first arbitrage I did, but one of the first arbitrage they did involve the company where they were offering cocoa beans in exchange for their stock. That was in 1955. And I bought the stock, turned in the stock, got warehouse certificates for cocoa beans and they happen to be a different type that were trading the cocoa exchange, but there was a basis differential, so I sold them. I mean that's just something that I was around at

至于长期资本管理公司，我们从业多年，对与证券相关的其他业务也很熟悉，其中之一就是套利。我做套利有 45 年了，此前格雷厄姆做套利有 30 年了。可惜的是，要做这门生意，我得一直守在电话旁边。我得到办公室待着，亲自下场指挥，才能掌握市场的最新动向，而我不想再做这种工作了。除非是很大的套利机会，而且得是我能弄懂的类型，不然我就不费这个劲。但我这辈子至少参与过 300 次套利，甚至更多。套利是一门好生意，一门非常好的生意。

长期资本管理公司的仓位非常分散，但前 10 大仓位可能就占了 90% 的风险资金，我对这 10 个仓位略知一二。我对长期资本管理公司的了解完全谈不上全面，但足够多了，能拿到大折扣的话，我觉得是值得收购的，而且我们有长期持有的耐心。在这样的事情上，我们可能会亏钱，但胜算很大。这是我能弄明白的游戏。我们还有其他一些所占比重不大的仓位，因为它们的规模做不大。其中涉及收益率曲线关系或新发行和旧发行的政府债券之类的东西。这些都是在证券市场中能够慢慢学到的东西，不是我们业务的基础。平均下来，它们可能在我们的年收益中占到 0.5%～0.75%。在投资行业有些资历，对此有一点了解，就有机会赚到这些钱。

首次套利……这不是我做的第一笔套利，是他们做的首批套利交易之一，那是在 1955 年，一家公司宣布可以用股票换可可豆。我买了股票，拿去换了可可豆的仓库凭单。这些可可豆正好和可可交易所里交易的可可豆品种不同，但是存在基差，所以我把它们卖掉了，这只是机缘巧合做成的一笔套利。从这件事里我了解了这类

---

37. arbitrage：*n.* 套利。

the time. So I learned about it. It hasn't have that cocoa bean deal since. 40-odd years I've been waiting for another cocoa bean deal. I haven't seen it, but it's there in my memory if it ever comes along. And Long-Term Capital is that on a big scale.

Question 13: What do you think about diversification?

Buffett: The question is about diversification. I have got a dual answer to that. If you are not a professional investor, if your goal is not to manage money in such ways to get a significantly better return than the world, then I believe in extreme diversification. I believe 98%-99%, maybe more than 99% of people who invest should extensively diversify and not trade, so that leads them to an index fund type of decision with very low costs. All they are going to do is own a part of America. And they have made a decision that owning a part of America is worthwhile. I don't quarrel with that at all. That is the way they should approach it unless they want to bring an intensity to the game to make a decision and start evaluating businesses. But once you are in the businesses of evaluating businesses and you decide that you are going to bring the effort and intensity and time involved to get that job done, then I think diversification is a terrible mistake to any degree. I got to ask that question the other day at Sun Trust. If you really know businesses, you probably shouldn't own more than six of them. If you can identify six wonderful businesses, that is all the diversification you need. And you can make a lot of money. And I will guarantee you that going into a seventh one instead of putting more money into your first one is gotta be a terrible mistake. Very few people have gotten rich on their seventh best idea. But a lot of people have gotten rich on their best idea. So I would say for anyone working with normal capital who really knows the businesses they have gone into, six is plenty, and I probably have half of it and what I like best. I don't diversify personally. All the people I've known that have done well with the exception we have mentioned, Walter Schloss[38].

生意，但之后再也没能碰上第二笔可可豆交易。我等了 40 多年都没能遇上，要是遇到了，我肯定不会忘记。长期资本管理公司就是这样一个机会，只是规模更大。

问题十三：您对分散投资怎么看？

巴菲特：这位同学问的是对分散投资的看法。对这个问题，我有两个答案。如果不是专业投资者，且投资目标不是获得超额回报，那就应该选择高度分散的投资方式。我相信，98% 至 99%，乃至 99% 以上的投资者都应该选择高度分散投资，而且要长期持有，这样一来，他们大概会投资成本很低的指数基金之类的。他们要做的就是拥有美国经济的一部分，假如确实认为拥有美国经济的一部分值得的话。我对这种做法毫无异议，绝大多数投资者是该这么做，除非想投入更多精力来做决策和评估企业。但如果开始以评估企业的方式来做投资决策，决定投入时间精力、提高工作强度来把投资做好，那分散投资就万万使不得，不管分散程度如何都一样。那天我在太阳信托谈到了这个问题。如果真的能看懂生意，就应该持有不超过 6 家公司。要是能找出 6 家好公司，那风险就已经够分散了，已经可以赚很多钱了。我敢保证，买入第 7 家是大错特错，绝对比不上往最看好的那家公司多投点钱。很少有人能靠第 7 家看好的公司致富，但是很多人都靠最看好的公司致富了。所以我想说，如果真正了解自己投资的业务，资金量又一般，持有 6 家公司就足够了。如果是我，只会持有 3 家最看好的，我个人是不搞分散投资的。我认识的投资者中比较成功的一般都不搞分散投资，除了沃尔特·施洛斯。沃尔特的投资高度分散，什么

---

38. Walter Schloss：沃尔特·施洛斯，同巴菲特一样，也是本杰明·格雷厄姆的门生。在近 50 年投资生涯中，他管理的基金整体收益远超同期大市，年化收益率表现亮眼，是价值投资领域的传奇。

Walter diversifies a lot. He owns a little of everything. I call him Noah—he has two of everything.

Question 14: How do you distinguish the Cokes of the world from the Proctor & Gamble [39] of this world?

Buffett: Well, Proctor & Gambles is a very, very good business with strong distribution capability, lots of brand names and everything, but if you ask me that I am going to go away for twenty years and put all my family's net worth into one business, would I rather have Proctor & Gamble or Coke? Actually Proctor & Gamble is more diversified among product line, but I would feel sure of Coke than Proctor & Gamble. I wouldn't be unhappy if someone told me I had to own Proctor & Gamble during the twenty-year period. I mean that would be in my top 5 percent, because they are not going to get killed. But I would feel better about the unit growth and the pricing power of a Coke over twenty or thirty years than I would about Proctor & Gamble.

Right now the pricing power might be tough, but you think a billion servings a day, extra penny, $10 million per day. We own 8% of that, so that is $800,000 per day for Berkshire Hathaway. You could get another penny out of the stuff. It doesn't seem impossible, does it? I mean it is worth another penny. Right now it would be a mistake to try and get it in most markets. But over time, Coke will make more per serving than it does now. Twenty years from now I guarantee they will make more per serving, and they will be selling a whole lot more servings. I don't know how many or how much more, but I know that.

P&G's main products—I don't think they have the kind of dominance, and they don't have the kind of unit growth, but they are good businesses. I would not be unhappy if you told me that I had to put my family's net worth into P&G and that was the only stock I would own. I might prefer some other name, but there are not 100 other names I would prefer.

都买一点。我管他叫诺亚，什么都来一点。

问题十四：可口可乐和宝洁这两类公司有什么区别？

巴菲特：宝洁是一家非常非常好的企业，分销能力强大，旗下品牌众多，优势很多。但如果问我，假设我要离开20年，把全副身家投入一家企业，我会选择宝洁还是可口可乐？其实宝洁的产品线更多元，但我对可口可乐比对宝洁更有信心。不过，如果说必须持有宝洁20年，我也不会不高兴。我的意思是，宝洁将是前5%的选择，因为宝洁不会被市场淘汰。但就未来二三十年的销量增长潜力和定价权来说，我更看好可口可乐，而不是宝洁。

现在可口可乐要提价可能不太容易，但想想看，每天10亿份，只要涨一分钱，每天就是1000万美元。我们拥有8%的股份，也就是说可口可乐每天为伯克希尔·哈撒韦公司赚80万美元。涨一分钱，这也不是没有可能，不是吗？我的意思是可口可乐涨一分钱也不贵。对大多数国际市场来说，可口可乐想涨价还不是时候，但未来可期。我敢保证，20年后，每份可口可乐能够比现在赚得更多，销量也高得多。上升空间有多少还不好说，但肯定是有的。

我不认为宝洁的主要产品在行业内具有这样的主宰地位，其销量增长潜力也不大，但这门生意是不错的。如果说我的全副身家必须尽数投入宝洁，我不能再持有其他股票，我也不会不高兴。我更喜欢别的公司，但更喜欢的公司也不会超过100个。

---

39. Proctor & Gamble：宝洁，简称P&G，美国日用品公司，始创于1837年，总部位于美国俄亥俄州，主营产品有织物及家居护理、美发美容、婴儿及家庭护理、健康护理、食品及饮料等。宝洁曾宣布专注于65个左右的品牌，在全球拥有多个技术中心。

Question 15: Would you buy McDonald's and go away for twenty years?

Buffett: McDonald's has a lot of things going for it, particularly abroad again. Their position abroad in many countries is stronger rather than it is here. It is a tougher business over time. People don't want to eat—exception to the kids when they are giving away Beanie Babies or something—at McDonald's every day. If people drink five Cokes today, they will probably drink five of them tomorrow. The fast food business is tougher than that. But if you had to pick one hand to have in the fast food business, which is going to be a huge business worldwide, you would pick McDonald's. I mean it has the strongest position.

It doesn't win taste test with adults. It does very well with children and it does fine with adults, but it is not like it is a clear winner. And it has gotten into the game in recent years of being more price promotional—you remember the experiment a year ago or so. It has gotten more dependent on that rather than just selling the product by itself. I like the product by itself. I feel better about Gillette[40] if people buy the Mach 3 because they like the Mach 3 than if they get a Beanie Baby with it. So I think fundamentally it is a stronger product if that is the case. And it probably is. We own a lot of Gillette and you can sleep pretty well at night if you think of a couple billion men with their hair growing on their faces. It is growing all night while you sleep. Women have two legs, it is even better. So it beats counting sheep. And those are the kinds of business …(you look for).

But if you got to think what promotion am I going to put out there against Burger King next month or what if they sign up Disney and I don't get Disney? I like the products that stand alone, absent promotion or price appeals although you can build a very good business based on that. And McDonald's is a terrific business. It is not as good a business as Coke. There are really hardly any. It is a very good business and if you bet on one company in that field, I'll pick

问题十五：您会买入麦当劳，然后放心地离开 20 年吗？

巴菲特：麦当劳有很多优势，尤其是在国际市场上。麦当劳在许多国家的行业地位都在比美国国内要高。未来这门生意会更难做。没人会天天在麦当劳吃东西——除了想要豆豆娃之类玩具的孩子们。可乐就不一样了，如果今天喝了五瓶可乐，明天就还有可能喝五瓶。快餐业比这更难做，但如果必须在快餐业中选择一家公司，而且还要有规模庞大的全球化业务，那就选麦当劳。我的意思是，麦当劳的行业地位最牢固。

在饮食赛道上，麦当劳并没有赢得成年人的青睐。麦当劳在孩子当中非常受欢迎，在成年人当中受欢迎程度还可以，但并不是毋庸置疑的赢家。近年来，麦当劳的促销活动越来越多——还记得一年前的试验吧？麦当劳越来越依赖促销而不是靠产品本身来提高销量。我喜欢产品本身卖得好的生意。我更喜欢吉列，大家买速锋 3 是因为喜欢，这比为了拿到豆豆娃玩偶而吃麦当劳更好。所以我认为，从根本上说，如果我分析得没错，吉列的产品更出色。很可能是这样。我们持有很多吉列的股份，一想到几十亿男人睡觉的时候都在长胡子，我们晚上就能睡得很安稳。胡子会长一整晚，而女人有两条腿需要刮毛，那就更棒了。这种催眠方式比数羊有效得多。这才是（你要的）生意。

但如果你想的是，下个月要搞什么活动来对抗汉堡王，万一汉堡王抢先和迪士尼联名了怎么办，那还怎么睡得好？虽然靠搞促销也能把生意做得红火，但我还是喜欢不靠低价促销就能卖得好的产品。麦当劳是一家很棒的企业，但这门生意不如可口可乐好。当然，比可口可乐好的生意几乎没有。快餐行业是一个非常好的行业，

---

40. Gillette：吉列，美国剃须护理品牌，创办于 1901 年，为宝洁旗下品牌，后文的速锋 3 是吉列的一款剃须刀产品。

Dairy Queen. We bought Dairy Queen here a while back. That is why I am plugging it shamelessly here.

Question 16: What do you think about the utility industry?

Buffett: I have thought about that a lot because you can put big money in it. I have even thought of buying the entire businesses. There is a fellow in Omaha actually that has done a little of that through Cal Energy. But I don't quite understand the game in terms of how it is going to develop with deregulation. I can see how it destroys a lot of value through the high cost producer once they are not protected by a monopoly territory.

I don't for sure see who benefits and how much. Obviously the guy with very low cost power or some guy that has got hydro-power at two cents a kilowatt has a huge advantage. But how much of that he's gonna get to keep everything or how extensively he can send that outside his natural territory. I haven't been able to figure that out with a sieve so that I really think I know what the industry will look like in ten years. But it is something I think about and if I ever develop any insights that call for action, I will act on them, because I think I can understand the attractiveness of the product. All the aspects of certainty of users need and the fact it is a bargain and all of that. I understand. I just don't understand who is going to make the money in ten years from now on. And that keeps me away.

Question 17: Why do large caps overperform small caps?

Buffett: We don't care if a company is large cap, small cap, middle cap, micro cap. It doesn't make any difference. The only questions else is:

· Can we understand the business?

· Do we like the people running it?

· And does it sell for a price that is attractive?

From my personal standpoint running Berkshire now because we've got, pro forma for Gen. Re or we have maybe $75 to $80 billion to invest in and I

如果要从中挑一家公司，我会选 DQ 冰淇淋。我们不久前买入了 DQ 冰淇淋，这就是为什么我厚着脸皮在这里给它做宣传。

问题十六：您怎么看待公用事业行业？

巴菲特：关于这个问题我想了很多，因为这个行业可以投入大笔资金。我甚至想过对公用事业公司来个整体收购。其实在奥马哈，有个人通过卡尔能源初步做到了类似的事。但我还没弄明白，随着管制的放松，这个行业的游戏将会有什么样的发展。可以预见的是，高成本生产商一旦失去了垄断的保护，就将遭受巨大的价值损失。

我不确定谁会从中受益，又能受益多少。显然，能源生产成本低的生产商，水电发电成本低至每千瓦时 2 美分的那帮人，有着巨大的优势。但是这种优势能持续多少年？其市场又能扩张到什么程度？我还没有完全摸清这些问题，也没有什么工具能帮助我预测这个行业在十年后的状态。但我会继续考虑，如果想通了，到了该采取行动的时候，我就会采取行动，因为我觉得这个产品确实颇有吸引力。用户的需求是确定的，这个行业的价格现在又很便宜，很多特质都很吸引我。我能看懂这些。我只是没弄明白未来十年会赚到钱的是哪家公司，所以暂时还没有在这方面投资。

问题十七：为什么大盘股比小盘股表现好？

巴菲特：一家公司是大盘股还是小盘股，是中盘股还是微盘股，我们都不关心。这种分类没有任何意义。唯一的问题是：

- 我们能弄懂公司业务吗？
- 我们欣赏公司的管理者吗？
- 当前的价格是否有吸引力？

从我这个伯克希尔经营者的角度来说，考虑到通用再保险公司的预估情况，我

only want to invest in five things, so I am really limited to very big companies. But if I were investing $100,000, I wouldn't care whether something was large cap or small cap or anything. I would just look for businesses I understood. Now, I think, on balance, large cap companies as businesses have done extraordinarily well the last ten years—and way better than people anticipated they would do.

You really have American businesses earning close to 20% on equity. And that is something nobody dreamed of and that is being produced by very large companies in aggregate. So you have had this huge revaluation upward because of lower interest rates and much higher returns on capital. If American business is really a disguised bond that earns 20%, as a 20% coupon is much better than a bond with a 13% coupon. And that has happened with big companies in recent years—whether it is permanent or not is another question. I am skeptical of that. I wouldn't even think about it. Except for questions of how much money we run, I wouldn't even think about the size of the business. See's Candies was a $25 million business when we bought it. If I can find one just like it now, even as big as we are, I would love to buy it. It is the certainty of it that counts.

Question 18: One thing though the last five years is that real estate has been primarily private. How do you think about the securitization of real estate?

Buffett: There has been enormous securitization[41] of the debt too, of real estate. And that is one of the items right now that is really clogging up the capital markets. The mortgage-backed securities are just not moving, in commercial mortgage backed, not residential mortgage backed. But I think you are directing your question at equities probably. The corporate form has been a lousy way to own equities. You have interjected a corporate income tax into something that people individually have been able to own with a single tax, and by having the normal corporate form you get a double taxation in there. You really don't need it and it takes way too much of the return.

们大概有750亿到800亿美元的资金可供投资，而我只想投资5家公司，所以我只投资大公司。但如果投资金额只有10万美元，我不会在意是大盘股还是小盘股，只会寻找能弄懂的公司。现在来看，总的来说，大盘股所代表的公司在过去十年中表现得非常好，业绩远超人们的预期。

美国公司的净资产收益率高达20%。大家做梦也想不到这些大公司的净资产收益率平均下来能有这么高。低利率加上更高的资本回报率，这些公司大幅升值。如果把美国企业当作一种债券，从前收益率是13%，现在是20%，当然更吸引人了。近年来，一些大公司确实做到了，能不能保持下去就另当别论了。我对此表示怀疑。我甚至不会去考虑这种可能性，要不是因为管理的资金量太大，我根本不在乎公司规模。收购喜诗糖果花了2500万美元，如果现在能找到像喜诗一样的公司，即使我们规模已经很大了，我也很乐意买。关键在于投资的确定性。

问题十八：过去五年，房地产主要是私营的，您如何看待房地产证券化？

巴菲特：债务和房地产的高度证券化，是当前资本市场真正的顽疾之一。抵押贷款支持的证券，无论是商业抵押贷款还是非住宅抵押贷款，都难以流通。不过我猜你想问的是资产证券化的问题。以公司的形式持有房地产是一种糟糕的做法。个人持有房地产只要缴单一税，可是通过公司持有，又添了一重企业所得税，成了双重征税。这种做法完全没必要，而且还会大大侵蚀投资回报。

---

41. securitization：*n.* 证券化。

REITs[42] have, in effect, created a conduit so that you don't get the double taxation, but they also generally have fairly high operating expenses. If you get real estate, let's just say you can buy fairly simple types of real estate on an 8% yield, or thereabouts, and you take away close to 1% to 1.5% by the time you count stock options and everything, it is not a terribly attractive way to own real estate. Maybe the only way a guy with a $1,000 or $5,000 can own it but if you have $1 million or $10 million, you are better off owning the real estate properties yourself instead of sticking some intermediary in between who will get a sizable piece of the return for himself. So we have found very little in that field. You will see an announcement in the next couple of weeks that may belie what I am telling you today. I don't want you to think I am double crossing you up here. But generally speaking we have seen very little in that field that gets us excited. People sometimes get very confused about—they will look at some huge land company. I'll take one that won't evoke any emotional reactions on the part of anybody, like Texas Pacific Land Trust, which has been around over 100 years and got a couple of million acres in Texas. And they will sell 1% of their land every year and they will take that as applying everything and come up with some huge value compared to the market value. But that is nonsense if you really own the property. I mean, you can't move. You can't move 50% of the properties or 20% of the properties. It is way worse than an illiquid stock.

So you get these, I think, you get some very silly valuations placed on a lot of real estate companies by people who don't really understand what it is like to own one and try to move large quantities of properties.

REITs have behaved horribly in the market this year as you know and it is not at all inconceivable that they would become a class that would get so unpopular that they would sell at significant discounts from what you could sell the properties for. And they could get interesting as a class and then the question is whether the management would fight you in that process because

房地产投资信托基金（REITs）实际上已经创造了一个避免双重征税的渠道，但其运营费用通常相当高。假设投资相对简单的房地产类型能拿到8%左右的收益率，算上股票期权之类的成本，收益会减少1%～1.5%，这种投资房地产的方式并不怎么吸引人。如果手上只有1000美元或5000美元，只能靠这种方式来投资房地产，那没话说。但如果手上有100万或1000万美元，直接买下房地产会更好，用不着让中间商吃掉相当一部分收益。所以说，我们在房地产领域没发现什么投资的好机会。接下来几周里，你们会看到一则公告，其中的内容可能和我今天所说的相矛盾。希望大家不会觉得我在骗人。但总的来说，我们在这个领域鲜少看到激动人心的机会。大型地产公司的估值有时很令人困惑。我挑一个大家都能冷静看待的公司来举例，得克萨斯太平洋土地信托，这家公司已有百年历史，在得州拥有百万英亩土地。他们每年出售1%的土地，然后据此来为公司名下所有土地估个总价，得出的数字往往远高于其市场价值。然而，真拥有这些地产的话就会知道，这种计算方式是不合理的，因为这些土地实际上无法轻易卖出，尤其不可能一次性卖出50%或20%。在流动性方面，土地比流动性差的股票还要糟糕。

所以你看，有些人对许多房地产公司做出了非常可笑的评估，因为他们并不真正了解拥有房地产公司是什么感觉，不知道想要卖出大批房地产有多难。

REITs今年的市场表现非常糟糕，它们可能变得特别冷门，甚至可能会比其所代表的资产价格更低，这是完全有可能发生的事。到了那个时候，REITs会变得很

---

42. REITs: Real Estate Investment Trusts 的缩写，即房地产投资信托基金，汇集资金投房地产，收益分配给投资者。

they would be giving up their income stream for managing things and their interests might run counter to the shareholders on that. I have always wondered about REITs that say their assets are so wonderful, and they are so cheap and then they (management) go out and sell stock. There is a contradiction in that. They say our stock at $28 is very cheap and then they sell a lot of stock at $28 less an underwriting commission. There is a disconnect there. But it is a field we look at. Charlie and I can understand real estate, and we would be open for very big transactions periodically. If there was a Long-Term Capital Management situation translated to real estate, we would be open to that. The trouble is so many other people would be too ... that it would be unlikely to go at a price that would really get us excited.

Question 19: Do you prefer the down market more?

Buffett: I have got no idea where the market is going to go. I prefer it going down. But my preferences have nothing to do with it. The market knows nothing about my feelings. That is one of the first things you have to learn with a stock. You buy 100 shares of General Motors (GM). Now all of a sudden you have this feeling about General Motors. It goes down, you may be mad at it. You may say, "Well, if it just goes up for what I paid for it, my life will be wonderful again." Or if it goes up, you may say how smart you were and how you and General Motors have this love affair. You have got all these feelings. The stock doesn't know you own it. The stock just sits there; it doesn't care what you paid or the fact that you own it. Any feeling I have about the market is not reciprocated. I mean it is very cold-shouldered we are talking about here.

Practically anybody in this room is more likely to be a net buyer of stocks over the next ten years than they are a net seller, so everyone of you should prefer lower prices. If you are gonna be a net eater of hamburger in the next ten years, you want hamburger to go down unless you are a cattle producer. If you are going to be a buyer of Coca-Cola and you don't own Coke stock, you hope

有吸引力，但问题在于，公司的管理层会不会和股东对着干，因为他们得放弃管理这些资产的收益，会与股东产生利益冲突。我就纳闷了，有些 REITs 的管理层老是说自家公司的资产非常好，被市场低估得厉害，背地里却把股票卖掉。这不是自相矛盾吗？他们一方面说我们的股票才卖 28 美元，被市场严重低估，一方面又以 28 美元的价格大量卖出，而且所得收益中还得扣除承销费。这有点说不过去。不过，这个领域我们确实有关注。我和查理都懂房地产，我们也随时准备来笔大买卖。如果出现那种类似长期资本管理公司的房地产机会，我们当然会有兴趣。但麻烦的是，很多其他人也会有兴趣……所以价格不太可能低到让我们非常动心的程度。

问题十九：您更喜欢低迷的市场吗？

巴菲特：我不知道市场会走向何方。我更喜欢下跌，但我喜欢什么没用，市场不会跟着我的喜好走。搞投资，首先得明白这个道理。比如你们买了 100 股通用汽车的股票，市场才不管你怎么想呢。它跌了，你们可能气得跳脚。你们可能会想："哎呀，只要能涨回到我的买入价，我的生活就又美好起来了。"要是它涨了，你们可能会沾沾自喜，觉得自己真是太有眼光了，觉得自己和通用汽车之间简直是真爱。你会产生各种各样的情绪。可股票不知道你持有它。它就在那儿，并不在乎你花了多少钱或你持有它这件事。我对市场产生的任何情绪都没有得到回应。我的意思是，股票是非常冷酷无情的。

未来十年，在座的各位几乎个个都会是股票的净买入者，不会是净卖出者，所以你们大家应该都盼着股价低一点。如果未来十年要大吃特吃汉堡，你肯定希望汉

the price of Coke goes down. You are looking for it to be on sale this weekend at your supermarket. You want it to be down on the weekends, not up on the weekends when you tend to the supermarket.

The NYSE is one big supermarket of companies. And you are going to be buying stocks, what you want to have happen? You want to have those stocks go down, way down; you will make better buys then. Later on twenty or thirty years from now when you are in a period when you are dissaving, or when your heirs dissave for you, then you may care about higher prices. There is Chapter 8 in Graham's *Intelligent Investor* about the attitude toward stock market fluctuations—that and Chapter 20 on the Margin of Safety are the two most important essays ever written on investing as far as I am concerned. Because when I read Chapter 8 when I was 19, I figured out what I just said is obvious, but I didn't figure it out myself. It was explained to me. I probably would have gone another 100 years and still thought it was good when my stocks were going up. We want things to go down, but I have no idea what the stock market is going to do. I never do and I never will. It is not something I think about at all. When it goes down, I look harder at what I might buy that day because I know there is more likely to be some merchandise there that I can use my money effectively in.

Moderator: Okay, Warren, we will take one more question from the audience ...

Buffett: I will let you pick who get it. You can be the guy ... (laughter)

Question 20: What would you do to live a happier life if you could live over again?

Buffett: This will sound disgusting. The question is, what would I do if I can live over again to have a happier life? What I might do is to select a gene pool[43] where people lived to be 120 or something I came from.

But I have been extraordinarily lucky. I mean, I use this example and I

堡降价，除非你是养牛户。想买但还没有买可口可乐股票的人，肯定希望价格能降下来。周末要去逛超市的人肯定盼着超市的可乐搞促销，而不是涨价。

纽约证券交易所就是一个卖公司的大超市。你们要是准备买股票，会希望看到什么呢？会希望股票下跌，跌得很惨，这样才能捡到便宜。等到二三十年后开始动用储蓄了，或者子孙开始花积蓄了，你才会盼着股价上涨。在格雷厄姆的《聪明的投资者》中，第 8 章讲的是对股市波动应持有的态度，第 20 章讲的是关于安全边际的内容，我觉得这是投资方面最重要的两篇文章。因为我 19 岁那年读了第 8 章，我发现我刚才说的那个道理其实挺直观的，但自己之前没想通，是看了书才明白过来的。要不是看了书，可能再过 100 年，我还觉得股票上涨是好事。我们希望股价下跌，但我不知道股市接下来会怎么走。我从不知道，将来也不会知道。我也完全不考虑这一点。股市跌的时候，更容易找到能让钱花得值的东西，我会更认真地考虑可以买些什么。

主持人：好了，沃伦，接下来是最后一个问题了……

巴菲特：你来挑让谁问吧。你负责选人……（笑）

问题二十：如果能重活一次，你会做什么来让自己过得更幸福？

巴菲特：对这个问题，我的回答可能有点倒人胃口。这个问题是在问，如果我能重活一次，为了过上更幸福的生活，我会怎么做。我可能会挑一挑基因，让自己活到 120 岁。

但我其实是非常幸运的。我有一个例子，接下来我会花一两分钟讲一下，因为

---

43. gene pool：基因库。

will take a minute or two because I think it is worth thinking about a little bit. Let's just assume that it was 24 hours before you were born and a genie[44] came to you and he said, "You look very promising and I have got a big problem. I've got to design the world in which you are going to live in." And he said, "I decided to hell with it. It is too tough; you design it." So you have got twenty-four hours, you figure out what the social rules should be, the economic rules and the governmental rules and you, your kids and their kids will live under those rules.

You say, "I can design anything?" And genie said, "Yeah, you can do it." And you say, "Well, there must be a catch?" He says, "Well, there is a catch." You don't know if you are going to be born black or white, rich or poor, male or female, infirm or able-bodied, bright or retarded. All you know is you are going to take one ball out of a barrel with 5.8 billion (balls). You are going to participate in what I called the ovarian[45] lottery. You're going to get one ball out of there. And that is the most important thing that is ever gonna happen in your life, because that is going to control whether you are born here or in Afghanistan and whether you are born with an IQ of 130 or an IQ of 70. It is going to determine a whole lot. What type of world do you want to design?

I think it is a good way to look at social questions, because not knowing which ball you are going to hit, you are going to want to design a system that is going to provide lots of goods and services because you want people on balance to live well. And you are gonna want it to produce more and more so your kids live better than you do and your grandchildren live better than their parents. But you're also going to want a system, if it does produce lots of goods and services, that does not leave behind a person who accidentally got the wrong ball and is not well wired for this particular system. I am ideally wired for the system I fell into here. I came out and got into something that enables me to allocate capital. Nothing so wonderful about that. If all of us were stranded on

我认为它很发人深思。假设在你出生前 24 小时，一个精灵说："你看起来很有前途，我现在有个大难题，我需要设计你投胎的世界。这实在这太难了，还是你自己来设计吧。"你有 24 小时来制定社会规则、经济规则和政治规则，你和子孙后代将在这些规则下讨生活。

你问："设计成什么样都可以吗？"精灵说："是的，随你的便。"你会说："这里面一定有陷阱吧？"精灵回答："好吧，是有个陷阱。"你不能决定自己投胎成什么样的人，是黑人还是白人，是富人还是穷人，是男性还是女性，是体弱多病还是身强体壮，是聪明还是迟钝。这相当于要从装着 58 亿个球的桶里拿一个球出来。我管这叫作投胎彩票。拿一个球出来，就是你一生中最重要的事情，因为这将决定你出生在美国还是阿富汗，智商是 130 还是 70，会决定太多事情。你们会想设计一个什么样的世界？

我认为这是一个看待社会问题的好方法。既然不知道自己会抽到哪一个球，那就会想要设计一个商品和服务都非常丰富的世界，让所有人都过上好日子。你们会希望社会产出越来越多，让子子孙孙越过越好。同时还会考虑到，万一自己手气太差，拿到的球天生就适应不了这个物质丰盈的世界，那也不能被世界抛弃。我生来就很适合如今这个世界，我生来就有理财天赋，这没什么了不起的。如果所有人都

---

44. genie：*n.* 精灵；（阿拉伯故事中，尤指瓶子或灯里的）杰尼。
45. ovarian：*adj.* 卵巢的；子房的。

a desert island, we all landed there and we were never going to get off of it, the most valuable person there would be the one who could raise the most rice over time. I can say, "I can allocate capital!" You wouldn't be very excited about that. So I am in the right place.

Gates says that if I had been born three million years ago, I would have been some animal's lunch. He says, "You can't run very fast; you can't climb trees; you can't do anything. You would just be chewed up the first day. You are lucky; you were born today." And I am. Getting back, one question you can ask yourself incidentally is that here is this barrel with 5.8 billion balls, everybody in the world, if you could put your ball back, and they took out at random a 100 balls and you had to pick one of those, would you put your ball back in? Now those 100 balls you are going to get out, roughly 5 of them will be American, so there is 95/5. So if you want to be in this country, you will only have 5 balls. Half of them will be women and half will be men. I will let you decide how you will vote on that one. Half of them are going to be below average in intelligence and half are going to be above. Do you want to put your ball in there?

Most of you will not want to put that ball back to get 100. So what you are saying is: I am in the luckiest one percent of the world right now sitting in this room—the top one percent of the world. Well, that is the way I feel. I've been lucky to be born where I was because it was 50 to 1 against me in the United States when I was born. Lucky with parents, lucky with all kinds of things and lucky to be wired in a way that in a market economy, pays off like crazy for me. It doesn't pay off for someone who is absolutely as good a citizen as I am, (by) leading Boy Scout troops, teaching Sunday School or whatever, raising fine families, but it just doesn't happen to be wired in the same way I am. So I have been extremely lucky. So I would like to be lucky again.

And if I'm lucky then the way to do it is to play out the game and do

被困在荒岛上回不来，那最厉害的人就是最会种地的人。我可以说："我会理财！"但没人会搭理我。所以我算是投胎投对地方了。

盖茨说，我要是出生在300万年前，很可能会成为野兽的午餐。他说："你跑得慢，又不会爬树，什么都不会做，生出来就会被吃掉。能出生在现在这个世界，是你走运。"他说得没错。回到刚才的话题上来，你们可以问问自己，一个桶里有58亿个球，每个球都代表世界上一个人，如果给你一个机会，让你把自己的球放回去，重新随机抽取100个球出来，你们再从中挑一个出来作为自己的命运，你们愿意吗？这100个球里，大概有5个是美国球，95∶5。所以，如果想继续做美国人，就得选中那5个球之一，这5个球中一半是女性，一半是男性，你们愿意选什么？其中一半的智力低于平均水平，一半的智力高于平均水平。你们愿意把自己的球放进去吗？

把球放回去，再从100个里重新抽，你们中的大多数人都不愿意。也就是说，在座的各位都承认，自己就是地球人中前百分之一的幸运儿。我也这么想。能出生在美国，我很走运，在那个年代，出生在美国的比例是50∶1。我很幸运，拥有很好的父母，拥有各种各样的东西，拥有理财头脑，还凭借这一点从市场经济中获得了高得离谱的回报。很多人和我一样是个不容置疑的好公民，有的领导童子军，有的周末教书，有的养儿育女，但他们并未得到这样的回报。只是因为他们的天赋不在理财上。所以说，我非常幸运，所以我想再幸运一次。

如果我足够幸运的话，那么我要做的就是享受人生的游戏，从事终身热爱的事

> *If I'm lucky then the way to do it is to play out the game and do something you enjoy all your life and be associated with people you like.*
>
> *如果我足够幸运的话，那么我要做的就是享受人生的游戏，从事终身热爱的事业，和喜欢的人交往。*

something you enjoy all your life and be associated with people you like. I only work with people I like. If I could make $100 million by buying a business with some guy that causes my stomach to churn, I would say no, because I say that is just like marrying for money which is probably not a very good idea in any circumstances. But if you are already rich, it is crazy. I am not going to marry for money. I would really do almost exactly what I have done except I wouldn't have bought the US Air.

Thanks.

业，和喜欢的人交往。我只和喜欢的人共事。哪怕和讨厌的人一起搞投资能赚到 1 亿美元，我也会拒绝，要我说这简直就像是为了钱结婚一样，无论如何也谈不上是好主意。而要是已经很有钱了还做这种事，那简直就是疯了。我不会为了钱结婚的。要是重活一遍，我还是会按照原先的轨迹走，只是不会再买美国航空了。

谢谢大家。

语录 Quotes

- The chains of habit are too light to be felt until they are too heavy to be broken.

  习惯的枷锁先是轻得难以察觉，后来便重得难以打破。

- You already own 100% and you are stuck with it. So you might as well be that person, that somebody else.

  每个人都拥有自己 100% 的股份，而且无法卖出。所以，不如亲自成为那个理想的投资人选。

- But time is the friend of the wonderful business; it is the enemy of the lousy business.

  时间是优秀生意的益友，却是糟糕生意的敌手。

- If you risk something that is important to you for something that is unimportant to you, it just doesn't make any sense.

  为了得到不重要的东西，拿重要的东西去冒险，是毫无意义的。

- The people who are going broke in this situation are just of two types, the ones who know nothing and the ones who know everything.

  如今破产的人只有两种，一种是一无所知的人，一种是无所不知的人。

- I urge you to work in jobs that you love. I think you are out of your mind if you keep taking jobs that you don't like because you think it will look good on your resume.

  我强烈建议大家从事自己喜欢的工作。如果为了简历好看而一直干不喜欢的工作，那真是太糊涂了。

第三章

主动的力量
成功是失败再往前走一步

主动 *Initiative*

The Benefits of Failure and the Importance of Imagination

失败的好处和想象力的重要性

——J. K. 罗琳 2008 年在哈佛大学毕业典礼上的演讲

简介 Profile

J. K. 罗琳
J. K. Rowling

1965年，J. K. 罗琳出生于英国的格温特郡，原名乔安娜·罗琳。罗琳自小学起便非常热爱写作与讲故事，展现出了极强的写作天赋。

1983年，为了精进学业，罗琳开始在英国埃克塞特大学进修法语与古典文学。大学毕业后，罗琳在一次火车旅途中，看到了一位瘦弱、戴着眼镜的黑发小巫师，一直在车窗外对着她微笑。这使她灵感迸发，并以这个小巫师的人物形象为蓝本，创造出了一个11岁小男孩，这就是未来风靡全球的童话人物——哈利·波特。随着"哈利·波特"系列的陆续出版与影视化，罗琳以其丰富的想象力和细腻的文笔为人们编织出了一个充满魔幻色彩的"魔法世界"，而她自己也从一个贫困潦倒、默默无闻的"灰姑娘"，一跃成为尽享尊荣、财产甚至超过英国女王的作家。

在依靠写作获得名利之前，罗琳历经磨难，在年纪尚轻时便踏入一段令她伤痕累累的婚姻。后来几经周折，她带着女儿逃出牢笼，长期靠微薄的救济金维生。这段经历让她对贫穷与失败格外感同身受，因此，罗琳多年来坚持参与社会慈善活动。2020年，她为那些在疫情时期无家可归的人和家庭暴力的受害者捐赠了100万英镑。面对弱势群体，她说："贫穷这种困境，有时会给生命带来无法弥补的摧残。"

2008年，J. K. 罗琳在哈佛大学毕业典礼上，通过回顾自己的人生经历，给哈佛毕业生们分享了自己宝贵的人生经验。她以设想自己毕业时最想知道什么为出发点，讲述了自己的所见所闻与经历过的困苦，告诉大家要坚持梦想、不怕失败，同时也要富有同情心、关爱世界。

演讲 Speech

President Faust, members of the Harvard Corporation and the Board of Overseers, members of the faculty, proud parents, and, above all, graduates.

The first thing I would like to say is "thank you." Not only has Harvard given me an extraordinary honour, but the weeks of fear and nausea I've endured at the thought of giving this commencement address have made me lose weight. A win-win situation! Now all I have to do is take deep breaths, squint at[1] the red banners and convince myself that I am at the world's Largest Gryffindor[2] reunion.

Delivering a commencement address is a great responsibility; or so I thought until I cast my mind back to my own graduation. The commencement speaker that day was the distinguished British philosopher Baroness Mary Warnock[3]. Reflecting on her speech has helped me enormously in writing this one, because it turns out that I can't remember a single word she said. This liberating discovery enables me to proceed without any fear that I might inadvertently influence you to abandon promising careers in business, the law or politics for the giddy[4] delights of becoming a gay[5] wizard.

You see? If all you remember in years to come is the "gay wizard" joke, I've come out ahead of Baroness Mary Warnock. Achievable goals: the first step to self improvement.

Actually, I have wracked my mind and heart for what I ought to say to you

福斯特校长、哈佛大学法学院和监事会成员、教职员工、自豪的家长们,当然还有毕业生们,大家好。

首先,我要说声"谢谢"。这不仅是因为哈佛给我的殊荣,还因为一想到这场毕业典礼演讲,我就又害怕又紧张,一连几周的煎熬让我成功减肥。这真是一个双赢的局面!现在我要做的就是深呼吸,眯起眼睛看红色的横幅,假装是在参加全世界最盛大的格兰芬多聚会。

发表毕业典礼演讲是一项重大的责任,至少在回想起自己的毕业典礼之前,我是这样认为的。那时的毕业典礼演讲嘉宾是杰出的英国哲学家玛丽·沃诺克。回想她的演讲对我撰写这篇演讲大有帮助,因为我发现自己完全不记得她说了什么。这一发现让我释然,让我可以毫无顾虑地继续写下去,而不必担心我会无意中耽误了你们,害你们放弃了商、法、政的大好前程,转而昏了头地想要成为快乐的巫师。

你们明白吗?若干年后,如果你们还能记得巫师的这个笑话,那我就已经胜过玛丽·沃诺克了。设定可实现的目标是自我提升的第一步。

实际上,为了写出今天要说的话,我伤透了脑筋。我问过自己,什么是我希

---

1. squint at: 眯着眼睛看。
2. Gryffindor: 格兰芬多学院,出自 J. K. 罗琳的奇幻小说"哈利·波特"系列,是霍格沃茨四学院之一,象征四大元素之一的火。根据小说的设定,格兰芬多学院始建于 9 世纪,以创办人戈德里克·格兰芬多的名字命名。学院以勇敢为择生条件,培养出了诸如邓布利多校长、哈利·波特及其父母等优秀的巫师和女巫。
3. Baroness Mary Warnock: 玛丽·沃诺克(1924—2019),英国哲学家,毕业于牛津大学,先后任教于牛津大学和剑桥大学。她的研究领域包括道德哲学、教育哲学和心灵哲学,曾被授予"荣誉院士"头衔。其代表作品有《萨特的哲学》《存在主义伦理学》《存在主义》等。
4. giddy: *adj.* 轻率的,激动不已的。
5. gay: 有"快乐的"和"同性恋的"两个意思,这里是罗琳在玩双关。

失败的好处和想象力的重要性　239

today. I have asked myself what I wish I had known at my own graduation, and what important lessons I have learned in the 21 years that has expired between that day and this.

I have come up with two answers. On this wonderful day when we are gathered together to celebrate your academic success, I have decided to talk to you about the benefits of failure. And as you stand on the threshold of what is sometimes called "real life," I want to extol the crucial importance of imagination.

These might seem quixotic[6] or paradoxical choices, but bear with me.

Looking back at the 21-year-old that I was at graduation, is a slightly uncomfortable experience for the 42-year-old that she has become. Half my lifetime ago, I was striking an uneasy balance between the ambition I had for myself, and what those closest to me expected of me.

I was convinced that the only thing I wanted to do, ever, was to write novels. However, my parents, both of whom came from impoverished backgrounds and neither of whom had been to college, took the view that my overactive imagination was an amusing personal quirk[7] that would never pay a mortgage, or secure a pension.

I know that the irony strikes with the force of a cartoon anvil[8], now. But ...

So they hoped that I would take a vocational degree; I wanted to study English Literature. A compromise was reached that in retrospect satisfied nobody, and I went up to study Modern Languages. Hardly had my parents' car rounded the corner at the end of the road than I ditched German and scuttled off down the Classics corridor.

I cannot remember telling my parents that I was studying Classics; they might well have found out for the first time on graduation day. Of all subjects on this planet, I think they would have been hard put to name one less useful than Greek mythology when it came to securing the keys to an executive bathroom.

望自己在毕业典礼上就能知道的，毕业到现在的 21 年里，我又学到了什么重要的教训。

我得出了两个答案。在这个美好的日子里，我们欢聚一堂，庆祝你们学业有成，那就来聊一聊失败的好处吧。而既然你们即将踏入所谓的"现实生活"，我也想强调一下想象力的重要性。

这两点看起来可能有点不切实际，也有点自相矛盾，但请容我细细道来。

对如今 42 岁的我来说，回忆起 21 岁刚毕业的自己，感觉往事略有些不堪回首。前半生，我一直挣扎于自己的抱负和身边人的期望之间，处于难以平衡的状态之中。

我那时候坚信，我这辈子唯一想做的事情就是写小说。然而，我的父母出身贫困，而且都没有上过大学，在他们看来，我那过于活跃的想象力是一种有趣的个人小癖好而已，没法帮我还贷，也给不了养老金的保障。

现在看来，他们都错了，这种对比就像动画片里铁砧砸下来的那一下那么有戏剧性。但是当初……

父母希望我拿到一个职业学位，而我想学英国文学。我们得出了一个折中的方案——我去学现代语言学。如今回想起来，这个方案没能让任何人满意。父母的车刚转过路尽头的拐角，我就放弃德语，报名学习古典文学。

我都想不起来有没有跟我爸妈说过我在学古典文学，他们很可能在毕业典礼那天才知道。如果想要赢得高管专用洗手间的钥匙，在这个星球上的所有学科中，大概很难找出一个比希腊神话更不实用的学科。

---

6. quixotic：*adj.* 不切实际的，异想天开的。
7. quirk：*n.* 怪癖，奇事。
8. anvil：指铁铸的砧板；锻捶金属用的垫座，大多数两头突起。

I would like to make it clear, in parenthesis, that I do not blame my parents for their point of view. There is an expiry date on blaming your parents for steering you in the wrong direction; the moment you are old enough to take the wheel, responsibility lies with you. What is more, I cannot criticise my parents for hoping that I would never experience poverty. They had been poor themselves, and I have since been poor, and I quite agree with them that it is not an ennobling experience. Poverty entails fear, and stress, and sometimes depression; it means a thousand petty humiliations and hardships. Climbing out of poverty by your own efforts, that is something on which to pride yourself, but poverty itself is romanticised only by fools.

What I feared most for myself at your age was not poverty, but failure.

At your age, in spite of a distinct lack of motivation at university, where I had spent far too long in the coffee bar writing stories, and far too little time at lectures, I had a knack for passing examinations, and that, for years, had been the measure of success in my life and that of my peers.

Now I am not dull enough to suppose that because you are young, gifted and well-educated, you have never known hardship or heartbreak, hardship or heartache. Talent and intelligence never yet inoculated anyone against the caprice of the fates, and I do not for a moment suppose that everyone here has enjoyed an existence of unruffled privilege and contentment.

However, the fact that you are graduating from Harvard suggests that you are not very well-acquainted with failure. You might be driven by a fear of failure quite as much as a desire for success. Indeed, your conception of failure might not be too far remove from the average person's idea of success—so high have you already flown.

Ultimately, we all have to decide for ourselves what constitutes failure, but the world is quite eager to give you a set of criteria if you let it. So I think it fair to say that by any conventional measure, a mere seven years after my

顺便澄清一下，我并不会因为意见相左而埋怨父母。父母不可能为孩子的人生航向承担一辈子责任，一旦长大成人，能自己掌舵了，责任就落在了自己的肩上。何况，父母只是盼着我永远不受穷，我不能因此怪罪他们。他们自己有过艰苦的岁月，而我后来也穷过，我完全同意他们的观点——贫穷并不是一种高尚的经历。贫穷意味着恐惧、压力，有时还有抑郁，意味着一千种琐碎的屈辱和艰辛。凭一己之力摆脱贫困，这是值得骄傲的事情，但只有傻子才会把贫穷本身浪漫化。

在你们这个年纪，我最害怕的不是贫穷，而是失败。

像你们这么大的时候，尽管我在大学里没什么进取心，总是待在咖啡馆里写故事，不怎么听课，但考试总能通过，在那些年里，这一直是我和同龄人眼中衡量人生成功的标准。

现在，我不想愚蠢地假设，你们因为年轻、才华横溢、受教育程度高，就没有经历过挑战和心碎，艰难和心痛。在反复无常的命运面前，天赋和智慧从未使任何人幸免于难，我从不认为这里每个人都能享受一帆风顺、称心如意的生活。

然而，哈佛的毕业生大概没怎么尝过失败的滋味。你们可能既害怕失败，又渴望成功。实际上，你们眼中的失败，在普通人眼中可能是成功，毕竟你们的起点太高了。

我们终究都必须自己确定怎样才算失败，但如果愿意听别人的，外界会迫不及

Climbing out of poverty by your own efforts, that is something on which to pride yourself, but poverty itself is romanticised only by fools.

凭一己之力摆脱贫困，这是值得骄傲的事情，但只有傻子才会把贫穷本身浪漫化。

graduation day, I had failed on an epic scale. An exceptionally short-lived marriage had imploded, and I was jobless, a lone parent, and as poor as it is possible to be in modern Britain, without being homeless. The fears that my parents had had for me, and that I had had for myself, had both come to pass, and by every usual standard, I was the biggest failure I knew.

Now, I am not going to stand here and tell you that failure is fun. That period of my life was a dark one, and I had no idea that there was going to be what the press has since represented as a kind of fairy tale resolution. I had no idea then how far the tunnel extended, and for a long time, any light at the end of it was a hope rather than a reality.

So why do I talk about the benefits of failure? Simply because failure meant a stripping away of the inessential. I stopped pretending to myself that I was anything other than what I was, and began to direct all my energy into finishing the only work that mattered to me. Had I really succeeded at anything else, I might never have found the determination to succeed in the one arena where I believed I truly belonged. I was set free, because my greatest fear had been realised, and I was still alive, and I still had a daughter whom I adored, and I had an old typewriter and a big idea. And so rot bottom became the solid foundation on which I rebuilt my life.

You might never fail on the scale I did, but some failure in life is inevitable. It is impossible to live without failing at something, unless you live so cautiously that you might as well not have lived at all—in which case, you fail by default.

Failure gave me an inner security that I had never attained by passing examinations. Failure taught me things about myself that I could have learned no other way. I discovered that I had a strong will, and more discipline than I had suspected; I also found out that I had friends whose value was truly above the price of rubies.

待地给你们一套标准。可以说，以任何传统的标准来看，我毕业仅仅七年就遭遇了史诗级的失败。一段极其短暂的婚姻破裂了，我失业了，成了单亲妈妈，穷到了当代英国的最低限度，好在还没有流落街头。父母的担忧、我自己的担忧，全都应验了。按照世俗的标准来看，我是自己圈子里最彻底的失败者。

现在，我站在这里可不是来告诉你们失败有多好玩的。那是我人生中的灰暗时期，当时根本没料到后来会迎来媒体描绘的那种童话般的结局。我当时不知道这黑暗的隧道还有多长。很长一段时间里，尽头的那点光不过是个希望，不是现实。

那么，为什么我要聊失败的好处呢？简单来说，因为失败帮我摒弃了不重要的东西。我不再对自己装模作样，而是开始将所有精力倾注于唯一重要的工作之中。倘若真的在其他领域取得了成就，我或许永远也不会下定决心，去追寻真正属于我的舞台。我获得了自由，因为我最害怕的事情已经成真了，而我熬过来了。我还有心爱的女儿，还有一台旧打字机和一个宏大的构想。于是，人生的谷底反而成了我重建生活的基石。

你们也许永远不会遇到我那种程度的失败，但人生中总有一些失败是不可避免的。活着就免不了会失败，除非谨慎过头，几乎等于白活。那样的话，就是默认失败了。

失败给了我一种内心的安定感，这是应付考试从未给过我的。失败让我更深入地认识了自己，这是通过别的途径学不到的。我发现自己原来意志坚强，比想象中更加自律，我还发现自己拥有比红宝石更珍贵的友谊。

Talent and intelligence never yet inoculated anyone against the caprice of the fates.

在反复无常的命运面前，天赋和智慧从未使任何人幸免于难。

The knowledge that you have emerged wiser and stronger from setbacks means that you are, ever after, secure in your ability to survive. You will never truly know yourself, or the strength of your relationships, until both have been tested by adversity. Such knowledge is a true gift, for all that it is painfully won, and it has been worth more than any qualification I ever earned.

So given a Time Turner, I would tell my 21-year-old self that personal happiness lies in knowing that life is not a check-list of acquisition or achievement. Your qualifications, your CV, are not your life, though you will meet many people of my age and older who confuse the two. Life is difficult, and complicated, and beyond anyone's total control, and the humility to know that will enable you to survive its vicissitudes[9].

Now you might think that I chose my second theme, the importance of imagination, because of the part it played in rebuilding my life, but that is not wholly so. Though I personally will defend the value of bedtime stories to my last gasp, I have learned to value imagination in a much broader sense. Imagination is not only the uniquely human capacity to envision that which is not, and therefore the fount of all invention and innovation. In its arguably most transformative and revelatory capacity, it is the power that enables us to empathise with humans whose experiences we have never shared.

One of the greatest formative experiences of my life preceded *Harry Potter*, though it informed much of what I subsequently wrote in those books. This revelation came in the form of one of my earliest day jobs. Though I was sloping off to write stories during my lunch hours, I paid the rent in my early 20s by the African research.

There in my little office I read hastily scribbled letters smuggled out of totalitarian regimes[10] by men and women who were risking imprisonment to inform the outside world of what was happening to them. I saw photographs of those who had disappeared without trace sent to me by their desperate families

吃了一堑，便也长了一智，变得更强大，明白这一点，就会对自己往后的生存能力充满信心。不经历磨难，永远不会真正了解自己，真正了解与身边人的情谊。这种认识是一份真正的礼物，尽管它是从痛苦中得来的，但它比我曾经获得的任何资格证书都更宝贵。

　　所以，要是能得到一个时间转换器，我会告诉 21 岁的自己，个人幸福在于领悟到，人生不是一张财产或成就的清单。资历和简历并不代表人生，尽管许多和我同龄或比我年长的人会把这两者混为一谈。你们会遇到许多这样的人。生活艰难而复杂，没人能够完全驾驭，认识到这一点，对生活怀有一颗谦逊的心，就能经受住生活的风风雨雨。

　　说到这里，你们或许认为，我选择第二个主题，即想象力的重要性，是因为它在我重建生活的过程中发挥了重要作用。并不完全是这样。虽然我个人誓死捍卫睡前故事的价值，但我已经学会了从更宽广的视角来珍视想象力。想象力让人类勾勒出并不存在的事物，是人类独有的能力，也是所有发明和创新的源泉。想象力拥有最具变革性和启示性的能力，能够让我们理解和感受那些未曾亲身体验过的生活。

　　我人生中最为重要的成长经历之一早在《哈利·波特》创作前就发生了，它极大地影响了这套书的内容。这份领悟源于早年的一份日常工作。20 岁出头时，尽管我会在午休时间偷偷写故事，但付房租还得靠我在非洲的研究工作。

　　在我那间小办公室里，我阅读了从极权主义政权中偷偷带出的信件。极权国家的人冒着坐牢的风险，告知外面的世界他们那里正在发生的事情。我看到了失踪人口的照片，是绝望的亲朋寄给我的。我读了酷刑受害者的证词，看到了伤情照片。

---

9. vicissitudes：*n.* 变化，变迁。
10. totalitarian regime：极权主义。

and friends. I read the testimony of torture victims and saw pictures of their injuries. I opened handwritten, eye-witness accounts of summary trials and executions, of kidnappings and rapes.

I shall never forget the African torture victim, a young man no older than I was at the time, who had become mentally ill after all he had endured in his homeland. He trembled uncontrollably as he spoke into a video camera about the brutality inflicted upon him. He was a foot taller than I was, and seemed as fragile as a child. I was given the job of escorting him back to the Underground Station afterwards, and this man whose life had been shattered by cruelty took my hand with exquisite courtesy, and wished me future happiness.

Every day, I saw more evidence about the evils humankind will inflict on their fellow humans, to gain or maintain power. I began to have nightmares, literal nightmares, about some of the things I saw, heard and read.

And yet I also learned more about human goodness than I had ever known before.

The power of human empathy, leading to collective action, saves lives, and frees prisoners. Ordinary people, whose personal well-being and security are assured, join together in huge numbers to save people they do not know, and will never meet. My small participation in that process was one of the most humbling and inspiring experiences of my life.

Unlike any other creature on this planet, human beings can learn and understand, without having experienced. They can think themselves into other people's places.

Of course, this is a power, like my brand of fictional magic—that is morally neutral. One might use such an ability to manipulate, or control, just as much as to understand or sympathise.

And many prefer not to exercise their imaginations at all. They choose to remain comfortably within the bounds of their own experience, never troubling

我看到了即决审判和处决、绑架和强奸的目击者的手写记录。

我永远不会忘记一位非洲的酷刑受害者，一个当时还没有我大的年轻男子，他在自己的国家遭受了百般折磨，精神失常。对着摄像机讲述所遭受的暴行时，他控制不住地颤抖。他大约比我高1英尺（约合30.48厘米），看起来脆弱得像个孩子。后来我被指派护送他去地铁站，这个生活因暴行而支离破碎的男人非常有礼貌地和我握手，祝我未来幸福。

一天天过去，越来越多的证据向我表明，人类会为了获得或维持权力而对同胞施加暴行。我开始做噩梦，做真正的噩梦，全都和我的所见所闻有关。

不过，我也对人类之善有了前所未有的认识。

人类同理心的力量可以促成集体行动，拯救生命，解放囚徒。那些个人福祉和安全有所保障的普通人团结起来，拯救素不相识，或许永不会相见的人们。在那项事业中微不足道的参与，成为我生命中最震撼、最鼓舞人心的经历之一。

人类与地球上其他生物都不同，无须亲身经历，即可学习和理解事物。人类能够换位思考。

当然，这种能力就像我笔下虚构的魔法一样，在道德上是中性的，可以用来理解和共情，也有人会用来操控他人。

许多人根本就不愿意发挥想象力。他们选择待在自身经历的舒适区内，从不费

> *I was set free, because my greatest fear had been realised, and I was still alive.*
>
> 我获得了自由，因为我最害怕的事情已经成真了，而我熬过来了。

to wonder how it would feel to have been born other than they are. They can refuse to hear screams or to peer inside cages; they can close their minds and hearts to any suffering that does not touch them personally; they can refuse to know.

I might be tempted to envy people who can live that way, except that I do not think they have any fewer nightmares than I do. Choosing to live in narrow spaces can lead to a form of mental agoraphobia[11], and that brings its own terrors. I think the wilfully unimaginative see more monsters. They are often more afraid.

What is more, those who choose not to empathise may enable real monsters. For without ever committing an act of outright evil ourselves, we collude with it, through our own apathy.

One of the many things I learned at the end of that Classics corridor down which I ventured at the age of 18, in search of something I could not then define, was this, written by the Greek author Plutarch[12]: What we achieve inwardly will change outer reality.

That is an astonishing statement and yet proven a thousand times every day of our lives. It expresses, in part, our inescapable connection with the outside world, the fact that we touch other people's lives simply by existing.

But how much more are you, Harvard graduates of 2008, likely to touch other people's lives? Your intelligence, your capacity for hard work, the education you have earned and received, give you unique status, and unique responsibilities. Even your nationality sets you apart. The great majority of you belong to the world's only remaining superpower. The way you vote, the way you live, the way you protest, the pressure you bring to bear on your government, has an impact way beyond your borders. That is your privilege, and your burden.

If you choose to use your status and influence to raise your voice on

心去想，如果自己活在别人的处境中会怎么样。他们对惨叫充耳不闻，也不愿去探查囚笼中的情形；他们会封闭思想和心灵，将未触及自身的痛苦拒之门外；他们拒绝去了解。

我可能会忍不住羡慕能这样活着的人，但我不认为他们做的噩梦比我少。选择局限于狭小空间里，可能会引发一种精神上的广场恐怖症，而这同样有其自身的恐怖之处。我认为那些刻意回避想象的人会看到更多怪物，往往更害怕。

更重要的是，选择不共情的人可能会催生真正的怪物出现。因为即使不曾亲自作恶，冷漠本身就是与恶共谋。

18岁的我为了寻找当时无法定义的东西，沿着古典文学的长廊探索，学到了很多东西，其中之一便是希腊作家普鲁塔克写的这句话：内心的成就将改变外部的现实。

这个观点挺让人吃惊，但每天都被无数次验证。它在一定程度上点出了我们与外部世界不可避免的联系，那就是，我们的存在本身就会影响他人的生活。

哈佛大学2008届的毕业生们，你们将来可能会对多少人的生活产生影响呢？智慧、辛勤工作的能力以及受到的教育赋予了你们独特的地位和责任。就连国籍也使你们与众不同。你们中的绝大多数人来自世界上仅存的超级大国。投票的方式、生活的方式、抗议的方式、对政府施加的压力，都会产生超越国界的影响。这是一项特权，也是一份责任。

倘若选择利用地位和影响力为没有话语权的人发声；倘若不仅与强者为伍，也

---

11. agoraphobia：广场恐怖症，指对一些特定场所（如广场、密闭空间、公共交通工具等）产生异乎寻常的恐惧或紧张，并出现明显的回避行为。
12. Plutarch：普鲁塔克（约46—约120），古罗马帝国时代的希腊作家、哲学家、历史学家，以其作品《平行列传》（又称《希腊罗马名人传》或《希腊罗马英豪列传》）闻名后世。

behalf of those who have no voice; if you choose to identify not only with the powerful, but with the powerless; if you retain the ability to imagine yourself into the lives of those who do not have your advantages, then it will not only be your proud families who celebrate your existence, but thousands and millions of people whose reality you have helped to change. We do not need magic to transform our world, we carry all the power we need inside ourselves already: We have the power to imagine better.

I am nearly finished. I have one last hope for you, which is something that I already had at 21. The friends with whom I sat on graduation day have been my friends for life. They are my children's godparents, the people to whom I've been able to turn in times of real trouble, people who have been kind enough not to sue me when I've used their names for Death Eaters[13]. At our graduation we were bound by enormous affection, by our shared experience of a time that could never come again, and, of course, by the knowledge that we held certain photographic evidence that would be exceptionally valuable if any of us ran for Prime Minister.

So today, I wish you nothing better than similar friendships. And tomorrow, I hope that even if you remember not a single word of mine, you remember those of Seneca[14], another of those old Romans I met when I fled down the Classics corridor, in retreat from career ladders, in search of ancient wisdom:

As is a tale, so is life: not how long it is, but how good it is, is what matters.

I wish you all very good lives.

Thank you very much.

同情弱者；倘若能够设身处地地为比自己弱势的人着想，那么不仅家人会因你们而骄傲，成千上万的人都会因你们而欢呼，感激你们改变了他们的现实生活。改变世界不需要魔法，力量早已藏于我们的内心：我们有能力去想象更美好的世界。

我快说完了。我对大家还有最后一个期望——希望大家能够拥有我 21 岁时就已经拥有的东西。毕业典礼那天和我坐在一起的朋友成了我一生的挚友。他们是我孩子的教父和教母，是我真正陷入困境时可以求助的人。他们都是好心人，没有因为我用他们的名字命名食死徒而起诉我。毕业的那天，我们难分难舍，因为我们有着深厚的感情，共同度过了一段一去不复返的时光，当然，还因为我们都知道彼此手上有某些照片，万一我们中有人竞选首相，这些照片将价值不菲。

因此，今天我能给你们最好的祝愿，莫过于你们能拥有同样的友谊。未来，我希望，即使你们把我的话全忘了，也能记得塞内加的一句话。我当年没有顺着事业的阶梯向上攀爬，转而与他在古典文学的殿堂相遇，他古老的智慧给了我人生的启迪：

人生就像故事，关键不在于长短，而在于是否精彩。

祝大家都拥有美好的人生。

感谢大家。

---

13. Death Eaters：食死徒，出自 J. K. 罗琳的奇幻小说《哈利·波特》，是该系列小说中伏地魔的党羽起初自称的称号，他们都是黑魔王的支持者和信徒（第一代的食死徒大都是伏地魔的同学），也有一部分是被迫成为的。他们精通黑魔法（部分由伏地魔传授），且左臂皆烙刻有黑魔标记。
14. Seneca：塞内加（约公元前 4—公元 65），古罗马悲剧家。生于罗马帝国行省西班牙，擅长演说，对哲学、伦理道德和自然科学都有研究和著作，是古罗马斯多葛派的代表人物之一。

语录 | Quotes

- Achievable goals: the first step to self improvement.
  设定可实现的目标是自我提升的第一步。

- Climbing out of poverty by your own efforts, that is something on which to pride yourself, but poverty itself is romanticised only by fools.
  凭一己之力摆脱贫困，这是值得骄傲的事情，但只有傻子才会把贫穷本身浪漫化。

- Talent and intelligence never yet inoculated anyone against the caprice of the fates.
  在反复无常的命运面前，天赋和智慧从未使任何人幸免于难。

- I was set free, because my greatest fear had been realised, and I was still alive.
  我获得了自由，因为我最害怕的事情已经成真了，而我熬过来了。

- You will never truly know yourself, or the strength of your relationships, until both have been tested by adversity.
  不经历磨难，永远不会真正了解自己，真正了解与身边人的情谊。

- Personal happiness lies in knowing that life is not a check-list of acquisition or achievement.
  个人幸福在于领悟到，人生不是一张财产或成就的清单。

- Without ever committing an act of outright evil ourselves, we collude with it, through our own apathy.
  即使不曾亲自作恶，冷漠本身就是与恶共谋。

Learn from Your Failures
在失败中成长
——奥普拉·温弗瑞 2013 年在哈佛大学毕业典礼上的演讲

简介 Profile

奥普拉·温弗瑞
Oprah Winfrey

　　1954 年，奥普拉·温弗瑞出生于美国密西西比州。父母离婚后，将年幼的她扔给外祖母照顾。温弗瑞的童年和青少年时期过得并不顺利。亲戚的侮辱、与母亲的不和使温弗瑞误入歧途，抽烟、吸毒、酗酒，她的生命浸泡在肮脏的大染缸里，几乎看不到任何未来的希望。就在这种情况下，温弗瑞的父亲拯救了她。14 岁时，温弗瑞住进父亲家，父亲与继母为温弗瑞制定了教育大纲，引导这个叛逆的女孩成长。在爱和教育中得到滋养的温弗瑞从此改头换面，而且还在费城举行的有 1 万名会员参加的校园俱乐部演讲比赛中，凭借一篇短小震撼的演讲《黑人·宪法·美国》拔得头筹，赢得 1000 美元的奖学金。

　　从此之后，温弗瑞找到了自己真正热爱的领域，开启了靠"铁嘴"功夫名声大噪的事业之旅。在天赋的加持与不懈的努力下，温弗瑞进入了美国知名的广播公司工作。1977 年，她主持了《人们在说话》脱口秀，收视率之火爆甚至打败了当年脱口秀名嘴菲尔·当纳的节目。随后，美国广播公司（ABC）芝加哥分部 WLS 电视台也邀请温弗瑞来主持一个名为《芝加哥早晨》的节目。仅在一个月的时间里，《芝加哥早晨》便成为家喻户晓的节目，而仅仅 30 岁出头的温弗瑞也因此成为人们心中无可争议的"脱口秀女皇"。美国《名利场》杂志评价她说："在大众文化中，她的影响力，除教皇外，可能比任何大学教授、政治家或者宗教领袖都大。"

　　2013 年，奥普拉·温弗瑞在哈佛大学的毕业典礼上告诉毕业生们要乐于接受挫折，视之为成长的契机。她还告诉毕业生们，遭遇困境在所难免，但你想创造的人生故事会带你走出低谷。

演讲 Speech

扫描二维码
获取本篇演讲原视频、音频

Oh my goodness! I'm at Haaaaaarvard! Wow! To President Faust, my fellow honorands[1]—Carl[2], that was so beautiful, thank you so much—and James Rothenberg, Stephanie Wilson, Harvard faculty, with a special bow to my friend Dr. Henry Louis Gates. All of you alumni, with a special bow to the class of '88, your $115 million.

And to you, members of the Harvard Class of 2013! Hello!

I thank you for allowing me to be a part of the conclusion of this chapter of your lives and the commencement of your next chapter. To say that I'm honored doesn't even begin to quantify the depth of gratitude that really accompanies an honorary doctorate from Harvard. Not too many little girls from rural Mississippi have made it all the way here to Cambridge[3]. And I can tell you that I consider today as I sat on the stage this morning getting teary for you all and then teary for myself, uh—I consider today a defining milestone in a very long and a blessed journey.

My one hope today is that I can be a source of some inspiration. I'm going to address my remarks to anybody who's ever felt inferior or felt disadvantaged, felt screwed by life; this is a speech for the Quad[4].

Actually, I was so honored I wanted to do something really special for you. I wanted to be able to have you look under your seats and there would be free Master and Doctor Degrees, but I see you got that covered already.

哦，天哪，我竟然在哈——佛！哇哦！福斯特校长，与我一同获得哈佛荣誉学位的各位——卡尔，这太美妙了，非常感谢你——还有詹姆斯·罗滕伯格、斯特凡妮·威尔逊、哈佛大学全体教员，特别要感谢我的朋友亨利·路易斯·盖茨博士。感谢所有的校友，特别要感谢1988届校友，感谢你们1.15亿美元的捐款。

还有你们，哈佛大学2013届毕业生，大家好！

感谢你们在人生的一个篇章即将结束之时，以及下一篇章即将开启之际，能让我参与其中。哈佛授予我荣誉学位，我想说我深感荣幸，但这不足以表达我内心深处的感激之情。能从密西西比的农村一路走到坎布里奇的小女孩并不多，我可以告诉你们，当我今天早晨坐在这个讲台上为你们所有人和我自己热泪盈眶的时候，我觉得今天是我漫长而幸运的人生旅途中的一个里程碑。

今天，我有一个心愿，就是希望能带给你们一些鼓舞。我将要说的这些话献给所有曾感到自卑、觉得自己处于弱势或者生活犹如一团乱麻的人；这是一场献给拉德克利夫学院的学生们的演讲。

说实话，我深感荣幸，所以我想为你们做一些真正特别的事情。我本想跟你们说，请看看你们自己的座位下面，那里为你们准备了免费的硕士或者博士学位证书，但我知道你们已经不缺这个了。

---

1. honorand：*n.* 获得名誉学位的人；受奖（或励）者。
2. Carl：指卡尔·穆勒（Carl Muller），哈佛大学校友会主席。
3. Cambridge：坎布里奇，美国马萨诸塞州东部城市，旧译剑桥，哈佛大学所在地。
4. Quad：此处指 Radcliffe Quadrangle，即以前的拉德克利夫学院，该学院于1999年被整合到哈佛大学。哈佛大学共有两所本科生院，即拉德克利夫学院与哈佛学院。从地理位置上看，拉德克利夫学院距离哈佛大学校园中心较远，因此有些学生认为该学院的学生比其他学院的学生地位更低（inferior）。奥普拉说这句话是为了呼应前句"我将要说的这些话献给所有曾感到自卑、觉得自己处于弱势或者生活犹如一团乱麻的人"。

I will be honest with you. I felt a lot of pressure over the past few weeks to come up with something that I could share with you that you hadn't heard before, because after all, you all went to Harvard; I did not. But then I realized that you don't have to necessarily go to Harvard to have a driven, obsessive Type A personality. But it helps. And while I may not have graduated from here, I admit that my personality is about as Harvard as they come.

You know my television career began unexpectedly. As you heard this morning, I was in the Miss Fire Prevention Contest. That was when I was 16 years old in Nashville, Tennessee, and you had the requirement of having to have red hair in order to win up, until the year that I entered. So they were doing the question-and-answer period because I knew I wasn't going to win under the swimsuit competition. So during the question-and-answer period, the question came: "Why, young lady, what would you like to be when you grow up?" And by the time they got to me, all the good answers were gone. So I had seen Barbara Walters on the *Today* show that morning, so I answered, "I would like to be a journalist. I would like to tell other people's stories in a way that makes a difference in their lives and the world." And as those words were coming out of my mouth, I went: "Whoa! This is pretty good! I would like to be a journalist. I want to make a difference."

Well, I was on television by the time I was 19 years old. And in 1986, I launched my own television show with a relentless[5] determination to succeed at first. I was nervous about the competition, and then I became my own competition, raising the bar every year, pushing, pushing, pushing myself as hard as I knew. Sound familiar to anybody here? Eventually, we did make it to the top, and we stayed there for 25 years. The *Oprah Winfrey Show* was number one in our time slot[6] for 21 years, and I have to tell you, I became pretty comfortable with that level of success.

But a few years ago, I decided, as you will at some point, that it was time

我可以坦诚地告诉你们，在过去几个星期里，我感受到了巨大的压力，我想和你们分享一些你们从来没有听过的东西，毕竟你们都上了哈佛，而我没有。不过后来我意识到，要想具备进取心的、强势的 A 型人格，并不一定得上哈佛，但能上哈佛还是有所帮助的。我虽然不是从这里毕业的，但我认为自己的性格特征跟哈佛培养出来的差不多。

　　你们都知道，我的电视事业是不期而至的。正如你们今天早上听到的，我曾经参加过"防火小姐大赛"。那时我 16 岁，在田纳西州的纳什维尔，要想赢得最后的比赛必须得是红头发，直到我参加的那年还是这样。我知道自己在泳装比赛中不会获胜。在问答环节中，他们问的问题是："嗨，小姑娘，你长大后想做什么呀？"轮到我回答时，所有好答案都被说完了。那天早上我正好看了芭芭拉·沃尔特斯的《今日秀》，于是我答道："我想成为一名新闻工作者，我要把人们的故事以某种方式讲出来，从而影响他们的生活，改变这个世界。"当这些话从我嘴里说出来的时候，我就想："哇！挺好的呀！我想要成为一名新闻工作者，我想要有所成就。"

　　后来，我 19 岁时上了电视。1986 年，我推出了自己的电视节目，并且一开始就下定决心，一定要不屈不挠，取得成功。我曾经对竞争感到紧张不安，后来我的竞争对手变成了我自己，我逐年提高对自己的要求，不断鞭策自己，用尽全力地鞭策自己。在座的各位有没有人听着耳熟的？终于，我们攀上了巅峰，而且保持了 25 年之久。《奥普拉脱口秀》的收视率连续 21 年排在同时段播出的电视节目的首位，我得告诉你们，对这样的成功我感到特别满足。

　　但是几年前，我决定是时候重新权衡了，去寻找新版图，实现新突破，正如你

> *Failure is just life trying to move us in another direction.*
>
> 失败只是生活试图让你转换前进的方向罢了。

---

5. relentless：*adj.* 不间断的，持续的；不屈不挠的。
6. slot：*n.*（时间表中的）位置。

to recalculate, find new territory, break new ground. So I ended the show and launched OWN: The Oprah Winfrey Network. The initials just worked out for me.

So, one year later, after launching OWN, nearly every media outlet had proclaimed that my new venture was a flop[7]. Not just a flop, but a big bold flop they call it. I can still remember the day I opened up *USA Today* and read the headline "Oprah, not quite standing on her OWN." I mean, really, *USA Today*? Now that's the nice newspaper! It really was this time last year the worst period in my professional life. I was stressed, and I was frustrated, and, quite frankly, I was actually … I was embarrassed.

It was right around that time that President Faust called and asked me to speak here, and I thought: "You want me to speak to Harvard graduates? What I … what could I possibly say to Harvard graduates—some of the most successful graduates in the world—in the very moment when I had stopped succeeding?"

So I got off the phone with President Faust, and I went to the shower. It was either that or a bag of Oreos. So I chose the shower. And I was in the shower for a long time, and as I was in the shower, the words of an old hymn came to me. You may not know it. It's "By and By When the Morning Comes." And I started thinking about when the morning might come because at the time I thought I was stuck in a hole. And the words came to me—"Trouble doesn't last always"—from that hymn. "This too shall pass," and I thought, as I got out of the shower. "I am gonna turn this thing around, and I would be better for it. And when I do, I'm going to go to Harvard, and I'm going to speak the truth of it!" So I'm here today to tell you I have turned that network around!

And it was all because I wanted to do it by the time I got to speak to you all, so thank you so much. You don't know what motivation you were for me, thank you. I'm even prouder to share a fundamental truth that you might not

们在某个时间点也会如此。于是我停播《奥普拉脱口秀》，推出了奥普拉·温弗瑞电视网，首字母缩写正好是"OWN"（自己）。

　　OWN 推出一年后，几乎每一家媒体都宣布我的新事业彻底失败了。用它们的话来说，不仅仅是"彻底失败"，简直是"一败涂地"。我依然能够记得，有一天我翻开《今日美国》，看到了一个大标题：《奥普拉：自立门户难成事》。我想，这是真的吗？《今日美国》？这可是份好报纸啊！去年的这个时候，真的是我职业生涯的低谷。我倍感压力，也十分沮丧，而且说实话，我也真的觉得很难堪。

　　就是在那个时候，福斯特校长给我打电话，邀请我来这里演讲，当时我想："你想让我去给哈佛大学的毕业生演讲？哈佛大学的毕业生可以跻身全世界最成功的毕业生之列，我能给他们讲些什么呢？而且还恰逢我不再成功的时候？"

　　挂掉福斯特校长的电话，我去冲了个澡。那个时候我要么去冲澡，要么吃一袋奥利奥饼干，所以我选择了冲澡。我冲了很久，在冲的时候，一首古老的圣歌闪过我的脑海。你们也许没听过，这首歌叫作《耐心等待曙光到来》。于是，我开始思考曙光何时才能到来，因为那时我觉得自己被困在了一个洞里。然后，我又想起了那首歌中的一句歌词"困难不会永存"。冲完澡出来我就想："我现在遇到的困难同样也会过去，我会扭转这件事情的局面，我会好起来的。等我做到了，我就要去哈佛大学，把这个真实的故事讲给大家听！"所以今天我来到了这里，告诉你们我已经扭转了那个电视网的困局！

　　我能做到这一点，完全是因为我希望自己在给你们所有人演讲前能做到这一点，所以非常感谢大家。你们不知道你们给了我多大的动力，谢谢你们！我甚至能更加

Trouble doesn't last always.

困难不会永存。

---

7. flop：*n.* [美口] 彻底的失败。

在失败中成长　263

have learned even as graduates of Harvard, unless you studied the ancient Greek hero with Professor Nagy. Professor Nagy, as we were coming in this morning, said, "Please, Ms. Winfrey, walk decisively."

I shall walk decisively. This is what I want to share. It doesn't matter how far you might rise. At some point, you are bound to stumble because if you're constantly doing what we do: raising the bar. If you're constantly pushing yourself higher, higher, the law of averages—not to mention the myth of Icarus[8]—predicts that you will at some point fall. And when you do, I want you to know this, remember this: There is no such thing as failure. Failure is just life trying to move us in another direction. Now, when you're down there in the hole, it looks like failure. So this past year I had to spoon-feed[9] those words to myself.

And when you're down in the hole, when that moment comes, it's really okay to feel bad for a little while. Give yourself time to mourn what you think you may have lost, but then here's the key: Learn from every mistake, because every experience, encounter and particularly your mistakes are there to teach you and force you into being more of who you are. And then figure out what is the next right move.

And the key to life is to develop an internal moral, emotional GPS that can tell you which way to go, because now and forever more when you Google yourself, your search results will read "Harvard, 2013." And in a very competitive world, that really is a calling card, 'cause I can tell you as one who employs a lot of people, when I see "Harvard," I sit up a little straighter and say: "Where is he or she? Bring them in." It's an impressive calling card that can lead to even more impressive bullets in the years ahead: lawyer, senator, CEO, scientist, physicist, winners of Nobel and Pulitzer Prizes, or late-night talk show host. But the challenge of life, I have found, is to build a resume that doesn't simply tell a story about what you want to be, but it's a story about who

自豪地与你们分享一个基本真理，即使你们是哈佛大学的毕业生，可能也不曾听说过这个真理，除非你们上过纳吉教授关于古希腊英雄的课。今天早上我们过来的时候，纳吉教授说："温弗瑞女士，请坚定前行。"

应当坚定地向前走，这就是我想要和你们分享的。无论你取得怎样的成就，到一定时候，你必然还是会跌倒，因为你会不断地做着我们现在正在做的事情：不断提高标准。如果你总是要求自己更进一步、更好一点，根据平均法则，可以预测你在某个时候注定会跌倒一次，就更不用提伊卡洛斯的神话了。当你跌倒时，我想让你了解并且记住这一点：世间并没有"失败"这回事。失败只是生活试图让你转换前进的方向罢了。现在，当你身处谷底、陷入困境，那只不过是看起来像失败而已。在过去的这一年里，我不得不给自己灌输这些话。

当你们身处谷底、陷入困境时，当那种时刻来临时，暂时的难过完全无妨。给自己一些时间，去为你认为自己可能已经失去的东西默哀，但这之后才是关键：要从每一次错误中吸取教训，因为你的每一次经历、遭遇，尤其是你犯下的错误，都将引导和促使你更好地实现自我。然后，再想清楚接下来该做什么。

人生的关键是建立起一种内在的道德上和情感上的 GPS，它会指引你前进的道路。因为不管是现在还是更远的将来，当你们在谷歌上搜索自己，搜索结果都会显示"哈佛大学 2013 届毕业生"。在这个竞争激烈的世界，这真的就是一张名片。我雇用过许多人，所以我可以告诉你们，当我看到"哈佛"二字时，我总会坐直一点才说："他/她在哪儿？请他们进来吧。"这是一张令人印象深刻的名片，在未来的日子里，这张名片会印上更加令人钦佩的头衔：律师、议员、首席执行官、科学家、物理学家、诺贝尔奖和普利策奖得主或深夜脱口秀节目主持人。然而我意识到，人

---

8. Icarus：伊卡洛斯，希腊神话中的人物，巧匠代达洛斯之子，与其父双双以蜡翼粘身飞离克里特岛，因飞得太高，蜡被阳光融化，坠入爱琴海而死。
9. spoon-feed：*v.* 填鸭式灌输。

you want to be. It's a resume that doesn't just tell a story about what you want to accomplish but why. A story that's not just a collection of titles and positions but a story that's really about your purpose. Because when you inevitably stumble and find yourself stuck in a hole, that is the story that will get you out.

What is your true calling? What is your dharma[10]? What is your purpose?

For me that discovery came in 1994 when I interviewed a little girl who had decided to collect pocket change in order to help other people in need. She raised a thousand dollars all by herself, and I thought, "Well, if that little 9-year-old girl with a bucket and big heart could do that, I wonder what I could do?" So I asked for our viewers to take up their own change collection, and in one month, just from pennies and nickels and dimes, we raised more than $3 million that we used to send one student from every state in the United States to college. That was the beginning of the Angel Network.

And so what I did was, I simply asked our viewers: "Do what you can wherever you are, from wherever you sit in life. Give me your time or your talent, your money if you have it." And they did. Extend yourself in kindness to other human beings wherever you can. And together, we built 55 schools in 12 different countries and restored nearly 300 homes that were devastated by hurricanes Rita and Katrina.

So the Angel Network—I have been on the air for a long time—but it was the Angel Network that actually focused my internal GPS. It helped me to decide that I wasn't just going to be on TV every day but that the goal of my shows, my interviews, my business, my philanthropy[11], all of it, whatever ventures I might pursue, would be to make clear that what unites us is ultimately far more redeeming[12] and compelling than anything that separates me. Because what had become clear to me—and I want you to know it isn't always clear in the beginning, because as I said, I'd been on television since I was 19 years old, but around '94, I got really clear. So don't expect the clarity

生的挑战在于编写这样一份履历：它不是简单地告诉别人你想从事什么职业，而是要讲清楚你想成为怎样的人；它介绍的不仅仅是你想有何成就，还有你为什么想有如此成就；它不是简单地罗列你的各种头衔和职位，而是要清楚地表明你的目标。因为我们难免会跌倒，会身陷困境，而这样一份人生履历将会令你摆脱困境。

你真正的向往是什么？你的处世哲学是什么？你的目标是什么？

对我而言，发现这一切是在 1994 年，我采访了一个小女孩，她决定筹集零花钱去帮助其他有需要的人。她凭借一己之力筹集到了 1000 美元。于是我想："如果那位 9 岁的小女孩可以靠着一个桶和一颗善心做成这件事，那么我能做点什么呢？"于是，我呼吁观看我们节目的观众捐出他们自己的零用钱。一个月的时间里，我们就是这样一角一分一厘地筹集到了 300 多万美元。我们从美国各个州分别挑选出一名学生，用这笔钱资助他们上大学。"天使网络"就是这样诞生的。

而我所做的就是简单地向我们的观众呼吁："无论你们身在何方，无论你们处境如何，请献出你们力所能及的时间、才智或者金钱。"他们这样做了。无论你在哪里，把你的善意传递给其他人。我们一起在 12 个不同的国家建立了 55 所学校，重建了近 300 个被丽塔和卡特里娜飓风摧毁的家园。

我做电视节目很久了，但正是"天使网络"令我的内在定位系统真正得以明确。它帮助我做了一个决定，那就是我不仅仅只是每天出现在电视上就可以了，我做脱口秀节目、做采访、做生意和做慈善，所有这一切，不论我是否追逐利益，目标都是要明确一点，那就是将我们凝聚在一起的事情远比将我孤立开来的事情更为可取、更令人信服。我自己已经弄清楚了，所以我想让你们也知道，事情并不总是在一开始就能明朗的，正如我所说的，我从 19 岁开始上电视，但直到 1994 年我才真正明了。所以，别指望一下子就能看透，也别指望立即就能明确你的目标。然而，我清

---

10. dharma：*n.* 法则；教规。
11. philanthropy：*n.* 慈善事业。
12. redeeming：*adj.* 可以弥补欠缺的；起补偿作用的。

to come all at once, to know your purpose right away. But what became clear to me was that I was here on earth to use television and not be used by it, to use television to illuminate the transcendent[13] power of our better angels.

So this Angel Network, it didn't just change the lives of those who were helped but the lives of those who also did the helping. It reminded us that no matter who we are or what we look like or what we may believe, it is both possible and, more importantly, it becomes powerful to come together in common purpose and common effort.

I saw something on the Bill Moyers show recently that so reminded me of this point. It was an interview with David and Francine Wheeler. They lost their 7-year-old son, Ben, in the Sandy Hook tragedy[14]. And even though gun safety legislation to strengthen background checks had just been voted down in Congress the time they were doing this interview, they talked about how they refused to be discouraged. Francine said this, she said: "Our hearts are broken, but our spirits are not. I'm gonna tell them what it's like to find a conversation about change, that is love, and I'm gonna do that without fighting them." And then her husband, David, added this: "You simply cannot demonize[15] or vilify[16] someone who doesn't agree with you, because the minute you do that, your discussion is over. And we cannot do that any longer. The problem is too enormous. There has to be some way that this darkness can be banished with light."

In our political system and in the media, we often see the reflection of a country that is polarized[17], that is paralyzed and is self-interested. And yet, I know you know the truth. We all know that we are better than the cynicism and the pessimism[18] that is regurgitated[19] throughout Washington and the 24-hour cable news cycle. Not my channel, by the way. We understand that the vast majority of people in this country believe in stronger background checks because they realize that we can uphold the Second Amendment, and also

楚自己来到这个世界上是要利用电视，而不是被电视利用，我要利用电视来展示我们更好的天使的神奇力量。

所以这个"天使网络"不仅仅改变了受助者的生活，也改变了那些提供帮助的人们的生活。它提醒我们，无论我们是谁，无论我们长相如何，也无论我们信仰什么，都有可能为了共同的目标走到一起，共同努力，而更重要的是，这样我们也会变得强大。

我最近在比尔·莫耶斯的节目中看到了一些东西，再次提醒了我这一点。那是对戴维·惠勒和弗朗辛·惠勒夫妇的一次访谈。在"桑迪·胡克惨案"中，他们失去了7岁的儿子本。他们在接受这次访谈时，国会刚刚投票否决了关于加强（枪支持有者）背景调查的枪支安全立法提案，但即便如此，他们仍说自己不会因此受到打击。弗朗辛是这么说的："我们的心碎了，但精神没有垮掉。我要告诉他们，如果我们要进行一个关于改变的对话，那就是爱。我会去做那件事，但不会与他们做斗争。"然后，她的丈夫戴维补充说："你不能随随便便地就妖魔化或者诋毁一个与你意见不合的人，因为在你那么做的时候，你们的对话就结束了。我们不能再这么做了，问题已经很严重，必须想办法让光明驱走黑暗。"

在我们的政治体系和新闻媒体中，我们常常看到对这个国家的评价：两极分化、瘫痪无能和自私自利。然而，我知道你们清楚真相是什么。我们都清楚，相比华盛顿和24小时滚动播出的电视新闻中涌动的愤世嫉俗和悲观主义，我们实际上要好得多。顺便说一句，这不是我的电视频道。我们清楚，这个国家的绝大多数人都支持开展更为严格的背景调查，因为他们意识到，我们可以支持宪法第二修正案，而且

---

13. transcendent：*adj.*［正式］超越一般范畴的；超然的。
14. Sandy Hook tragedy：桑迪·胡克惨案，指2012年12月发生在美国康涅狄格州费尔菲尔德县纽镇桑迪·胡克小学的枪击案，造成28人死亡，是美国历史上死亡人数第二多的校园枪击案。
15. demonize：*vt.* 使成为魔鬼；使似魔鬼。
16. vilify：*vt.* 污蔑，诋毁。
17. polarize：*vt.* 使两极分化，使分化。
18. pessimism：*n.* 悲观；悲观主义。
19. regurgitate：*vt.* 涌动。

reduce the violence that is robbing us of our children. They don't have to be incompatible[20].

And we understand that most Americans believe in a clear path to citizenship for the 12 million undocumented immigrants who reside in this country because it's possible to both enforce our laws and at the same time embrace the words on the Statue of Liberty that have welcomed generations of huddled masses to our shores. WE CAN DO BOTH.

And we understand—I know you do 'cause you went to Harvard—that people from both parties and no party believe that indigent[21] mothers and families should have access to healthy food and a roof over their heads and a strong public education because here, in the richest nation on Earth, we can afford a basic level of security and opportunity. So the question is: What are we going to do about it? Really, what are you going to do about it?

Maybe you agree with these beliefs. Maybe you don't. Maybe you care about these issues, and maybe there are other challenges that YOU, Class of 2013, are passionate about. Maybe you want to make a difference by serving in government. Maybe you want to launch your own television show. Or maybe you simply want to collect some change. Your parents would appreciate that about now. The point is your generation is charged with this task of breaking through what the body politic has thus far made impervious[22] to change.

Each of you has been blessed with this enormous opportunity of attending this prestigious school. You now have a chance to better your life, the lives of your neighbors and also the life of our country. When you do that, let me tell you what I know for sure: That's when your story gets really good.

Maya Angelou always says: "When you learn, teach. When you get, give. That, my friends, is what gives your story purpose and meaning." So you all have the power in your own way to develop your own Angel Network, and, in doing so, your class will be armed with more tools of influence and

也可以减少夺走我们孩子生命的暴力行为，两者并不矛盾。

我们知道，大多数美国人都相信，对于居住在这个国家的 1200 万无合法身份的移民而言，总会有一条明确的途径使他们成为公民。因为在执行法律的同时，我们也能践行镌刻在自由女神像上的话：欢迎芸芸众生世世代代来到我们的海岸。这两者，我们都能做到。

我们了解，我知道你们也了解，因为你们是哈佛大学的学生，来自两党和无党派的人都相信，贫困的母亲和家庭理应享有健康的食品、获得容身之所，并受到健全的公共教育，因为在这个地球上最富有的国度里，我们有能力提供最基本的安全和机遇保障。然而问题也随之而来：对此我们有何打算？说真的，你们打算为此做些什么呢？

你们也许赞同这些理念，也许持有异议。你们也许对这些问题很上心，也许其他的挑战才是你们 2013 届哈佛毕业生所热衷的。也许你想通过在政府工作来让这个社会有一些改变，也许你想推出自己的电视节目，又或许你仅仅只是想去筹集一些零用钱。你们的父母都会赞许你们现在所做的事情。关键在于，你们这一代人肩负着这样一种使命：打破这个国家迄今所造成的难以改变的现状。

你们每一个人都已经被赋予了上这所名校的巨大机会。现在你们有机会改善你们的生活，改善你们周围人的生活以及改变我们国家的命运。当你们这样做的时候，让我告诉你们我所确信的事情：那正是你们的人生变得真正精彩的时候。

玛娅·安杰洛常说："有所学，则去传递；有所得，则去给予。我的朋友们，这会赋予你们的人生目标和意义。"所以，你们都有能力用自己的方式去发展你们自己的天使网络。这样做的话，你们这一届的学生会比历史上任何一代人都拥有更多的工具去发挥你们的影响力和行使你们的权利。我在模拟世界里做到了。我有幸拥有

---

20. incompatible：*adj.* 不协调的；不相容的。
21. indigent：*adj.* 贫困的，贫穷的。
22. impervious：*adj.* 无动于衷的；不受影响的。

empowerment than any other generation in history. I did it in an analog world. I was blessed with a platform that at its height reached nearly 20 million viewers a day. Now, here in a world of Twitter and Facebook and YouTube and Tumblr[23], you can reach billions in just seconds. You're the generation that rejected predictions about your detachment[24] and your disengagement[25] by showing up to vote in record numbers in 2008. And when the pundits[26] said—they talked about you—they said you'd be too disappointed, you'd be too dejected to repeat that same kind of turnout in the 2012 election, and you proved them wrong by showing up in even greater numbers. That's who you are.

This generation, your generation, I know has developed a finely honed radar for b.s. Can you say "b.s." at Harvard? The spin and phoniness and artificial nastiness that saturates[27] so much of our national debate. I know you all understand better than most that real progress requires authentic—an authentic way of being honesty, and above all, empathy.

I have to say that the single most important lesson I learned in 25 years talking every single day to people was that there is a common denominator in our human experience. Most of us, I tell you, we don't want to be divided. What we want, the common denominator that I found in every single interview, is we want to be validated. We want to be understood. I have done over 35,000 interviews in my career, and as soon as that camera shuts off, everyone always turns to me and inevitably, in their own way, asks this question: "Was that okay?" I heard it from President Bush; I heard it from President Obama. I've heard it from heroes and from housewives. I've heard it from victims and perpetrators[28] of crimes. I even heard it from Beyonce in all her Beyonceness. She finishes performing, hands me the microphone and says, "Was that okay?" Friends and family, yours, enemies, strangers in every argument in every encounter, every exchange, I will tell you they all want to know one thing: Was that okay? Did you hear me? Do you see me? Did what I say mean anything to you?

一个平台，在鼎盛时期每天的观众人数将近 2000 万。现在，在推特、脸书、油管和汤博乐盛行的世界里，你在分秒之间便可达到几十亿的浏览量。你们这一代人，在人们都以为你们冷漠淡然、与世隔绝的时候，你们在 2008 年的大选中用创纪录的投票人数还击了这样的臆测。当那些权威人士说——当他们谈论起你们，说你们将会令人十分失望，以至于在 2012 年大选中不会重现相同数量的投票人数的时候，你们却用更高的投票纪录证明了他们是错的。这才是你们！

我所了解的你们这一代人对"胡说八道"极为敏感。你们在哈佛能说"胡说八道"这个词吗？在我们的全国性讨论中，充斥着太多欺骗、虚假和龌龊。我知道，你们比大多数人都更明白，真正的进步来自真诚——一种真正诚实的态度，最重要的是，一种感同身受的心理。

我不得不坦言，在我 25 年来每一天与人们的对话中，我所学到的最重要的一课是，我们的人生经历中都有一个共同特征。我告诉你们吧，我们大多数人都不愿意被分割。我在每一次的访谈中发现的共同特征就是，我们想要得到认可，我们想要被理解。在我的职业生涯中，我做了超过 35 000 次访谈，每次摄像机一关闭，每个人总会转向我，不可避免地以各自的方式问我这样一个问题："我的表现可以吗？"布什总统这样问过我，奥巴马总统这样问过我，无论是英雄还是家庭主妇，无论是罪案中的受害者还是罪犯，都这样问过我，甚至连碧昂斯都以她特有的方式这样问过我。表演结束后，她把话筒递给我，问道："我的表现可以吗？"朋友、家人、你们、敌人以及在每次争论中邂逅的陌生人，每一次交流，我可以告诉你们，他们都想知道一件事情：我的表现可以吗？你听得见我吗？你看得到我吗？我说的话对你有意义吗？

---

23. Tumblr：汤博乐，成立于 2007 年，是全球最大的轻博客网站，也是轻博客网站的始祖。汤博乐是一种介于传统博客和微博之间的全新媒体形态，既注重表达，又注重社交，而且注重个性化设置，广受年轻人欢迎。
24. detachment：*n.* 冷漠。
25. disengagement：*n.* 脱离；分离。
26. pundit：*n.* 权威人士，专家。
27. saturate：*vt.* 充塞；使饱和。
28. perpetrator：*n.* 犯罪者，作恶者。

And even though this is a college where Facebook was born, my hope is that you would try to go out and have more face-to-face conversations with people you may disagree with. That you'll have the courage to look them in the eye and hear their point of view and help make sure that the speed and distance and anonymity of our world doesn't cause us to lose our ability to stand in somebody else's shoes and recognize all that we share as a people. This is imperative[29] for you as an individual and for our success as a nation.

"There has to be some way that this darkness can be banished with light." says the man whose little boy was massacred[30] on just an ordinary Friday in December. So whether you call it soul or spirit or higher self, intelligence, there is, I know this, there is a light inside each of you, all of us, that illuminates your very human beingness if you let it.

And as a young girl from rural Mississippi, I learned long ago that being myself was much easier than pretending to be Barbara Walters. Although, when I first started, because I had Barbara in my head, I would try to sit like Barbara, talk like Barbara, move like Barbara. And then one night, I was on the news reading the news, and I called Canada "Can-a-da," and that was the end of me being Barbara. I cracked myself up on TV. Couldn't stop laughing. And my real personality came through, and I figured out, "Oh, gee, I can be a much better Oprah than I could be a pretend Barbara."

I know that—I know that you all might have a little anxiety now and hesitation about leaving the comfort of college and putting those Harvard credentials[31] to the test. But no matter what challenges or setbacks or disappointments you may encounter along the way, you will find true success and happiness if you have only one goal—there really is only one and that is this: to fulfill the highest, most truthful expression of yourself as a human being. You want to max out your humanity by using your energy to lift yourself up, your family and the people around you. Theologian Howard Thurman said

尽管这所学校是脸书诞生的地方，但我希望你们能够试着走出去，去和那些也许与你意见不合的人面对面地交流。你们会有勇气去直视他们的眼睛，去聆听他们的观点，去确信在这个世界上，无论我们发展有多快，无论我们距离有多远，无论我们是否匿名，都不会导致我们失去设身处地为别人着想的能力，意识到我们作为人类应当学会分享。无论作为个人，还是为了我们这个国家的成功，你都必须做到这一点。

　　那位在12月一个再平凡不过的星期五痛失幼子的男人说："一定存在某种方法让光明驱走黑暗。"不管你们称之为灵魂、精神还是更高自我或者悟性都好，我所知道的是，在你们每个人的心中，在我们所有人的心中，都有一盏明灯，只要你愿意，它就可以点亮你人性的光芒。

　　作为一个来自密西西比州乡村的小女孩，很早以前我就意识到，相比模仿芭芭拉·沃尔特斯，做自己要容易得多。虽然在一开始，因为我心里想着成为芭芭拉，我会试着让自己坐姿像芭芭拉，谈吐像芭芭拉，举止也像芭芭拉。后来有一天晚上，我在新闻节目中读新闻，把加拿大（Canada）念成了"Can-a-da"，我就再也不想变成芭芭拉了。我在电视上捧腹大笑，笑得停不下来。我真正的自我展露无遗，我想通了："哦，天哪，相比成为一个假装的芭芭拉，我能成为一个更为出色的奥普拉。"

　　我知道——我知道你们即将告别舒适的大学校园，去检验你们在哈佛所取得的成绩，对此，你们现在可能都会有些许焦虑不安和犹豫不决。但是，不管你们一路上可能会经历怎样的挑战、阻碍或失望，只要认准一个目标，你们就能获得真正的成功和快乐。而人生确实只有这一个目标，那就是作为一个人，最大限度地展现最

---

29. imperative：*adj.* 必要的；极重要的。
30. massacre：*vt.* 大屠杀；残杀。
31. credentials：*n.*（表明一个人有资格做某事或起某种作用的）成就；资历。

it best. He said: "Don't ask yourself what the world needs. Ask yourself what makes you come alive, and then go do that, because what the world needs is people who have come alive."

The world needs people like Michael Stolzenberg from Fort Lauderdale. When Michael was just 8 years old, Michael nearly died from a bacterial infection that cost him both of his hands and both of his feet. And in an instant, this vibrant little boy became a quadruple amputee[32], and his life was changed forever.

But in losing who he once was, Michael discovered who he wanted to be. He refused to sit in that wheelchair all day and feel sorry for himself, so with prosthetics[33] he learned to walk and run and play again. He joined his middle school lacrosse team, and last month, when he learned that so many victims of the Boston Marathon bombing would become new amputees, Michael decided to banish that darkness with light.

Michael and his brother Harris created MikeysRun.com to raise $1 million for other amputees by the time Harris runs the 2014 Boston Marathon. More than 1,000 miles away from here, these two young brothers are bringing people together to support this Boston community the way their community came together to support Michael. And when this 13-year-old man was asked about his fellow amputees, he said this: "First, they will be sad. They're losing something they will never get back, and that's scary. I was scared. But they'll be okay. They just don't know that yet."

We might not always know it. We might not always see it, or hear it on the news, or even feel it in our daily lives, but I have faith that no matter what, Class of 2013, you will be okay, and you will make sure our country is okay. I have faith because of that 9-year-old girl who went out and collected the change. I have faith because of David and Francine Wheeler. I have faith because of Michael and Harris Stolzenberg, and I have faith because of you,

真实的自己。你们要运用自己的力量鼓舞自己、家人和你们周围的人，从而最大限度地展示你的人性光辉。神学家霍华德·瑟曼说得最好，他说："不要问自己这个世界需要什么，问问自己是什么让你充满活力，然后就去做，因为这个世界所需要的就是充满活力的人。"

这个世界就需要像来自劳德代尔堡的迈克尔·斯托尔岑贝格这样的人。迈克尔在年仅8岁的时候险些死于细菌感染，那次感染夺去了他的双手和双脚，转瞬之间，这个生气勃勃的小男孩就成了一个被截去四肢的残疾人，而这也改变了他的一生。

但失去原来的自己的同时，迈克尔发现了自己想成为什么样的人。他拒绝整日坐在轮椅上为自己感到惋惜，所以他在假肢的帮助下重新学会了行走、奔跑和玩耍，还加入了他高中的长曲棍球队。就在上个月，当得知波士顿马拉松爆炸事件中很多受害者可能会被截肢的时候，迈克尔决定用光明去帮助他们驱走那片黑暗。

迈克尔和他的兄弟哈里斯创建了 MikeysRun 网站，希望到哈里斯参加 2014 年波士顿马拉松比赛的时候能够为其他被截肢者筹集到 100 万美元。1000 多英里以外的年轻兄弟俩正在将人们团结在一起，去支持波士顿社区，正如他们的社区聚集在一起支持迈克尔一样。在被问及如何看待和自己一样被截肢的人的时候，这个 13 岁的男孩是这么说的："一开始他们会伤心，他们失去的是他们永远无法找回的东西，那会很可怕。我也曾感到害怕。但他们会好起来的，只是他们暂时还不知道罢了。"

我们也许并不总是很了解这样的事情，也许并不总是亲眼看到或从新闻中听到这样的事情，甚至在我们的日常生活中也感觉不到它的存在。但是我坚信，无论发生什么事，作为 2013 届毕业生，你们一定会很好，你们也会确保我们的国家很好。我之所以这样坚信，是因为有那位走出去募集零钱的 9 岁女孩；我之所以这样坚信，

---

32. amputee：*n.* 被截肢者，肢体被截除的人。
33. prosthetics：*n.* 假肢。

the network of angels sitting here today. One of them, Khadijah Williams, who came to Harvard four years ago. Khadijah had attended 12 schools in 12 years living out of garbage bags amongst pimps and prostitutes and drug dealers, homeless, going in to department stores, Wal-Mart in the morning, to bathe herself so that she wouldn't smell in front of her classmates, and today she graduates as a member of the Harvard Class of 2013.

From time to time, you may stumble, fall. you will, for sure—count on this. No doubt, you will have questions, and you will have doubts about your path, but I know this: If you're willing to listen, to be guided by that still small voice that is the GPS within yourself, to find out what makes you come alive, you will be more than okay. You will be happy, you will be successful, and you will make a difference in the world.

Congratulations, Class of 2013. Congratulations to your family and friends. Good luck and thank you for listening. Was that okay?

是因为有戴维·惠勒和弗朗辛·惠勒夫妇；我之所以这样坚信，是因为有迈克尔·斯托尔岑贝格和哈里斯·斯托尔岑贝格兄弟俩；我之所以这样坚信，是因为有你们，今天坐在这里的"网络天使"们。四年前来到哈佛的卡迪亚·威廉姆斯就是其中一员。卡迪亚曾在12年里上过12所学校，靠捡食垃圾袋中的食物为生，她的身边曾充斥着皮条客、妓女和毒贩，她曾无家可归。为了不让同学们闻到自己身上的异味，她每天早晨都去百货大楼、沃尔玛超市洗澡。而就在今天，她成了2013届哈佛毕业生中的一员。

时不时地，你或许会步履蹒跚，会失足跌倒，谁都会有这么一天。毫无疑问，你会产生怀疑，怀疑自己所选择的道路，但是我知道：如果你愿意聆听，愿意让你体内的GPS定位系统那还很微小的声音引导你，找到你的动力所在，你会生活得更好。你会快乐，会成功，会让世界因你而不同。

祝贺你们，2013届的毕业生们！祝贺你们的家人和朋友！祝你们好运，感谢你们听我演讲！我的表现可以吗？

语录 Quotes

- Trouble don't last always.
  困难不会永存。

- Failure is just life trying to move us in another direction.
  失败只是生活试图让你转换前进的方向罢了。

- When you're down in the hole, when that moment comes, it's really okay to feel bad for a little while.
  当你们身处谷底、陷入困境时，当那种时刻来临时，暂时的难过完全无妨。

- The key to life is to develop an internal moral, emotional GPS that can tell you which way to go.
  人生的关键是建立起一种内在的道德上和情感上的GPS，它会指引你前进的道路。

- Real progress requires authentic—an authentic way of being honesty, and above all, empathy.
  真正的进步来自真诚——一种真正诚实的态度，最重要的是，一种感同身受的心理。

- There really is only one and that is this: to fulfill the highest, most truthful expression of yourself as a human being.
  人生确实只有这一个目标，那就是作为一个人，最大限度地展现最真实的自己。

Don't Be Afraid. We'll Make It out of This Mess

别怕犯错，勇敢向前

——泰勒·斯威夫特 2022 年在纽约大学毕业典礼上的演讲

> 简介 Profile

泰勒·斯威夫特
Taylor Swift

1989年，泰勒·斯威夫特出生于美国宾夕法尼亚州的雷丁市，她的童年是在宾夕法尼亚州蒙哥马利县的一个圣诞树农场度过的。

2001年，在看了乡村歌手菲丝·希尔在电视上的演出后，泰勒央求母亲让自己去田纳西州乡村民谣之乡纳什维尔追寻音乐梦想。她开始学习吉他，创作了自己的第一首歌 Lucky You。

凭借着天赋与努力，泰勒在追逐音乐梦想的道路上勇往直前。她的歌声与演唱风格引起了斯科特·波切塔的注意，彼时的斯科特刚成立了自己的独立唱片公司，急需招募歌手与作曲家。眼光独到的斯科特看到了泰勒的才华，决定与其签约，泰勒成为斯科特公司旗下的第一位歌手。

果然，泰勒不负众望，于2006年发行了同名专辑 Taylor Swift。该专辑发行的首周销售量就达到了39 000张，在公告牌二百强专辑榜首周排行第19名，于2007年达到第5名的峰值。在公告牌乡村专辑榜上，该专辑于发行后第2周首次登顶，累计拿下8周冠军，成为她乡村音乐生涯的重要起点。

时至今日，泰勒共获得14座格莱美奖，也是全美音乐奖获奖最多的歌手。格莱美节目制作人肯·爱因里希评价泰勒时说："泰勒·斯威夫特的歌曲为她赢得了最大的歌迷群——年轻人。她写歌的习惯也成为捕获年轻人的撒手锏。她以写自己的成长经历闻名，歌曲里都是青春的味道，这一点正好切合了年轻歌迷的心，他们能听懂歌曲的内容，自然就会产生共鸣。她播撒在乡村音乐土壤中的种子，发芽后越来越向流行音乐生长。"

2022年5月18日，泰勒·斯威夫特被纽约大学授予荣誉博士学位并发表演讲，她以幽默风趣的演讲为2022届毕业生们带来了真诚的建议：别怕犯错，因为我们会从中吸取教训，最终走出困境，所以勇敢地向前走吧！

演讲 Speech

Hi, I'm Taylor.

Last time I was in a stadium this size, I was dancing in heels and wearing a glittery leotard. This outfit is much more comfortable.

I'd like to say a huge thank you to NYU's Chairman of the Board of Trustees, Bill Berkeley, and all the trustees and members of the board, NYU's President Andrew Hamilton, Provost Katherine Fleming, and the faculty and alumni here today who have made this day possible.

I feel so proud to share this day with my fellow honorees Susan Hockfield[1] and Felix Matos Rodriguez[2], who humble me with the ways they improve our world with their work. As for me, I'm 90% sure the main reason I'm here is because I have a song called *22*. And let me just say, I am elated to be here with you today as we celebrate and graduate[3] New York University's Class of 2022.

Not a single one of us here today has done it alone. We are each a patchwork quilt[4] of those who have loved us, those who have believed in our futures, those who showed us empathy and kindness or told us the truth even when it wasn't easy to hear. Those who told us we could do it when there was absolutely no proof of that.

Someone read stories to you and taught you to dream and offered up some moral code of right and wrong for you to try and live by. Someone tried their best to explain every concept in this insanely complex world to the child that

大家好，我是泰勒。

我上次来到这么大的体育场，是为了跳舞，那时我穿着闪闪发光的紧身舞衣和高跟鞋。现在我身上这套衣服舒服多了。

我衷心感谢纽约大学校董会主席比尔·伯克利、所有校董会成员、纽约大学校长安德鲁·汉密尔顿、教务长凯瑟琳·弗莱明以及今天在座的全体教职员工和校友，是你们成就了我的今天。

能与苏珊·霍克菲尔德和菲利克斯·马托斯·罗德里格斯同获今天的荣誉，我感到无比自豪。他们二位凭借自己的工作让世界变得更好，这让我感到惭愧。至于我，我有90%的把握，我在这里主要是因为我有一首歌叫《22》。让我说一句，很高兴今天能和大家一起庆祝纽约大学2022届毕业典礼。

在座的各位当中，没有一个人是孤身一人走到今天的。我们就像是由一块块碎片拼凑而成的百衲被，而碎片是爱我们的人、相信我们未来的人、向我们表达同理心和善意的人、对我们直言相劝的人、在绝望中热切鼓舞我们的人。

有人给你们读故事，教会你们梦想，教导一些是非道德准则，让你们尝试去构筑人生。小时候的你们问了无数的问题，比如"月亮是怎么工作的""为什么我们能

> *You don't always get all the things in the bag that you selected from the menu in the delivery service that is life. You get what you get.*
>
> 生活就像点外卖，挑中的未必都能送达，得到什么就是什么。

---

1. Susan Hockfield：苏珊·霍克菲尔德，美国艺术与科学院院士，麻省理工学院建校以来首位女校长。
2. Felix Matos Rodriguez：菲利克斯·马托斯·罗德里格斯，纽约市立大学第8任校长。
3. graduate：*v.* 授予毕业文凭或学位证书，使毕业。
4. patchwork quilt：百衲被。

was you, as you asked a bazillion questions like "how does the moon work" and "why can we eat salad but not grass." And maybe they didn't do it perfectly. No one ever can. Maybe they aren't with us anymore. In that case I hope you'll remember them today. If they are here in this stadium, I hope you'll find your own way to express your gratitude for all the steps and missteps that have led us to this common destination.

I know that words are supposed to be my "thing", but I will never be able to find the words to thank my mom and my dad, and my brother, Austin, for the sacrifices they made every day so that I could go from singing in coffee houses to standing up here with you all today, because no words would ever be enough.

To all the incredible parents, family members, mentors, teachers, allies, friends and loved ones here today who have supported these students in their pursuit of educational enrichment, let me say to you now: Welcome to New York. It's been waiting for you.[5]

I'd like to thank NYU for making me technically, on paper at least, a doctor[6]. Not the type of doctor you would want around in the case of an emergency, unless your specific emergency was that you desperately needed to hear a song with a catchy hook[7] and an intensely cathartic[8] bridge section. Or if your emergency was that you needed a person who can name over 50 breeds of cats in one minute.

I never got to have the normal college experience, per se[9]. I went to public high school until tenth grade and finished my education doing home-school work on the floors of airport terminals. Then I went out on the road on a radio tour, which sounds incredibly glamorous but in reality it consisted of a rental car, motels, and my mom and I pretending to have loud mother-daughter fights with each other during boarding so no one would want the empty seat between us on Southwest.

吃沙拉却不能吃草"，有人尽其所能地向你们解释这个复杂世界中的每一个概念。也许他们的回答并不完美，毕竟没人能做到完美。也许他们已经不在了，要是这样，我希望你们今天能想起他们。如果他们就在这个体育场里，我希望你们能以自己的方式来感谢他们，感谢引领自己走向这个共同目的地的每一步，包括失误。

　　语言本该是我的强项，但我永远无法找到合适的词语来感谢我的父母和弟弟奥斯汀，任何词语都不足以表达我的感激。没有他们日复一日地牺牲，我就无法从咖啡馆歌手走到今天，来与大家分享这一时刻。

　　今天在座的所有家长、家庭成员、导师、老师、伙伴、亲朋，你们一直支持这些学生们在学业方面的追求，现在我想对你们说：欢迎来到纽约，纽约一直期盼着你们的到来。

　　我要感谢纽约大学让我在理论上，至少在纸面上，成为一名博士。但我不是那种大家希望紧急情况下能够在场的博士（医生），除非你们的紧急情况是迫切需要听一首歌，需要旋律抓耳的副歌和情感强烈的间奏，或者要找一个能在一分钟内说出五十多种猫咪品种的人。

　　我自己从来没有体验过正常的大学生活。我在公立高中读到十年级，在机场航站楼的地板上做家庭教育作业，就这样完成了学业。然后我开始了电台巡演，听起来光鲜亮丽，但实际上那时我开着租来的车，住在汽车旅馆。在西南航空登机的时候，我和妈妈会假装大声吵架，这样旁边那个空位就不会有人想坐了。

---

5. Welcome to New York. It's been waiting for you.：这两句是泰勒的单曲 *Welcome To New York* 中的歌词。
6. doctor：兼有"博士"和"医生"之义。
7. hook：本意指"钩子"，在音乐领域指一首歌曲中最勾人的部分。
8. cathartic：*adj.* 宣泄情绪的。
9. per se：*adv.* 本身，自身。

别怕犯错，勇敢向前　287

As a kid, I always thought I would go away to college, imagining the posters I'd hang on the wall of my freshmen dorm. I even set the ending of my music video for my song *"Love Story"* at my fantasy imaginary college, where I meet a male model reading a book on the grass and with one single glance, we realize we had been in love in our past lives, which is exactly what you guys all experienced at some point in the last 4 years, right?

But I really can't complain about not having a normal college experience to you because you went to NYU during a global pandemic, being essentially locked into your dorms and having to do classes on the Internet. Everyone in college during normal times stresses about test scores, but on top of that you also had to pass like a thousand tests.

I imagine the idea of a normal college experience was all you wanted too. But in this case you and I both learned that you don't always get all the things in the bag that you selected from the menu in the delivery service that is life. You get what you get.

And as I would like to say to you wholeheartedly, you should be very proud of what you've done with it. Today you leave New York University and then go out into the world searching for what's next. And so will I.

So as a rule, I try not to give anyone unsolicited advice unless they ask for it. I'll go into this more later. I guess I have been officially solicited in this situation, to impart whatever wisdom I might have and tell you the things that helped me so far in my life.

Please bear in mind that I, in no way, feel qualified to tell you what to do. You've worked and struggled and sacrificed and studied and dreamed your way here today and so, you know what you're doing. You'll do things differently than I did them and for different reasons.

So I won't tell you what to do because no one likes that. I will, however, give you some life hacks I wish I knew when I was starting out my dreams of a

小时候，我一直以为我会去上大学，想象着自己会在大一宿舍墙上挂什么样的海报。我甚至把我那首《爱情故事》的 MV 的结尾设定成这样：在幻想中的大学里，在草地上，我遇到了一个看书的男模，我们仅对视一眼，便认出对方是自己前世的恋人。你们过去四年中都经历过这样的时刻，对吧？

但我没法抱怨你们没有正常的大学经历，因为你们是在全球疫情期间来到纽约大学的，基本上都被锁在宿舍里，不得不上网课。在正常时期，大学生们只是为考试成绩而烦恼，而你们却还必须通过上千次检测。

我猜想，你们也同样满心渴望着正常的大学生活。但在如今这种情况下，我们都明白，生活就像点外卖，挑中的未必都能送达，得到什么就是什么。

我想真心实意地告诉你们，你们应该为自己所取得的成就感到骄傲。今天你们将离开纽约大学，走向世界，踏上寻找下一站的旅程。我也一样。

我的原则是，尽量不要不请自来地给人提建议。这一点稍后再进一步探讨。而今天，我想自己算是受到了正式邀请，来和你们分享我所领悟到的人生智慧，以及迄今为止的人生中让我受益良多的东西。

请记住，我决不认为自己有资格告诉你们该怎么做。你们历经努力、奋斗，为了理想在学海苦修，舍弃了许多，终于走到了今天，因此，你们清楚自己在做什么。你们将会因不同于我的理由，走上不同于我的道路。

所以我不会对你们指手画脚，因为没人乐意接受这样的指导。不过，我会分享一些生活技巧。我真希望自己能在追逐职业梦想之初，在应对生活、爱情、压力、

> *So as a rule, I try not to give anyone unsolicited advice unless they ask for it.*
>
> *我的原则是，尽量不要不请自来地给人提建议。*

career, and navigating life, love, pressure, choices, shame, hope and friendship.

The first of which is life can be heavy, especially if you try to carry it all at once. Part of growing up and moving into new chapters of your life is about catch and release. What I mean by that is, knowing what things to keep, and what things to release. You can't carry all things, all grudges, all updates on your ex, all enviable promotions your school bully got at the hedge fund his uncle started. Decide what is yours to hold and let the rest go.

Oftentimes the good things in your life are lighter anyway, so there's more room for them. One toxic relationship can outweigh so many wonderful, simple joys. You get to pick what your life has time and room for. Be discerning.

Secondly, learn to live alongside cringe. No matter how hard you try to avoid being cringe, you will look back on your life and cringe retrospectively. Cringe is unavoidable over a lifetime. Even the term "cringe" might someday be deemed "cringe."

I promise you, you're probably doing or wearing something right now that you will look back on later and find revolting and hilarious. You can't avoid it, so don't try to. For example, I had a phase where, for the entirety of 2012, I dressed like a 1950s housewife. But you know what? I was having fun. Trends and phases are fun. Looking back and laughing is fun.

And while we're talking about things that make us squirm but really shouldn't, I'd like to say that I'm a big advocate for not hiding your enthusiasm for things. It seems to me that there is a false stigma around eagerness in our culture of "unbothered ambivalence." This outlook perpetuates the idea that it's not cool to "want it," that people who don't try hard are fundamentally more chic[10] than people who do.

And I wouldn't know because I have been a lot of things but I've never been an expert on "chic." But I'm the one who's up here so you have to listen to me when I say this: Never be ashamed of trying. Effortlessness is a myth. The

抉择、羞耻、希望以及友谊时就知道这些技巧。

第一点，生活有时会变得很沉重，尤其当你们试图一股脑儿扛起一切时。学会取舍是成长和开启人生新篇章的一部分。我的意思是，你们得知道什么该留下，什么该放手。恩恩怨怨、前任的动态、校霸在他叔叔创办的对冲基金公司里获得了令人艳羡的晋升……把什么都带上是不可能的，决定好要留下什么，剩下的就任其随风散去吧。

美好的事物通常更加轻盈，因此不会占据太多生活空间。背负一段不健康的关系可能会让人失去许多美好而简单的乐趣。要用什么来填充自己的时间和空间，这取决于你。要擦亮眼睛。

第二点，学会与尴尬和平共处。无论多么努力地避免尴尬，回首往昔，仍然会感受到种种尴尬。在人的一生当中，尴尬是无可避免的。就连"尴尬"这个词本身，有朝一日或许也会被视为"尴尬"。

我敢保证，你们现在所做的某件事情，穿的某件衣服，等将来回头看，会觉得恶心又可笑。这一点无可避免，因而也不必花心思去规避。比如，我有个阶段，在2012年一整年里，我都穿得像个20世纪50年代的家庭主妇。可你们猜怎么着，那时我很开心。潮流趋势和人生阶段很有趣，回顾过往并自嘲一番也很有趣。

有些事情让人感到不自在，但其实不该如此。对于这一点，我想说，我提倡积极表达对事物的热情，不要掩藏起来。我认为，在我们这种"无所谓的淡漠"文化中，对于热情存在一种错误的耻辱感。这种观念让人们认为"渴望"是不酷的，不努力的人从根本上说比努力的人更时髦。

我不懂这种时髦，毕竟我尝试过很多事情，却从来不是"时髦"方面的权威。但既然站在这里的人是我，我就要对你们说一句：永远不要羞于尝试。不劳而获是

---

10. chic: *adj.*（穿着、品位、言谈举止等方面）优雅老练，十分入时。

people who wanted it the least were the ones I wanted to date and be friends with in high school. The people who want it the most are the people I now hire to work for my company.

I started writing songs when I was twelve and since then, it's been the compass guiding my life, and in turn, my life guided my writing. Everything I do is just an extension of my writing, whether it's directing videos or a short film, creating the visuals for a tour, or standing on stage performing.

Everything is connected by my love of the craft, the thrill of working through ideas and narrowing them down and polishing it all up in the end. Editing. Waking up in the middle of the night and throwing out the old idea because you just thought of a newer, better one, or a plot device that ties the whole thing together. There's a reason they call it a hook. Sometimes a string of words just ensnares me and I can't focus on anything until it's been recorded or written down.

As a songwriter I've never been able to sit still, or stay in one creative place for too long. I've made and released 11 albums and in the process, I've switched genres from country to pop, to alternative, to folk. And this might sound like a very songwriter-centric line of discussion, but in a way, I really do think we are all writers.

And most of us write in a different voice for different situations. You write differently in your Instagram stories than you do your senior thesis. You send a different type of email to your boss than you do your best friend from home. We are all literary chameleons and I think it's fascinating. It's just a continuation of the idea that we are so many things, all the time.

And I know it can be really overwhelming figuring out who to be, and when. Who you are now and how to act in order to get where you want to go. I have some good news: it's totally up to you. I have some terrifying news: it's totally up to you.

痴人说梦。读中学的时候，我会想和不爱尝试的人约会或者做朋友。而现在，我会为我的公司雇用最乐于尝试的人。

我 12 岁开始写歌，从那以后，歌曲就成了我生活的指南针，反过来，生活也指引着我的创作。我所做的一切都不过是创作的延伸，无论是拍摄视频和短片，为巡回演出打造视觉效果，还是站在舞台上表演。

一切皆因热爱而生，因将创意细化完善的激情而起。编辑也是如此。还有这种情形：半夜醒来，想到了更棒的创意或串联整个作品的情节设计，于是摒弃先前的想法。难怪人家管这个叫"钩子"。有时候，一串歌词会把我困住，我没办法专心做别的事，直到把它们录好或写好。

作为一名歌曲创作者，我向来坐不住，做不到长时间停留在同一种创意中。我已经制作并发行了 11 张专辑，在这个过程中，我从乡村音乐转向流行音乐，再到另类音乐，再到民谣。这听起来可能像是只针对写歌人的讨论，但从某种程度上说，我真的认为我们都是写作者。

大多数人在不同的情境下会采用不同的语气写作。在照片墙软件上发布的动态和毕业论文的风格不一样，给老板发的邮件和在家里给挚友发的邮件风格也不一样。我们都是文学变色龙，我对此十分着迷。我们始终在不断展现自身多面性，而创作是其延续。

你想成为谁？何时达成目标？你现在是谁？如何行动才能抵达理想之境？我明白，想要弄明白这些真的很难。事情完全取决于你。这是个好消息，也是个坏消息。

> *Part of growing up and moving into new chapters of your life is about catch and release.*
>
> 学会取舍是成长和开启人生新篇章的一部分。

I said to you earlier that I don't ever offer advice unless someone asks me for it, and now I'll tell you why. As a person who started my very public career at the age of 15, it came with a price. And that price was years of unsolicited advice. Being the youngest person in every room for over a decade meant that I was constantly being issued warnings from older members of the music industry, the media, interviewers, executives. This advice often presented itself as thinly veiled warnings.

See, I was a teenager at a time when our society was absolutely obsessed with the idea of having perfect young female role models. It felt like every interview I did included slight barbs by the interviewer about me one day "running off the rails." That meant a different thing to everyone person said it me. So I became a young adult while being fed the message that if I didn't make any mistakes, all the children of America would grow up to be perfect angels.

However, if I did slip up, the entire earth would fall off its axis and it would be entirely my fault and I would go to pop star jail forever and ever. It was all centered around the idea that mistakes equal failure and ultimately, the loss of any chance at a happy or rewarding life.

This has not been my experience. My experience has been that my mistakes led to the best things in my life. And being embarrassed when you mess up is part of the human experience. Getting back up, dusting yourself off and seeing who still wants to hang out with you afterward and laugh about it. That's a gift. The times I was told no or wasn't included, wasn't chosen, didn't win, didn't make the cut … looking back, it really feels like those moments were as important, if not more crucial, than the moments I was told "yes."

Not being invited to the parties and sleepovers in my hometown made me feel hopelessly lonely, but because I felt alone, I would sit in my room and write the songs that would get me a ticket somewhere else. Having label

我先前跟你们说过，除非有人问我，否则我不会不请自来地提供建议，现在我来说说原因。我 15 岁就步入公众视野，这是有代价的。代价就是多年以来那些不请自来的建议。十多年来，在各个场合我都是最年轻的人，所以不断受到音乐界前辈、媒体人、采访者和企业高管的告诫。他们的告诫往往是欲盖弥彰的警告。

你们看，我十几岁的时候，我们的社会热衷于打造完美的年轻女性典范。感觉在每场采访中，采访者都会稍微带刺地提到我终将"偏离正轨"。说这句话的每个人意思各不相同。所以我在成长过程中一直被灌输这样的信息：若是我不犯错，全美国的孩子长大后都会成为完美的天使。

但若我真的犯了错，整个地球就会脱离轨道，这全都得怪我，我会被终身监禁在流行歌星的监狱里。一切都围绕着这样一个观点展开：错误等于失败，最终，等于失去了让生活变得快乐和有意义的机会。

我的经验不是这样的。我的经验告诉我，错误让我遇到了生命中最美好的事情。搞砸事情，感到尴尬，也是人生体验的一部分。重新站起来，拍拍身上的灰尘，看看哪些人仍然愿意和我一起出去玩，和我一起对此付之一笑。这是一份礼物。回想起来，遭拒、落选、落败、未能晋级……我真心觉得，这些否定我的时刻和肯定我的时刻一样重要，甚至更为关键。

没人邀请我参加家乡的聚会和睡衣派对，这让我感到极其孤独，但因为孤独，所以我会坐在房间里写歌，而那些歌为我赢得了去往别处的通行证。纳什维尔唱片

Never be ashamed of trying. Effortlessness is a myth.

永远不要羞于尝试。不劳而获是痴人说梦。

executives in Nashville tell me that only 35-year-old housewives listen to country music and there was no place for a 13-year-old on their roster made me cry in the car on the way home. But then I'd post my songs on my MySpace[11] and—yes, MySpace—and would message with other teenagers like me who loved country music, but just didn't have anyone singing from their perspective. Having journalists write in depth, oftentimes critical, pieces about who they perceive me to be made me feel like I was living in some weird simulation, but it also made me look inward to learn about who I actually am.

Having the world treat my love life like a spectator sport in which I lose every single game was not a great way to date in my teens and twenties, but it taught me to protect my private life fiercely. Being publicly humiliated over and over again at a young age was excruciatingly[12] painful but it forced me to devalue the ridiculous notion of, minute by minute, ever fluctuating social relevance and likability. Getting canceled[13] on the internet and nearly losing my career gave me an excellent knowledge of all the types of wine.

I know I sound like a consummate[14] optimist, but I'm really not. I lose perspective all the time. Sometimes everything just feels completely pointless. I know the pressure of living your life through the lens of perfectionism. And I know that I'm talking to a group of perfectionists because you are here today graduating from NYU.

And so this may be hard for you to hear: In your life, you will inevitably misspeak, trust the wrong people, underreact, overreact, hurt the people who didn't deserve it, overthink, not think at all, self sabotage[15], create a reality where only your experience exists, ruin perfectly good moments for yourself and others, deny any wrongdoing, not take the steps to make it right, feel very guilty, let the guilt eat at you, hit rock bottom, finally address the pain you caused, try to do better next time, rinse, repeat. And I'm not gonna lie: These mistakes will cause you to lose things. I'm trying to tell you that losing things

公司的高管告诉我，只有 35 岁的家庭主妇才听乡村音乐，他们公司里没有 13 岁小孩的位置，这让我在回家的车里哭了起来。但后来我把我的歌发布在聚友网上，没错，我在聚友网和其他十几岁的乡村音乐同好交流。这些青少年热爱乡村音乐，只是找不到共鸣的声音来唱出他们的心声。记者们对我进行深度报道，讲述他们眼中的我，往往带有批评色彩，让我觉得像是活在怪异的模拟世界里，但这也促使我向内探索，去了解真实的自我。

全世界都把我的爱情故事当作观赏性体育赛事来看，而我每一场都输掉了，对于十几二十岁的我来说，这并不是理想的约会经历，但教会了我要极力捍卫自己的隐私。年轻时屡屡公开受辱是极其痛苦的，但这种经历让我逐渐学会了看淡社会热度和受欢迎程度这类时刻波动的荒谬概念。被互联网淡忘并几近失业，让我对各类葡萄酒有了透彻的了解。

我知道，我听起来像个十足的乐天派，但实际上并非如此。我并不能始终保持这种心态。有时候，一切似乎都变得毫无意义。我了解活在完美主义镜头下的压力。我知道，你们是一帮完美主义者，毕竟你们今天可是要从纽约大学毕业了。

所以，很多事情对你们来说可能很难接受：在生活中，难免会说错话、信错人、没反应过来、反应过激、伤害无辜、想得太多、没过脑子、自我折磨、自说自话、破坏氛围、拒绝认错、知错不改、羞愧难当、悔不当初、心灰意冷、亡羊补牢、想

---

11. MySpace：聚友网。该网站成立于 2003 年 9 月，是全球第二大社交网站。它为全球用户提供了一个集交友、个人信息分享、即时通讯等多种功能于一体的互动平台。
12. excruciatingly：*adv.* 极度痛苦地。
13. cancel："取消"，是 2010 年代后期至今流行的一种网络文化用语，特指因意见分歧而对名人或各类公众人物做出拒绝支持、声讨乃至抵制其相关作品等言论或行为。
14. consummate：*adj.* 完满的，绝顶的。
15. self sabotage：自暴自弃，自我折磨。

doesn't just mean losing. A lot of the time, when we lose things, we gain things too.

Now you leave the structure and framework of school and chart your own path. Every choice you make leads to the next choice which leads to the next, and I know it's hard to know which path to take. There will be times in life when you need to stand up for yourself. Times when the right thing is actually to back down and apologize. Times when the right thing is to fight. Times when the right thing is to turn and run. Times to hold on with all you have and times to let go with grace. Sometimes the right thing to do is to throw out the old schools of thought in the name of progress and reform. Sometimes the right thing to do is to sit and listen to the wisdom of those who have come before us. How will you know what the right choice is in these crucial moments? You won't.

How do I give advice to this many people about their life choices? I won't. The scary news is: you're on your own now. But the cool news is: you're on your own now.

I leave you with this: We are led by our gut instincts, our intuition, our desires and fears, our scars and our dreams. And you will screw it up sometimes. So will I. And when I do, you will most likely read about on the internet. Anyway hard things will happen to us. We will recover. We will learn from it. We will grow more resilient because of it.

And as long as we are fortunate enough to be breathing, we will breathe in, breathe through, breathe deep, breathe out. And I am a doctor now, so I know how breathing works.

I hope you know how proud I am to share this day with you. We're doing this together. So let's just keep dancing like we're the class of 22[16].

着下不为例但又重蹈覆辙。说实话,这些错误会让你们失去很多。我想告诉你,失去并不仅仅是失去。很多时候有失必有得。

如今,你们将要脱离学校的结构和框架,去规划自己的道路。你们的每一个选择都会引出下一个选择,而下一个选择又会引出下下个选择。我知道,选出自己要走的路并非易事。生活中总会有需要为自己站出来的时候。正确的做法有时是让步和道歉,有时是战斗,有时是转身逃跑,有时是坚守阵地,有时是优雅放手,有时是以进步和改革的名义抛弃旧思想,有时是坐下来倾听前人的智慧。在这些关键时刻,怎么才能知道什么是正确的选择?你没法知道。

我如何向这么多人提供人生建议呢?我不会做这种事。你们现在只能靠自己了。这是个坏消息,也是个好消息。

我要告诉你们的是,本能、直觉、欲望和恐惧、伤疤和梦想将引领我们前进。有时候你们会把事情搞砸。我也一样,而且要是我把事情搞砸了,你们大概率能在网上看到。我们总归免不了会跌倒,但我们会爬起来,会从中吸取教训,会因此而更加顽强。

只要我们有幸还在呼吸,我们就会吸气、呼气、深吸一口气、再呼出。我现在是博士(医生)了,所以我了解呼吸的工作原理。

能与你们共度今日,我心中无比自豪。我们一起毕业了。那么,就继续跳舞吧,就像我们都只有 22 岁那样。

---

16. Let's just keep dancing like we're the class of 22:这一句话巧妙化用了泰勒的单曲《22》中的歌词 "we just keep dancing like we're 22"。

语录 Quotes

- You don't always get all the things in the bag that you selected from the menu in the delivery service that is life. You get what you get.
  生活就像点外卖,挑中的未必都能送达,得到什么就是什么。

- So as a rule, I try not to give anyone unsolicited advice unless they ask for it.
  我的原则是,尽量不要不请自来地给人提建议。

- Part of growing up and moving into new chapters of your life is about catch and release.
  学会取舍是成长和开启人生新篇章的一部分。

- Learn to live alongside cringe.
  学会与尴尬和平共处。

- Never be ashamed of trying. Effortlessness is a myth.
  永远不要羞于尝试。不劳而获是痴人说梦。

- Being embarrassed when you mess up is part of the human experience.
  搞砸事情,感到尴尬,也是人生体验的一部分。

- Losing things doesn't just mean losing. A lot of the time, when we lose things, we gain things too.
  失去并不仅仅是失去。很多时候有失必有得。

Make Your Inexperience an Asset
让经验匮乏成为优势

——娜塔莉·波特曼 2015 年在哈佛大学毕业典礼上的演讲

简介 Profile

娜塔莉·波特曼
Natalie Portman

提起娜塔莉·波特曼，大多数人脑海中首先浮现的是电影《这个杀手不太冷》中的小女孩，参演那一年她13岁。在这部电影中，娜塔莉出演了一个叛逆的12岁小女孩，在全家被杀后跟随杀手里昂（让·雷诺饰）一起踏上了复仇之路。这部电影成了电影史上的一部经典之作，娜塔莉饰演的小女孩的角色形象也由此深入人心。

然而，与《这个杀手不太冷》中出身悲惨、性格叛逆的小女孩不同，娜塔莉生于一个家教严格的家庭，自幼学习优异。她在高中时参与撰写的一篇论文曾入围美国高中科学研究竞赛"英特尔科学奖"（Intel Science Talent Search）的评选。对于幼年的自己，娜塔莉曾这样评价道："我和其他孩子不一样。我更有野心。我知道我喜欢什么，想要什么，我很努力。我是一个非常认真的孩子。"

1999年，刚演完《星球大战前传1：幽灵的威胁》且演艺事业正当红的娜塔莉被哈佛大学录取，主修心理学。获得了文学学士学位后，她又回到出生地以色列，在耶路撒冷希伯来大学攻读研究生课程。在主演电影《V字仇杀队》期间，娜塔莉对影片所涉及的恐怖主义做了详尽的了解和研究，甚至一度成为哥伦比亚大学恐怖主义和反恐主义的客座教授。2011年，娜塔莉凭借在影片《黑天鹅》中的出色表演摘得奥斯卡最佳女主角的桂冠。显然，娜塔莉并不甘于做演艺圈的"花瓶"，而是选择做一个能够主宰自己人生的智慧女性。

2015年5月27日，娜塔莉·波特曼获邀到母校哈佛大学为2015届毕业生做毕业典礼致辞。演讲中，她谈及自己求学的经历和寻求人生目标时经历的迷茫与痛苦，鼓励毕业生好好利用"缺乏经验"这一优势来开辟属于自己的道路，找到为之奋斗的方向，拥有属于自己的人生。

演讲 Speech

扫描二维码
获取本篇演讲原视频、音频

Hello, class of 2015. I am so honored to be here today. Dean Khurana, faculty, parents, and most especially graduating students, thank you so much for inviting me. The Senior Class Committee: It's genuinely one of the most exciting things I've ever been asked to do. I have to admit, primarily because I can't deny it as it was leaked in the WikiLeaks release of the Sony hack, that when I was invited I replied, and I directly quote my own email, "Wow! This is so nice! I'm gonna need some funny ghost writers. Any ideas?" This initial response, now blessedly public, was from the knowledge that at my class day we were lucky enough to have Will Ferrel[1] as class day speaker and, that many of us were hungover or even freshly high, mainly wanted to laugh. So I have to admit that today, even 12 years after graduation, I'm still insecure about my own worthiness. I have to remind myself: Today you're here for a reason.

Today I feel much like I did when I came to Harvard Yard as a freshman in 1999, when you guys were, to my continued shocked and horror, still in kindergarten. I felt like there had been some mistake; that I wasn't smart enough to be in this company, and that every time I opened my mouth, I would have to prove that I wasn't just a dumb actress. So I start with an apology. This won't be very funny. I'm not a comedian, and I didn't get a ghost writer. But I am here to tell you today: Harvard is giving you all diplomas tomorrow. You are here for a reason.

2015 届的毕业生,你们好。我非常荣幸今天能来到这里。库拉纳教学主任、教职员工们、家长们,尤其是毕业生们,非常感谢你们邀请我。毕业生委员会,这真的是我受邀所做的最令人激动的事情之一。我不得不承认,主要是因为我也否认不了,在维基解密披露的索尼遭到黑客入侵事件的那些文件里,我写的电子邮件被曝光了。当我接到邀请时,我是这么回复的:"哇!太棒了!我需要找一些有意思的写手。有什么建议吗?"这封如今幸运地得以公开的最初回复邮件之所以这么写,是因为我受到了一件事情的启发:我毕业那天,我们很幸运地邀请到威尔·法瑞尔担当毕业演讲嘉宾,而我们很多人都宿醉未醒,甚至由于之前玩得太"嗨",大多都只想傻笑。所以我不得不承认,即便是毕业 12 年后的今天,我仍然不确定自己配不配在这里讲话。我必须提醒自己:今天你来这儿是有原因的。

今天我的感觉和我 1999 年作为大一新生来到哈佛园时很像,那时你们还在读幼儿园——这真是让我感到震惊和害怕。那时我觉得是不是有什么地方搞错了;我觉得我不够聪明,不够格来这里上学,而且我每次开口说话时,都不得不去证明我不是个愚蠢的女演员。所以我首先要道个歉。这次演讲不会很搞笑。我不是喜剧演员,我也没有找写手。但我今天来这儿是要告诉你们:哈佛大学明天将给你们所有人颁发毕业证书。你们来这儿是有原因的。

> *You can harness that inexperience to carve out your own path, one that is free of the burden of knowing how things are supposed to be, a path that is defined by its own particular set of reasons.*
> 你们也可以利用这种缺乏经验的状态去开拓一条属于自己的路,一条不必费心去了解事情本该如何的路,一条由其自身特定的一套理由而定义的路。

---

1. Will Ferrel:威尔·法瑞尔(1967—),美国演员、制片人、编剧。

Sometimes your insecurities and your inexperience may lead you, too, to embrace other people's expectations, standards, or values. But you can harness that inexperience to carve out your own path, one that is free of the burden of knowing how things are supposed to be, a path that is defined by its own particular set of reasons.

The other day I went to an amusement park with my soon-to-be 4-year-old son. And I watch him play arcade games. He was incredible focused, throwing his ball at the target. Jewish mother than I am, I skipped 20 steps and was already imagining him as a Major League player with his aim and his arm and his concentration. But then I realized what he want. He was playing to trade in his tickets for the crappy plastic toys. The prize was much more exciting than the game to get it. I, of course, wanted to urge him to take joy and the challenge of the game, the improvement upon practice, the satisfaction of doing something well, and even feeling the accomplishment when achieving the game's goals. But all of these aspects were shaded by the little 10-cent plastic men with sticky stretchy blue arms that adhere to the walls. That—that was the prize. In a child's nature, we see many of our own innate tendencies. I saw myself in him and perhaps you do too.

Prizes serve as false idols everywhere: prestige, wealth, fame, power. You'll be exposed to many of these, if not all. Of course, part of why I was invited to come to speak today, beyond my being a proud alumna, is that I've recruited some very coveted toys in my life, including a not-so-plastic, not-so-crappy one—an Oscar. So we bump up against the common trope[2], I think, of the commencement address: people who have achieved a lot telling you that the fruits of the achievement are not always to be trusted. But I think that contradiction can be reconciled, and is in fact instructive. Achievement is wonderful when you know why you're doing it. And when you don't know, it can be a terrible trap.

有时候，你们也可能会因为不自信或缺乏经验而欣然接受他人的期望、标准或价值观。但你们也可以利用这种缺乏经验的状态去开拓一条属于自己的路，一条不必费心去了解事情本该如何的路，一条由其自身特定的一套理由而定义的路。

　　前几天，我和快4岁的儿子一起去了游乐场。我看着他玩街机游戏，他朝球靶扔球，玩得格外专注。我这个犹太裔母亲略过了20步，已经把他想象成了职业棒球大联盟的球员，目标明确，挥棒有力，精神集中。但很快我就意识到他想要的是什么，他玩游戏只是为了换券领取劣质的塑料玩具。奖品比赢得奖品的游戏本身更让人激动。我当然想鼓励他感受游戏中挑战的乐趣，在练习中进步的乐趣，做好一件事获得满足感的乐趣，甚至感受完成游戏目标时的成就感。但所有这些都被那个10美分的塑料小人掩盖了，这个塑料小人的蓝色弹性手臂有黏性，可以粘在墙上。这就是奖品。在孩子的天性中，我们看到很多自己固有的倾向。我从他身上看到了我自己，也许你们也可以（从孩子身上看到自己）。

　　威信、财富、名望、权力，不管在哪里，这些奖品都是错误的崇拜对象。这些你们即使不会全部接触到，也将会接触到其中的很多。当然，我今天被邀请来演讲的部分原因，除了我是一个充满自豪的校友，还因为我人生中得到了一些令人向往的玩具，包括一个既不是塑料做的也不劣质的玩具———一座奥斯卡小金人。我想正因为这样，我们会听到有关毕业演讲的一种常见的比喻：有很多成就的演讲者告诉你，不要总是相信成就的果实。但我认为这种矛盾可以调和，实际上也很有教育意义。当你知道你为何而做时，成就是很美好的；但如果你不知道，它就会是一个可怕的陷阱。

> *Achievement is wonderful when you know why you're doing it. And when you don't know, it can be a terrible trap.*
> 当你知道你为何而做时，成就是很美好的；但如果你不知道，它就会是一个可怕的陷阱。

---

2. trope：*n.* 修辞，比喻。

I went to a public high school on Long Island: Syosset High School. Ooh, hello, Syosset! The girls I went to school with had Prada bags and flat-ironed hair. And they spoke with an accent, I who had moved there at age 9 from Connecticut, mimicked to fit in: Florida oranges, chocolate cherries. Since I'm ancient and the Internet was just starting when I was in high school, people didn't really pay that much attention to the fact that I was an actress. I was known mainly at school for having a backpack bigger than I was and always having white-out on my hands because I hated seeing anything crossed out in my notebooks. I was voted for my senior year book "most likely to be a contestant on *Jeopardy*[3]": or code for nerdiest.

When I got to Harvard just after the release of *Star Wars: Episode I*, I knew I would be starting over in terms of how people viewed me. I feared people would have assumed I'd gotten in just for being famous, and that they would think that I was not worthy of the intellectual rigor here. And it would not have been far from the truth. When I came here, I had never written a 10-page paper before. I'm not even sure I've written a 5-page paper. I was alarmed and intimidated by the calm eyes of fellow students who came here from Dalton or Exeter, who thought that compared to high school the workload here was easy. I was completely overwhelmed and thought that reading 1000 pages a week was unimaginable, that writing a 50-page thesis is just something I could never do. I had no idea how to declare my intentions. I couldn't even articulate them to myself.

I've been acting since I was 11. But I thought acting was too frivolous and certainly not meaningful. I came from a family of academics and was very concerned of being taken seriously.

In contrast to my inability to declare myself, on my first day of orientation freshman year, five separate students introduced themselves to me by saying, "I'm going to be president. Remember I told you that." Their names, for the

我是在长岛的锡塞特公立中学上的高中。噢，你们好啊，锡塞特的毕业生们。和我一起上学的女生都挎着普拉达包包，拉直了头发。她们说话带着口音，我9岁从康涅狄格州搬到长岛，为了融入也学着说这种口音："佛罗里达橘子、巧克力樱桃。"由于我高中时看起来年纪比较大，而且那时网络才刚兴起，所以人们并不会特别注意我是演员这个事实。大家知道我主要是因为我在学校背着一个比我人还要大的书包，而且手上总是沾着涂改液，因为我讨厌在我的笔记本上看到任何被划掉的东西。在高中最后一年的年鉴上，我被选为"最有可能上《危险边缘》节目的参赛选手"，或者说白了，就是最书呆子气的人。

就在《星球大战前传1：幽灵的威胁》上映后，我来哈佛大学读书，我知道我又得重新应对别人如何看我这种事了。我害怕别人都以为我能上哈佛只不过是因为我很有名，害怕别人会认为我不适合这里严谨治学的氛围。但别人这么想也不算太离谱。来这儿之前，我从未写过10页的论文。我甚至都不确定自己有没有写过5页的论文。我被来自道尔顿或埃克塞特的同学们淡定的眼神吓坏了，他们认为和高中相比，这里的课业负担就是小菜一碟。我完全招架不住，觉得一周读1000页书不可想象，而写一篇50页的论文简直就是我永远无法做到的事情。我不知道该怎么表明我的意图，我甚至跟自己都说不清。

我11岁就开始演戏了。但我当时认为演戏太过轻浮，当然也没有意义。我出身于一个学者家庭，非常看重别人是否把我当回事。

在我参加大一迎新会的第一天，我还不能很好地介绍自己，与此相反，有五位同学是这样向我介绍他们自己的："我以后会成为总统。记住我跟你说过这句话。"大家记好了，这几个同学的名字是伯尼·桑德斯、马尔科·鲁比奥、特德·克鲁兹、

---

3. Jeopardy：《危险边缘》，美国一档电视智力竞赛节目。

record, were Bernie Sanders, Marco Rubio, Ted Cruz, Barack Obama, Hilary Clinton. In all seriousness, I believed every one of them: Their bearing and self-confidence alone seemed proof of their prophecy, where I couldn't shake my self-doubt. I got in only because I was famous. This was how others saw me and it was how I saw myself. Driven by these insecurities, I decided that I was going to find something to do in Harvard that was serious and meaningful that would change the world and make it a better place.

At the age of 18, I'd already been acting for 7 years and assumed I'd find a more serious and profound path in college. So freshman fall I decided to take neurobiology and advanced modern Hebrew literature because I was serious and intellectual. Needless to say, I should have failed both. I got Bs, for your information, and to this day, every Sunday I burn a small effigy to the pagan gods of grade inflation. But as I was fighting my way through Aleph-Bet Yod Y'shua in Hebrew[4] and the different mechanisms of neuro-response, I saw friends around me writing papers on sailing and pop culture magazines, and professors teaching classes on fairy tales and *The Matrix*. I realized that seriousness for seriousness's sake was its own kind of trophy, and a dubious one; a pose I sought to counter some half-imagined argument about who I was. There was a reason that I was an actor. I love what I do. And I saw from my peers and my mentors that that was not only an acceptable reason, it was the best reason.

When I got to my graduation, sitting where you sit today, after four years of trying to get excited about something else, I admitted to myself that I couldn't wait to go back and make more films. I wanted to tell stories, to imagine the lives of others and help others do the same. I'd found or perhaps reclaimed my reason. You have a prize now, or at least you will tomorrow. The prize is a Harvard degree in your hand. But what is your reason behind it? My Harvard degree represents, for me, the curiosity and invention that were

巴拉克·奥巴马、希拉里·克林顿。说实在的，我相信他们每一个人说的话——单是他们的举止和自信似乎就能证明他们的预言，而我在这方面还摆脱不了自我怀疑。我能进入哈佛只是因为我很有名，别人是这么看我的，我也是这么看我自己的。在这种不自信的驱使下，我决定要在哈佛找点严肃且有意义的事做，找点将能改变世界并使之变得更美好的事做。

18岁那年，我已经演了7年戏了，我以为自己会在大学找到一条更严肃、更有深度的路。所以大一那年秋天，我决定学习神经生物学和当代高级希伯来语文学课程，因为我是个严肃认真的人，智商也不低。不用说，我本该两门课都不及格的。告诉你们，我两门课都得了B，所以直到今天，每周日我都要向主管打高分的那些异教神灵们烧一幅小神像（以表谢意）。但当我苦学希伯来语和神经反应的不同机制时，我看到周围的朋友们在航海和流行文化杂志上发表文章，看到教授们开班讲授童话和《黑客帝国》。我意识到，为了严肃而严肃本身就是一种比喻，一种靠不住的比喻，一种我试图用来反驳有关我是谁的争论的姿态，而这种争论有一半是我想象出来的。我当演员是有理由的——我喜爱我做的事情。我从我的同辈和导师们身上看到，这不仅是一个可以接受的理由，还是最好的理由。

经过4年的时间竭力让自己对别的事情感兴趣之后，我迎来了毕业，就坐在你们今天坐的地方，那时我才向自己承认，我迫不及待地想要回去拍电影，拍更多的电影。我想去讲故事，去想象别人的生活，并帮助别人做同样的事情。我已经找到或者说重新找回了我的理由。你们现在有了一个奖品，或者至少明天会有。这个奖品就是你们手上的哈佛大学文凭。但在这个奖品背后，你们的理由是什么呢？对我而言，我的哈佛大学文凭象征着我在这里被激发的好奇心和创造力；象征着我维系的友谊；象征着格雷厄姆教授跟我说的，不要讲述阳光如何照耀花朵，而要讲述花

---

4. Aleph-Bet Yod Y'shua in Hebrew：希伯来语字母表，这里指代希伯来语。

encouraged here, the friendships I've sustained, the way Professor Graham told me not to describe the way light hit a flower but rather the shadow the flower cast, the way Professor Scarry talked about theater as a transformative religious force, how professor Coslin showed how much our visual cortex is activated just by imagining. Now granted[5] these things don't necessarily help me answer the most common question I'm asked: What designer you are wearing? What's your fitness regime? Any make-up tips? But I have never since been embarrassed to myself as what I might previously have thought was a stupid question. My Harvard degree and other awards are emblems of the experiences which led me to them—The wood-paneled lecture halls, the colorful fall leaves, the hot vanilla Toscaninis, reading great novels in overstuffed library chairs, running through dining halls screaming, "Ooh! Ah! CityStep[6]! CityStep! CityStep! CityStep! Wohoo!"

It's easy now to romanticize my time here. But I had some very difficult times here too. Some combination of being 19, dealing with my first heartbreak, taking birth control pills that have since been taken off the market for their depressive side effects, and spending too much time missing daylight during winter months, led me to some pretty dark moments, particularly during sophomore year. There were several occasions I started crying in meetings with professors, overwhelmed with what I was supposed to pull off when I could barely get myself out of bed in the morning. Moments when I took on the motto for my schoolwork: Done, not good. If only I could finish my work, even if it took eating a jumbo pack of sour Patch Kids to get me through a single 10-page paper, I felt that I'd accomplished a great feat. I repeat to myself: Done, not good.

A couple of years ago, I went to Tokyo with my husband, and I ate at the most remarkable sushi restaurant. I don't even eat fish. I'm vegan, so that tells you how good it was. Even with just vegetables, this sushi was the stuff

朵投下的阴影；象征着斯凯瑞教授说的，戏剧是革命性的宗教力量；象征着柯思兰教授展示的，我们的视觉皮质仅凭想象就能够被很好地激活。的确，这些知识现在并不一定能帮我回答我被问到的那些最普遍的问题：你穿的是哪个设计师设计的衣服？你有什么健身方法？有什么化妆技巧？但自此以后，我再也不会因为我以前可能认为是很愚蠢的问题而感到尴尬了。我的哈佛学位和其他的奖励象征着那些引导我获得这些奖励的经历——镶嵌着木板的礼堂，五颜六色的秋叶，大受欢迎的香草托斯卡尼尼冰淇淋，在铺有加厚软垫的图书馆椅子上读经典小说，在餐厅里边跑边叫："哦！啊！城市阶梯！城市阶梯！城市阶梯！城市阶梯！呜呼！"

　　现在要想美化我在这里读书的时光很容易，但我在这里也度过了一段非常艰难的日子。那时，我才19岁，经历了第一次心碎，服用了因有抑郁副作用而退出市场的避孕药，冬天的那几个月里长时间见不到阳光，这些因素加起来，让我陷入了十分黑暗的日子，尤其是在大二那年。有好几次，我一见教授就哭，因为我那时早上几乎无法起床，可还要克服困难完成我应完成的作业，这让我喘不过气来。有段时间，我对待功课的座右铭就是：做完就行，不求多好。只要我能完成任务就行，即便我要吃一大包酸味水果软糖才能写完10页论文，我也觉得我已经完成一项伟大的壮举了。我不断地对自己说：做完就行，不求多好。

　　几年前，我和丈夫一起去东京，在一家最有名的寿司店吃饭。我是个素食者，连鱼都不吃，所以你们由此可知那里的寿司有多好吃。即便只有蔬菜，那些寿司也是你梦寐以求的食物。饭店只有六个座位。我和丈夫很惊讶，怎么会有人把米饭做得比其他所有米饭都好吃。我们很好奇他们为什么不开个更大的饭店，成为市区最

---

5. granted：*adj.*（表示某事属实，然后再对其做出评论）不错，的确。
6. CityStep：城市阶梯，是哈佛大学最大的学生组织之一，完全由在校学生运营，为大学生提供接触艺术、展示自我的平台和机会。

you dreamed about. The restaurant has 6 seats. My husband and I marveled at how anyone can make rice so superior to all other rice. We wondered why they didn't make a bigger restaurant, and be the most popular place in town. Our local friends explained to us that all the best restaurants in Tokyo are that small and do only one type of dish: sushi or tempura or teriyaki. Because they want to do that thing well and beautifully. And it's not about quantity. It's about taking pleasure in the perfection and beauty of the particular. I'm still learning now that it's about good and maybe never done, that the joy and work ethic and virtuosity[7] we bring to the particular can impart a singular[8] type of enjoyment to those we give to, and of course to ourselves.

In my professional life, it also took me time to find my own reasons for doing my work. The first film I was in came out in 1994. Again, appallingly, the year most of you were born. I was 13 years old upon the film's release, and I can still quote what *The New York Times* said about me verbatim, "Miss Portman poses better than she acts." The film had a universally tepid critic response and went on to bomb commercially. That film was called *The Professional*, or *Leon* in Europe. And today, 20 years and 35 films later, it is still the film people approach me about the most, to tell me how much they loved it, how much it moved them, how it's their favorite movie. I feel lucky that my first experience releasing a film was initially such a disaster by all standards and measures. I learned early that my meaning had to be from the experience of making the film and the possibility of connecting with individuals, rather than the foremost trophies in my industry; financial and critical success. And also those initial reactions could be false predictors of your works' ultimate legacy. I started choosing only jobs that I'm passionate about, and from which I knew I could glean meaningful experiences. This thoroughly confused everyone around me: agents, producers, and audiences alike. I made *Goya[9]'s Ghosts*, a foreign independent film, and studied art history, visiting the Prado[10] every day

受欢迎的地方。当地的朋友告诉我们，东京所有最好的饭店都是那么小，而且只做一类菜：寿司或天妇罗或照烧。因为他们想把东西做好、做漂亮。这与数量无关，而是以把一件事情做得尽善尽美为乐。我现在仍旧在学习：将事情做好，虽然可能永远也做不完；它关乎我们做某件事时的快乐、职业道德和精湛技艺可以给我们所服务的那些人带来一种非凡的享受，当然也会给我们自己带来非凡的享受。

在我的职业生涯中，我也是花了很长时间才找到我工作的理由。我参演的第一部电影是1994年上映的。好吧，这也太吓人了，那年你们大部分人才刚出生。电影上映时我13岁，如今我还能一字不差地说出当时《纽约时报》对我的评价："波特曼小姐摆的造型好过她的表演。"电影在评论界反应平平，商业上则是惨败。那部电影叫作《这个杀手不太冷》，在欧洲叫《杀手里昂》。今天，20年过去了，我演过35部电影，可人们来找我绝大多数情况下仍然是因为这部电影，他们跟我说他们当年有多爱这部电影，这部电影多让他们感动，这是他们最喜欢的电影。我觉得很幸运，无论用什么标准来衡量，我有关电影上映的首次体验在最初是那么糟糕。这让我早早就懂得，我的意义必须来自拍电影的经历以及与他人建立联系的机会，而不是我在电影领域获得的最重要的成就——商业上和评论上的成功。而且，那些最开始的反馈完全可能错误预测你的工作最终会产生什么影响。于是，我开始只选择那些我喜欢的工作，从这些工作中我知道自己能慢慢收获有意义的经验。这使我周围的人，包括经纪人、制作人以及观众，感到很困惑。我拍外国独立电影《戈雅之魂》，研究艺术史，连续4个月每天都去参观普拉多博物馆，同时阅读关于戈雅和西班牙审判的资料。我拍动作片《V字仇杀队》，为了拍这部影片，我学习了我所能了解到的关于自由战士——也有人称之为恐怖分子——的所有资料，从梅纳赫姆·贝京到地下

---

7. virtuosity：*n.*（艺术家、运动员等的）精湛技艺，高超技巧。
8. singular：*adj.* 非凡的；突出的；显著的。
9. Goya：弗朗西斯科·德·戈雅（1746—1828），西班牙浪漫主义画派画家。
10. Prado：普拉多博物馆，建于18世纪，位于西班牙马德里，被认为是世界上最伟大的博物馆之一，亦是收藏西班牙绘画作品最全面、最权威的美术馆。

for four months as I read about Goya and the Spanish Inquisition. I made *V for Vendetta*, a studio action movie for which I learned everything I could about freedom fighters, whom otherwise may be called terrorists, from Menachem Begin[11] to the Weather Underground[12]. I made *Your Highness*, a pothead comedy[13] with Danny McBride, and laughed for three months straight[14]. I was able to own my meaning and not have it be determined by box office receipts or prestige.

By the time I got to making *Black Swan* the experience was entirely my own. I felt immune to the worst things anyone could say or write about me and to whether the audience felt like going to see my movie or not. It was instructive for me to see the ballet dancers. For ballet dancers, once your technique gets to a certain level, the only thing that separates you from others is your quirks or even flaws. One ballerina was famous for how she turned slightly off balance. You can never be the best technically. Someone will always have a higher jump or a more beautiful line. The only thing you can be the best at is developing your own self. Authoring your own experience was very much what *Black Swan* itself was about. I worked with Darren Aronofsky, the film director that changed my last line in the movie, too. It was perfect because my character Nina is only artistically successful when she finds perfection and pleasure for herself, not when she was trying to be perfect in the eyes of others. So when *Black Swan* was successful financially and I began receiving accolades, I felt honored and grateful to have connected with people, for the true core of my meaning I had already established. And I needed it to be independent of people's reactions to me. People told me that Black Swan was an artistic risk. A scary challenge to try to portray a professional ballet dancer. But it didn't feel like courage or daring that drew me to it. I was so oblivious to my own limits that I did things I was woefully unprepared to do. And so the very inexperience that in college had made me feel insecure, and made me want

气象组织。我和丹尼·麦克布赖德拍大麻喜剧《王子殿下》，连续笑了三个月。我变得能拥有我自己的意义，而不是将其交由票房收入或名声来决定。

到我拍《黑天鹅》时，那经历就全都是我自己的了。我已经不再在乎别人可能会把我说得或写得多烂，也不管观众是否想来看我的电影。对我来说，看芭蕾舞演员让我得到了启发。对芭蕾舞演员而言，技巧一旦达到一定的高度，你和别人的唯一区别就只在于你的怪异甚至是你的瑕疵——有一个芭蕾舞演员就因旋转时稍稍有点不平衡而闻名。严格说来，你永远都不可能是最好的。总会有人跳得更高，或有更优美的身段。你唯一能做到最好的，就是发展自我。《黑天鹅》这部影片本身所讲的就是书写你自己的经历。我和达伦·阿罗诺夫斯基导演合作，他也修改了我在电影里的最后一句台词。这很棒，因为我饰演的尼娜只有在发现自己完美且快乐，而不是尽力让别人认为她完美的时候，才获得了艺术上的成功。所以当《黑天鹅》取得商业上的成功，我开始得到赞誉时，我感到荣幸且感激能够与观众产生共鸣，因为我已经确立了自己内心意义的真正核心。而且我需要这种意义独立于人们对我的反应之外。人们跟我说《黑天鹅》是艺术上的冒险：试图出演一个职业芭蕾舞演员，这是一个可怕的挑战。但吸引我去这么做的并不是勇气或胆量。我完全没注意到自己的能力边界，才会去做我毫无准备去做的事。我在大学时的缺乏经验让我感到不自信，让我想按照他人的规则做事，而现在恰恰是这种缺乏经验让我真正敢去冒险。我甚至没有意识到演芭蕾舞演员存在风险。当导演达伦问我是否能跳芭蕾时，我告诉他我差不多算是一个芭蕾舞演员，而且我也坚信，我是个芭蕾舞演员。准备拍摄时，我很快就意识到，我距离芭蕾舞演员可能还有 15 年的距离，这逼着我去付出

---

11. Menachem Begin：梅纳赫姆·贝京（1913—1992），以色列政治家，1977 年至 1983 年任以色列总理。
12. Weather Underground：地下气象组织，美国激进左翼组织，由一批大学生于 1969 年组织成立，目的是成立一个秘密党派来推翻美国政府。该组织制造过不少暴动，最后于 1977 年解散。
13. pothead comedy：大麻喜剧，指以大麻的使用、交易、相关文化或其对社会和个人的影响等为主要或重要情节元素的电影，通常具有比较强烈的黑色幽默或荒诞色彩。
14. straight：*adj.* 连续的；不间断的。

to play by others' rules, now is making me actually take risks. I didn't even realize were risks. When Darren asked me if I could do ballet, I told him that I was basically a ballerina; which by the way I wholeheartedly believed. When it quickly became clear in preparing for the film that I was maybe 15 years away from being a ballerina, it made me work a million times harder. And of course the magic of cinema and body doubles helped the final effect. But the point is, if I had known my own limitations, I never would have taken the risk. And the risk led to one of my greatest artistic, personal experiences, and that I not only felt completely free, I also met my husband during the filming.

Similarly, I just directed my first film, *A Tale of Love and Darkness*. I was quite blind to the challenges ahead of me. The film is a period film, completely in Hebrew, in which I also act with an 8-year-old child as a costar. All of these are challenges I should have been terrified of, as I was completely unprepared for them. But my complete ignorance to my own limitations looked like confidence and got me into the director's chair. Once there, I had to figure it all out, and my belief that I could handle these things contrary to all evidence of my ability to do. So was half the battle. The other half was very hard work. The experience was the deepest and most meaningful one of my career. Now clearly I'm not urging you to go perform heart surgery without the knowledge to do so. Making movies admittedly has less drastic consequences than most professions, and allows for a lot of effects that make up for mistakes. The thing I'm saying is, make use of the fact that you don't doubt yourself too much right now. As we get older, we get more realistic, and I guess that includes about our abilities or lack thereof. And that realism does us no favors.

People always talk about diving into[15] things you're afraid of. That never worked for me. If I'm afraid, I run away. And I would probably urge my child to do the same. Fear protects us in many ways. What has served me is diving into my obliviousness[16]. Being more confident than I should be, which

成百上千万倍的努力。当然,电影艺术和替身使电影最后呈现出来的效果很好。但关键是,如果我知道自己的局限,我就不会冒这个风险。而这次冒险使我有了最难忘的个人艺术经历之一,而且我在电影拍摄期间不仅感到十分自由,还遇到了我的丈夫。

与此类似,我刚刚导演了我的第一部电影《爱与黑暗的故事》。那时我根本不清楚前方会有什么挑战。这是一部年代戏,整部电影都使用希伯来语,影片中我要和一个8岁的孩子合作。我本应该对所有这些挑战感到害怕,因为我对这些完全没有准备。但我完全看不到自己的局限,看起来好像很自信,这让我坐上了导演的位置。一旦坐到那个位置上,我就不得不把所有事情搞清楚,虽然所有证据都表明我不行,但我还是相信自己能够把这些事情都处理好。这只是战斗的一半,另一半是艰辛的工作。这次经历是我事业中最深刻、最有意义的一次。我现在显然不是敦促你们在没有相关知识的情况下去做心脏手术。我承认,跟大多数职业相比,拍电影没有什么严重的后果,还可以用很多特效来弥补失误。我现在所说的是,你们要利用好现在你们还不那么怀疑自己这一事实。随着我们年纪越来越大,我们变得越来越现实,我想这也包括我们会怀疑自身能力,考虑自己的不足。而这种现实主义的态度对我们没有好处。

人们总说要勇于投身于自己害怕的事情。这对我从来都没用。如果我害怕,我会跑开。而且我可能也会让我的孩子这么做。从很多方面来讲,恐惧保护着我们。对我来说,有用的是好好利用我的无知无觉。人们常谴责美国孩子,以及我们这些考试得高分且自我膨胀的人,说我们过度自信。其实,过度自信可以是件好事,如

---

15. dive into:全身心地投入。
16. obliviousness: n. (尤指对周围发生的事情)毫不在意、毫无知觉、未察觉。

everyone tends to decry[17] in American kids, and those of us who have been grade inflated and ego inflated. Well, it can be a good thing if it makes you try things you never might have tried. Your inexperience is an asset, and will allow you to think in original and unconventional ways. Accept your lack of knowledge and use it as your asset.

I know a famous violinist who told me that he can't compose because he knows too many pieces, so when he starts thinking of the note, an existing piece immediately comes to mind. Just starting out one of your biggest strengths is not knowing how things are supposed to be. You can compose freely because your mind isn't cluttered with too many pieces. And you don't take for granted the way things are. The only way you know how to do things is your own way. You here will all go on to achieve great things. There is no doubt about that. Each time you set out to do something new, your inexperience can either lead you down a path where you will conform to someone else's values, or you can forge your own path, even if you don't realize that's what you're doing. If your reasons are your own, your path, even if it is a strange and clumsy path, will be wholly yours, and you will control the rewards of what you do by making your internal life fulfilling.

At the risk of sounding like a Miss America contestant, the most fulfilling things I've experienced have truly been the human interactions: spending time with women in village banks in Mexico with a FINCA microfinance organization; meeting young women who were the first and the only in their communities to attend secondary schools in rural Kenya, with the Free the Children group that built sustainable schools in developing countries; tracking with gorilla conservationists in Rwanda. It's a cliche, because it's true, that helping others ends up helping you more than anyone. Getting out of your own concerns and caring about someone else's life for a while reminds you that you are not the center of the universe. And that in the ways we're generous or not,

果这样能促使你去尝试你从未尝试过的事情。没有经验是你的优势，它将使你用独创的、非常规的方式进行思考。接受你知识匮乏的这一现实，并将此作为你的优势吧！

我认识一个著名的小提琴家，他曾跟我说他无法作曲，因为他知道的曲子太多了，所以当他开始想音符时，现有的某首曲子会立即出现在他的脑海里。而你们最大的优势之一就是不知道事情应该怎么做，就从这个优势着手吧。你们可以自由谱曲，因为你们的脑子里没有塞满曲子。你们不会想当然地认为事情就该是那样。你们知道的做事情的唯一方法就是你们自己的方法。你们在座的各位都将成就伟大的事业，这是毫无疑问的。每次你们要开始做新的事情时，缺乏经验会促使你们要么走别人的路，遵从别人的价值，要么开拓自己的路，即便你们没有意识到那是你们正在做的。如果你拥有自己的理由，那么即使你的这条路奇怪而坎坷，它也将完全属于你，而你也将能够通过让自己的内心得到满足，来掌控所做事情的回报。

下面说的话听起来可能像美国小姐参赛者说的话，尽管这样，我还是要说。我经历过的最令人满足的事情真的就是人与人的互动：和国际社会援助基金会小额金融组织一起，在墨西哥乡村银行里与妇女们共度时光；和解放儿童组织一起在肯尼亚农村与那里的年轻女孩见面，她们是各自社区最早也是唯一上中学的人，解放儿童组织致力于在发展中国家修建可持续学校；在卢旺达同大猩猩保护者一起行走。帮助别人最后就是帮助自己，这是陈词滥调，却是真的。忘掉自己的烦恼，偶尔关心一下别人的生活，这样会提醒你，你不是宇宙的中心。不管我们是否慷慨，我们都能够改变他人的生活轨迹。甚至在工作中，工作人员、导演、同行演员给我的一

---

17. decry: *vi.*（强烈）谴责，抨击，反对。

we can change the course of someone's life. Even at work, the small feats of kindness crew members, directors, fellow actors have shown me, have had the most lasting impact.

And of course, first and foremost, the center of my world is the love I share with my family and friends. I wish for you that your friends will be with you through it all, as my friends from Harvard have been together since we graduated. My friends from school are still very close. We have nursed each other through heartaches and danced at each others' weddings. We've held each other at funerals and rocked each other's new babies. We've worked together on projects, helped each other get jobs, and thrown parties for when we've quit bad ones. And now our children are creating a second generation of friendship, as we look at them toddling together, haggard[18], and disheveled[19] working parents that we are. Grab the good people around you. Don't let them go. The biggest asset this school offers you is a group of peers that will be both your family and your school for life.

I remember always being pissed at the spring here in Cambridge, tricking us into remembering a sunny yard full of laughing Frisbee throwers, after eight months of dark, frigid, library dwelling. It was like the school had managed to turn on the good weather, as a last memory we should keep in mind that would make us want to come back. But as I get farther away from my years here, I know that the power of this school is much deeper than weather control. It changed the very questions I was asking. To quote one of my favorite thinkers, Abraham Joshua Heschel, "To be or not to be is not the question. The vital question is: how to be and how not to be."

Thank you.

I can't wait to see how you do all the beautiful things you will do.

点点善举也产生了最持久的影响。

当然，最重要的是，我世界的中心是我与家人和朋友分享的爱。我希望你们的朋友会一直和你们在一起，就像我毕业后仍然和哈佛大学的朋友在一起一样。现在我与我上学时的朋友关系仍然很紧密。我们在彼此伤心时互相照顾，在彼此的婚礼上跳舞，在葬礼上互相扶持，抱着彼此新诞生的孩子轻摇。我们在各种项目中合作，帮助彼此找工作，在辞掉烂工作时一起聚会庆祝。现在我们的孩子正在发展第二代友谊。作为面容憔悴、蓬头垢面的上班族家长，我们看着他们一起学步。抓住身边的好人，不要让他们离去。这所学校给你的最大资产就是一群同龄人，他们将是你一生的家人，一生的同学。

我记得我们总是被坎布里奇的春天惹恼，因为它骗我们记住一个洒满阳光的院子里人们扔着飞盘欢声笑语的场景，而此前八个月我们都待在昏暗寒冷的图书馆里。就好像学校能够把天气变好似的，让我们最后记在脑海里的是这样的好天气，让我们还想回来。但毕业多年后，我知道，这所学校的力量比控制天气还要强大得多，它改变了我过去所问的那些问题。用我最喜欢的思想家亚伯拉罕·约书亚·赫舍尔的话来说："生存还是灭亡，这都不是问题，关键问题是，如何生存以及如何灭亡。"

谢谢。

我迫不及待想看看你们如何去做你们将要做的所有美好事情。

---

18. haggard：*adj.* 憔悴的，形容枯槁的。
19. disheveled：*adj.*（人或其外表）不整洁的，乱糟糟的。

语录 | Quotes

- You can harness that inexperience to carve out your own path, one that is free of the burden of knowing how things are supposed to be, a path that is defined by its own particular set of reasons.
  你们也可以利用这种缺乏经验的状态去开拓一条属于自己的路，一条不必费心去了解事情本该如何的路，一条由其自身特定的一套理由而定义的路。

- Achievement is wonderful when you know why you're doing it. And when you don't know, it can be a terrible trap.
  当你知道你为何而做时，成就是很美好的；但如果你不知道，它就会是一个可怕的陷阱。

- I was able to own my meaning and not have it be determined by box office receipts or prestige.
  我变得能拥有我自己的意义，而不是将其交由票房收入或名声来决定。

- Your inexperience is an asset, and will allow you to think in original and unconventional ways.
  没有经验是你的优势，它将使你用独创的、非常规的方式进行思考。

- If your reasons are your own, your path, even if it is a strange and clumsy path, will be wholly yours, and you will control the rewards of what you do by making your internal life fulfilling.
  如果你拥有自己的理由，那么即使你的这条路奇怪而坎坷，它也将完全属于你，而你也将能够通过让自己的内心得到满足，来掌控所做事情的回报。

第四章

勇气的力量
真正的成长是向死而生

勇气 Courage

This Is Water
这就是水

——大卫·福斯特·华莱士 2005 年在凯尼恩学院毕业典礼上的演讲

简介 Profile

大卫·福斯特·华莱士
David Foster Wallace

  大卫·福斯特·华莱士于 1962 年出生在美国纽约州，家庭环境优渥。在考入亚利桑那大学后，他攻读了自己热爱的写作专业，并且取得了优异的成绩。

  然而，金无足赤，人无完人，华莱士的心理问题却成了他一生的困扰。9 岁时，华莱士便出现了抑郁与焦虑的症状，于是在精进学业的同时，他还需要花时间去对抗抑郁。后来，他被确诊为患有"非典型抑郁症"，并开始服用名叫苯乙肼的药物来治疗。这段艰难的历程后来被华莱士写进了他的小说《无尽的玩笑》。这部小说出版后取得了巨大成功，华莱士也因此名声大噪，被《纽约时报》誉为"他那一代作家中最具天才的一位"。

  华莱士的作品中有着对这个世界和对整个人生清醒的思考和认识，而他的文字又有着让人无法抗拒的魅力，他以诙谐、讥讽、犀利的笔触带领读者从纷繁复杂的社会中找回真正的自我，去独立思考，去掌控自己的人生。

  然而他自己却无时无刻不遭受着精神的折磨，清醒地看着自己在痛苦中挣扎、沉沦。或许是感到自己愈来愈难掌控自身，2008 年的 9 月 12 日，华莱士在家中自杀，结束了自己年仅 46 岁的生命。

  华莱士写的小说，真正能看懂的人寥寥无几，连曾经出版《无尽的玩笑》的编辑在收到华莱士寄来的 1000 多页的书稿，面对密密麻麻的脚注、缩写词和糅杂的后现代语言时，都感到难以呼吸。但是，华莱士生前的唯一一篇演讲稿却在社交网络上风靡，后来还被改编成一本小书《生命中最简单又最困难的事》，在华莱士去世后得以出版。

  这篇演讲是华莱士于 2005 年在凯尼恩学院的毕业典礼上发表的，其内容直指教育的本质，充满了哲学的洞见，堪称照亮迷茫、庸碌人生的一盏明灯。

演讲 Speech

Greetings, thanks and congratulations to Kenyon's graduating class of 2005.

There are these two young fish swimming along and they happen to meet an older fish swimming the other way, who nods at them and says, "Morning, boys. How's the water?" And the two young fish swim on for a bit, and then eventually one of them looks over at the other and goes, "What the hell is water?"

This is a standard requirement of US commencement speeches, the deployment of didactic little parable-ish[1] stories. The story thing turns out to be one of the better, less bullshitty conventions of the genre, but if you're worried that I plan to present myself here as the wise, older fish explaining what water is to you younger fish, please don't be. I am not the wise old fish. The point of the fish story is merely that the most obvious, important realities are often the ones that are hardest to see and talk about. Stated as an English sentence, of course, this is just a banal platitude[2], but the fact is that in the day to day trenches of adult existence, banal platitudes can have a life-or-death importance, or so I wish to suggest to you on this dry and lovely morning.

Of course the main requirement of speeches like this is that I'm supposed to talk about your liberal arts education's meaning, to try to explain why the degree you are about to receive has actual human value instead of just a

大家好，感谢并祝贺凯尼恩学院 2005 届的毕业生们。

两条小鱼在水里游，碰巧遇到一条老鱼，老鱼朝他们点点头说："早上好，孩子们。水怎么样呀？"两条小鱼又游了一会儿，其中一条终于看着同伴问道："水到底是什么啊？"

讲一讲富有教育意义的寓言体小故事，是美国毕业典礼演讲的常规要求。事实证明，讲故事是演讲的好传统，故事总归没那么多废话。不过不必担心，我不会扮演老鱼来向你们这些小鱼解释水是什么，我并不是一条睿智的老鱼。鱼的故事只是为了指出，最明显、最重要的事实往往也最难被看到和讨论。用英语说出来，这句话不过是陈词滥调，但在成人日常生活的战壕中，陈词滥调可能生死攸关，至少，在这个清爽怡人的早晨，这一点正是我想要告诉你们的。

当然，这类演讲的主要要求是要阐述人文教育的意义，阐释为何即将到手的学位中蕴含着真正的人文价值，而不仅仅是物质回报。那么，我们就来讨论一下毕业

> *The most obvious, important realities are often the ones that are hardest to see and talk about.*
> 最明显、最重要的事实往往也最难被看到和讨论。

---

1. parable-ish：寓言式的。
2. banal platitude：平庸的陈词滥调。

这就是水　331

material payoff. So let's talk about the single most pervasive cliché[3] in the commencement speech genre, which is that a liberal arts education is not so much about filling you up with knowledge as it is about quote, "teaching you how to think." If you're like me as a student, you've never liked hearing this, and you tend to feel a bit insulted by the claim that you needed anybody to teach you how to think, since the fact that you even got admitted to a college this good seems like proof that you already know how to think. But I'm going to posit to you that the liberal arts cliché turns out not to be insulting at all, because the really significant education in thinking that we're supposed to get in a place like this isn't really about the capacity to think, but rather about the choice of what to think about. If your total freedom of choice regarding what to think about seems too obvious to waste time discussing, I'd ask you to think about fish and water, and to bracket for just a few minutes your skepticism about the value of the totally obvious.

Here's another didactic little story. There are these two guys sitting together in a bar in the remote Alaskan wilderness. One of the guys is religious, the other is an atheist, and the two are arguing about the existence of God with that special intensity that comes after about the fourth beer. And the atheist says: "Look, it's not like I don't have actual reasons for not believing in God. It's not like I haven't ever experimented with the whole God and prayer thing. Just last month I got caught away from the camp in that terrible blizzard[4], and I was totally lost and I couldn't see a thing, and it was fifty below, and so I tried it: I fell to my knees in the snow and cried out 'Oh, God, if there is a God, I'm lost in this blizzard, and I'm gonna die if you don't help me.'" And now, in the bar, the religious guy looks at the atheist all puzzled. "Well then you must believe now," he says, "After all, here you are, alive." The atheist just rolls his eyes. "No, man, all that was was a couple Eskimos happened to come wandering by and showed me the way back to camp."

典礼演讲中最常见的陈词滥调吧,即人文教育重在"教会学生如何思考",而不是灌输知识。如果你们和我当学生时一样,那想必不会喜欢听这种话。这话说得好像你们需要别人教自己如何思考似的,你们也许会觉得受到了侮辱。因为事实上,能被这么好的大学录取,似乎已经证明了你们具备思考的能力。但我要告诉你们的是,人文教育中的陈词滥调其实一点也不侮辱人,因为在这样一个环境中,我们理应接受的思考教育的关键不在于思考能力,而在于思考对象的选择。如果你们觉得自己对思考对象的选择拥有完全的自由,不值得浪费时间讨论,那么,请思考一下鱼与水的问题,暂时把质疑搁置几分钟。

　　我要再讲一个有教育意义的小故事。在遥远的阿拉斯加荒野上,有两个人坐在酒吧里,一个是信教的,一个是无神论者,二人在争论上帝是否存在。四杯啤酒下肚,争论越发激烈起来。无神论者说:"瞧,我认为上帝不存在是有切实依据的。我也不是从来没有向上帝祈祷。就在上个月,我遇到了一场可怕的暴风雪,被困在营地外面,完全迷失了方向,什么也看不见,气温是零下 50 摄氏度,所以我试了一下。我跪在雪地里,喊道'噢,上帝,如果你真的存在,帮帮我吧,我在暴风雪中迷路了,如果你不帮我,我就要死了。'"现在,那个信教的家伙困惑地看着无神论者:"那你现在肯定相信上帝存在了,毕竟,你还活着。"无神论者只是翻了个白眼:"不,伙计,只不过是有一对因纽特夫妻碰巧路过,给我指了回营地的路。"

---

3. cliché: *n.* 陈词滥调。
4. blizzard: *n.* 暴风雪。

It's easy to run this story through kind of a standard liberal arts analysis: the exact same experience can mean two totally different things to two different people, given those people's two different belief templates and two different ways of constructing meaning from experience. Because we prize tolerance and diversity of belief, nowhere in our liberal arts analysis do we want to claim that one guy's interpretation is true and the other guy's is false or bad. Which is fine, except we also never end up talking about just where these individual templates and beliefs come from. Meaning, where they come from inside the two guys. As if a person's most basic orientation toward the world, and the meaning of his experience were somehow just hard-wired, like height or shoe-size; or automatically absorbed from the culture, like language. As if how we construct meaning were not actually a matter of personal, intentional choice. Plus, there's the whole matter of arrogance. The nonreligious guy is so totally certain in his dismissal of the possibility that the passing Eskimos had anything to do with his prayer for help. True, there are plenty of religious people who seem arrogantly and certain of their own interpretations, too. They're probably even more repulsive than atheists, at least to most of us. But religious dogmatists[5]' problem is exactly the same as the story's unbeliever: blind certainty, a close-mindedness that amounts to an imprisonment so total that the prisoner doesn't even know he's locked up.

The point here is that I think this is one part of what teaching me how to think is really supposed to mean. To be just a little less arrogant. To have just a little critical awareness about myself and my certainties. Because a huge percentage of the stuff that I tend to be automatically certain of is, it turns out totally wrong and deluded. I have learned this the hard way, as I predict you graduates will, too.

Here is just one example of the total wrongness of something I tend to be automatically sure of: Everything in my own immediate experience supports

用所谓人文教育的标准来分析这个故事并不难：同样的经历在两个人的解读中迥然不同，因为两个人信念框架不同，从经历中构建意义的方式不同。人文分析珍视宽容和信仰的多元化，所以不会说谁对谁错，谁优谁劣。这本身没有问题，只是我们也从未讨论过个人框架和信仰究竟源自何处。换句话说，它们在这两个人内心的起源是什么。就好像一个人最根本的世界观以及赋予经历的意义，某种程度上是预设好的，就像身高或者鞋码一样；或者就像语言那样，自然而然地从文化中习得。就好像构建意义的方式实际并非个人有意的选择。另外，傲慢的问题也很大。无神论者坚信过路的因纽特人与求助祈祷毫无关联。诚然，也有不少宗教人士自高自大，对自己的见解深信不疑。这种人比无神论者更令人反感，至少对大多数人来说是这样。但是，宗教教条主义者的问题与故事中无神论者的问题完全一致：盲目确信，思想封闭得等同于彻头彻尾的监禁，而囚犯甚至没发现自己被囚禁了。

重点在于，它也是"教人如何思考"的一部分真正意义。少一点自大，多一点对自我认知的批判意识。我发现，很多的东西我不假思索地深信不疑，但实际上是错误的，是有误导性的。我经受了惨痛的教训才明白这一点，我猜你们这些毕业生也一样。

关于这一点我举个例子。我自己的所有直接经验都让我深信，自己是宇宙的绝对中心，是最真实、最生动、最重要的存在。我们不大讨论这种天生且根本的自我

---

5. dogmatist：*n.* 教条主义者。

my deep belief that I am the absolute center of the universe; the realist, most vivid and important person in existence. We rarely talk about this sort of natural, basic self-centeredness because it's so socially repulsive. But it's pretty much the same for all of us. It is our default setting, hard-wired into our boards at birth. Think about it: there is no experience you have had that you are not the absolute center of. The world as you experience it is there in front of you or behind you, to the left or right of you, on your TV or your monitor, and so on. Other people's thoughts and feelings have to be communicated to you somehow, but your own are so immediate, urgent, real.

Please don't worry that I'm getting ready to lecture you about compassion or other-directedness or all the so-called virtues. This is not a matter of virtue. It's a matter of my choosing to do the work of somehow altering or getting free of my natural, hard-wired default setting which is to be deeply and literally self-centered and to see and interpret everything through this lens of self. People who can adjust their natural default setting this way are often described as being "well-adjusted," which I suggest to you is not an accidental term.

Given the triumphant academic setting here, an obvious question is how much of this work of adjusting our default setting involves actual knowledge or intellect. This question gets very tricky. Probably the most dangerous thing about an academic education—least in my own case—is that it enables my tendency to over-intellectualize stuff, to get lost in abstract argument inside my head, instead of simply paying attention to what is going on right in front of me, paying attention to what is going on inside me.

As I'm sure you guys know by now, it is extremely difficult to stay alert and attentive, instead of getting hypnotized by the constant monologue[6] inside your own head—may be happening right now. Twenty years after my own graduation, I have come gradually to understand that the liberal arts cliché about teaching you how to think is actually shorthand for a much deeper, more

中心，因为它在社交上很招人嫌，但它在我们每个人身上都差不多。这是我们的默认设置，一出生就固化在我们的系统中了。想想看：在所有的经历中，自己都是绝对的中心。你们感知到的世界就在前面、后面、左边或右边，电视或电脑屏幕里，等等。别人的想法和感受必须以某种方式传达给你们自己，但自己的想法和感受是如此直接、迫切且真实。

别担心，我没打算给你们讲什么同理心、利他主义之类的所谓美德。这与美德无关，只是我选择要以某种方式改变或摆脱自己自然固有的默认设置，即深度地、真正地以自我为中心，并通过自我这个视角来看待和解读一切。能这样调整自己固有的默认设置的人，常被形容为"适应良好的"，我得指出，我觉得这个表述并非偶然。

鉴于这里学术氛围浓郁，一个显而易见的问题在于，调整默认设置在多大程度上涉及实际知识或智力。这个问题非常复杂。也许学术教育最危险之处在于，它助长了对事物过度分析的倾向，让人迷失于头脑里的抽象论证之中，而不是直接观察眼前之事，关注内心的动态。至少在我的个人经历中是这样。

我敢肯定你们现在都知道，想要持续保持警觉和专注，不被脑海中说个不停的独白所催眠，是一件极为困难的事——也许这种情况现在就在你们的头脑中上演。

> *Blind certainty, a close-mindedness that amounts to an imprisonment so total that the prisoner doesn't even know he's locked up.*
>
> *盲目确信，思想封闭得等同于彻头彻尾的监禁，而囚犯甚至没发现自己被囚禁了。*

---

6. monologue：*n.* 独白；滔滔不绝的讲话。

serious idea: learning how to think really means learning how to exercise some control over how and what you think. It means being conscious and aware enough to choose what you pay attention to and to choose how you construct meaning from experience. Because if you cannot exercise this kind of choice in adult life, you will be totally hosed. Think of the old cliché about quote, "the mind being an excellent servant but a terrible master." This, like many clichés, so lame and unexciting on the surface, actually expresses a great and terrible truth. It is not the least bit coincidental that adults who commit suicide with firearms almost always shoot themselves in the head. They shoot the terrible master. And the truth is that most of these suicides are actually dead long before they pull the trigger.

And I submit that this is what the real, no bullshit value of your liberal arts education is supposed to be about: how to keep from going through your comfortable, prosperous, respectable adult life dead, unconscious, a slave to your head and to your natural default setting of being uniquely, completely, imperially alone day in and day out. That may sound like hyperbole, or abstract nonsense. Let's get concrete. The plain fact is that you graduating seniors do not yet have any clue what "day in day out" really means. There happen to be whole, large parts of adult American life that nobody talks about in commencement speeches. One such part involves boredom, routine, and petty frustration. The parents and older folks here will know all too well what I'm talking about.

By way of example, let's say it's an average adult day, and you get up in the morning, go to your challenging, white-collar, college-graduate job, and you work hard for eight or ten hours, and at the end of the day you're tired and somewhat stressed and all you want is to go home and have a good supper and maybe unwind for an hour, and then hit the sack early because, of course, you have to get up the next day and do it all again. But then you remember

毕业二十年后，我逐渐明白，人文教育中"教人如何思考"的陈词滥调，实际上是一种更深刻、更严肃观念的简略表达：学习如何思考，实际上是指学习如何控制思考方式和思考内容。也就是说，要有足够的意识去筛选关注对象，选择如何从经验中构建意义。倘若成年了还没法做出这样的选择，就彻底完了。想想那句老话："头脑是优秀的仆人，却也是恐怖的主人。"这句话和许多陈词滥调一样，听起来平平无奇，实则道出了深刻且沉重的真理。开枪自杀的成年人几乎都是对着头开枪，这绝非巧合。他们射杀了可怕的主人。实际上，对大多数自杀者来说，远在扣动扳机之前，他们就已经"死"了。

我认为，人文教育的真正价值在于：如何避免在优渥安乐的生活中成为思维和默认设置的俘虏，变得唯我独尊、孤高自傲，从而迷失甚至"死去"。这或许听起来过于夸张，或像是抽象的废话。我们来说点实在的。明摆着的事实是，你们这些即将毕业的学生根本还不懂"日复一日"到底是什么感觉。在美国成人的生活中，其实有很大一部分内容是人们在毕业典礼演讲中从不会提起的，比如乏味的例行公事、琐碎的烦恼挫败。在场的家长和长辈肯定对此深有体会。

我们来看看一个普通成年人的一天会是什么样的。早上起床，去做一份富有挑战性的白领工作，大学毕业生会做的那种，努力工作8到10个小时，等到一天结束时筋疲力尽，压力很大，只想回家，好好吃顿晚饭，最好还能放松一小时，然后早点睡觉，毕竟明天这些还得再来一遍。但紧接着你想起来，家里的食物吃完了。由

> *The mind being an excellent servant but a terrible master.*
>
> 头脑是优秀的仆人，却也是恐怖的主人。

这就是水　339

there's no food at home. You haven't had time to shop this week because of your challenging job, and so now after work you have to get in your car and drive to the supermarket. It's the end of the work day and the traffic is apt to be very bad. So getting to the store takes way longer than it should, and when you finally get there, the supermarket is very crowded, because, of course, it's the time of day when all the other people with jobs also try to squeeze in some grocery shopping. And the store is hideously lit and infused with soul-killing muzak or corporate pop and it's pretty much the last place you want to be but you can't just get in and quickly out; you have to wander all over the huge, over-lit store's confusing aisles to find the stuff you want and you have to maneuver your junky cart through all these other tired, hurried people with carts, etc. etc., cutting stuff out because this is a long ceremony and eventually, you get all your supper supplies, except now it turns out there aren't enough check-out lanes open even though it's the end-of-the-day rush. So the checkout line is incredibly long, which is stupid and infuriating. But you can't take your frustration out on the frantic lady working the register, who is overworked at a job whose daily tedium and meaninglessness surpasses the imagination of any of us here at a prestigious college.

But anyway, you finally get to the checkout line's front, and you pay for your food, and you get told to "Have a nice day" in a voice that is the absolute voice of death. And then you have to take your creepy, flimsy, plastic bags of groceries in your cart with the one crazy wheel that pulls maddeningly to the left, all the way out through the crowded, bumpy[7], littery parking lot, and then you have to drive all the way home through slow, heavy, SUV-intensive, rush-hour traffic, etc. etc.

Everyone here has done this, of course. But it hasn't yet been part of you graduates' actual life routine, day after week after month after year.

But it will be. And many more dreary, annoying, seemingly meaningless

于工作很有挑战性，这周还没能抽出时间去购物，所以下班后必须开车去超市一趟。这是工作日的最后一天，路上会很堵，所以花了比平时长得多的时间才到超市。你千辛万苦到了超市，却发现超市里非常拥挤，这是理所当然的，毕竟所有上班族都只能在这个时间来买东西。超市里亮得晃眼，充斥着令人窒息的背景音乐或偶像团体的流行歌曲，这简直是你最不愿意待的地方，但又不能拿了东西就走人，得在亮得刺眼的大商场里、在混乱的货架之间来回转悠，才能找齐要买的东西，而且还得推着那个破旧的推车，避开其他疲惫又匆忙的人和他们的推车等。还会因为太麻烦了不得不放弃购物清单上的一些东西，最终，你找齐了晚餐需要的所有东西，但现在问题是，即使是晚高峰，超市还是没有开放足够的收银通道，结账的人们大排长龙。这种安排很蠢，很让人恼火，但你不能冲忙疯了的收银员女士发火，她的工作已经超负荷了，她每天的工作单调乏味，毫无意义，远超名牌大学毕业生的想象。

  不管怎样，你终于排到了收银台的前面，付了钱，然后听到人家死气沉沉地说"祝你今天愉快"。然后，你必须把那令人不安的、薄得要命的、装着杂货的塑料袋放在推车里，车上还有个轮子令人抓狂地向左偏，一路穿过拥挤、颠簸[7]、垃圾遍地的停车场，然后在缓慢、拥堵、SUV密集的交通高峰中一路开车回家，等等等等。

  当然，在场的每个人都经历过这些，但对于你们这些毕业生而言，这还尚未成为日复一日，年复一年的日常生活的一部分。

  但你们终将过上这样的生活，而且还会有更多沉闷、烦人、找不到意义之所在

---

7. bumpy: *adj.* 颠簸的，不平的。

routines besides. But that is not the point. The point is that petty, frustrating crap like this is exactly where the work of choosing is gonna come in. Because the traffic jams and crowded aisles and long checkout lines give me time to think, and if I don't make a conscious decision about how to think and what to pay attention to, I'm gonna be pissed and miserable every time I have to shop, because my natural default setting is the certainty that situations like this are really all about me, about my hungriness and my fatigue and my desire to just get home, and it's going to seem for all the world like everybody else is just in my way. And who are all these people in my way? And look at how repulsive[8] most of them are, and how stupid and cow-like and dead-eyed and nonhuman they seem in the checkout line, or at how annoying and rude it is that people are talking loudly on cell phones in the middle of the line. And look at how deeply and personally unfair this is.

Or, of course, if I'm in a more socially conscious liberal arts form of my default setting, I can spend time in the end-of-the-day traffic being disgusted about all the huge, stupid, lane-blocking SUV's and Hummers and V-12 pickup trucks, burning their wasteful, selfish, forty-gallon tanks of gas, and I can dwell on the fact that the patriotic or religious bumper-stickers always seem to be on the biggest, most disgustingly selfish vehicles, driven by the ugliest. This is an example of how not to think, though, biggest most disgustingly selfish vehicles, driven by the ugliest, most inconsiderate and aggressive drivers.

And I can think about how our children's children will despise us for wasting all the future's fuel, and probably screwing up the climate, and how spoiled and stupid and selfish and disgusting we all are, and how modern consumer society just sucks, and so on and so forth.

You get the idea.

If I choose to think this way in a store and on the freeway, fine. Lots of us do. Except thinking this way tends to be so easy and automatic that it doesn't

的日常琐事。这不是重点。重点在于，正是面对这种看似微不足道的挫折和烦恼之时，选择开始发挥作用了。堵塞的交通、拥挤的过道和结账的长队给了我思考的时间。如果不能有意识地决定如何思考和注意什么，每次购物我都会生气，都会感到痛苦，因为天生的默认设置让我觉得一切都与我挂钩，都与我的饥饿、疲劳和想回家的心情挂钩，就好像全世界都挡住了我的去路。这些拦路虎都是些什么人？看看他们中的多数人，多么讨人厌啊，他们在排队结账时看起来愚蠢、呆滞、眼神空洞、没个人样，看看那些一边排队一边打电话的人，多么烦人，真没礼貌啊。不得不承受这一切，对我来说多么不公平啊。

当然了，如果我处于更具社会意识的人文教育默认模式中，我会在晚高峰交通中花时间厌恶那些庞大、蠢笨、挡道的 SUV、悍马和 V-12 皮卡车，它们毫无节制地挥霍着 40 加仑（约合 151.42 升）油箱里的汽油。我会放任自己沉浸在这样的想法里：那些爱国或宗教主体的保险杠贴纸似乎总是贴在那些最庞大、最自私、最恶心的车辆上，司机也都是最丑陋的人。这便是放弃思考的例子，只需要放任自己的情绪，坚信车都是自私自利得令人作呕的大块头，司机都是最丑陋、最自私和最野蛮的人。

我可以想象子孙后代会如何鄙夷我们这代人，毕竟我们浪费了本该属于未来的燃料，或许还破坏了气候，这代人多么任性、愚蠢、自私和恶心，现代消费社会实在是糟透了，诸如此类。

你们懂的。

在商店和高速公路上，如果我选择了这种想法，那也没关系。很多人都是这样

---

8. repulsive：*adj.* 令人厌恶的、令人反感的。

have to be a choice. It is my natural default setting. It's the automatic way that I experience the boring, frustrating, crowded parts of adult life when I'm operating on the automatic, unconscious belief that I am the center of the world, and that my immediate needs and feelings are what should determine the world's priorities.

The thing is that, of course, there are totally different ways to think about these kinds of situations. In this traffic, all these vehicles stopped and idling in my way. It's not impossible that some of these people in SUV's have been in horrible auto accidents in the past, and now find driving so terrifying that their therapist has all but ordered them to get a huge, heavy SUV so they can feel safe enough to drive. Or that the Hummer that just cut me off is maybe being driven by a father whose little child is hurt or sick in the seat next to him, and he's trying to get this kid to the hospital, and he's in a way bigger, more legitimate hurry than I am: it is actually I who am in his way.

Or I can choose to force myself to consider the likelihood that everyone else in the supermarket's checkout line is just as bored and frustrated as I am, and that some of these people probably have much harder, more tedious and painful lives than I do.

Again, please don't think that I'm giving you moral advice, or that I'm saying you are supposed to think this way, or that anyone expects you to just automatically do it. Because it's hard. It takes will and effort, and if you are like me, some days you won't be able to do it, or you just flat out won't want to.

But most days, if you're aware enough to give yourself a choice, you can choose to look differently at this fat, dead-eyed, over-made-up lady who just screamed at her kid in the checkout line. Maybe she's not usually like this. Maybe she's been up three straight nights holding the hand of a husband who is dying of bone cancer. Or maybe this very lady is the low-wage clerk at the motor vehicle department, who just yesterday helped your spouse resolve a

做的。只是，这种思维方式往往太容易自发产生了，根本不需要刻意选择。这就是我固有的默认设置。我自发地、无意识地把自己视作世界的中心，认为全世界都应该优先照顾我的即时需求和感受。面对成年生活的无聊、挫折和拥挤时，我就会无意识地采取这种应对方法。

可问题是，我们本可以用截然不同的视角来看待这种情况。在这样的交通状况下，所有车都停了下来，挡了我的道，那些SUV车主没准出过严重车祸，吓破了胆，所以听治疗师的话，换成了又大又重的SUV，他们才得以放心开车。刚才超车的那辆悍马也许是一个父亲开的，副驾驶上的孩子受伤或生病了，他要送孩子去医院，比我更着急，也急得更有理：其实是我挡了他的道。

也许，我可以选择逼自己这么想：在超市收银台前排队的每个人都和我一样，无聊又沮丧，他们中某些人可能活得比我更艰难、乏味和痛苦得多。

再次声明，我不是在给你们上道德课，也不是在劝你们以这种方式思考，更没有人盼着你们能自发去做。因为这是很难的，很需要意志力和努力，像我，有时候就做不到，或者完全不想做。

只是大多数时候，如果有意识地给自己更多选择的机会，就能够用不同的眼光看待别人，比如收银台前一个一边排队一边冲孩子大喊大叫的、浓妆艳抹的死鱼眼胖女人。也许她平时不是这样的。也许她的丈夫患有骨癌、生命垂危，她已经连着三个晚上没睡了，一直握着丈夫的手。也许这位女士是车辆管理所的基层职员，就

> *If you worship money and things, if they are where you tap real meaning in life, then you will never have enough, never feel you have enough.*
>
> 崇拜金钱和物质，将其视作生活的真正意义，那便会贪得无厌，永不餍足。

这就是水　345

horrific, infuriating, red-tape[9] problem through some small act of bureaucratic kindness. Of course, none of this is likely, but it's also not impossible. It just depends what you what to consider. If you're automatically sure that you know what reality is, and who and what is really important, on your default setting, then you, like me, probably won't consider possibilities that aren't annoying and miserable. But if you really learn how to think, how to pay attention, then you will know you have other options. It will actually be within your power to experience a crowded, hot, slow, consumer-hell type situation as not only meaningful, but sacred, on fire with the same force that lit the stars: love, fellowship, the mystical oneness of all things deep down.

Not that that mystical stuff is necessarily true. The only thing that's capital-T True is that you get to decide how you're gonna try to see it. This, I submit, is the freedom of a real education, of learning how to be well-adjusted. You get to consciously decide what has meaning and what doesn't. You get to decide what to worship, because here's something else that's weird but true: in the day-to-day trenches of adult life, there is actually no such thing as atheism. There is no such thing as not worshipping. Everybody worships. The only choice we get is what to worship. And the compelling reason for maybe choosing some sort of god or spiritual-type thing to worship—be it JC or Allah, be it JHWH[10] or the Wiccan Mother Goddess, or the Four Noble Truths[11], or some inviolable set of ethical principles—is that pretty much anything else you worship will eat you alive. If you worship money and things, if they are where you tap real meaning in life, then you will never have enough, never feel you have enough. It's the truth. Worship your own body and beauty and sexual allure and you will always feel ugly. And when time and age start showing, you will die a million deaths before they finally plant you. On one level, we all know this stuff already. It's been codified as myths, proverbs, clichés, epigrams[12], parables; the skeleton of every great story. The whole trick is

在昨天，她发挥公职人员的力量，做了件好事，帮你们的爱人处理了一个繁文缛节的糟心问题。当然，可能性不高，但也不是完全不可能，关键在于你们自己怎么想。如果不假思索地就认为自己对于现实和真相了如指掌，任凭默认设置运作，那你我便不会想到事情还有其他并不烦人、并不让人痛苦的可能性。但倘若当真学会了思考，学会了关注，你们就会发现原来还有别的选择。你们会发现，原来即使是拥挤、闷热、滞缓、地狱般的购物情境，也可以富有意义，神圣非凡，燃烧着与点亮星星同样的力量：爱、友谊、万物深处神秘的合一。

并不是说玄妙就是真理。唯一正确的是，你们可以决定如何去看待它。我认为，这是真正的教育自由——学习自我调整，掌握赋予事物意义的能力，自主选择信仰。

因为这里有一个奇怪的事实：在成年人日常生活的战壕里，实际上并不存在无神论这回事，不存在不崇拜的情况。每个人都有自己的信仰，唯一可选的是信仰对象。无论是耶稣基督还是安拉，无论是耶和华还是威卡教母神，无论是佛教的四圣谛还是某些不可侵犯的道德原则，也许选择崇拜这类神或灵性事物的原因，是崇拜别的事物会被生吞活剥。崇拜金钱和物质，将其视作生活的真正意义，那便会贪得无厌，永不餍足。事实如此。崇拜肉体、美貌和性魅力，就永远都会觉得自己丑陋，不必等到入土，只要岁月的痕迹浮现出来，就会先死去无数回。道理我们多多少少都懂。神话、谚语、陈词滥调、警句、寓言，每一个伟大故事的骨架之中，都有这

---

9. red-tape：*adj.* 繁文缛节。
10. JHWH：耶和华，来源于《圣经·旧约》。古希伯来人崇拜的独一真神，出于敬畏不敢直呼其名，在经卷中把它的名字写作"JHWH"，只记辅音，不记元音，无法拼读，读经或祈祷时，就用"阿特乃"（adhonay，意为"吾主"）来代替。后来基督教神学家把"adhonay"一词中的元音嵌入"JHWH"之中，拼写成 Jehovah，读作"耶和华"，约定俗成，沿用至今。
11. Four Noble Truths：四圣谛，佛教用语，是释迦牟尼体悟的苦、集、灭、道四条人生真理，四圣谛告诉人们人生的本质是苦，以及之所以苦的原因、消除苦的方法和达到涅槃的最终目的。
12. epigram：*n.* 警句；隽语；诙谐短诗。

keeping the truth up front in daily consciousness.

Worship power, you will end up feeling weak and afraid, and you will need ever more power over others to numb you to your own fear. Worship your intellect, being seen as smart, you will end up feeling stupid, a fraud, always on the verge of being found out. But the insidious thing about these forms of worship is not that they're evil or sinful, it's that they're unconscious. They are default settings. They're the kind of worship you just gradually slip into, day after day, getting more and more selective about what you see and how you measure value without ever being fully aware that that's what you're doing.

And the so-called real world will not discourage you from operating on your default settings, because the so-called real world of men and money and power hums merrily along in a pool of fear and anger and frustration and craving and worship of self. Our own present culture has harnessed these forces in ways that have yielded extraordinary wealth and comfort and personal freedom. The freedom all to be lords of our own tiny skull-sized kingdoms, alone at the center of all creation. This kind of freedom has much to recommend it. But of course there are all different kinds of freedom, and the kind that is most precious, you will not hear much, talk about much, in the great outside world of wanting and achieving and displaying. The really important kind of freedom involves attention and awareness and discipline, and being able truly to care about other people and to sacrifice for them over and over in myriad[13] petty[14], unsexy ways every day.

That is real freedom. That is being educated, and understanding how to think. The alternative is unconsciousness, the default setting, the rat race, the constant gnawing sense of having had, and lost, some infinite thing.

I know that this stuff probably doesn't sound fun and breezy or grandly inspirational the way a commencement speech is supposed to sound. What it is, as far as I can see, is the capital-T Truth, with a whole lot of rhetorical niceties

些道理。诀窍只有一个，那就是，在一个个平凡的日子践行这些道理。

崇拜权力者，终会感到软弱和恐惧，所以永远在追求更多的权力，好凌驾于他人之上，麻痹自己的恐惧。崇拜才智者，被人当作聪明人，终究会觉得自己愚蠢，是个骗子，总是战战兢兢地怕人发现。但这些信仰的险恶之处不在于邪恶、罪恶，而在于它们是无意识的默认设置。人们会日渐深陷其中，对所见所闻的评价日益片面化，自己却察觉不到。

所谓的"现实世界"不会阻拦默认设置的运作，因为由人、金钱和权力组成的所谓"现实世界"，在恐惧、愤怒、沮丧、渴望和自我崇拜的泥潭里畅游哼歌。当代文化利用这些力量收获了财富、舒适与个人自由。所有人都可以自由地主宰头颅大小的王国，独立于万物中央。这种自由值得称道。在这个充斥着欲望、辉煌和夸耀的广袤世界里，自由多种多样，而最珍贵的那种自由却少有人论及。真正重要的自由是关注、觉察和自制，是能够真心实意地关心他人，能够日复一日地、平淡琐碎地付出。

那才是真正的自由。那才是受到了教育，明白了如何思考。若非如此，就只是无意识地活着，是活在默认设置中，是困于无尽竞争中，是挥之不去的蚀心失落，就像曾经拥有而又失去了某种宝贵至极的东西。

我知道，这些东西听起来可能不像毕业典礼演讲该有的那么轻松、有趣或鼓舞人心。但在我看来，它是大写的真理，剥去了辞藻修饰。当然，你们想怎么看待它

> *Everybody worships. The only choice we get is what to worship.*
>
> 每个人都有自己的信仰，唯一可选的是信仰对象。

---

13. myriad：*adj.* 无数的。
14. petty：*adj.* 琐碎的。

stripped away. You are, of course, free to think of it whatever you wish. But please don't just dismiss it as just some finger wagging Dr. Laura[15] sermon. None of this stuff is really about morality or religion or dogma or big fancy questions of life after death.

The capital-T Truth is about life before death.

It is about the real value of a real education, which has almost nothing to do with knowledge, and everything to do with simple awareness; awareness of what is so real and essential, so hidden in plain sight all around us, all the time, that we have to keep reminding ourselves over and over:

"This is water."

"This is water."

It is unimaginably hard to do this, to stay conscious and alive in the adult world day in and day out. Which means yet another grand cliché turns out to be true: your education really is the job of a lifetime. And it commences: now.

I wish you way more than luck.

都行。但请不要只把它看作劳拉博士式的说教。它实际上无关道德、宗教、教条或来世之类的深奥议题。

这一真理讲的是现世之事。

它讲的是真正教育的真正价值，它几乎无关知识，而全然关乎简单的觉察；觉察到那些真实和本质的东西，那些极为隐蔽却又无处不在的东西，那些显而易见却需要时时自我警醒的东西：

"这就是水。"

"这就是水。"

在成人世界里，想要日复一日地保持清醒和活力，难度超乎想象。这意味着又一个陈词滥调被证实了：教育是终生的事业。而这项事业即将开启。

愿大家拥有的不只是好运。

---

15. Dr. Laura：劳拉·马卡姆博士，美国著名亲子育儿专家、哥伦比亚临床心理学博士、《父母平和孩子快乐》的作者。

语录 Quotes

- The most obvious, important realities are often the ones that are hardest to see and talk about.

  最明显、最重要的事实往往也最难被看到和讨论。

- The really significant education in thinking that we're supposed to get in a place like this isn't really about the capacity to think, but rather about the choice of what to think about.

  在这样一个环境中，我们理应接受的思考教育关键不在于思考能力，而在于思考对象的选择。

- Blind certainty, a close-mindedness that amounts to an imprisonment so total that the prisoner doesn't even know he's locked up.

  盲目确信，思想封闭得等同于彻头彻尾的监禁，而囚犯甚至没发现自己被囚禁了。

- The mind being an excellent servant but a terrible master.

  头脑是优秀的仆人，却也是恐怖的主人。

- If you're automatically sure that you know what reality is, and who and what is really important, on your default setting, then you, like me, probably won't consider possibilities that aren't annoying and miserable.

  如果不假思索地就认为自己对于现实和真相了如指掌，任凭默认设置运作，那你我便不会想到事情还有其他并不烦人、并不让人痛苦的可能性。

- Everybody worships. The only choice we get is what to worship.

  每个人都有自己的信仰，唯一可选的是信仰对象。

这就是水

Thirteen Lessons on Life
十三堂人生课

——马修·麦康纳 2015 年在休斯敦大学毕业典礼上的演讲

简介 Profile

马修·麦康纳

Matthew McConaughey

马修·麦康纳1969年出生于美国得克萨斯州，1993年毕业于美国得克萨斯大学奥斯汀分校，获广播电视电影学士学位。作为炙手可热的明星，毫无疑问，马修·麦康纳拥有非常迷人的外表：黝黑健康的肌肤、完美的肌肉曲线，浑身散发着一股阳光、野性、自信的气质，是个不折不扣的"得克萨斯之子"。

1993年，马修在电影《年少轻狂》中扮演一个派对男孩，这是他的第一部电影。虽然在片中只有三句台词，但是他的天分展露无遗，凭借突破性的表演得到关注。作为一名演员，在最初的很长一段时期内，马修因为参演《婚礼专家》《十日拍拖手册》等浪漫喜剧片，一直被称作"浪漫喜剧之王"。后来，马修·麦康纳试着挑战自我，开始在电影中饰演复杂的角色。事实证明，他的选择是正确的，这些影片让他成为名副其实的演技派。

2013年，马修在电影《达拉斯买家俱乐部》中扮演一位被医生告知生命只剩30天却坚持与病魔抗争的艾滋病患者。凭借此片，马修·麦康纳获得了当年的金球奖最佳男主角和奥斯卡金像奖最佳男主角。2014年，马修又在科幻电影《星际穿越》中担任男主角，广受好评。

目睹马修短时间内从"花瓶"到"演技派"这样脱胎换骨的变化，美国媒体创造了一个新词"麦康纳的复兴"（McConaissance），由"麦康纳"（McConaughey）和"文艺复兴"（Renaissance）两个词组合而成，意为"重获新生"。

2015年5月，马修·麦康纳在休斯敦大学做毕业演讲。在40多分钟的演讲中，他和毕业生们分享了13条人生哲理，告诉他们，在人生高速发展的关键时期，应该持有什么样的观念和心态才能持续精进，少走弯路。

演讲 Speech

Congratulations, class of 2015. You guys and gals and young men and women are the reason I'm here. I'm really looking forward to talking with ya'll tonight. You heard my dad played football here, and I believe he even graduated from here, as an extra incentive for me to come. Short and sweet or long and salty? A sugar donut or some oatmeal? Out of respect for you and your efforts in getting your degree, I thought long and hard about what I could share with you tonight. You know, did I want to stand up here at a podium and read you your rights? Did I want to come up here to share some really funny stories? I thought about what you would want. I thought about what you might need. I also thought about what I want to say and what I need to say. Hopefully, we're both going to be happy on both accounts. As the saying goes: Take what you like; leave the rest. Thank you for having me.

So, before I share with you some what I do know, I want to talk with you about what I don't know.

Now, I have two older brothers. One was in high school in the early 1970s. This was a time when a high school GED[1] got you a job and college degree was exemplary.

My other brother, Pat, was in high school in the early 80s, and by this time the GED wasn't enough to guarantee employment—you needed a college degree. And if you got one, you had a pretty good chance of getting the kind of

恭喜你们，2015届的毕业生。正是因为你们这些少男少女，我才来到了这里。我真的很期待今晚同你们所有人聊一聊。你们都知道我老爸曾在这里踢过足球，我相信他甚至是从这里毕业的，这是让我来到这里的另一个动机。你们是想要简短愉快的聊天，还是尖锐辛辣的长篇大论呢？甜甜圈还是燕麦粥？出于对你们以及你们为获得学位而付出的努力的尊重，我苦思冥想了许久，想着今晚该和你们分享些什么。你们以为我想站在讲台上告诉你们应享有的权利，还是来这里和你们分享几个有趣的故事？我思考过你们想要什么，你们可能会需要什么。我还思考过我想说什么以及我需要说什么。我希望能两者兼顾，皆大欢喜。俗话说得好，拿走你们喜欢的，其余的留下来。多谢你们邀请我。

在我同你们分享一些我知道的事情之前，我想先谈谈我不知道的事情。

我有两个哥哥。一个哥哥在20世纪70年代初上高中。在那个年代，拥有高中同等学力就能找到工作，而拥有大学文凭就更是模范了。

我的另一位哥哥派特，在20世纪80年代初上高中，而那时，只有高中同等学力已经不能保证找到工作了，你需要大学文凭。如果你有大学文凭，毕业后就很有

> *Do not fall into the trap, the entitlement trap, of feeling like you're a victim: you are not. Get over and get on with it.*
>
> 别掉进陷阱里，那些权利陷阱——让你们感觉自己像个受害者的陷阱。你们不是。要克服这种感觉，行动起来。

---

1. GED：General Equivalent Diploma 的缩写，意为"同等学力"。

job that you wanted after you graduated.

Now me, I graduated from high school in 1988, got my college degree in 1993. And that college degree in '93 did not mean as much. It was not a ticket; it was not a voucher; it was not a free pass go to anything.

So, I ask the question: what does your college degree mean?

It means you got an education; it means you have more knowledge in a specific subject, vocation; it means you may have more expertise in what your degree is in.

But what's it worth? In the job market? Out there, today?

We know the market for college graduates is more competitive now than ever. Now some of you already have a job lined up, you've got a path where today's job is going to become tomorrow's career, but for most of you the future's probably still pretty fuzzy—you don't have that job that directly reflects the degree you just got. Many of you don't even have a job at all. Think about it: You've just completed your scholastic educational curriculum in life—the one you started when you were 5 years old in kindergarten up until now, and your future may not be any more clear than it was 5 years ago. You don't have the answers and it's probably pretty damn scary.

And I say, that's OK, 'cause that is how it is: This is the reality that many of you are facing. This is the world that we live in. And well, I'm not here to discourage you or in any way belittle your accomplishments. But tonight, which I'd like to applaud that one more time—you graduated. Now I'm not here to be a downer on that. Let's get that straight, but I am here to talk brass tacks[2]. I want to skip the flattery and the attaboys[3], 'cause I do know this: the sooner that we become less impressed with our life, with our accomplishments, with our career, with whatever that prospect is in front of us, the sooner we become less impressed and more involved with that and these things, the sooner we get a whole lot better at doing them.

可能找到心仪的工作。

现在轮到我了。我 1988 年高中毕业，1993 年拿到大学文凭。然而在 1993 年，大学文凭已经不算什么了。它不是门票，不是凭证，不是去任何地方的免费入场券。

所以我要问的问题是：你们的大学文凭意味着什么？

它意味着你们受过教育，意味着你们在某一具体学科、行业上具有更多的知识，意味着你们在获得学位的那个领域中拥有更多的专业知识。

但是这个学位价值何在？在就业市场上，在那里，就在当下，有什么价值？

我们知道，对于大学毕业生来说，如今就业市场里的竞争史无前例的激烈。你们中的一些人已经找到了一份工作，现在的工作将会变为未来的事业，你们已经走在这样的道路上。但对你们中的多数人而言，未来可能仍然相当模糊——你们找不到和你们刚刚获得的学位相匹配的工作。你们中的许多人甚至根本找不到工作。想想看：你们刚刚完成了人生中的学校教育课程——从 5 岁上幼儿园时就开始一直到现在的课程。你们的未来可能并不比 5 年前更清晰。你们找不到答案，而这可能相当吓人。

我认为这没什么，因为事实如此：这正是你们中的许多人面对的现实。这就是我们生活的世界。我今晚来这里不是让你们气馁，也不是要用任何方式来贬低你们的成就。今晚，我要再次为你们的成就鼓掌——你们毕业了。我不是来这里泼冷水的。坦白地说，我是来这里讨论基本事实的。我想跳过那些恭维和安慰的话，因为我知道，对于我们的人生、我们的成就、我们的职业、我们的前程，我们越快以平常心待之，越快地投入其中，我们就越快做得更好。

2. brass tack：基本实情；铁证。
3. attaboy：n. 好小伙，用于表示赞许、钦佩或鼓励。

So, I'm gonna talk to you about some things I've learned in my journey—most from experience, some I heard in passing, many I'm still practicing, but all of them, I do believe are true.

Now they may be truths to me, but don't think that makes them mine, because you cannot own a truth. So please think of these as signposts, approaches, paradigms, that give some science to satisfaction. They are yours to steal. They are yours to share, liken to your own lives, to personally apply in your own lives, in your own way, should you choose to. So, here we go:

No.1: This should come up to the Jumbotron[4]. Life's not easy.

It's up there. Life is not easy. It is not. Don't try to make it that way. Life's not fair; it never was; it isn't now; it won't ever be. Do not fall into the trap, the entitlement trap, of feeling like you're a victim: you are not. Get over and get on with it. And yes, most things are more rewarding when you break a sweat to get 'em. Fact.

No. 2: "Unbelievable" is the stupidest word in the dictionary.

It shouldn't ever come out of our mouths. Think about it. To say, "Oh wow, what an unbelievable play!" "It was an unbelievable book, unbelievable film, unbelievable act of courage …" Really?

It may be spectacular, maybe phenomenal, most excellent or outstanding, but unbelievable? Uhuh! Give others and yourself more credit. It just happened; you witnessed it; you just did it; believe it!

What about the other side of unbelievable? You know that side when we humans underperform or act out of our best character. For instance, a man flies a suicide jet into the World Trade Center. Millions die from diseases every day that we have cures for. Bob, the builder, swears that he's gonna have your house built by Thanksgiving and you can't move in until Christmas, the next year. Our best friends lie to us, and we lie to ourselves all the time. Unbelievable? I don't think so. Again, it just happened, and it happens every day.

所以，我想和你们谈谈我在我的人生之旅中学到的一些东西——多数是亲身经历，另有一些是我听说的，许多我现在还在践行中，但我相信所有这些都是正确的。

不过，虽然它们对我来说可能是真理，但不要以为它们就是属于我的，因为你是不可能占有一条真理的。所以请把它们视作给幸福提供一些技巧的路标、途径和范例。这些东西属于你，你可以偷偷地拿走，也可以与人分享；可以比作你们自己的生活，也可以亲自将其应用于你自己的人生，用你自己的方式。如果你们选择那么做，好，我们开始。

第一点，这一点应当出现在大屏幕上：生活不容易。

就在大屏幕上，生活不容易，不容易。别试图让它变得一帆风顺。生活是不公平的，之前如此，现在也是，将来也不会公平。别掉进权利陷阱里，那种让你们感觉自己像个受害者的陷阱。你们不是。要克服这种心态，行动起来。是的，只要你们付出努力，多数情况下都会得到回报。事实如此。

第二点："难以置信"是词典里最愚蠢的词。

这个词永远都不应该从你们的嘴里说出来。想想看，"噢哇，多么难以置信的戏剧！""这是本难以置信的书，难以置信的电影，难以置信的英勇之举……"之类的话。当真如此吗？

它可能很壮观，可能很惊人，极其出色或优异，但是它难以置信吗？不！给别人和自己多些信任。它就是发生了，你见证了它，你刚完成了它，所以相信它！

"难以置信"的另一面又是怎样的呢？当我们人类表现不佳或者未能竭尽全力时，你们就知道另一面是什么样的了。例如，一个人驾驶一架喷气式飞机自杀性地撞向世贸大厦。每天都有数百万人死于我们能够治愈的疾病。建筑商鲍勃发誓他能在感恩节之前造好你的房子，可你直到来年圣诞节也未能搬入新家。最好的朋友对我们撒谎，我们也一直对自己撒谎。这些都难以置信吗？我不这么认为。再次强调，它已经发生了，每天都在发生。

---

4. jumbotron：*n.* 大屏幕。

Nothing that we homo sapiens[5] earthlings[6] to do is unbelievable and if there's one thing you can depend on people being is people. So we shouldn't be surprised. We us are the trickiest mammal walking on the planet! I'm not worried about the monkeys. I'm worried about you and me.

So acknowledge the acts of greatness as real, and do not be naive about mankind's capacity for evil, nor be in denial of our own shortcomings. Nothing we do is unbelievable. It is a stupid word. I think it is an un-be-lievably stupid word. That's No. 2.

So … No. 3: Happiness is different than joy.

You hear that all the time, don't ya? "I just want to be happy." Hum … just wanna be happy. But what's happiness? Happiness is an emotional response to an outcome. If I win I will be happy; if I don't I won't. It's an if-then, cause and effect, quid pro quo[7] standard that we cannot sustain because we immediately raise it every time we attain it. You see happiness … happiness demands a certain outcome. It is result-reliant.

And I say if happiness is what you're after, then you are gonna be let down frequently and you're gonna be unhappy much of your time. Joy, though, Joy's a different thing; it's something else. Joy is not a choice. It's not a response to some result. It's a constant. Joy is the feeling that we have from doing what we are fashioned to do, no matter the outcome.

Personally, as an actor, I started enjoying my work and literally being more happy when I stopped trying to make the daily labor a means to a certain end. For example, I need this film to be a box office success; I need my performance to be acknowledged; I need the respect of my peers.

All those are reasonable aspirations[8], but the truth is, as soon as the work, the daily making of the movie, the doing of the deed, became the reward in itself, for me? I got more box-office, more accolades[9], and more respect than I'd ever had before. See, joy is always in process; it's under construction; it's

我们现代的凡人所做的事情没有一件是难以置信的。如果还有一件事可以相信，那就是相信人类是人。所以我们不应当感到吃惊，我们是这个星球上最复杂的哺乳动物！我不担心猴子。我担心的是你们和我自己。

所以，要承认那些伟大之举是真实的，也不要天真地低估人类作恶的能力，或者否认我们自己的缺点。我们所做的事情没有一件是难以置信的。这是个愚蠢的单词。我认为这是个愚蠢得难以置信的单词。这就是第二点。

那么……**第三点：快乐不同于喜悦。**

你们常听到这种说法吧："我只不过是想快乐。"嗯……只不过是想快乐。但是什么是快乐？快乐是对结果的情绪反应。如果我赢了，我就会快乐；如果我输了，我就不快乐。这是一种"如果—那么"、因果关系、等价交换的标准，我们无法让它持久，因为每次我们获得快乐，我们立刻就将标准提高。你瞧，快乐需要结果，它依赖于结果。

我说，如果你们追求的就是快乐，那么你们就会不断地感到失望，多数时候你们都不会快乐。可是喜悦却不是。它和快乐不同。喜悦不是一种选择，不是对某种结果的反应。喜悦是一种恒常的状态。喜悦来源于做我们喜欢做的事，与结果无关。

就我个人而言，作为演员，当我不再试图将每天的劳动作为达到某种特定目的的手段时，我开始享受我的工作，并且的确变得更快乐了。这种目的可以是我需要这部电影票房大卖，我需要我的表演获得认可，我需要得到同龄人的尊重。

所有这些都是合理的愿望，但事实是，一旦工作本身、每天的影片拍摄、做事本身变成了回报，那对于我的意义呢？我得到了比以往更高的票房、更多的赞誉和更多的尊重。瞧，喜悦总是在过程之中，在不断构建当中；它会不经意地到来，就

---

5. homo sapien：现代人。
6. earthling：*n.* 凡人，俗人。
7. quid pro quo：*n.* 补偿物；等价交换。
8. aspiration：*n.* 渴望，期望。
9. accolade：*n.* 荣誉。

inconstant approach, alive and well in the doing of what we are fashioned to do and enjoying it.

No. 4: Define success for yourself.

You all really like that one? Define success for yourself. Now check this out: I'm in the south of New Orleans a few years ago. I went to a voodoo shop, and they had this wooden partition against the wall, these columns. And in these columns were all these vials of these magic potions, right. And headings above each potion defining what they would give you were things like fertility, health, family, legal help, energy, forgiveness, money.

Guess which column was empty? Money. Let's admit it. Money is king today. It's what makes the world go round. It is success. The more we have, the more successful we are, right?

Now I'd argue that our cultural values have even been financialized—humility is not in vogue anymore; it's too passive. It's a get-rich-quick on the Internet, riches' 15-minutes-of-fame world that we live in. And we see it every day.

But, we all want to succeed, right? So the question we have to ask ourselves is what success is to us. What success is to you? Is it more money? That's fine. I got nothing against money. Maybe it's a healthy family; maybe it's a happy marriage; maybe it's to help other, to be famous, to be spiritually sound, to leave the world a little bit better place than you found it.

Continue to ask yourself that question. Now your answer may change over time. That's fine, but do yourself this favor: Whatever your answer is, don't choose anything that will jeopardize your soul. Prioritize who you are, who you want to be. And don't spend time with anything that antagonizes your character. Don't drink the Kool-Aid, man! It tastes sweet, but it will give you cavities tomorrow. Life is not a popularity contest. Be brave; take the hill, but first, answer the question: "What's my hill?"

在我们从事自己喜欢做的事情并享受这一过程当中。

第四点：定义自己的成功。

你们都喜欢这一点吗？自己定义成功。现在，来看看这个。几年前我在新奥尔良南部待过。我去过一家伏都巫术商店，店内靠墙处有一个木制隔断，上面有一些竖栏。在那些竖栏里全是装有魔法药剂的小瓶子。每瓶药剂上面都标明了它们会带给你的东西，诸如生育、健康、家庭、法律援助、能量、宽恕、金钱等。

猜猜哪个竖栏是空的？金钱。我们承认，现在金钱至上。它让世界运转。它就是成功。我们的钱越多，我们就越成功，对吗？

我认为我们的文化价值观甚至都被金钱化了——谦逊已经不再流行，那样太被动了。我们生活在一个可以在互联网上快速致富，富人的名声又转瞬即逝的世界。我们每天都看到这样的事情发生。

可是我们所有人都想获得成功，对吧？所以我们必须问自己的问题就是，对我们来说，成功是什么。成功对你们来说意味着什么？是挣更多的钱吗？这没问题。我并不反对金钱。成功也许是拥有一个健康的家庭；也许是快乐的婚姻；也许是帮助别人，名扬天下，心灵健全，让这个世界比你发现它时变好了一点点。

你要不断地问自己这个问题，答案可能随着时间而改变。没有关系，但是一定要帮你自己这个忙：不论答案是什么，不要做任何出卖灵魂的事情。首先要考虑一下你是谁，你想成为什么人。不要花费时间在任何有违本性的事情上。伙计，不要喝"酷爱牌"饮料！它喝起来很甜，但明天会让你长龋齿。人生并非一场声望竞赛。要勇敢，要攻占山头，但首先得回答这个问题："我要的是哪座山？"

Do not fall into the trap, the entitlement trap, of feeling like you're a victim—you are not. Get over and get on with it.

别掉进权利陷阱里，那种让你们感觉自己像个受害者的陷阱。你们不是。要克服这种心态，行动起来。

So me, how do I define success? For me, myself. For me, it's a measurement of five things. We got fatherhood; we got being a good husband; we got my health: mind, body, spirit; we got career; and we got friendships. These were important to me in my life right now.

So, I try to measure these five things each day. I check in with them. I like to see whether or not I'm in the debit section or the credit section with each one. Am I in the red or am I in the black, you follow?

For instance, sometimes, say, my career is rolling. It's way appearing in the black. But I see my relationship with my wife maybe could use a little bit more of my attention. I gotta pick up the slack on being a better husband; get that one out of the red. Or say my spiritual health could use some maintenance—it's down here. But hey man, my friendships and my social life are in high gear. Right? I gotta recalibrate; checks and balances; I gotta go to church; remember to say "thank you" more often. Something. But I gotta take the tally, because I want to keep all five in healthy shape, and I know that if I don't take care of them, if I don't keep up maintenance on them, one of them is gonna get weak, man. It's gonna dip too deep into the debit section. It's gonna go bankrupt. It's gonna get sick, die even.

So first, we have to define success for ourselves and then we have to put in the work to maintain it: Take that daily tally, tend our garden, keep the things that are important to us in good shape.

Let's admit it. We've all got two wolves in us: a good one and a bad one, and they both wanna eat. Best I can tell, we just gotta feed that good one a little more than the other one. Here we go.

No. 5: Process of elimination is the first step to our identity, a.k.a.[10] where you are not is as important as where you are.

All right, 1992, I got my first job as an actor. Three lines, three days' work, in a film called *Dazed and Confused*. All right, all right, all right.[11] All right.

那么我呢，我是如何定义成功的呢？对我自己而言，成功就是对五件事的考量：做个好父亲，做个好丈夫，心灵、肉体和精神的健康，事业成功，拥有友谊。这些就是我目前生活中重要的东西。

因此我每天都试图考量这五件事。我审视它们。我喜欢看自己在每一项上是处于借方还是贷方的位置，是亏欠还是有结余。你们明白我的意思吧？

例如，有时我的事业进展顺利。这一项看上去是盈余。但我发现我可能需要多关注一下与妻子的关系。我得紧张起来，做个更好的丈夫，把这一项的欠账补上。抑或是我的精神健康需要维护——最近情绪低落。不过我和朋友们的关系以及我的社交生活却高速运转，对吧？我得重新调整，得协调平衡。我得上教堂，要记得多说"谢谢"。诸如此类。但我得记账，因为我想要这五件事情全都保持良好状态。而且我知道，如果我对它们不上心，不及时维护它们的话，它们中的某一项就会变得糟糕，深陷入亏欠的部分里。这会导致破产，会生病，甚至丧命。

因此，首先我们得为自己定义成功，然后我们得付出努力维护它：每天记账，修整花园，让那些对我们而言重要的东西保持良好的状态。

不容否认，我们心里都有两头狼：一头好的，一头恶的。它们都想吃东西。我能说的就是，我们得让好狼比恶狼多吃点。就是这样。

第五点：**不断进行清减是构建我们身份的第一步，也就是说，你不在的地方同你所在的地方一样重要。**

好吧，1992年，我获得了我作为演员的第一份工作。三行台词，三天的工作，

---

10. a.k.a.：also known as 的缩写，意为"亦称，或者说"。
11. All right, all right, all right.：出自马修·麦康纳的第一部电影《年少轻狂》，这是其中最著名的一句话。

There we go.

So the director of that film, Richard Linklater, he kept inviting me back to set each night, putting me in more scenes which led to more lines, all of which I happily said yes to. I mean, I'm having a blast; people are telling me I'm good at what I'm doing, and they write me a check for $325 a day. I mean hell, yeah, give me more scenes; I love what I'm doing. Well, by the end of the shoot, by the end of the film, those three lines had turned into over three weeks, work, and it was mine; it was Wooderson's 1970 Chevelle that we went to get Aerosmith tickets in. Yeah. It was bad ass.

Well, a few years ago I'm watching this film again, and I notice two scenes that I really shouldn't have been in. In one of these scenes, my character Wooderson, I exited screen left to head somewhere, then I re-entered the screen to double-check if any of the other characters wanted to go with me. Now, in re-watching the film, and you'll agree if you know Wooderson, Wooderson was not a guy who would ever say later, and then come back to see if you were sure you didn't wanna go. Now when Wooderson leaves, Wooderson is gone. He does not stutter step, flinch, rewind, ask twice, or solicit[12]. You know what I'm talking about. Wooderson has better things to do, like liking those high school girls, man, 'cause I get older and they stay the same age.

My point is I should not have been in that scene. I shouldn't come back. I should have exited screen left and never come back.

But back then, making my first film, getting invited back to the set, cashing that check and having a ball, I wanted more screen time. I wanted to be in the scene longer and more and come back into the scene, right? But I shouldn't have been there: Wooderson shouldn't have been there.

It is just as important where we are not as it is where we are.

The first step that leads to our identity in life is usually not "I know who I am." I know who I am. That's not the first step. The first step's usually "I know

在电影《年少轻狂》里。好吧，好吧，好吧。好吧。这样就对了。

这部电影的导演理查德·林克莱特每晚都邀请我返回片场，让我拍更多的镜头，所以就有更多的台词，我对这一切都愉快地接受了。我是说，我非常开心，因为人们告诉我，我很擅长做正在做的事情，而且他们支付我每天 325 美元的酬劳。我的意思是，是的，让我多拍些镜头吧，我喜欢正在做的事情。好啦，拍摄结束、影片完成时，原来的三行台词已经变成了三个多星期的工作，它变成我的电影了；我们开着伍德森的 1970 年雪佛兰去买空中铁匠乐队的演出票。是的，酷极了。

几年之后我又看了一遍这部影片，我注意到有两个场景我不该出现。在其中一个场景里，我扮演的角色伍德森从左边退场前往某处，然后又重新进入镜头，再次确认是否有其他人想和我一起去。现在再次看电影，如果你了解伍德森的话，你会同意下面这一点：他不是一个会过后折返确定你是否的确不想去的人。当伍德森离开时，他就走了。他不会犹豫、退缩、绕回来、再次询问，或者请求。你们明白我的意思。伍德森有更重要的事情要做，例如追求那些高中女孩儿，嘿，因为我在变老，而她们却永葆青春。

我要说的是，我不该出现在那个场景里，我不该回去。我应该从屏幕的左边退场，不再返回。

但在当时，那是我的第一部电影，被邀请返回片场，兑现那张支票，举办舞会，我想要拍更多的镜头。我想在电影场景里多待会儿，想要返回到里面。但我本不该在那儿：伍德森本不该在那儿。

我们不在的地方和我们所在的地方同样重要。

要确定我们在生活中的身份，首先要做的通常不是"我知道我是谁"。我知道我

---

12. solicit：*vi.* 征求，请求。

who I am not." Process of elimination.

Defining ourselves by what we are not is the first step that leads us to really knowing who we are.

You know, that group of friends that you hang out with, that really might not bring out the best in you? You know, they gossip too much, or they're kind of shady, and they really aren't gonna be there for you in a pinch? Or how about that bar that we keep going to, that we always seem to have the worst hangover from? Or that computer screen, right, that computer screen that keeps giving us an excuse not to get out of the house and engage with the world and get some real human interaction. Or how about that food that we keep eating, that stuff that tastes so good going down, makes us feel like crap the next week when we feel lethargic and we keep putting on weight?

Well, those people, those places, those things—stop giving them your time and energy. Just don't go there; I mean, put them down. And when you do this, when you do put'em down, when you quit going there, when you quit giving them your time, you inadvertently find yourself spending more time and in more places that are healthy for you, that bring you more joy. Why? Because you just eliminated the whos, the wheres, the whats, the whens that were keeping you from your identity. Trust me, too many options, I promise you, too many options makes tyrants of us all. So get rid of the excess, the wasted time, decrease your options. And if you do this, you will have accidentally, almost innocently, put in front of you what is important to you by process of elimination.

Knowing who we are is hard. It's hard. Give yourself a break. Eliminate who you are not first, and you're gonna find yourself where you need to be.

No. 6: "Don't leave crumbs" and the beauty of delayed gratification.

So what are crumbs? The crumbs I'm talking about are the choices that we make—that make us have to look over our shoulder in the future.

是谁，那不是第一步。第一步通常是"我知道我不是谁"。这是一个不断清减的过程。

根据我们不是谁来定义我们自己，这是引导我们真正了解自己是谁的第一步。

你们知道吗，那群你们常厮混在一起的朋友并不能让你展现出最好的一面。他们太爱传闲话，或者名声不好，在你需要的时候，他们并未在你身边。又比如那个酒吧，我们常去那里，总是喝得烂醉。又比如那个电脑屏幕。对，那个电脑屏幕一直给我们借口，让我们足不出户，不去和世界打交道，不去获取真正的人际交流。再比如我们一直在吃的食物，那种吃下去口感很棒，但第二周却让我们感觉糟透了，让我们无精打采、体重飙升的食物。

对于那些人、那些地方、那些东西，不要再花费时间和精力在上面。别再去那里；我的意思是，放下它们。当你这么做的时候，当你真的放下的时候，当你不再去那里，不再在那上面浪费时间的时候，不经意间你就会发现，你有了更多的时间，去更多对你有益并带给你快乐的地方。为什么呢？因为你们清除了那些阻碍你们找到自我的人物、地点、事情和时间。相信我，选择太多——我向你们保证——会让我们变成暴君。所以，丢掉那些多余的东西，无意义的时间，减少选择。如果你这么做了，你就会通过这种清减过程，在不经意间，几乎是在毫无意识中，得到对你重要的东西。

知道我们是谁，这件事很难。真的很难。放轻松，首先清除掉不属于你的东西，你就会发现你需要成为什么样的人。

第六点："不要留下麻烦"，以及延迟享乐的好处。

那么什么是麻烦呢？我所说的麻烦就是那些让我们在将来不得不担惊受怕的选择。

> *Joy is the feeling that we have from doing what we are fashioned to do, no matter the outcome.*
> 喜悦来源于做我们喜欢做的事，与结果无关。

You didn't pay that guy back the money that you owed him and tonight you just saw him three rows behind you, shit! You slept around on your spouse, and you just found out that tomorrow she and the lady you're having an affair with are gonna be at the same PTA meeting. Shit again. You drank too much last night; you're too hangover to drive your son to his 8 a.m. Saturday morning baseball practice. These are the crumbs! They come in the form of regret, guilt, and remorse[13]. You leave crumbs today. They will cause you more stress tomorrow, and they disallow you from creating a customized future in which you do not have to look over your shoulder.

So let's flip the script. Instead of creating outcomes that take from us, let's create more outcomes that pay us back, fill us up, keep your fire lit, turn you on, for the most amount of time in your future.

These are the choices I'm talking about and this is the beauty of delayed gratification.

Tee yourself up. Do yourself a favor. Make the choices, the purchases today that pay you back tomorrow. Residuals[14], in my business, we call it "mailbox money." If I do my job well today, and that movie keeps re-running on TV, five years from now I'm getting checks in the mailbox. It's a heck of a deal.

So, whether its prepping the coffee maker the night before so all you gotta do is press the button in the morning, or getting ready for the job interview early so you don't have to cram the night before, or choosing not to hook up with that married woman because you know you're gonna feel horrible about tomorrow and her husband carries a gun. Or paying your debts on time so that when you do see that guy three rows back tonight you don't have to hunker down in your seat hoping he doesn't see you. Get some R.O.I.[15]. You know what that is? Return on investment. Your investment. You customize your future. Don't leave crumbs.

你欠某个人的钱没有还，而今晚你却看见他就坐在你后面三排的地方，见鬼！你背着配偶与别人厮混，却发现第二天她将与那个和你发生风流韵事的女人参加同一场家长会，真是见鬼！昨晚你喝得太醉了，没法开车送孩子去参加周六早上八点钟的棒球训练。这些就是麻烦！它们以遗憾、愧疚和悔恨的形式出现。今天你留下麻烦，明天它们就会给你带来更多的困扰。它们将会使你无法创造一个你想要的无忧的未来。

那让我们摆明立场吧。在未来的大部分时间里，不要制造会让你付出代价的后果，而是要创造出更多能给你以回报、令你感到充实、让你激情不减、使你身心愉快的结果。

这些就是我所谈的选择，这就是延迟享乐的好处。

做好准备，帮自己个忙。只做那些未来给你回报的选择和努力。在我们这行，电影复映追加酬金被称为"邮箱钱"。如果我今天干得好，拍出的影片一直在电视上反复播出，那么五年后我的邮箱里还会收到支票。这划算极了。

所以，头天晚上准备好咖啡机，第二天早上需要做的就是按下按钮；早早为工作面试做好准备，就不必在前一天晚上临时抱佛脚；不要选择和那个已婚妇女搭讪，因为你知道明天会感觉很糟糕，而且她丈夫将拿着枪来找你；记得及时还债，那样当你今晚看到坐在你三排之后的那个人时，你就不必缩在椅子里希望他不要看见你。你们要有 R.O.I.。你们知道那是什么吧？投资回报率。你们自己的投资，建构你们自己的未来。不要留下麻烦。

---

13. remorse：*n.* 悔恨。
14. residuals：*n.* 剩余工资；（电影、电视节目等）复播复映追加酬金。
15. R.O.I.：return on investment 的缩写，即投资回报率。

No. 7: Dissect your successes and reciprocity of gratitude.

We so often focus on failure, don't we? We study failure. We obsess with failure. We dissect failure and our failures. We dissect them so much. We end up intoxicated with them to the point of disillusion.

When we write in our diary, usually? When we're depressed. What do we gossip about? Other people's flaws and limitations. We can dissect ourselves into self-loathing if we're not careful. I find that most of the times our obsession with what is wrong just seems breeding more wrong, more failure.

Now the easiest way to dissect success is through gratitude. Giving thanks for that which we do have, for what is working, appreciating the simple things we sometimes take for granted. We give thanks for these things, and that gratitude reciprocates, creating more to be thankful for. It's really simple and it works.

I'm not saying being denial of your failures. No, we can learn from them too, but only if we look at them constructively, as a means to reveal what we are good at, what we can get better at, what we do succeed at.

Now personally, I've read a whole lot of my bad reviews, all right? I've had quite a few. Written by the more talented critics, they're the ones who give constructive bad reviews. They reveal to me what did translate in my work, what came across, what was seen, or what wasn't. Now I don't obsess on the unfavorable aspect of their review, but I do seek what I can learn from it, because their displeasure actually uncovers and makes more apparent what I do well, what I am successful at, and then I dissect that.

Life's a verb. We try our best. We don't always do our best. Well, architecture is a verb as well. Yes, it is. Since we are the architects of our own lives, let's study the habits, the practices, the routines that we have that lead to and feed our success, our joy, our honest pain, our laughter, our earned tears. Let's dissect that and give thanks for those things, and when we do that, guess what

第七点：剖析你们的成功和感激的互惠性。

我们总是太过于关注失败，不是吗？我们研究失败。我们对失败耿耿于怀。我们剖析失败本身以及我们遭遇的各种失败。我们如此沉迷于剖析失败，乃至最后无法自拔，终于幻灭。

我们通常什么时候写日记？当我们沮丧的时候。我们都八卦些什么？别人的缺陷和短处。如果不当心，我们就会剖析自己直到自我嫌弃。我发现多数时候我们对错误的过分痴迷似乎只会制造更多的错误、更多的失败。

要剖析成功，最简单的方法就是感恩。感谢我们所拥有的，感谢那些进展顺利的事情。珍惜那些我们有时视作理所当然的寻常事物。我们感激这些东西，而这种感激之情会回报我们，创造出更多值得感恩的事情。就是这么简单，而且很管用。

我不是说要否认失败。不是的，我们也能够从失败中学到东西，但只有当我们积极看待失败，把它们作为一种展现我们所擅长的、能做得更好的、成功做到的事情的途径时才会如此。

就个人而言，我看过许多对我的差评，真的。我有不少差评。那些更有天赋的批评家写出了具有建设性的差评。他们向我展示了我的作品表达了什么，给人的印象是什么，展现了什么，或者没有展现什么。如今我已不再纠结于他们的评论中不友善的一面，而是在其中寻找使我受益的东西。因为他们的批评其实暴露并揭示出了我的确做得不错的地方、我成功做到的事情，然后我就剖析这些东西。

人生是一个动词。我们全力尝试，但我们并不总是尽己所能。建筑也是一个动词。确实是。既然我们是自己人生的建筑师，就让我们研究我们拥有的那些习惯、做法和日常事务吧，它们不停地给我们带来成功、喜悦、痛苦、欢笑和泪水。让我们剖析这些东西并对它们表示感激。如果我们真这么做了，你们猜会发生什么？我

happens? We get better at 'em, and we have more to dissect.

No. 8: Make voluntary obligations.

All right, Mom and Dad, since we were young, they teach us things as children. Teachers, mentors, the government, and laws, they all give us guidelines by which to navigate this life, rules to abide by in the name of accountability.

I'm not talking about those obligations. I'm talking about the ones that we make with ourselves, with our God, with our own consciousness. I'm talking about the you versus you obligations. We have to have 'em. Again, these are not societal laws and expectations that we acknowledge and endow for anyone other than ourselves. These are faith-based obligations that we make on our own.

These are not the lowered insurance rates for a good driving record; you will not be fined to put in jail if you do not gratify these obligations I speak of. No one else governs these but you. They are your secrets with yourself; your own private council, personal protocols; and while nobody throws you a party when you abide by them, no one's going to arrest you when you break them either, except yourself, or some cops who got a "disturbing the peace" call at 2:30 in the morning because you were playing bongos in your birthday suit[16]. That was me.

An honest man's pillow is his peace of mind, and when you lay down on the pillow at night, no matter who's in your bed, we all sleep alone. These are your personal *Jiminy Crickets*[17]. And there are not enough cops in the entire world to police them. It's on you. It's on you.

No. 9: From can to want.

All right, check this out. In 1995 I got my first big paycheck as an actor. I think it was 150 grand. The film I was on was *Boys on the Side*, and we're shooting in Tucson, Arizona, and I had this sweet little adobe guesthouse on the

们会做得更好，我们会拥有更多可剖析的东西。

第八点：履行自愿义务。

好吧，自打我们小时候起，妈妈和爸爸就教我们东西。老师、导师、政府、法律，全都以负责人的名义，为我们提供把控人生的参考和需要遵守的规则。

我不是在谈那些义务。我说的是我们对我们自己，对上帝，对我们自己的良心所负有的责任。我说的是你和你自己的责任。我们必须负起这些责任。重申一下，这些责任不是我们赋予他人的社会法律和期许，而是仅适用于我们自己的。这些是建立在信仰基础上的义务，是我们主动履行的义务。

这些不是因为驾驶记录良好而降低了的保险利率，你们不会因为未能履行我所说的这些义务而被罚入狱。除了自己，没有人能控制这些。这些是你和自己之间的秘密，是你的私人议会、个人协议。当你履行这些义务时，没人会为你开派对庆祝，而当你违背这些义务时，也没人逮捕你，除了你自己，或者某些警察，他们在凌晨2点半接到"扰乱安宁"的报警电话，说你正一丝不挂地演奏小手鼓。那就是我。

对于诚实的人来说，安宁的心境是他最好的枕头。晚上躺在这个枕头上时，不论床上还有谁，你们都能独自入眠。这些是你们个人的道理。整个世界上没有足够多的警察来监督这些义务。这得靠你们自己，靠你们自己。

第九点：从我能到我想。

好吧，来说一下这一点。1995年，我获得了当演员以来的第一张大支票，我想那是15万美元。我出演的那部电影是《潇洒有情天》，它是我们在亚利桑那州的图森拍摄的。当时我住在萨格鲁国家公园旁边一处舒适的土砖小客房里。房子有一个

---

16. in one's birthday suit：什么都没穿。
17. *Jiminy Cricket*：《蟋蟀杰明尼》，科普类教育动画片。在这里引申为"道理"。

edge of the Saguaro National Park. The house came with a maid, my first maid. It was awesome. So, I got a friend over one Friday night and we're having a good time, and I'm telling her about how happy I am with my set-up in the house, the maid, especially, the maid. I'm telling her, "Look, this lady, she cleans the place up after I go to work; she washes my clothes, the dishes; puts fresh water by my bed; leaves me cooked meals sometimes; she even presses my jeans!" And my friend, she smiles at me, happy that I'm excited over this, and she says, "Well, that's great Matthew, if you like your jeans pressed."

And I kind of looked up at her, my jaw caught hanging open, stuttered a moment, had that dumb ass look you get when you've just been told the truth and you didn't think about it. And it hit me: I hate that line going down the front my jeans! I hate that line! And it was then, for the first time, that I noticed it. I've never thought about not liking that starched line down the front of my jeans because I'd never had a maid to iron my jeans before! And since she did, now, for the first time in my life, I just liked it because I could get it. I never thought about if I really wanted it. Well, I didn't want it there, that line. That night I learned something.

Just because you can? Nah, come on. It's not a good enough reason to do something. Even when it means having more. Be discerning[18]. Choose it because you want it. Do it because you want to. Never had my jeans pressed again. I hate that line.

No. 10: A roof is a man-made thing.

This may cut a little close to the bone, since the geography, but I think we all were there and we'll all remember where we were. But on January 3, 1993, it was the NFL playoffs, and your Houston Oilers were playing the Buffalo Bills. The Oilers were up 28–3 at halftime, 35–3 early in the 3rd. Frank Reich and the Bills come back to win 41–38 in overtime for one of the greatest comebacks in NFL history. The Bills won, but they didn't really beat the Oilers.

女佣，我的第一个女佣。真是太棒了。一个周五的晚上，我有个朋友过来，我们过得很愉快。我告诉她我对房子里的配置和女佣感到很满意，尤其对女佣。我对她说："瞧这位女士，我上班后她打扫这里，替我洗衣服和碗碟，在我的床头放上新鲜的水，有时还给我做好饭，她甚至把我的牛仔裤都熨烫好了！"我的朋友对我笑着，看我对这些感到兴奋，她很高兴。她说："嗯，太棒了，马修，如果你喜欢你的牛仔裤被熨烫的话。"

我抬眼望着她，嘴巴张得老大，一时间瞠目结舌，脸上的愚蠢表情就是那种你被告知了从未想到过的真相时的样子。我突然想到：我讨厌牛仔裤的正面有一条褶！我讨厌那条褶！正是在那一刻，我第一次注意到了这一点。我从未想过自己不喜欢牛仔裤正面有条僵硬的褶，因为以前从未有女佣为我熨过牛仔裤！如今她既然这么做了，生平第一次有人为我熨烫牛仔裤，我就欣然接受了，只因为我能享受到这些。我从没想过自己是否真的想要这样。好吧，我不想要裤子上有条褶。那一晚我学到了些东西。

只是因为你能？不，才不是。这并不是让你做某事足够好的理由。即便当这意味着你会获得更多东西时，也是如此。要有识别力。你想要的时候才选它。你想做的时候才去做。自那以后我再也不熨烫牛仔裤了。我讨厌那条褶。

第十点："屋顶"是人造的。

由于地理的原因，这话可能有点儿尖刻，但我认为我们当时都在场，而且我们全都记得我们当时在哪里。1993年1月3日，美国职业橄榄球大联盟季后赛，你们的休斯敦油人队对阵布法罗·比尔队。中场休息时油人队28：3领先，第三局开局时35：3领先。到加时赛时，弗兰克·赖克带领比尔队以41：38扳回比分，赢了比赛，那是美国橄榄球联盟历史上最惊人的逆转之一。比尔队赢了，但他们并未真

---

18. discern：*vi.* 辨别，识别。

The Oilers lost that game; they beat themselves. You all remember that, huh?

Why? Why'd they beat themselves, or how? Was it because at halftime they put a ceiling, a roof, a limit on their belief in themselves, a.k.a the prevent defense? Or maybe they started thinking about the next opponent in the playoffs at halftime. I mean, they were up. Then they came out, played on their heels, lost the mental edge the entire second half. And voila: they lost. In a mere two quarters, defensive coordinator Jim Eddy went from being called the defensive coordinator of the year and the man first in line to be a head coach next year, to a man without a job in the NFL.

You've choked? Nobody has ever choked? I have. You know I'm talking about: fumbled at the goal line, stuck your foot in your mouth once you got the microphone, had a brain freeze on the exam that you were totally prepared for, forgot the punch line to a joke in front of four thousand graduating students at the University of Houston Commencement? Or maybe you've had that feeling of "Oh my God, life just cannot get any better than this moment." And asked yourself, "Do I deserve this?"

Now what happens when we get that feeling? We tense up. We have this sort of outer body experience where we are literally seeing ourselves in the third person. And we realize that the moment just got bigger than us. You ever felt that way? I have.

And it's because we have created a fictitious ceiling, a roof, to our expectations of ourselves, a limit where we think it's all too good to be true. But it's not. And it's not our right to say or believe it is.

We shouldn't create these restrictions on ourselves: a blue ribbon, a statue, a score, a great idea, the love of our life, a euphoric bliss. Who are we? To think that we don't deserve or haven't earned these gifts when we get 'em? It's not our right.

But, if we stay in process, all right, within ourselves, in the joy of the

正击败油人队。油人队输了比赛，他们败给了自己。你们都记得吧？

为什么呢？他们为什么会被自己打败，或者他们是怎么被打败的？是不是因为在中场休息时，他们在自己的信心上加了一个天花板，一个屋顶，一个限制，也就是采用了预防式防守战术？或许他们在中场休息时已经开始考虑季后赛的下一个对手了。我是说，他们当时处于领先地位。然后他们上场了，小心翼翼地打球，在整个下半场失去了心理优势。看，他们输了。在短短两节的时间里，防守协调员吉姆·埃迪从被称作年度最佳防守协调员的人和下一年总教练的首要人选，变成了美国橄榄球联盟中的失业人员。

你曾经搞砸过吗？没人搞砸过吗？我搞砸过。你们知道我的意思：在球门线上漏接球；一拿到麦克风就说错话；在准备充分的考试当中大脑停顿；在休斯敦大学的毕业典礼上，当着四千名毕业生的面开个玩笑却想不起来其中好笑的句子。或者你可能曾经有过那种感觉："哦，天哪，人生再没有比此刻更棒的时候了。"你问自己："我配得到这一切吗？"

现在，当我们有那样的感觉时会发生什么？我们会紧张，我们会有灵魂出窍的体验，仿佛真的以第三人视角看自己。我们意识到那一刻超出了我们的预期。你们有过那样的感觉吗？我有过。

那是因为我们为自己制造了一个虚假的天花板，一个屋顶，加在自我期许之上；我们设立了一个限度，到了那个限度时我们就认为事情好得不真实。但事实并非如此。我们无权那么说或者那么认为。

我们不应当给自己设定这些限制：一条蓝丝带、一尊雕像、一个得分、一个好主意、人生挚爱、愉快幸福。我们是谁？在我们得到礼物时，认为我们不配拥有或者获得这些？我们没有权利那么去想。

然而，如果我们一直前进，对，保持自我，保持做事的快乐，我们将永远不会

doing, we will never choke at the finish line. Why? Because we aren't thinking of the finish line, because we're not looking at the clock, we're not watching ourselves on the Jumbotron performing the very act that we're in the middle of. No, we're in process. The approach is the destination and we are never finished.

Bo Jackson[19], what did he do? He used to run over the goal line, through the end zone[20] and up the tunnel. The greatest snipers and marksmen in the world, they don't aim at the target. They aim on the other side of the target.

We do our best when our destinations are beyond the measurement, when our reach continually exceeds our grasp, and when we have immortal finish lines.

Now when we do this, the race is never over. The journey has no port. The adventure never ends because we are always on the way. So, do this! Do this and let them, let somebody else come up and tap you on the shoulder and say, "Hey, you scored." Let them run up and tap you on the shoulder and say, "Man, you won." Let them come tell you, "You go home now." Let them say, "I love you too." Let them say, "Thank you."

Take the lid off the man-made roofs that we put above ourselves and always play like an underdog. Here we go.

No. 11: Turn the page.

The late, great University of Texas football coach, Daryl Royal, I don't know if you remember him. He won a national championship in '69; he won a couple of national championships. You know Daryl Royal? He was a friend of mine and a good friend to many people. Now a lot of people looked up to this man. One of the people who looked up to him was a musician named Larry. Now at this time in his life Larry was in the prime[21] of his country music career. He had No.1 hits and his life was rolling. He had picked up a bad habit of a snort in the white stuff somewhere along the line, and at one particular

在终点线前功亏一篑。为什么呢？因为我们没有考虑终点线，没有盯着时钟，没有观看大屏幕上自己正在做的事情。没有，我们在进程当中。接近就是目标，而且我们永远不会结束。

博·杰克逊，他是怎么做的？他常常跑过球门线，穿过达阵区，跑进球员通道里面去。世上最伟大的攻击队员或射手们，他们是不会瞄准目标的。他们瞄准的是目标的另外一面。

当我们与终点的距离难以量度时，当我们一直无法抓住目标时，当我们总是到达不了终点线时，我们就要竭尽全力。

当我们这么做时，比赛就永不终止，旅程不会停止，冒险也永不结束，因为我们一直在路上。所以，就这么做，就这么做。让别人走过来拍着你的肩膀说："嘿，你得分了。"让他们跑过来拍着你的肩膀说："伙计，你赢了。"让他们来告诉你："你现在可以回家了。"让他们说："我也爱你。"让他们说："谢谢你。"

去除我们为自己设定的限制吧，就当自己是占下风的人。开始吧。

第十一点：翻篇。

得克萨斯大学已故的、伟大的橄榄球教练达里尔·罗伊尔，我不知道你们是否记得他。他在1969年得过一次全国冠军。他得过不少全国冠军。你们知道达里尔·罗伊尔吗？他是我的朋友，也是许多人的好朋友。现在，有许多人敬重这个人。敬重他的人中有个叫拉瑞的音乐家。当时拉瑞正处于他乡村音乐事业的黄金时期，他的歌多次登过榜首，他的生活风生水起。不知从什么时候开始，他染上了吸毒的

---

19. Bo Jackson：博·杰克逊（1962— ），美国前棒球与美式足球运动员，曾两度拿下十项全能州冠军。1994年结束职业生涯。
20. end zone：达阵区，也称端区，是美式足球的得分区域，位于场地两端。
21. prime：*n.* 黄金时期。

party after a "bathroom break," Larry went confidently up to his mentor Daryl and he started telling him a story. Coach Royal listened as he always had, and when Larry finished his story and was about to walk away, coach Royal put a gentle hand on his shoulder and he very discreetly said, "Hey Larry, you got something on your nose there, bud." Larry immediately hurried to the bathroom mirror where he saw some of the white powder that he hadn't cleaned off his nose. He was ashamed. He was embarrassed. As much because he felt so disrespectful to coach Royal, and as much because he'd obviously gotten too comfortable with the drug to even hide it as well as he should.

Well, the next day Larry went to coach's house. He rang the doorbell. Coach answered and he said, "Coach, I need to talk to you." Daryl said, "Sure, come on in."

Larry confessed. He purged his sins to coach. He told him how embarrassed he was, and how he had lost his way in the midst of all this fame and fortune. And towards the end of an hour, Larry, who was in tears, he asked coach. He said: "Coach, what do you think I should do?" The coach, being a man of few words, just looked at him and calmly said, "Larry, I have never had any trouble turning the page in the book of my life." Larry got sober[22] that day and he has been sober for the last 40 years.

You ever get in a rut? You know what I'm talking about. You get in a funk? Stuck on the merry-go-round of a bad habit? I have. Look, we are going to make mistakes—you gotta own them, then you gotta make amends, and then you gotta move on. Guilt and regret kills many a man before their time. So turn the page; get off the ride. You are the author of the book of your life. Turn that page.

No. 12: Give your obstacles credit.

You know those No Fear T-shirts that were out. I don't know maybe somewhere continue to go. No Fear? Anybody remember those, or is it just me?

坏习惯，吸食某种白色毒品。在某次派对上，在"上厕所"过后，他自信满满地来找他的导师达里尔，开始讲故事。罗伊尔教练一如既往地仔细聆听，拉瑞讲完准备离开时，罗伊尔教练把一只手轻轻地放在他的肩膀上，不露痕迹地说道："嘿，拉瑞，你鼻子那里有东西，伙计。"拉瑞立刻匆匆地跑到厕所里照镜子，发现鼻子上有一些未擦净的白色粉末。他羞愧异常，无比尴尬，既是因为他感到自己太不尊重罗伊尔教练了，也是因为他发现自己对毒品太安之若素了，甚至在应当掩饰的时候都不费心掩饰了。

第二天，拉瑞去了教练家。他按了门铃，教练打开门。他说："教练，我需要和你谈谈。"达里尔答道："没问题，进来吧。"

拉瑞坦白了一切。他向教练供出了自己的罪过。他告诉教练自己有多尴尬，以及他是怎样在盛名和财富中迷失了方向。在拉瑞讲了近一个小时后，他流着泪问教练："教练，你认为我该怎么办？"教练是个少言寡语之人，他只是看着拉瑞，平静地说："拉瑞，当我为人生翻开新的一页时，从没有过困难。"那一天，拉瑞清醒了，在后来的40年里，他一直保持清醒。

你曾经一成不变吗？你知道我的意思。你曾恐慌过吗？你曾陷入坏习惯的恶性循环里吗？我曾经如此。我们都会犯错误——你们得承认错误，然后补偿损失，然后你们才能继续前进。内疚和悔恨曾使很多人提早丧命。所以要翻开新的一页，重新来过。你们是自己生命之书的作者。翻过那一页。

第十二点：承认挫折的价值。

你知道，那些印有"无畏"的T恤衫已经过时了，我不知道是不是有些地方还

---

22. sober：*adj.* 冷静的，清醒的。

I saw them everywhere. I don't get 'em, and I never did. I mean, hell, I try to scare myself at least once a day. I mean I get butterflies every morning before I go to work. I was nervous before I got here to speak tonight. I think fear is a good thing. You know why? Because it increases our need to overcome that fear.

Say your obstacle is fear of rejection. You wanna ask her out. You wanna ask him out. But you fear that she may say no. You want to ask your boss for that promotion, but you're scared he's gonna think you're overstepping your bounds.

Well, instead of denying those fears, declare them; say the fear out loud; admit them; give them the credit they deserve. Don't get all macho and act like they're no big deal, and don't get paralyzed by denying that they exist and therefore abandoning your need to overcome them. I mean, I'd even subscribe to the belief that we're all destined to have to do the thing we fear the most anyway, at some point.

So, you give your obstacles credit, and you will, one, find the courage to overcome them; or you will, two, see more clearly that they are not really worth prevailing over.

So be brave; have courage, and when you do, you get stronger; you get more aware; you get more respectful of yourself and that which you fear.

No. 13: So how do we know when we cross the truth?

Thirteen. Thirteen. Someone was asking why did I pick thirteen—that's not an lucky number. Well, I don't know when thirteen got the bad rap and become the mongrel of numerology. It's never done me wrong, thirteen. In fact, thirteen has been a pretty lucky number for me, and I wanna tell you how.

I've always taken these 21-day trips by myself to far off places where I usually don't know the language and nobody knows my name. They're adventures, one, but they're also a purge—all right, they're a cleanse for me.

在流行。那种"无畏"？大家都记得，还是只有我记得？曾经到处都可以看到。我不穿，我从不穿。我是说，见鬼，我每天都要至少吓唬自己一次。我是说每天早晨去工作之前，我都感到忐忑不安。在今晚来这里演讲之前我也紧张。我认为恐惧是个好东西。为什么呢？因为恐惧增加了我们克服恐惧的需要。

承认吧，你们的障碍就是害怕被拒绝。你想约他/她出去，但你担心他/她可能拒绝。你想要上司给你升职，但你害怕他会觉得你越界了。

不要否认这些恐惧，相反，宣布出来，大声地把恐惧说出来，承认它们，承认它们的价值。不要总是扮演男子汉，就仿佛那些恐惧无足轻重一样，也不要因为拒绝恐惧的存在而变得麻木，以至因此放弃克服恐惧的需要。我是说，我甚至相信，在某个时候，我们都注定要做我们最害怕的事情。

所以要承认挫折的价值，第一，你会找到克服它们的勇气；第二，或许你会更加清晰地看到，它们其实不堪一击。

所以要勇敢，要有勇气。而当你有勇气时，你会变得更强大，会变得更清醒；你会更尊重自己，以及自己害怕的东西。

第十三点：我们如何知道我们遇到了真理？

十三，十三。有人问我为何要用十三，那是个不吉利的数字。好吧，我不知道十三是什么时候背上恶名，成为数字命理学中的倒霉蛋。十三从来没有得罪过我。事实上，十三对我来说是个相当幸运的数字，我想告诉你原因。

我经常独自前往偏远地区进行 21 天的旅行。在那里，我通常不懂他们的语言，也没人知道我的名字。这些旅行是冒险，但它们也是一种净化，好吧，它们净化了我。它们就像 21 天的斋戒，让我摆脱关注，摆脱我那按部就班的人生中的所有事

They're like a 21-day fast from attention, from all the things I have in my well-appointed life. They're a check out, so I can check in with me. See how I'm doing, be forced to be my own and my only company, to have a look in my mirror. And we all know what can happen when we do that, sometimes we do not like what we see.

Well, in 1996, right after I got famous from a film I did called *A Time to Kill*, I headed out on one of this 21-day walkabout, and this time to the jungles and mountains of Peru. The sudden fame that I'd just gotten was somewhat unbalancing. My face was everywhere; everyone wanted a piece of me; people I'd never met were swearing that they loved me. Everywhere I went, there I was, on a billboard, a magazine cover. It was just weird, overall. You know, I was asking myself: What was this all about? What was reality in this, and what's the bullshit? Did I deserve all this? These were all questions I was asking myself.

"Who was I?" was another.

Now, there's always an initiation period with these trips. An amount of time that it takes for the place to initiate the traveler. The time it takes to disconnect from the world we just left, and become completely present in the one we are traveling in. Now for me, that initiation period usually last about thirteen days. Thirteen hellish days until I'm out of my own way. After that, the whole trip is really fun and smooth sailing.

Well, it was the night of the twelfth day of my 21-day trip. I'm settling into camp. I'd already hiked 80 miles to this point and I had a three-day trek to Machu Pichu. And I was full-on sick of myself. Wrestling with the loss of my anonymity, I was guilt ridden for sins of my past, I was a lot of regret. I was lonely, disgusted with my company: mine, and I was doing a pretty good job of mentally beating the shit out of myself.

Anyway, grappling with[23] these demons on this night, I couldn't sleep. All

情。它们就像是登记离开，那样我自己才能再次登记入住。看看当我被迫自力更生，独身自处时，被迫看着镜子中的自己时，我过得怎么样。我们都知道我们那样做会发生什么，有时候我们并不喜欢自己看到的样子。

在 1996 年，我刚因电影《杀戮时刻》成名，就出发进行一次 21 天的徒步旅行，那次是去秘鲁的丛林和山区。一夜爆红使我有点儿失衡。到处都能看到我的脸，每个人都想要一张我的照片，从未见过我的人发誓他们爱我。无论我去哪儿，都能看到自己——在广告板上，在杂志封面上。整体而言，这种感觉很怪。什么情况？真相如何，到底怎么一回事？我配拥有这一切吗？这些都是我问自己的问题。

"我是谁？"这是另一个问题。

这些旅行总是有一个初始阶段，就是旅行目的地引起旅行者兴趣所需要的时间，是我们切断同刚刚离开的世界之间的联系，然后完全进入我们正在其中旅行的世界所需要的时间。对于我而言，酝酿阶段通常持续 13 天。13 天糟透了的日子，直到我彻底放松了自己。在那之后，整个旅程就变得真正有趣和平稳。

那是在 21 天旅行中第 12 天的晚上。我在帐篷里安置了下来。当时我已经徒步走了 80 英里（约合 128.75 公里），我还要坐 3 天的牛车前往马丘比丘。我对自己厌烦透了。不能再隐匿身份，这令我很纠结。我为自己过去的罪过感到惭愧无比，满是悔恨。我很孤独，对我的同伴，也就是我自己，充满厌恶之情，在心里狠狠批斗了自己一番。

> *Life is not a popularity contest. Be brave; take the hill, but first, answer the question "What's my hill?"*
>
> *人生并非一场声望竞赛。要勇敢，要攻占山头，但首先得回答这个问题："我要的是哪座山？"*

---

23. grapple with：斗争。

of these badges and banners and expectations and anxieties that I was carrying with me—I needed to free myself from them. "Who was I?" I asked myself, not only on this trip, but in this life. So I stripped down[24] to nothing. I took every moniker that gave me pride and confidence, all the window dressings, the packaging around the product. I discard them all. I got rid of my lucky and faithful American cap. I stripped off my talismans[25] from adventures past. I even discarded my late father's gold ring with an M on it that he gave to me, and it was a meltdown of he and my mom's class rings and gold from my mom's teeth. I even got rid of that.

I was naked. Literally and figuratively. And I got sick. Soaked in sweat, I threw up until there was no bile left in my belly, and finally passed out from exhaustion.

Now, a few hours later, I awoke on this thirteenth morning to a rising sun. Surprisingly fresh and energized. I dressed, made some tea and I went for a morning walk. Not towards my destination Machu Pichu, but rather to nowhere in particular. My gut was still a bit piqued from last night's purge, but I curiously felt pretty good: felt alive, felt clean, felt free and light.

Along a muddy path on this walk, I turned a corner, and there in the middle of the road was this mirage[26] of the most magnificent pinks and blues and red colors that I had ever seen. It was electric glowing and vibrant, just hovering just off the surface of the jungle floor, as if it was plugged in to some neon power plant.

I stopped. I stared. There was no way around it. The jungle floor in front of me was actually thousands of butterflies, there in my path. It was spectacular, so I stayed awhile. Somewhere in my captivation, I heard this little voice inside my head say these words, "All I want is what I can see, and all I can see is what's in front of me."

Now at that moment, for the first time on this trip, I had stopped

不管怎么说，由于那一晚同那些魔鬼斗争，我无法入睡。我随身携带的所有的奖章、旗帜、期待和焦虑——我需要使自己摆脱它们。不光是在这次旅行中，在整个一生之中，我都在扪心自问："我曾经是谁？"所以我把自己剥得干干净净。我清除了所有给我带来骄傲和信心的标记，所有的窗户装饰物、产品外包装。我把它们全都扔了。我丢掉了一直戴着的、给我带来幸运的美式帽子。我摘掉了以往探险中得到的护身符。我甚至丢掉了已经过世了的父亲给我的金戒指，上面有个字母"M"，那是他和我妈妈的毕业戒指再加上妈妈的金牙融化后制成的。我把它也扔了。

我赤身裸体，不论是字面意思还是比喻意思都是如此。我感到恶心。我大汗淋漓，呕吐不止，直到吐光了胆汁，最终筋疲力尽，昏迷了过去。

几个小时后，我在旅行的第13天的早晨醒了过来，看到一轮初升的太阳。我感到不可思议的精神抖擞。我穿好衣服，泡了点儿茶喝，然后出去散步。不是去我的目的地马丘比丘，而是漫无目的地闲逛。由于前一晚的呕吐，我的肠道仍然有些不适，但奇怪的是我感觉相当不错：充满活力，洁净，自由，轻盈。

我沿着一条泥泞小道走着，转过一个弯，就在道路的中间出现了我从未见过的最绚烂的粉色、蓝色和红色构成的幻景。那是电光在闪烁着，跳跃着，就在丛林的地面之上盘绕，仿佛接通了一座霓虹灯发电厂似的。

我停了下来，盯着看。没路可绕行。我面前的丛林地面上真真切切地落着成千上万只蝴蝶，就在我走的小路上。那景象真是叹为观止，所以我停留了一会儿。就在我着迷地看着时，我听到脑子里有个小小的声音说了这些话："我要的就是我能看见的，我能看见的就是眼前的。"

就在那一刻，在那次旅行中，我第一次不再预测转角会有什么。我第一次不再

---

24. strip down：脱去，摘下。
25. talisman：*n.* 护身符。
26. mirage：*n.* 幻想；海市蜃楼。

anticipating what was around the corner. For the first time I stopped thinking about what was coming up next; what was up ahead. Time slowed down. I was no longer in a rush to get anywhere. And my anxieties were greatly eased.

A few hours later I returned to camp, packing for my continued journey. I had a bounce in my step, new energy. Even the local Sherpas I was traveling with even noticed, calling out to me, "sois luz Mateo, sois luz!!!" Which means "you are light" in Spanish.

You see, I forgave myself that morning. I let go of the guilt, the weight that was on my shoulders lifted, my penance was paid, and I got back in good graces with my God. And I shook hands with myself, my best friend, the one that we're all stuck with anyway: ourselves. From that morning on, the adventure was awesome. I was present; I was out of my own way, I was not anticipating next, I was embracing only what was in front of my eyes and giving everything the justice it deserved.

You see, I crossed a truth that morning. Now did I find it? I don't know. I think it found me. Why? Because I put myself in a place to be found. I put myself in a place to receive the truth. So, how do we know when we cross the truth?

Well I think the truth is all around us, all the time. I mean, I think the answer, you know, is always right there, or right there. I think it's all around us, we just don't always see it; we don't always grasp it, hear it, access it—usually because we're not in the right place to do so.

So what do we do?

First, I believe we gotta put ourselves in the place to receive the truth. Let's admit it; we live in an extremely noisy world, with all kinds of frequencies coming at us. We got commitments, deadlines; fix this; do that; plans, expectations, and they all make it hard to get clarity and peace of mind. So we have to consciously put ourselves in places to receive that clarity. Now that

想接下来会发生什么，前方会遇到什么。时间的脚步慢了下来，我不再仓促赶往任何地方，我的焦虑也极大地减轻了。

几个小时之后，我返回了营地，整理行装继续旅行。我脚步轻快，精神焕发。就连和我同行的当地的夏尔巴人也注意到了，他们朝我喊道："sois luz Mateo, soisluz!!!"那是西班牙语，意思是"你的脚步很轻巧"。

看吧，那天早晨我原谅了自己。我抛掉了负罪感，我肩上的重负被拿掉了，我的忏悔有了回报，我又重新获得了上帝的眷顾，我同我最好的朋友——自己，那个无论怎样都与我纠缠在一起的自己握手言和。从那天早晨起，旅行变得棒极了。我活在当下，放开了自己，不再预测未来，只关注眼前的事物，并且认真平等地对待每一个事物。

你们看，那天早晨我遇到了真理。是我找到真理的吗？我不知道，我认为是它找到了我。为什么？因为我把自己放在了一个可以被找到的位置上。我把自己放在了一个能够接受真理的位置上。那么我们如何知道我们遇到了真理？

我想真理就在我们身边，一直都在。我是说，我认为答案，你们知道的，答案总是在那里，或者说就在那里。我想它就在我们身边，只不过我们并不常看见它罢了。我们并不总是能抓住它，听见它，接触到它，这通常是因为我们没有在正确的位置上去那样做。

那么我们该怎么做？

首先，我认为我们要把自己放在可以接受真理的位置上。我们不得不承认，我们生活在一个极度喧闹的世界里，各种频率的声音向我们涌来。我们有任务，有最后期限，搞定这个，做好那个，各种计划、预期，它们都让我们很难神志清醒，心境平和。所以我们必须有意识地把自己放置在能够让自己清醒的位置上。那可能是

may be prayer, that may be meditation[27], that may be a walkabout, that may be being in right company, a road trip, whatever that is for you, schedule that time. Schedule it.

So, if we do that, if we hear it, if we put ourselves in a place to hear it and we do, and it's become clear: a truth, natural and infinite. Then the second part comes, which is to personalize it. Ask yourself how it works for you, how it applies to you personally, why you need it in your life, specifically. And if you do that, then comes the third part: Have the patience to internalize it and get it from our intellectual head, thinking about it, and into our bones and soul and our instinct. Now we can't rush this part; it does take time.

So if we get that far, we receive it; we personalize it; and we internalize it. If we make it that far, then comes the biggie man; this comes the following: gotta have the courage to act on it. To actually take it into our daily lives and practice it; to make it an active part of who we are and live it.

When do that, all right, when do that, then we have what I believe is heaven right here on earth.

That's the place where what we want is also just what we need. I mean that's the ticket, isn't it? Think about it. I know that's where I want to live.

So while we're here, and they're gonna run across the Jumbotron. Let's make it a place where we break a sweat, where we believe, where we enjoy the process of succeeding in the places and ways that we are fashioned to, where we don't have to look over our shoulder because we are too busy doing what we're good at. Voluntarily keeping our own council because we want to, traveling towards immortal finish lines, we write our own book, overcoming our fears. We make friends with ourselves.

And that is the place that I'm talking about.

Thank you, good luck and just keep living.

做祈祷，可能是冥想，可能是徒步旅行，可能是有个好伴，可能是公路旅行。不论对你们来说是什么，都要定好计划。定计划吧。

如果我们那么做了，如果我们听见了它，如果我们把自己放置在能够听见它的位置上，并且行动，那么它就会出现：一条真理，自然而无限。然后就是第二步，也就是要使之个人化。问问你自己，它怎样才能对你有用，它如何才能应用在你身上，具体说来，你为什么在生活中需要它。如果你那么做了，就到了第三步：要有耐心将之内化，把它从我们聪明的头脑中取出，好好思索一下，将它融入我们的骨髓、灵魂和本能当中。我们对这一步不能草率了事。它需要时间。

如果我们到了那一步，我们就会接受它，将它个人化，将它内化。如果我们已经走了那么远，接下来就该到最难的部分了：接下来要有勇气将真理付诸实践。要把它真正融入我们的日常生活，践行它，让它成为自己和生活的一个活跃部分。

当我们那么做时，好，当我们那么做时，我们就在地球上拥有了我相信是天堂的地方。

在那里，我们想要的东西也正是我们需要的东西。我是说那就是入场券，不是吗？想想看。我知道那就是我想生活的地方。

所以当我们在这里时，它们会在大屏幕上闪过。让我们把它变成一个流汗努力的地方，我们相信的地方，我们以适合的方式、在适合的位置享受成功过程的地方，一个我们忙着做擅长的事而无暇悔恨的地方。自发地监督自己，因为我们想那样做。朝着不朽的终点线行进，写我们自己的书，克服我们的恐惧，和自己成为朋友。

那就是我所说的地方。

谢谢你们，祝你们好运，继续前进。

---

27. meditation：*n.* 冥想。

语录 Quotes

- Do not fall into the trap, the entitlement trap, of feeling like you're a victim—you are not. Get over and get on with it.

  别掉进权利陷阱里，那种让你们感觉自己像个受害者的陷阱。你们不是。要克服这种心态，行动起来。

- Acknowledge the acts of greatness as real, and do not be naive about mankind's capacity for evil, nor be in denial of our own shortcomings.

  要承认那些伟大之举是真实的，也不要天真地低估人类作恶的能力，或者否认我们自己的缺点。

- Joy is the feeling that we have from doing what we are fashioned to do, no matter the outcome.

  喜悦来源于做我们喜欢做的事，与结果无关。

- Life is not a popularity contest. Be brave; take the hill, but first, answer the question "What's my hill?"

  人生并非一场声望竞赛。要勇敢，要攻占山头，但首先得回答这个问题："我要的是哪座山？"

- Defining ourselves by what we are not is the first step that leads us to really knowing who we are.

  根据我们不是谁来定义我们自己，这是引导我们真正了解我们是谁的第一步。

Life Is Too Short to Live Empty-Handed
生命太过短暂，不能空手走过

——朱棣文 2009 年在哈佛大学毕业典礼上的演讲

> 简介 Profile

朱棣文
Steven Chu

  1948 年，朱棣文生于美国密苏里州的圣路易斯。他的祖籍是江苏太仓，其家族非常重视教育，对后代的培养也是不遗余力。朱棣文的哥哥朱筑文不仅是麻省理工学院博士，还成了斯坦福大学医学系教授；而他的弟弟朱钦文 21 岁就获得了政治学博士学位，后来还考进了世界知名的哈佛大学法学院。一家人都可谓是学霸，而朱棣文小时候成绩平平，一直被两个兄弟的光芒所笼罩，也难怪他曾自嘲是"家里最笨的人"。

  朱棣文从小就喜欢动手，做各种奇怪又有趣的实验。幸运的是，他遇到了一位发现他长处的物理启蒙老师，领着他进入了自己热爱的天地。1970 年，朱棣文毕业于罗切斯特大学。在随后的二十几年中，他埋首于实验研究之中，在原子物理、激光科学技术领域持续精进。多年的孜孜以求终于换来了人生的第一个高峰：1997 年，凭借激光冷却和捕获原子的方法发明，朱棣文获得诺贝尔物理学奖，成为第五位拿到诺贝尔奖的华裔科学家。随后，朱棣文在 1998 年当选为中国科学院外籍院士。2008 年，在奥巴马提名下，朱棣文成为美国第 12 任能源部部长，甚至还被选定为"指定幸存者"，即意外情况下美国总统的继承人。

  从小城市里"并不聪明"的华裔少年到第一位成为美国内阁部长的诺贝尔奖得主，朱棣文一路走来的人生经历能给予人很多启示。或许在大多数人眼里，朱棣文幸运地走上了人生坦途，但他认为更重要的是，"我从未为未来担忧，因为我乐在其中"。2009 年，朱棣文出席哈佛大学的毕业典礼，为毕业生们带来了他的衷心建议：追寻自己内心的热爱，在成长过程中要心怀感激，成为一个能够回馈社会的人。

演讲 Speech

扫描二维码
获取本篇演讲原视频、音频

Madam President Faust, members of the Harvard Corporation and the Board of Overseers, faculty, family, friends, and, most importantly, today's graduates, thank you for letting me share this wonderful day with you.

I am not sure I can live up to the high standards of Harvard Commencement speakers. Last year, J.K. Rowling, the billionaire novelist, who started as a classics student, graced this podium. The year before, Bill Gates, the mega-billionaire philanthropist and computer nerd stood here. Today, sadly, you have me. I am not a billionaire, but at least I am a nerd.

I am grateful to receive an honorary degree from Harvard, an honor that means more to me than you might care to imagine. As you may have heard this morning, I was the academic failure of my family. Both my brothers have degrees from Harvard.

My older brother Gilbert, after getting a Ph.D. in Physics from that other school down the river, got and M.D. Ph.D. from Harvard; while my younger brother Morgan Chu, who you just heard name today at the Board of Overseers, has a law degree.

When I was awarded a Nobel Prize, I thought my mother would be pleased. Not so. I called her on the morning of being announced, she replied, "That's nice, but when are you going to visit me next?" Now, as the last brother with a degree from Harvard, maybe, at last, she will be pleased.

福斯特校长女士、哈佛大学董事会的各位成员、监管委员会的各位理事、各位教职员工、各位家人、各位朋友，以及今天最重要的各位毕业生们，感谢大家与我分享这美好的一天。

哈佛毕业典礼演讲者的标准很高，我不确定自己是否能够达标。去年登上这个讲坛的，是古典文学专业出身的亿万富翁小说家 J. K. 罗琳，而前年则是亿万富翁、慈善家和电脑痴比尔·盖茨。今天就很遗憾了，由我来给大家演讲。我虽然不是亿万富翁，但总归也是个痴人。

我很感激哈佛大学授予我荣誉学位，这对我的来说意义重大，重大得也许超出你们的想象。今天早上你们可能已经听说了，在我家里，我算是个学渣。我的两个兄弟都是哈佛出身。

我的哥哥吉尔伯特在查尔斯河下游的学校获得物理学博士学位后，又在哈佛大学拿到了医学博士学位；而我的弟弟摩根·朱，就是你们今天在监事会上听到的那个名字，他拿到了法学学位。

拿到诺贝尔奖的时候，我以为我母亲会很高兴，但她并没有。消息公布的那天早上，我给她打了电话，她回答说："不错，那你下次什么时候来看我？"现在好了，家里三兄弟都有哈佛学位了，也许她终于会高兴了。

> *In order to be heard, it is important to deliver the same message more than once.*
>
> 要想让人听进去，有必要反复传达同一个信息。

Another difficulty with giving a Harvard commencement address is that some students may disapprove of the fact that I will borrow material from my previous speeches as well as from others. I ask that you forgive me for two reasons.

First, in order to be heard, it is important to deliver the same message more than once. Second, authors who borrow from others are following in the footsteps of the best. Ralph Waldo Emerson[1], who graduated from Harvard at the age of 18, noted, "All my best thoughts were stolen by the ancients." Picasso declared, "Good artists borrow. Great artists steal." Why should commencement speakers be held to a higher standard?

I also want to point out the irony of speaking to graduates of an institution that would have rejected me, had I the chutzpah[2] to apply. I am married to "Dean Jean," a former dean of admissions at Stanford. She assures me that she would have rejected me, if given the chance. When I showed her a draft of this speech, she objected strongly to my use of the word "rejected." She never rejected applicants; her letters stated that "we are unable to offer admission." I have great difficulty understanding the difference. After all, deans of admissions of highly selective schools are in reality, "deans of rejection." Clearly, I have a lot to learn about marketing.

So my address will follow the classical sonata[3] form of commencement addresses. The first movement, just presented, were light-hearted remarks. This next movement consists of unsolicited advice, which is rarely valued, seldom remembered, never followed. As Oscar Wilde said, "The only thing to do with good advice is to pass it on. It is never of any use to oneself." So, here comes the advice.

First, every time you celebrate an achievement, be thankful to those who made it possible. Thank your parents and friends who supported you, thank your professors who were inspirational, and especially thank the other

在哈佛大学毕业典礼上发表演讲还有一处难点，有些学生可能不喜欢我重复自己先前的和前人的演讲内容。这一点请谅解，原因有二。

第一，要想让人听进去，有必要反复传达同一个信息。第二，借鉴是在追随伟人的脚步。拉尔夫·瓦尔多·爱默生18岁毕业于哈佛大学，曾经说过这样一句话："我最好的想法都让古人给偷走了。"毕加索也说过："优秀艺术家借鉴，伟大艺术家剽窃。"为什么毕业典礼演讲者适用的标准更高呢？

我得指出，今天有幸为哈佛毕业生演讲，这一点还挺讽刺的，当年如果我有胆子申请哈佛，想必会遭到拒绝。我的爱人是吉恩主任，曾任斯坦福大学招生主任。她明确指出，要是换了她，她也会拒绝我。她看了我的演讲草稿，强烈反对我用"拒绝"这个词，说自己从不"拒绝"申请者，只会在信中写道："我们无法提供入学机会。"我很难看出这有什么差别，毕竟，高门槛学校的招生主任与其说是"招生主任"，不如说是"拒生主任"。显然，我得好好学学如何推销自己。

我的演讲将按照毕业典礼演讲的常规奏鸣曲式进行。刚才讲的那些，就是第一部分，都是些轻松的话。接下来的内容是一些不请自来的忠告，它们往往不受重视，很少被人记住，也几乎不会被采纳。正如奥斯卡·王尔德所说："忠告对自己毫无用处，唯一该做的就是传给别人。"所以，我的忠告来了。

首先，每当你庆祝自身成就时，都要感谢身后的帮手。感谢给予支持的父母和朋友，感谢给予启发的教授，尤其要感谢讲课不太精彩、让你们不得不自学的教授。

---

1. Ralph Waldo Emerson：拉尔夫·沃尔多·爱默生（1803—1882），出生于马萨诸塞州波士顿，毕业于哈佛大学，是美国著名思想家、文学家、诗人，被思想界誉为"美国的文艺复兴领袖"。
2. chutzpah：*n.* 无所顾忌。
3. sonata：*n.* 奏鸣曲。

professors whose less-than-brilliant lectures forced you to teach yourself. Going forward, the ability to teach yourself is the hallmark of a great liberal arts education and will be the key to your success. To your fellow students who have added immeasurably to your education during those late night discussions, hug them, and go off the strip a little bit. Also, of course, thank Harvard. Should you forget, there's an alumni association to remind you.

Second, in your future life, cultivate a generous spirit. In all negotiations, don't bargain for the last, little advantage. Leave the change on the table. In your collaborations, always remember that "credit" is not a conserved quantity. In a successful collaboration, everybody gets 90 percent of the credit.

Jimmy Stewart[4], as Elwood P. Dowd in the movie *Harvey*[5] got it exactly right. Forgive me, I don't really … can't really imitate Jimmy Stewart very well, but … He said: "Years ago my mother used to say to me, 'In this world, Elwood, you must be … she always used to call me Elwood … in this world, Elwood, you must be oh so smart or oh so pleasant.'" Well, for years I was smart. I recommend pleasant. You may quote me on that.

My third piece of advice is as follows: As you begin this new stage in your lives, follow your passion. If you don't have a passion, don't be satisfied until you find one. Life is too short to go through it without caring deeply about something. When I was your age, I was incredibly single-minded in my goal to be a physicist. After college, I spent eight years as a graduate student and postdoc at Berkeley, and then nine years at Bell Labs. During that time, my central focus and professional joy was physics.

Here is my final advice. Pursuing a personal passion is important, but it should not be your only goal. When you are old and gray, and look back on your life, you will want to be proud of what you have done. The source of that pride won't be the things you have acquired or the recognition you have received. It will be the lives you have touched and the difference you have made.

从长远来看，自学能力是高水平人文教育的标志，也将成为成功的关键。对于在夜谈会上极大丰富了你们教育经历的同学们，给他们一个拥抱；偶尔也要离开人群，独自探索一番。当然，也要感谢哈佛。如果你们忘了，校友会会提醒你们的。

其次，在未来的人生中，要培养一种慷慨的精神。在任何谈判中都别锱铢必较，别把谈判桌上的钱全都拿走。在合作关系中，要永远记得，荣誉并不是恒定不变的量。成功的合作中，每个人都能获得 90% 的荣誉。

吉米·斯图尔特在电影《我的朋友叫哈维》里扮演的艾尔伍德·P. 多德说得很对。请原谅，我模仿得不太像，他是这么说的："多年以前，我母亲曾对我说，'艾尔伍德——她总是叫我艾尔伍德——在这个世界上，要么就得聪明绝顶，要么就得讨人喜欢。'"我当了很多年聪明人，如今更推崇讨人喜欢。我这句话你们也可以直接引用。

我的第三个忠告如下：开启人生新篇章时，要追随热爱。如果还没有热爱，那就一直找，不要将就。生命很短，必须对某样东西倾注热情，方不虚此生。我在你们这个年纪的时候，一门心思地想要成为物理学家。大学毕业后，我在伯克利度过了 8 年研究生和博士后生涯，随后又进贝尔实验室工作了 9 年。在此期间，我的人生重心和职业乐趣都是物理学。

接下来是我的最后一个忠告。追求个人热爱固然重要，但不该是唯一目标。待到白发苍苍之时，回首过往人生，你们会希望能够为自己曾做过的事而自豪。这份自豪并不源于获得的财富和荣誉，而源于向他人伸出的援手、为世界带来的改变。

---

4. Jimmy Stewart：即詹姆斯·斯图尔特（James Stewart），美国电影、电视、舞台剧演员，奥斯卡最佳男主角奖、奥斯卡终身成就奖及其他多数主要电影组织的奖项得主。其作品类型横跨西部片、文艺片、家庭喜剧、悬疑片、传记电影等，多部作品名列美国电影学会各类百年最佳影片，被美国国家电影保护局典藏。他活跃的年代大致与好莱坞的黄金时期重合，而他本人也已经成为一种文化象征，以及一个经典时代的传奇化身。

5. *Harvey*：《我的朋友叫哈维》是一部题材古怪的、导人向善的美国主旋律喜剧电影。詹姆斯·斯图尔特扮演的艾尔伍德几十年来一直与只有他能看见的 6 英尺（约合 1.83 米）高的白兔精灵哈维为伍。虽然如此，由于他的热情、淳朴、乐于助人的个性，镇上的人都很喜欢他。对他不满的是他那嗜好社交、有点神经质的姐姐和其貌不扬、待嫁闺中的侄女。两人打算把他送至精神病院。一系列阴差阳错的喜剧情节之后，无论是医院还是家人都被他和哈维所征服。

After nine years at Bell labs, I decided to leave the warm, cozy ivory tower for what I considered to be the "real world," a university. Bell Labs, to quote what was said about Mary Poppins[6], was "practically perfect in every way," but I wanted to leave behind something more than just scientific articles. I wanted to teach and I wanted to give birth to my own set of scientific children.

Ted Geballe, a friend and distinguished colleague of mine at Stanford, who went from Berkeley to Bell Labs to Stanford years earlier, described our motives best and I quote:

"The best part of working at a university is the students. They come in fresh, enthusiastic, open to ideas, unscarred by the battles of life. They don't realize it, but they're the recipients of the best our society can offer. If a mind is ever free to be creative, that's the time. They come in believing textbooks are authoritative, but eventually they figure out that textbooks and professors don't know everything, and then they start to think on their own. And then, I begin learning from them."

My students, postdoctoral fellows, and the young researchers who worked with me at Bell Labs, Stanford, and Berkeley have been extraordinary. Over 30 former group members are now professors, many at the best research institutions in the world, including Harvard. I have learned much from them. And even now, in rare moments on weekends, the remaining members of my biophysics group meet with me in the ether world of cyberspace.

I began teaching with the idea of giving back; I received more than I gave. This brings me to the final movement of this speech. It begins with a story of an extraordinary scientific discovery and a new dilemma that it poses. It's a call to arms and about making a difference.

So here's the movement. In the last several decades, our climate has been changing. Climate change is not new: the Earth went through six ice ages in the past 600,000 years. However, recent measurements show that the climate has

在贝尔实验室工作 9 年后，我决定离开温暖安逸的象牙塔，投身于我眼中的"真实世界"——大学。套用评价玛丽·波平斯的话来讲，贝尔实验室"无可挑剔"，但我希望自己给世界留下的不仅仅是科学论文。我想教书育人，培养自己在科学上的后辈。

我在斯坦福大学有一位朋友，同时也是一位优秀的同事，叫作泰德·格巴尔，几年前他也从伯克利去了贝尔实验室，后来又进了斯坦福。他对我们这种行为的动机解读得最到位，他是这么说的：

"在大学里工作，最好的一点是能够和学生待在一起。他们朝气蓬勃，满腔热情，思想开放，没有在生活的战役中受过伤。他们是我们社会中最好的受众，尽管他们自己并未察觉到这一点。如果存在思想可以自由发挥创造力的时候，那就是大学时期。他们抱着对教科书的绝对信任而来，但最终会发现教科书和教授并非无所不知。从此，他们开始独立思考，而我则开始向他们学习。"

我的学生、博士后研究员以及在贝尔实验室、斯坦福大学和伯克利大学与我共事的年轻研究人员都非常优秀。前小组成员中有 30 多人如今已成为教授，其中不少任职于全球顶尖研究机构，包括哈佛大学。我从他们身上学到了很多。即使是现在，我周末偶尔还会上网，和还在从事生物物理学研究的旧友在网络世界里碰头。

我抱着回馈社会的心态执教，得到的却比付出的多。这就引出了我演讲的最后一节。一切始于一个了不起的科学发现及其带来的新困境。这是一个号召行动和改变的故事。

我开始讲了。近几十年来，我们的气候一直在变化。气候变化并不是新鲜事：地球在过去 60 万年里经历了 6 个冰河时期。然而，最近的测量数据表明，气候已

---

6. Mary Poppins：玛丽·波平斯，是电影《欢乐满人间》里的仙女，她喜爱孩子并教授孩子们如何在受挫后寻找快乐之道。

begun to change rapidly. The size of the North Polar Ice Cap in the month of September is only half the size it was a mere 50 years ago. The sea level which has been rising since direct measurements began in 1870 is now five times faster, that rate is now five times faster than it was at the beginning of recorded measurements. Here's the remarkable scientific discovery. For the first time in human history, science is now making predictions of how our actions will affect the world 50 and 100 years from now. These changes are due to an increase in carbon dioxide put into the atmosphere since the beginning of the Industrial Revolution. The Earth has warmed up by roughly 0.8 degrees Celsius since the beginning of this Revolution. There is already approximately a 1 degree rise built into the system, even if we stop all greenhouse gas emissions today. Why? It will be decades to warm up the deep oceans before the temperature reaches a new equilibrium.

If the world continues on a business-as-usual[7] path, the Intergovernmental Panel on Climate Change[8] predicts that there is a fifty-fifty chance the temperature will exceed 5 degrees by the end of this century. This increase may not sound like much, but let me remind you that during the last ice age, the world was only 6 degrees colder. During this time, most of Canada and the United States down to Ohio and Pennsylvania were covered year round by a glacier. A world 5 degrees warmer will be very different. The change will be so rapid that many species, including Humans, will have a hard time adapting. I've been told, for example, that in a much warmer world, insects were bigger. I wonder if this thing buzzing around is a precursor[9].

We also face the specter of nonlinear "tipping points" that may cause much more severe changes. An example of a tipping point is the thawing[10] of the permafrost[11]. The permafrost contains immense amounts of frozen organic matter that have been accumulating for millennia. If the soil melts, microbes will spring to life and cause this debris to rot. The difference in biological

经开始急剧变化。9月，北极冰盖的面积仅为50年前的一半。自1870年有直接测量记录以来，海平面一直在上升，现在上升的速度比有记录的测量开始时快了5倍。这就是我说的那个了不起的科学发现。在人类历史上，科学首次预测出人类活动对50年乃至100年后的影响。这些变化归咎于工业革命以来大气中二氧化碳排放量的增加。自革命伊始，地球已升温约0.8摄氏度。即使如今停止一切温室气体的排放，预计仍会继续上升约1摄氏度。原因何在？因为要等深海完全吸收这些热量，让地球达到新的气候平衡状态，这一过程需要几十年时间。

如果世界保持现状，预计到20世纪末，气温将有50%的概率会上升超过5摄氏度。这种上升听起来可能不多，但容我指出，在上一个冰河时期，全球的气温只比现在低6摄氏度。而在那期间，加拿大和美国的大部分地区，直到俄亥俄州和宾夕法尼亚州，一年到头都覆盖着冰川。地球变暖5摄氏度将会引发巨变。变化将来得非常迅猛，包括人类在内的许多物种将难以适应。例如，我听说，在温度高得多的世界里，昆虫的体形也会大得多。这让我忍不住想，耳边嗡嗡作响的东西会不会就是一个预兆。

非线性"引爆点"的幽灵同样威胁着我们，还可能会导致更严重的变化。例如，永冻层融化就是一个引爆点。永冻层中封存着千年来积累的大量冻结有机物。若永冻层融化，微生物就会活跃起来，使得有机物腐化。我们都很清楚冰点温度前后生物活动的变化。冷冻食品在冰箱里长期保存，仍然可以食用，但一旦解冻，就会很

---

7. business-as-usual：照旧的。
8. Intergovernmental Panel on Climate Change：联合国政府间气候变化专门委员会，是世界气象组织（WMO）及联合国环境规划署（UNEP）于1988年联合建立的政府间机构。其主要任务是对气候变化科学知识的现状，气候变化对社会、经济的潜在影响以及如何适应和减缓气候变化的可能对策进行评估。
9. precursor：*n.* 前兆；先驱。
10. thaw：*v.* 解冻，溶解。
11. permafrost：*n.* 永冻层。

activity below freezing and above freezing is something we are all familiar with. Frozen food remains edible for a very long time in the freezer, but once thawed, it spoils quickly. How much methane and carbon dioxide might be released from the rotting permafrost? If even a fraction of the carbon is released, it could be greater than all the greenhouse gases we have released since the beginning of the industrial revolution. Once started, a runaway effect could occur.

The climate problem is the unintended consequence of our success. We depend on fossil energy to keep our homes warm in the winter, cool in the summer, and lit at night; we use it to travel across town and across continents. Energy is a fundamental reason for the prosperity we enjoy, and we will not surrender this prosperity. The United States has 3 percent of the world population, and yet, we consume 25 percent of the energy. By contrast, there are 1.6 billion people who don't have access to electricity. Hundreds of millions of people still cook with twigs or dung. The life we enjoy may not be within easy reach of the developing world, but it is within sight, and they want what we have.

Here is the dilemma. How much are we willing to invest, as a world society, to mitigate the consequences of climate change that will not be realized for at least 100 years? Deeply rooted in all cultures, is the notion of generational responsibility. Parents work hard so that their children will have a better life. Climate change will affect the entire world, but our natural focus is on the welfare of our immediate families. Can we, as a world society, meet our responsibility to future generations?

While I am worried, I am hopeful we will solve this problem. I became the director of the Lawrence Berkeley National Laboratory, in part because I wanted to enlist some of the best scientific minds to help battle against climate change. I was there only four and a half years, the shortest serving director

快变质。永冻层腐烂，可能会释放出多少甲烷和二氧化碳呢？哪怕只有一小部分碳释放出来，其总量也可能超过工业革命以来人类排放的所有温室气体。这种事情一旦发生，局势便会失控。

气候问题是人类成就带来的意外后果。凭借化石能源，我们让家中冬暖夏凉，为夜晚照明，穿越城市，跨越大洲。能源是繁荣的根本，我们不会放弃繁荣。美国拥有全球3%的人口，却消耗了世界25%的能源。相比之下，还有16亿人用不上电，数亿人仍然用树枝或粪便生火做饭。发展中国家难以触及我们这样的生活，却看在眼里，惦记在心里。

这是一个两难的问题。全世界作为一个整体社会，愿意投入多少资金来缓解至少100年之内都不会显现的气候变化问题？代际责任深深植根于所有文化之中。父母努力工作，是为了让孩子过上更好的生活。气候变化将影响全世界，但我们天生更关注直系亲属的福祉。作为一个全球性的社会，我们能履行我们对子孙后代的责任吗？

对于这个问题的解决，我忧心忡忡，却仍抱有期望。我之所以出任劳伦斯伯克利国家实验室主任，部分原因是想召集顶尖科学家，共同应对气候变化。我在那里只待了4年半，是实验室78年历史中任期最短的主任，但在我离开时，伯克利实验

Deeply rooted in all cultures, is the notion of generational responsibility.

代际责任深深植根于所有文化之中。

in the 78-year history of the Lab, but when I left, a number of very exciting energy institutes at the Berkeley Lab and UC Berkeley had been established.

I am extremely privileged to be part of the Obama administration. If there ever was a time to help steer America and the world towards a path of sustainable energy, now is the time. The message the President is delivering is not one of doom and gloom, but of optimism and opportunity. And I share this optimism. The task ahead is daunting, but we can and will succeed.

We know some of the answers already. There are immediate and significant savings in energy efficiency and conservation. Energy efficiency is not just low-hanging fruit; it is fruit lying on the ground. For example, we have the potential to make buildings 80 percent more efficient with investments that will pay for themselves in less than 15 years. Buildings consume 40 percent of the energy we use, and a transition to energy efficient buildings will cut our carbon emissions by one-third.

We are revving up the remarkable American innovation machine that will be the basis of a new prosperity. We will invent much improved methods to harness the sun, the wind, nuclear power, and capture and sequester[12] the carbon dioxide emitted from our power plants. Advanced bio-fuels and the electrification of personal vehicles will make us less dependent on foreign oil.

In the coming decades, we will almost certainly face higher oil prices and be in a carbon-constrained economy. We have the opportunity to lead in development of a new, industrial revolution. The great hockey player, Wayne Gretzky[13], when asked, how he positions himself on the ice, he replied, " I skate to where the puck is going to be, not where it's been." America should do the same.

The Obama administration is laying a new foundation for a prosperous and sustainable energy future, but we don't have all of the answers. That's where you come in. In this address, I am asking you, the Harvard graduates, to join

室和加州大学伯克利分校已经建立了几个令人振奋的能源研究所。

能成为奥巴马政府的一员，我倍感荣幸。如果引导美国和世界走上可持续能源的道路也要择时，那么现在时机正好。总统传达的信息是，未来并非在劫难逃，我们还能乐观地把握好机会。我也持这种乐观态度。前路漫漫，令人望而生畏，但我们定将成功。

我们已经找到了一部分答案。很多方法可以立竿见影地提高能效和节约能源。如果把能效比作果子，那它不仅仅是低垂于枝头，而是早已瓜熟蒂落。例如，我们可以将建筑物的能效提高 80%，而成本不到 15 年时间即可收回。建筑消耗在能源使用中占 40%，推广节能建筑将使我们的碳排放量减少 1/3。

我们正在加速运转美国卓越的创新机器，这将为新一轮的大繁荣奠定基础。我们将发明更先进的方法来利用太阳能、风能、核能，来捕获和贮存发电厂排放的二氧化碳。先进的生物燃料和私家车的电气化将使我们减少对外国石油的依赖。

在未来的几十年里，我们几乎必将迎来更高的油价，并进入碳减排经济时代。我们有机会引领一场新的工业革命。杰出的冰球运动员韦恩·格雷茨基曾被问及冰面跑位心得，他回答道："我滑向冰球将要去往之处，而非它去过的地方。"美国也应该这样做。

奥巴马政府正在为可持续的繁荣未来奠定新的能源基础，但许多问题尚未找到答案。这就是你们大展身手的舞台。在这次演讲中，我请求你们这些哈佛毕业生加入我们。作为未来的智慧型领袖，请花时间去了解更多的利害关系，并采取行动。

---

12. sequester：*v.* 使隔绝。
13. Wayne Gretzky：韦恩·格雷茨基，加拿大职业冰球运动员，得到 2857 分的"伟大冰球手"，全球冰球传奇人物。

us. As our future intellectual leaders, take time to learn more about what's at stake, and then act on that knowledge. As future scientists and engineers, I ask you to give us better technology solutions. As future economists and political scientists, I ask you to create better policy options. As future business leaders, I ask that you make sustainability an integral part of your business.

Finally, as humanists, I ask that you speak to our common humanity. One of the cruelest ironies about climate change is that the ones who will be hurt the most are the most innocent: the worlds poorest and those yet to be born.

The coda[14] to this last movement is borrowed from two humanists.

The first quote is from Martin Luther King, when he spoke on ending the war in Vietnam in 1967. His message seems so fitting for today's climate crisis. I quote:

"This call for a worldwide fellowship that lifts neighborly concern beyond one's tribe, race, class, and nation is in reality a call for an all-embracing and unconditional love for all mankind. This oft[15] misunderstood, this oft misinterpreted concept, so readily dismissed by the Nietzsches of the world as a weak and cowardly force, has now become an absolute necessity for the survival of man … We are now faced with the fact, my friends, that tomorrow is today. We are confronted with the fierce urgency of now. In this unfolding conundrum[16] of life and history, there is such a thing as being too late."

The final message is from William Faulkner[17]. On December 10th, 1950, his Nobel Prize banquet speech was about the role of humanists in a world facing potential nuclear holocaust. I quote:

"I believe that man will not merely endure. He will prevail. He is immortal, not because he among creatures has an inexhaustible voice, but because he has a soul, a spirit capable of compassion and sacrifice and endurance. The poet's, the writer's, duty is to write about these things. It is his privilege to help man endure by lifting his heart, by reminding him of the courage and the honor and

作为未来的科学家和工程师，请提供更好的技术方案。作为未来的经济学家和政治学家，请制定更好的政策方案。作为未来的商业领袖，请将可持续发展纳入业务之中。

最后，作为人道主义者，请为我们共同的人道主义发声。气候变化的影响中有一点既残酷至极又讽刺至极，最受伤的人恰恰是最无辜的人：贫苦之人和未生之人。

尾声的内容是两位人道主义者的话。

第一句话来自马丁·路德·金，是他在 1967 年针对越南战争结束这一话题所说，用在当下的气候危机问题上也恰到好处，他是这么说的：

"我呼吁抛开部落、种族、阶级和国家之间的成见，在全世界构建友爱关系。我呼吁对全人类的包容和无条件的爱。这一理念常遭误读和误解，被尼采等人随意贬低为懦弱和畏缩的力量，现在却攸关人类存亡……朋友们，我们现在要直面的事实是，明天已然成为今天。我们面临着当下极其紧迫的问题。对这个在生活与历史中缓缓浮出水面的难题来说，有一种东西叫作悔之晚矣。"

最后再引用威廉·福克纳的一句话。1950 年 12 月 10 日，他在诺贝尔奖宴会做了一场演讲，提及在核浩劫的阴影之下，人道主义者应当扮演何种角色。他是这么说的：

"我相信，人类会生存下去，更会取得胜利。人是不朽的，不是因为万物中唯人类独具不竭之声，而是因为人类拥有灵魂，有共情、奉献和持之以恒的精神。诗人和作家的责任就是将之付诸纸上。他们拥有这样的荣幸——鼓舞人心，弘扬勇气、

---

14. coda：*n.* 尾声，乐曲的后奏。
15. oft：*adv.* 时常，再三。
16. conundrum：*n.* 复杂难题；谜语。
17. William Faulkner：威廉·福克纳（1897—1962），美国文学史上最具影响力的作家之一，意识流文学在美国的代表人物，1949 年诺贝尔文学奖得主，其代表作为《喧哗与骚动》。

hope and pride and compassion and pity and sacrifice which have been the glory of his past."

Graduates, you have an extraordinary role to play in our future. As you pursue your private passions, I hope you will also develop a passion and a voice to help the world in ways both large and small. Nothing will give you greater satisfaction.

Please accept my warmest congratulations. May you prosper, may you help preserve and save our planet for your children, and all future children of the world.

荣誉、希望、骄傲、同情、怜悯和奉献等昔日的光辉品格，帮助人类坚持下去。"

毕业生们，你们在人类未来中扮演着非比寻常的角色。希望你们在追求个人志趣的同时，也能发展出为世界做贡献的激情和力量，无论贡献是大是小。再没有什么能比这个更能带给人满足感了。

衷心祝贺大家。祝大家有所成就，愿大家能够献出自己的力量，护佑地球，护佑你们的孩子，护佑世界上所有未来的孩子。

语录 Quotes

- In order to be heard, it is important to deliver the same message more than once.
  要想让人听进去，有必要反复传达同一个信息。

- Every time you celebrate an achievement, be thankful to those who made it possible.
  每当你庆祝自身成就时，都要感谢身后的帮手。

- Going forward, the ability to teach yourself is the hallmark of a great liberal arts education and will be the key to your success.
  从长远来看，自学能力是高水平人文教育的标志，也将成为成功的关键。

- Life is too short to go through it without caring deeply about something.
  生命很短，必须对某样东西倾注热情，方不虚此生。

- Deeply rooted in all cultures, is the notion of generational responsibility.
  代际责任深深植根于所有文化之中。

- One of the cruelest ironies about climate change is that the ones who will be hurt the most are the most innocent: the worlds poorest and those yet to be born.
  气候变化的影响中有一点既残酷至极又讽刺至极，最受伤的人恰恰是最无辜的人：贫苦之人和未生之人。

生命太过短暂，不能空手走过

Ten Suggestions for Life
人生的十个建议

——本·伯南克 2013 年在普林斯顿大学毕业典礼上的演讲

> 简介 Profile

本·伯南克
Ben Shalom Bernanke

　　1953 年，本·伯南克出生于美国佐治亚州的奥古斯塔。他自幼天资过人，素有"神童"的称号。大学入学考试时，他以近乎满分的优异成绩被哈佛大学录取。

　　作为美联储前主席，本·伯南克执掌美联储 8 年。2009 年，《时代》杂志将他评为"年度风云人物"。他是当之无愧站在全球经济顶峰的权势人物，不仅有着超前的经济眼光和独到的政治手腕，而且头脑聪慧，在学术领域同样值得称道。

　　在就任美联储主席前，伯南克曾在普林斯顿大学任教 17 年，并担任经济系主任，成为美国知名的宏观经济学家，主要研究方向是货币政策和宏观经济史，编著了《宏观经济学原理》《微观经济学原理》等教材。2022 年，因对银行和金融危机的研究，本·伯南克获得了诺贝尔经济学奖。

　　尽管本·伯南克因在美联储当权期间出色的成绩而声名大噪，但他本人却极具学者风范，骨子里始终饱含对学术研究的执着和热情。在美联储，伯南克凭借诸多新想法为自己赢得了"个人创意工厂"的称号。他自由的思想方式在那些早就习惯了美联储高度谨慎行事风格的银行家和投资者中很受欢迎。

　　2013 年 6 月 2 日，伯南克在普林斯顿大学 2013 届本科生毕业典礼上发表了演讲。演讲中，伯南克以其自身的经历和对现实世界的观察对毕业生们提出了十条建议，涉及人生、事业、价值观等诸多方面，句句发自肺腑，却不乏幽默。最后，伯南克还特别强调，选择终身伴侣时除了看外表，更重要的是找到一个能够与你互相支持和慰藉的人，并劝诫毕业生们成功后不要忘记常和父母联系。

演讲 Speech

Hi! Well, it's nice to be back at Princeton. I find it difficult to believe that it's been almost 11 years since I departed these halls for Washington. I wrote recently to inquire about the status of my leave in the university, and the letter I got back began, "Regrettably, Princeton receives many more qualified applicants for faculty positions than we can accommodate[1]."

I'll extend my best wishes to the seniors later, but first I want to congratulate the parents and families sitting all out on the lawn. As a parent myself, I know that putting your kid through college these days is no walk in the park. Some years ago I had a colleague who sent three kids through Princeton even though neither he nor his wife attended this university. He and his spouse were very proud of that accomplishment, as they should have been. But my colleague also used to say that, from a financial perspective, the experience was kind of like buying a new Cadillac every year and then driving it off a cliff. I should say that he always added that he would do it all over again in a minute. So, well done, Moms and Dads.

This is indeed an impressive and appropriate setting for a commencement. I am sure that, from this lectern, any number of distinguished spiritual leaders have ruminated[2] on the lessons of the Ten Commandments[3]. I don't have that kind of confidence, and, anyway, coveting your neighbor's ox or donkey[4] is not the problem it used to be, so I thought I would use my few minutes today

大家好！嗯，回到普林斯顿感觉很好。很难相信，从我离开这些讲堂前往华盛顿已有近11个年头了。最近，我写信询问了我在普林斯顿大学的教职状态，得到的回信开头写道："很遗憾，普林斯顿收到很多更为合格的人员的申请，而我们所能提供的教职有限。"

我稍后会向大四的毕业生们致以我最美好的祝愿。但是首先，我想祝贺坐在外面草坪上的各位父母和家人们。我也为人父，了解这年头供孩子读完大学绝非像在公园里散步那么轻松。几年前，我有位同事供他的三个孩子读完了普林斯顿，而他和他的妻子都没有上过这所大学。他们对这一成就非常自豪，而他们也本该引以为傲。但是我的同事也曾这么说过：从财务的角度来看，这一经历有点像是每年买一辆崭新的凯迪拉克，然后开着它冲下悬崖。我该说，他总是补充道，他愿意马上重新再做一遍。所以说，在座的父母们，你们干得不错。

这里的确是一个适合举行毕业典礼的场所，能给人留下深刻的印象。我肯定，很多杰出的精神领袖都在这个讲台旁思考过"十诫"的训诫。我没有那样的自信，

> *If you are not happy with yourself, even the loftiest achievement is not going to bring you much satisfaction.*
>
> 如果你不为自己感到快乐，纵使最高的成就也无法给你带来太多的满足。

---

1. accommodate：*vt.* 向……提供。
2. ruminate：*vi.* 沉思；反复思考。
3. Ten Commandments：十诫（犹太教、基督教的戒条）。
4. covet your neighbor's ox or donkey：出自"十诫"，原句为："You shall not covet your neighbor's wife, or his manservant or maidservant, his ox or donkey, or anything that belongs to your neighbor."（不可觊觎你邻居的妻子、男女仆人、牛或驴和任何其他属于你邻居的东西。）covet：*vt.* 觊觎；垂涎。

to make Ten Suggestions, or maybe just Ten Observations, about the world and your lives after Princeton. Please note, these points have nothing to do with interest rates. My qualification for making such suggestions, or observations, besides being kindly invited to speak here today by President Tilghman, is the same reason that your obnoxious[5] brother or sister got to go to bed later—I am older than you. All of what follows has been road-tested in real-life situations, but past performance is no guarantee of future results.

1. The poet Robert Burns once said something about the best-laid plans of mice and men ganging aft agley[6], whatever "agley" means. A more contemporary philosopher, Forrest Gump, said something similar about life and boxes of chocolates and not knowing what you are going to get.[7] They were both right. Life is amazingly unpredictable; any 22-year-old who thinks they know where they will be in 10 years, much less in 30, is simply lacking imagination. Look what happened to me: A dozen years ago I was minding my own business teaching Economics 101 in Alexander Hall and thinking of good excuses for avoiding faculty meetings. Then I got a phone call ... In case you are skeptical of Forrest Gump's insight, here's a concrete suggestion for each of the graduating seniors. Take a few minutes the first chance you get and talk to an alum participating in their 25th, or 30th, or 40th reunion—you know, somebody who was near the front of the P-rade. Ask them, back when they were graduating 25, 30, or 40 years ago, where they expected to be today. If you can get them to open up, they will tell you that today they are happy and satisfied in various measures, or not, and their personal stories will be filled with highs and lows and in-betweens. But, I am willing to bet, those life stories will in almost all cases be quite different, in large and small ways, from what they expected when they started out those many years ago. This is a good thing, not a bad thing: Who wants to know the end of a story that's only in its early chapters? Don't be afraid to let the drama play out.

再说，觊觎邻居家的牛或驴已不再像过去那样是个问题，所以我想我会用几分钟时间就这个世界和你们从普林斯顿毕业后的生活提出十条建议，或者可能只是十点观察心得。请注意，这些建议与利率毫无关系。我之所以有资格提出这些建议或观察心得，除了因为蒂尔曼校长诚挚地邀请我今天来这里演讲，理由和你们讨厌的哥哥姐姐可以比你们晚睡是一个道理——我比你们年长。下面要讲的所有内容都已经在真实的生活场景中被验证过了，但是以往的表现并不能确保未来的结果。

第一条，诗人罗伯特·彭斯曾经说过一些有关"鼠与人之最周密的计划也常有乖误"的话，不管"乖误"是什么意思。一位更加现代的哲学家福里斯特·冈普（阿甘）说过类似的关于生活、一盒巧克力和不知道你将得到什么的话。他们二位说得都对。人生令人惊奇地难以预料；任何一个22岁的人，如果他们觉得自己知道今后10年将在哪里，更别说今后30年，那他就是缺乏想象力。不妨看看我的经历：十几年前，我只关心自己的事，在亚历山大教室讲授"经济学101"，琢磨着合理的借口不去参加教职工会议。后来我接到一个电话……以防你们怀疑阿甘的洞察力，这里我给每位大四毕业生一个具体的建议。一旦有机会就花几分钟时间，与参加第25、30或40周年聚会的校友谈一谈——你们知道，就是靠近游行队伍前列的人。问问他们，在25、30或40年前他们即将毕业的时候，他们期待自己今天在哪里。如果你能让他们敞开心扉，他们就会告诉你，如今他们在不同程度上感到幸福和知足，或者不幸福、不满足，他们的个人经历充满高潮、低谷和过渡状态。但是，我愿意打赌，这些人生经历不论从大还是小的方面，几乎与他们多年前毕业时所期待的颇为不同。这是好事，而不是坏事；谁想在小说的头几章就知道它的结局呢？不要害怕，让人生的大戏演下去。

---

5. obnoxious：*adj.* 使人非常不快的，惹人讨厌的。
6. the best-laid plans of mice and men ganging aft agley：再周密的计划也不能确保成功。这句谚语出自苏格兰诗人罗伯特·彭斯（Robert Burns）的《致老鼠》(*To a Mouse*)，原句为："The best laid schemes of mice and men, gang aft agley." 直译为："不管是人是鼠，即使最如意的安排设计，结局也往往会出其不意。"
7. 此处是指影片《阿甘正传》(*Forrest Gump*) 中的主人公阿甘的一句经典台词："Life is like a box of chocolates. You never know what you're going to get."（人生就像是一盒巧克力，你永远不知道下一块会是什么口味。）

2. Does the fact that our lives are so influenced by chance and seemingly small decisions and actions mean that there is no point to planning, to striving? Not at all. Whatever life may have in store for you, each of you has a grand, lifelong project, and that is the development of yourself as a human being. Your family and your friends and your time at Princeton have given you a good start. Well, what will you do with it? Will you keep learning and thinking hard and critically about the most important questions? Will you become an emotionally stronger person, more generous, more loving, more ethical? Will you involve yourself actively and constructively in the world? Many things will happen in your lives, pleasant and not so pleasant, but, paraphrasing a Woodrow Wilson School adage[8] from the time I was here, "Wherever you go, there you are." If you are not happy with yourself, even the loftiest achievement is not going to bring you much satisfaction.

3. The concept of success leads me to consider so-called meritocracies[9] and their implications. We have been taught that meritocratic institutions and societies are fair. Putting aside the reality that no system, including our own, is really entirely meritocratic, meritocracies may be fairer and more efficient than some alternatives. But are they fair in an absolute sense? Think about it. A meritocracy is a system in which the people who are the luckiest in their health and genetic endowment[10]; luckiest in terms of family support, encouragement, and, probably, income; luckiest in their educational and career opportunities; and luckiest in so many other ways difficult to enumerate[11]—those are the folks who reap the largest rewards. The only way for even a putative[12] meritocracy to hope to pass ethical muster[13], to be considered fair, is if those who are the luckiest in all of those respects also have the greatest responsibility to work hard, to contribute to the betterment of the world, and to share their luck with others. As the Gospel of Luke says (and I am sure my rabbi[14] will forgive me for quoting the New Testament in a good cause): "From everyone to whom

第二条，我们的人生受到机缘巧合和看似微小的决定及行动的影响如此之大，这一事实难道就意味着规划和奋斗毫无意义吗？完全不是。无论生活可能为你预留了什么，你们每个人都有一个宏大的终身项目，那就是你作为个人的自身发展。你们的家人、朋友和你们在普林斯顿度过的时光给你们开了个好头。那么你们要怎样利用呢？你们会继续学习，上下而求索并批判性地思考最重要的问题吗？你们会成为在情感方面更加坚强的人，变得更加大度、更有爱心、更有道德吗？你们会积极地并有建设性地投身于这个世界吗？你们的一生中将会发生很多事情，有愉快的，也有不那么愉快的，但是用当初我在普林斯顿时伍德罗·威尔逊学院的一句格言来说："不论你去哪里，都要随遇而安。"如果你不为自己感到快乐，纵使最高的成就也无法给你带来太多的满足。

第三条，成功的概念促使我思考所谓的任人唯贤及其含义。我们已被教导过，任人唯贤的机构和社会是公平的。任何制度，包括我们自己的，都无法真正做到完全意义上的任人唯贤，但抛开这一现实不说，任人唯贤可能比一些其他可供替代的选择更加公平和高效。但它们绝对公平吗？想想看。任人唯贤这种制度中，都是在健康和遗传禀赋方面最幸运的人，在家庭支持、鼓励可能还有收入方面最幸运的人，在教育和职业机遇方面最幸运的人，在很多其他难以罗列的方面最幸运的人——正是这些人获得了最大的回报。即便是一个假定存在的任人唯贤制度，它所希望能经得起道德检验并被认为公平的唯一方法就是，让那些在方方面面都最幸运的人也担负起努力工作、致力于让世界变得更好并与他人分享好运的最大责任。正如《路加福音》所言（我肯定我的拉比会原谅我出于正当原因引用《圣经·新约》）："多给谁，

---

8. adage：*n.* 谚语；格言。
9. meritocracy：*n.* 任人唯贤；精英管理（的社会）。
10. endowment：*n.* 天赋；天生的气质（或才能）。
11. enumerate：*vt.* 逐一举出；列举。
12. putative：*adj.* 假定存在的。
13. pass ethical muster：通过道德检验。"pass muster" 是一个英语习语，意为通过考核、达到标准或符合要求。
14. rabbi：*n.* 拉比；犹太宗教领袖（尤指有资格传授犹太教义且精于犹太法典的犹太教堂主管）。

much has been given, much will be required; and from the one to whom much has been entrusted[15], even more will be demanded." It's kind of like grading on the curve.

4. Who is worthy of admiration? The admonition[16] from Luke—which is shared by most ethical and philosophical traditions, by the way—helps with this question as well. Those most worthy of admiration are those who have made the best use of their advantages or, alternatively, coped most courageously with their adversities. I think most of us would agree that people who have, say, little formal schooling but labor honestly and diligently to help feed, clothe, and educate their families are deserving of greater respect—and help, if necessary—than many people who are superficially more successful. And also more fun to have a beer with. That's all that I know about sociology.

5. Since I have covered what I know about sociology, I might as well say something about political science as well. In regard to politics, I have always liked Lily Tomlin's line, in paraphrase: "I try to be cynical, but I just can't keep up." We all feel that way sometimes. Actually, having been in Washington now for almost 11 years, as I mentioned, I feel that way quite a bit. Ultimately, though, cynicism is a poor substitute for critical thought and constructive action. Sure, interests and money and ideology all matter, as you learned in political science. But my experience is that most of our politicians and policymakers are trying to do the right thing, according to their own views and consciences, most of the time. If you think that the bad or indifferent results that too often come out of Washington are due to base motives and bad intentions, you are giving politicians and policymakers way too much credit for being effective. Honest error in the face of complex and possibly intractable[17] problems is a far more important source of bad results than are bad motives. For these reasons, the greatest forces in Washington are ideas, and people prepared to act on ideas. Public service as I've discovered is not easy. But,

就向谁多取；多托谁，就向谁多要。"（《路加福音》第 12 章第 48 节，新修订标准版《圣经》）。这有点像曲线评分法。

第四条，谁值得钦佩？路加的告诫也有助于解答这个问题——顺便补充一句，多数道德和哲学传统都认同这一点。最值得钦佩的人是那些充分利用其自身优势的人，或者换句话说，那些最勇敢地应对逆境的人。我想我们多数人都会同意，那些没怎么正式上过学但诚实勤恳地工作来供家人吃穿、上学的人比那些表面看似更成功的人值得更多的尊重——以及帮助，如果他们需要的话。与他们一起喝啤酒也更加有趣。这就是我所了解的社会学的全部内容。

第五条，既然谈到了对社会学的了解，那我不妨也聊聊政治学吧。关于政治，我一直喜欢莉莉·汤姆林的那句台词，按我的理解来说就是"我试着让自己愤世嫉俗，但就是无法继续下去"。有时候，我们所有人都会有这种感觉。实际上，正如我刚才所提到的，如今在华盛顿待了近 11 年后，我对此颇有同感。然而，愤世嫉俗终究是批判性思维和建设性行动的可悲替代品。当然，正如你们在政治科学里所学过的，利益、金钱和意识形态都很重要。但我的感受是，多数时候，我们的多数政客和政策制定者都在凭借自己的看法和良心尽量做正确的事。如果你们认为华盛顿经常出现的那些糟糕或无关紧要的结果都归咎于卑鄙的动机和恶劣的图谋，那你们也太看得起这些政客和政策制定者的效能了。在复杂且可能难以处理的问题面前，诚实的错误远比卑鄙的动机更能引致糟糕的结果。出于这些原因，在华盛顿最强大的力量是想法，人们则准备好基于这些想法采取行动。我发现投身公共服务并非易事。

---

15. entrust：*vt.* 交托；委托。
16. admonition：*n.* 告诫；警告。
17. intractable：*adj.*（问题或情况）难以对付的。

in the end, if you are inclined in that direction, it is a worthy and challenging pursuit.

6. Having taken a stab at sociology and political science, let me wrap up economics while I'm at it. Economics is a highly sophisticated[18] field of thought that is superb at explaining to policymakers precisely why the choices they made in the past were wrong. About the future, not so much. However, careful economic analysis does have one important benefit, which is that it can help kill ideas that are completely logically inconsistent or wildly at variance with the data. This insight covers at least 90 percent of proposed economic policies.

7. I'm not going to tell you that money doesn't matter, because you wouldn't believe me anyway. In fact, for too many people around the world, money is literally a life-or-death proposition. But if you are part of the lucky minority with the ability to choose, remember that money is a means, and not an end. A career decision based only on money and not on love of the work or a desire to make a difference is a recipe for unhappiness.

8. Nobody likes to fail but failure is an essential part of life and of learning. If your uniform isn't dirty, you haven't been in the game.

9. I spoke earlier about definitions of personal success in an unpredictable world. I hope that as you develop your own definition of success, as you will be able to do so, I hope that you're able to do it, with a close companion on your journey. In making that choice, remember that physical beauty is evolution's way of assuring us that the other person doesn't have too many intestinal[19] parasites[20]. But don't get me wrong; I am all for beauty, romance, and sexual attraction—where would Hollywood and Madison Avenue be without them? But while important, those are not the only things to look for in a partner. The two of you will have a long trip together, I hope, and you will need each other's support and sympathy more times than you can count. Speaking as somebody

不过最终如果你倾向于此，这是个值得的追求，并且充满了挑战。

第六条，谈完社会学和政治科学，就让我趁这个机会讲讲经济学吧。经济学是一个高度复杂的思想领域，它非常善于向政策制定者们精确地解释他们以往的选择为何是错误的。而对于未来，经济学就不这么善于做出解释了。不过，细致的经济分析确实有一个重大益处，那就是它有助于将完全不合逻辑或与现实数据完全对不上号的想法扼杀掉。这适用于至少90%的经济政策草案。

第七条，我不会跟你们说钱无关紧要，因为反正你们也不会相信我。实际上，对全球很多人而言，钱是关乎生死存亡的大事，这一点毫不夸张。不过，如果你们属于幸运的少数人，有能力去选择，请记住钱只是途径，而非最终目的。如果一个职业决定仅仅只是基于金钱，而不考虑对工作的热爱或改变世界的意愿，那就会造成不幸。

第八条，没有人喜欢失败，但失败是生活和学习的必修课。如果你的队服不脏，那你还没有进入比赛。

第九条，我刚才谈了在无法预测的世界中个人成功的定义。我希望你们在形成自身对成功的定义时——你们一定能够做到，我希望在你们能够做到的同时，还有一位人生旅途中的亲密伴侣。在选择伴侣时，记住外表之美只是进化的一种方式，使我们确认此人肠内没有太多寄生虫。但是别误解我，我完全欣赏美丽、浪漫和异性的吸引力——没有了这些，好莱坞和麦迪逊大街会是什么样子？不过这些固然重要，但并不是寻找伴侣时考虑的唯一因素。我希望你们会结伴走很远，你们会需要对方数不清的支持和同情。作为一个享受了35年幸福婚姻的人，我想象不出对人生

---

18. sophisticated：*adj.* 复杂的，尖端的。
19. intestinal：*adj.* 肠的。
20. parasite：*n.* 寄生虫。

who has been happily married for 35 years, I can't imagine any choice is consequential for a lifelong journey than the choice of a traveling companion.

10. Call your mom and dad once in a while. A time will come when you will want your own grown-up, busy, hyper-successful children to call you. Also, remember who paid your tuition to Princeton.

Well, those are my ten suggestions. They're probably worth exactly what you paid for them. But they come from someone who shares your affection for this great institution and who wishes you the best for the future.

Congratulations, graduates. Give 'em hell.

的旅途而言，有比挑选旅伴更为重要的抉择。

第十条，时不时给你的爸爸妈妈打个电话。总有一天，你会想让你那已经长大成人、忙忙碌碌、超级成功的孩子们给你打电话。还有，别忘了是谁给你支付的普林斯顿的学费。

嗯，这些就是我的十条建议。它们的价值可能与你们为此支付的费用一样（不值一文）。但是这些建议来自一个跟你们一样对这所伟大的院校抱有感情并祝愿你们未来一切顺利的人。

恭喜你们，毕业生们。放手去拼搏吧！

语录 Quotes

- Who wants to know the end of a story that's only in its early chapters? Don't be afraid to let the drama play out.

  谁想在小说的头几章就知道它的结局呢？不要害怕，让人生的大戏演下去。

- Wherever you go, there you are.

  不论你去哪里，都要随遇而安。

- If you are not happy with yourself, even the loftiest achievement is not going to bring you much satisfaction.

  如果你不为自己感到快乐，纵使最高的成就也无法给你带来太多的满足。

- Those most worthy of admiration are those who have made the best use of their advantages or, alternatively, coped most courageously with their adversities.

  最值得钦佩的人是那些充分利用其自身优势，或者换句话说，那些最勇敢地应对逆境的人们。

- Honest error in the face of complex and possibly intractable problems is a far more important source of bad results than are bad motives.

  在复杂且可能难以处理的问题面前，诚实的错误远比卑鄙的动机更能引致糟糕的结果。

- If you are part of the lucky minority with the ability to choose, remember that money is a means, and not an end.

  如果你们属于幸运的少数人，有能力去选择，请记住钱只是途径，而非最终目的。

The Last Lecture
最后一课

——兰迪·波许 2008 年在卡内基梅隆大学毕业典礼上的演讲

> 简介 Profile

兰迪·弗雷德里克·波许
Randy Frederick Pausch

美国很多知名高校有一个特别的传统：在每位教授退休前，学校会为其安排一堂面向全校师生的"最后一课"。在"最后一课"的演讲者中，有一个人格外特殊，他叫兰迪·波许，是卡内基梅隆大学的计算机科学、人机交互及设计教授。他尚未到退休的年龄，便站上了"最后一课"的讲台。

2006年，波许被诊断出患有晚期胰腺癌。次年8月，他被告知可能仅剩不到6个月的生命。虽时日无多，但波许并未因此消沉度日，他把这仅剩的岁月看作人生难得的体验，将无情的病魔看成一个艰难的挑战。2007年9月18日，兰迪·波许在他的母校卡内基梅隆大学做了一场题目为《真正实现你的童年梦想》的讲座。这场讲座轰动全美，《华尔街日报》称之为"一生难觅的最后的讲座"。

"最后一场演讲"走红的同时，波许也被ABC新闻网评为"年度人物"，被《时代》周刊选入"影响世界的100人"；卡内基梅隆大学所在的城市匹兹堡将11月9日定为"兰迪·波许日"；就连当时的美国总统小布什也给他写信说："您的努力反映了美国人灵魂中最好的一面。"除了美国，波许的"最后一课"的影响力甚至辐射全球，他的故事不仅被拍成电影，出版的《最后的演讲》一书更是成为全球最为畅销的图书之一。

2008年7月25日，兰迪·波许因胰腺癌并发症在家中去世，终年47岁。而他在卡内基梅隆大学2008届毕业典礼上的演讲，也成了他人生最后的绝唱，是真正意义上的最后一课。他在人生尽头用充满眷恋的目光回望过往，用了短短的6分钟向毕业生传递了时光淬炼的人生智慧：追寻心之所向，以满腔热情充实地度过每一天。

演讲 Speech

扫描二维码
获取本篇演讲原视频、音频

I am glad to be here today. Hell, I am glad to be anywhere today.

President Cohon asked me to come and give the charge to the graduates. I assure you, it's nothing compared to the charge you have just given me.

This is an incredible place. I have seen it through so many lenses. I saw it when I was a graduate student that didn't get admitted and then somebody invited me back and said: OK, we'll change our mind.

And I saw it as a place that hired me back to be on the faculty many years later and then gave me the chance to do what anybody wants to do, which is, follow their passion, follow their heart and do the things they're excited about.

And the great thing about this university, unlike almost all the other ones I know of, is that nobody gets in your way when you try to do it. And that's just fantastic.

And to the degree that a human being can love an institution. I love this place and I love all of the people and I am very grateful to Jerry Cohon and everyone else for all the kindness that have been shown me.

Last August I was told that in all likelihood I had three to six months left to live. I am on month nine now and I am gonna get down and do any push-ups[1]… But there will be a short pick-up basketball game later.

Somebody said to me, in light of those numbers, wow, so you are really

很高兴今天能来到这里。不过坦白说，不论去哪里，我今天都会很高兴。

科恩校长让我来鼓励鼓励毕业生，但我保证，我的演讲和大家刚才给我的鼓励相比，根本不算什么。

这是一个令人惊叹的地方。我用各种各样的视角观察过它。我申请过这所学校的研究生，起初未被录取，随后有人邀我回来，告诉我说，学校改变主意了。

多年以后，学校将我聘回来担任教职。这是一个人人艳羡的机会，在这里，我可以跟随热爱，跟随内心，投身于让自己心潮澎湃的事业之中。

这所大学与我所知的其他大学几乎都不一样。不同之处在于，要是我打算做些什么，没有人会阻挠。这真是太棒了。

某种层面上来说，人可以爱上一个机构。我爱这个地方，我爱这里所有的人，我非常感激杰瑞·科恩以及所有对我表达过善意的人。

去年 8 月，我被告知自己很可能只剩下 3 到 6 个月的生命了。从那时算起，我已经活到了第 9 个月，我还能趴下来做几个俯卧撑……还是别了，一会儿还要有一小场篮球赛呢。

有人对我说：从数据来看，哇，你真的战胜了死神。我想都没想就回答道：战

> *We don't beat the Reaper by living longer. We beat the Reaper by living well, and living fully.*
>
> 战胜死神不能靠活得更久，要活得好、活得充实，才能战胜死神。

---

1. I am gonna get down and do any push-ups：波许在他的演讲《最后一课》中，幽默地说不要同情他，他开玩笑说自己还可以做几个俯卧撑。

beating the Grim Reaper[2]. And what I said without even thinking about is that we don't beat the Reaper by living longer. We beat the Reaper by living well, and living fully.

For the Reaper will come for all of us. The question is: What do we do between the time we are born and the time he shows up?

'Cause he shows up—it is too late to do all the things that you're always gonna kind of "get round to". So I think the only advice I can give you on how to live your life well is, first off, remember, it's a cliche, but love cliches, "It is not the things we do in life that we regret on our deathbed, it is the things we do not".

'Cause I assure you I've done a lot of really stupid things and none of them bother me. All the mistakes, and all the dopy[3] things and all the times I was embarrassed, they don't matter. What matter is that I can kind of look back and say, "Pretty much anytime I got a chance to do something cool, I tried to grab for it." And that's where my solace[4] come from.

The second thing I would add to that—and I didn't coordinate on the subject of this word but I think it's the right word that comes up—is passion. And you will need to find you passion. Many of you have already done it; many of you will later; many of you may take till your 30s or 40s. But don't give up on finding it. Alright? Because then all you're doing is waiting for the Reaper. Find you passion and follow it.

And if there's anything I have learned in my life, you will not find that passion in things. And you will not find that passion in money. Because the more things and the more money you have, the more you will just look around and use that as the metric, and there will always be some one with more.

So your passion must come from the things that fuel you from the inside. And honors and awards are nice things but only to be the extent that they regard the real respect from your peers. And to be thought well of by other people that

胜死神不能靠活得更久，要活得好、活得充实，才能战胜死神。

谁也无法逃脱死神的镰刀，关键在于，从出生到被死神收割的时光里，我们做了些什么？

一旦死神现身，那些打算"将来有空再做"的事情就来不及了。所以，就如何活得充实而言，我能给予的唯一建议是一句陈词滥调，虽然听着有点老套，但我喜欢老套的话："临终前不会对做过的事感到后悔，而是会对没做过的事情感到遗憾。"

坦白说，我干过很多蠢事，但我不会为此内耗。犯的错、犯的蠢以及随之而来的尴尬都不重要。重要的是，回首过往之时，我可以说："只要有机会去做很酷的事情，我都会尽力去争取。"这句话将会成为我的慰藉。

我还要补充一点。虽然本来没有打算说这个主题，但我觉得它很合适，那就是热爱。要找到自己所热爱的事物。你们当中有些人已经找到了，有些人以后会找到，有些人要等到三四十岁才能找到。要永不言弃，好吗？放弃等同于等死。要找到自己的热爱，并追随它前进。

若是说我从生活中学到了什么，那就是，人在外物和钱中找不到热爱。因为拥有的外物和钱越多，就越会以此来丈量世界。然而，总会有人比自己更富有。

热爱必须源于能够予人以心灵能量的事物。荣誉和奖励是好东西，前提是它们

> *Find you passion and follow it.*
>
> 要找到自己的热爱，并追随它而前进。

---

2. Grim Reaper：*n.* 狰狞的收割者（指骷髅状死神，身披斗篷，手持长柄大镰刀）。
3. dopy：*adj.* 恍惚的，迟钝的。
4. solace：*n.* 安慰，慰藉。

you think even more highly of is a tremendous honor that I've been granted.

Find you passion, and in my experience, no matter what you do at work or what you do in official settings, that passion would be grounded in people. And it will be grounded in the relationships you have with people, and what they think of you, when you time comes. And if you can gain the respect of those around you, and the passion and true love, and I've said this before, but I waited till 39 to get married because I had to wait that long to find someone where her happiness was more important than mine. And if nothing else I hope that all of you can find that kind of passion and that kind of love in your life. Thank you!

代表着同行发自内心的敬佩。而得到自己敬仰之人的认可，对我来说是无上的荣耀。

去寻找自己的热爱吧。根据我的经验，无论在何种工作和环境之中，热爱都是以人为基础的。热爱会建立在你们与他人的关系上，以及盖棺论定之时你们所得的评价。如果你能获得身边人的尊重，就能获得他们的热情与爱。正如我之前所说，我之所以39岁才结婚，是因为等了那么久，我才等来了能够让我把她的幸福看得比我自己的（幸福）还重的人。抛开一切不论，衷心祝愿大家都能在人生中找到热爱和真爱。谢谢大家！

语录 Quotes

- We don't beat the Reaper by living longer. We beat the Reaper by living well, and living fully.
  战胜死神不能靠活得更久，要活得好、活得充实，才能战胜死神。

- It is not the things we do in life that we regret on our deathbed, it is the things we do not.
  临终前不会对做过的事感到后悔，而是会对没做过的事情感到遗憾。

- Find you passion and follow it.
  要找到自己的热爱，并追随它前进。

- Your passion must come from the things that fuel you from the inside.
  热爱必须源于能够予人以心灵能量的事物。

- No matter what you do at work or what you do in official settings, that passion would be grounded in people. And it will be grounded in the relationships you have with people, and what they think of you, when you time comes.
  无论在何种工作和环境之中，热爱都是以人为基础的。热爱会建立在你们与他人的关系上，以及盖棺论定之时你们所得的评价。

本书部分作者尚未取得联系，请权利人见声明后与我们联系，以便奉寄稿酬。

本书内容源自公开资料，版权归原作者所有。编者已尽力核实内容，但因客观条件限制，不保证完全准确，相关责任由引用方承担。

书中观点仅代表作者立场，与出版方无关。

特此声明。